"Nations Are Built of Babies"

"Nations Are Built of Babies"

Saving Ontario's Mothers and Children 1900–1940

CYNTHIA R. COMACCHIO

McGill-Queen's University Press
Montreal & Kingston • London • Buffalo

ISBN 0-7735-0991-7

Legal deposit fourth quarter 1993
Bibliothèque nationale du Québec

Printed in Canada on acid-free paper

This book has been published with the help of a
grant from the Social Science Federation of Canada,
using funds provided by the Social Sciences and
Humanities Research Council of Canada. Funding has
also been provided by Wilfrid Laurier University and
by the Canada Council through its block grant
program.

Photo credits, pages 178–9:
Public Archives of Ontario, RG 10–30 series,
Department of Health. Thanks to A.J. MacDonald,
J. Dirks, and C. Niarchos-Bonrolias.

Canadian Cataloguing in Publication Data

Comacchio, Cynthia R., 1957–
   Nations are built of babies: saving Ontario's mothers
   and children, 1900–1940
   Includes bibiographical references and index.
   ISBN 0-7735-0991-7
   1. Infants – Ontario – Death – Social aspects.
   2. Mothers – Ontario – Death – Social aspects.
   3. Maternal health services – Ontario – Social aspects.
   4. Infants – Health and hygiene – Ontario – Social
   aspects. 5. Child rearing – Ontario – Social aspects.
   I. Title.
   R463.06C65 1993   613'.0432'0971   C93-090264-5

Typeset in Baskerville 10/12
by Caractéra production graphique inc., Quebec City

To my parents
Bruno and Maria Comacchio
and my children
Stefanie Anne Marie and
Evan Robert John Abeele
with much love

Contents

Figures and Tables

Illustrations

Preface

This project began as a personal quest for enlightenment. Ten years ago, awaiting the birth of my first child, I joined the continuum of expectant mothers who – before and since my time – have known the thrill and terror of impending parenthood. With little knowledge of babies and a desperate eagerness to learn, I did as required of graduate students: I made urgent treks to libraries, scanned child care tomes, took earnest notes. I purposefully interviewed my mother and every woman I knew who had had children. I consulted my doctor faithfully. By the time that my daughter arrived late one steamy August afternoon, I felt I had attained the requisite level of preparedness and then some. I was confident that I had grasped the latest childrearing precepts and that I had only to apply them for assured success.

Like countless other mothers, what I did not know, and could not have known, was that flesh-and-blood babies are not much like their textbook counterparts. By all objective medical standards, my daughter was "normal" and healthy. But she would not eat, sleep, or be comforted according to the books. She did not cry at the appropriate intervals sanctioned by the experts. Instead she ate little, slept fitfully, and cried incessantly. As did I, in light of what appeared to be futile hours of study, consultation, and stockpiling of child care manuals. The fledgling social historian learned the value of "lived experience" the hard way.

My personal experiment with scientific parenting led me to a series of historical questions. How, I wondered, had mothers learned about babies in the past? In particular, how had they learned the tricks of child care in the pre-Spockian dark ages? Had "professional" advisers for mothers always existed in some form? When and how had doctors come to predominate in this area traditionally belonging to women? What kind of medical help was available to mothers before state medicare made health care accessible to all families regardless of their economic position? How had medicine's "onward march" during the past century influenced the health and well-being of mothers and children?

When I began this study of the child and maternal welfare campaign in early twentieth century Ontario, I was prepared to believe in the progressive model of medical advance. I learned that, much as with parenting experiences, the story is neither that simple nor that linear in development. The result is this book. It attempts to uncover, within the specific context of Ontario in the years 1900 to 1940, some of the social, economic, and ideological complexities underlying what have so long been considered the biologically ordained experiences of pregnancy, childbirth, and child nurture.

As always, there are a great many people to thank. At the University of Guelph, Terry Crowley was an astute and good-humoured supervisor in this project's earliest incarnation as my doctoral thesis. My colleagues at Wilfrid Laurier University merit much appreciation, especially Terry Copp, Suzanne Zeller, David Monod, and Joyce Lorimer, all of whom provided necessary criticism and even more necessary encouragement, as did Marlene Shore of York University. Robert Abeele helped me immeasurably with charts, graphs, and statistics, as did Dan Gallivan, particularly with respect to design. The McGill-Queen's University Press team – Philip Cercone, Don Akenson, and Joan McGilvray – was patient and supportive, and their faith in this project sustained me. Victoria Grant was both efficient and personally engaged in the copy-editing process, guiding me through the final hurdles. Evelyn Jones and Lynne Doyle helped with typing and many other such details. My sister Linda Calanchie, my brother John Comacchio, and their spouses Murray and Lorna were called on to fill the parenting role on occasions when my work took me away from my children, a contribution for which no parent can be too grateful. Catherine Voight and Susan Scadding were empathic listeners to whom mere thanks fall far short of the mark. Finally, research grants from the Social Sciences and Humanities Research Council and Wilfrid Laurier University facilitated this project's completion.

This book is dedicated with much love and appreciation to my children and my parents, from whom I have learned more than could be found in any number of documents, texts, and statistical tables. My children Stefanie (now 10) and Evan (now 5) literally inspired this study and have witnessed its entire development since its infancy and their own. They are both healthy and bright despite their mother's anxieties, preoccupations, and outright mistakes. My parents, Bruno and Maria Comacchio, not only raised their children while making their difficult way in an unfamiliar culture, but have never failed to believe in us, and to help us wholeheartedly with our own. I can say it to them now: you were right.

"Nations Are Built of Babies"

CHAPTER ONE

Introduction

Next to love, the most profound emotion infusing the parent-child relationship is fear. At the very heart of childrearing is an eternal nexus of hope and dread. Until the unforeseeable moment when parents can control all factors working against the child's welfare, parental anxiety is likely to remain an historical constant. Yet while such fear has been and conceivably always will be intrinsic to parenting, its nature and causes have varied over time according to its specific historical context. The fundamental threats to the child remain unchanged: disease, mental illness, familial and societal violence, poverty. What has changed is their relative importance as dangers to the child, and consequently as sources of parental anxiety.

At the beginning of the twentieth century in Canada, one in five babies regularly lost its life before its second birthday. Maternity was doubly fearsome: not only did infants fall prey to a scourge of illnesses, but the very process of childbirth was potentially hazardous to the health of both mother and child. Canadian interest in child and maternal welfare originally stirred reformist groups, especially women's organizations, at the turn of the century. Infant mortality was perceived as one of the most tragic and wasteful effects of rapid industrialization and urbanization. Reformers' perceptions were confirmed by medical data, which indicated that it was a class mortality afflicting primarily the ill-housed and ill-fed families of workers. Early twentieth-century medical surveys publicized the child welfare cause, while the impact of World War One transformed this incipient movement into a concerted campaign to save mothers and infants and improve national health.

Although voluntary associations and interested lay people continued to participate actively in child welfare concerns, by the time of the Great War, health care professionals, both private practitioners and public employees, had effectively taken the reins of leadership. The solution they advocated was "scientific motherhood." From the medical perspective, Canadian mothers were handicapped in their childrearing duties by an ignorance that could be remedied only through expert tutoring and supervision. Medically designed information about child health and childrearing methods was delivered to mothers through state-sponsored advice literature, diagnostic clinics, and visiting nurse services.

Behind the objective of saving infants and mothers from unnecessary death was a conscious attempt to "modernize" Canadian families by means of "modern" childrearing methods. Although the "child welfare problem" was fundamentally a health issue, it was defined from the viewpoint of the material realities and ideological imperatives of industrial capitalism. In order to ensure both social reproduction and economic productivity – never so important as in times of war – the requisite human qualities had to be instilled in children at the earliest possible moment. Doctors reasoned that, if infants could be saved and their physical, mental, and moral health regulated, the benefits in socio-economic terms would more than offset any individual or state investment. The result would be a modern Canada worthy of the most favourable implications of modernity: progress, efficiency, productivity, and the triumph of reason that was signified by advances in science and technology.

This study is concerned with the process that saw child welfare shift out of the voluntarist, female-ordered reform sphere to become the object of a male-dominated professional body and a state-sponsored campaign. It seeks to examine how child nurture and family health were appropriated as state interests in the years 1900 to 1940. No argument was made by medicine or the state against the view that these subjects should be the primary concern of women. But increasingly in the early twentieth century, the state came to be seen as the most effective instrument for the protection of children and the regulation of family life.[1] Patriarchal ideas and class dynamics shaped medical understanding of the child welfare problem, and the solutions prescribed sought to reinforce the family and the state as mutually supportive entities. For all the rhetoric of separate spheres that sustained patriarchy, it was recognition of the permeability of boundaries between the private and public that led to attempts by medicine and the state to intervene in intimate human relationships.

The questions addressed in this study are straightforward. What forces contributed to the medicalization of motherhood that amounted to a much wider medical dominance of modern society? What role was ascribed to the state within the campaign and with respect to the modern family itself? How did families targeted for medical regulation respond to this authoritative intervention in an area that was traditionally their domain? The answers that emerge reveal more than anything the many ambiguities and contradictions that characterize the reformulation of historical relationships between the professions and society, between society and state, between family and state, and within the family itself.

That these relationships are intertwined and dialectical barely requires stating. Ultimately, the medical profession rose to social authority, not only because doctors wanted that authority, but because the public accepted its premise. The state became involved in child welfare, not only because the medical profession invoked the state's responsibilities, but because policy-makers recognized that contemporary socio-economic realities compelled new functions for the state. And the working-class mothers who were the primary targets of child welfare initiatives not only accepted this aid but expected it – and more that was not forthcoming – because they understood that their families would benefit from even limited medical services that were otherwise beyond their grasp. Without denying the centrality of class and gender relationships of dominance and subordination, it is significant that the clients did not simply submit to ideas and methods that were thrust upon them. They took what suited their purposes, resisted what did not, and voiced their needs when these were all too often left unmet. Their lack of success is testimony, not of their passivity, but of the force of medical politics and the unaccountability of the state to those it was supposed to serve.

Health care is typically analysed in terms of scientific progress, the professional ethic of service, and the cultural context that profoundly influences both needs and the way that they are met. While these are important considerations, the crucial determinant of health care is its relationship to the nature of production. In capitalist societies, health becomes a commodity. The profit motive necessitates the exploitation and alienation of a large sector of the population, to the detriment of its health and well-being. In turn, health care delivery is shaped by profit and efficiency objectives: care is bought and sold in the marketplace at whatever price the market will sustain. The distribution of health care also reflects the status of the medical profession as a vital sector of the dominant class.[2]

In effect, the health care system mirrors the priorities and organization of the larger socio-economic system in a number of ways: in its concentration of economic and political power at the top, in its class and gender stratification, in its division of labour, in its general lack of accountability, and even in its definitions of health and illness.[3]

The predominant health difficulties, then, are those defined by the conditions of work and life that are the common experience of the majority of the population.[4] Differences in individual and class behaviour and in cultural patterns obviously make an impact. In the end, however, the explanation for ill health remains materialist, in that these individual choices and broader patterns are themselves derived from socio-economic inequalities.[5]

By the nineteenth century, the medical profession favoured a mechanistic conception of the body that emphasized the objective, organic basis of illness. Doctors also espoused a cultural/behavioural explanation of class differences that located predisposing factors to ill health in individual lifestyle choices. This medical model made prescribed changes in behaviour the most efficacious approach to both illness and the personal failings at its source.[6] From an historical perspective, however, cultural and behavioural patterns cannot be separated from their broader structural and environmental context, essentially what the doctors themselves were attempting to do. By examining this relationship between health and day-to-day existence, we can begin to understand the connections between illness, medicine, and the nature of production in different societies at specific moments in history.

Like wealth and power, health is a social resource that is unequally distributed. Marx and Engels noted the correlation of poverty, disease, and social deviance in the nineteenth-century working class, as did British social scientists Booth and Rowntree. Canadian historians writing within the Marxist tradition have remarked upon the "potent force" of generalized ill health and specific diseases in undermining the resistance of nineteenth-century workers to the incursions of factory discipline.[7] Also, like wealth and power, the unequal distribution of health and health care corresponds to gender and age.[8] Women and children were the earliest victims of the new industrial order, and it was their situation that sparked the concern of those advocating state protection and regulation of families.[9]

Capitalism obviously cannot perpetuate itself unless the population is able to produce, consume, and reproduce. Yet the wage labour system by definition threatens to absorb all existing labour and capital. In order to continue this dynamic, the reproductive sphere must be drained to an untenable point. The system's innate potential for self-destruction was revealed in the early stages of industrialization when its repercussions for living standards and public health became all too apparent.[10] Reproduction is more than procreation: it encompasses the socialization, physical maintenance, and emotional nurture of family members. What happens in the home on every level affects the capacity of human beings to work, to function socially, to continue to exist.[11] It is important, therefore, to consider the family's relation to the economy, especially its contribution to the reproduction of labour power and the consequences for the social position of women.

Witness this 1929 debate in the House of Commons when J.S. Woodsworth discussed the relationship between industry, the family, and the state in terms of "the debt that industry owes to the family": "Industry is entirely dependent upon the family for its labour. Every industrial manager provides a certain amount in his estimates for the installation of machinery, and he also provides for the replacement of same ... There is no provision of like nature made with regard to labour ... from the standpoint of labour as a factor in industry, we should arrange that industry recognizes in a very material way something of its responsibility to the family which provides the labour that is needed in industry."[12] Woodsworth understood the family's role in sustaining industrial capitalism by its reproductive as well as its productive functions, and wanted that critical relationship acknowledged by both capital and the state.

While it is clearly in the general interest that families be healthy in every sense, when the requirements of production conflict with those of reproduction, the family is no longer able to protect the health and welfare of its members on its own. Moreover, while healthy workers are essential to production and profit, maintaining their health and welfare also gives rise to costs that capitalists prefer to avoid. The state is then obliged to play a more active role in regulating and providing services for the workforce to ensure its reproduction.[13] One of the state's functions is to legitimize the continuing dominance of certain classes and interest groups in decision-making processes that relate to the development of health care. Professional bodies under state protection play an invaluable part in the economic and political functioning of the system, contributing directly to the management and surveillance of the working class by regulating on behalf of capital under the auspices of the state.[14]

The Marxist critique of health, health care delivery, and the professions in capitalist systems exposes the continuing tension between the requirements of capitalism and those of health. But Marxist sociology does not distinguish between historically specific modes of capitalist production and their effects for societal and state approaches to health and health care. The turn-of-the-century transition to monopoly capitalism from its earlier competitive form, and the onslaught of a "second industrial revolution" fuelled by technological innovation changed the labour process. Production now required an intensification of labour that made worker efficiency paramount.[15] Emerging interest in the "psycho-physics" of industrial labour in early twentieth-century Europe also turned the attention of scientists and social scientists to the physiological and mental impact of the altered nature of work. The "science of work" investigated the relationship between machine and human being to allow for the "calibration" of workers – literally the fine-tuning of their bodies – to fit them to machinery.[16] The corresponding definition of health also shifted from emphasis on sheer physical endurance, which could be secured by simple replacement of workers, to optimum labour efficiency, which had to be promoted and instilled in all workers and potential workers. The metaphors of mass production, as Emily Martin has noted, were borrowed by the medical profession to describe biological functions like sex and reproduction.[17]

Marxist theorists have also tended to downplay crucial variables such as age and gender, both definitive components of power relations with respect to their impact on health and the prescribed mode of health care. Feminists depict the medical profession as a privileged occupational group exercising authority and control over subordinate social groups, especially women.[18]

The feminist perspective also recognizes that childrearing and all forms of unpaid domestic work are central to capitalist production because the household does not simply consume, but also produces and reproduces labour power. Women cheapen labour costs by their domestic work in the household and their "feminine" labour in the workforce.[19] In the medical context, predominantly female occupations such as nursing and midwifery are subordinated within the profession itself, closely regulated, or even excluded outright. As Wendy Mitchinson has shown, doctors reinforced patriarchal values through their supposedly scientific constructions of normal womanhood. For its part, the state has also attempted to meet the changing, at times conflicting, requirements of both capitalism and patriarchy by institutionalizing class relations and upholding gender distinctions.[20]

Doctors played an integral role in delineating both the targets of social and moral reform in the early twentieth century and the means to approach these.[21] Studies of such reform movements in Canada present a lengthy list of motives: socio-economic transformation, class anxieties, changing gender roles, xenophobia intensified by prevalent racialist theories and state-sponsored immigration.[22] The outcome was an enhanced sense of collective responsibility for problems that were increasingly defined as social. This is perhaps best interpreted as a self-imposed collective culpability on the part of middle-class, urban, Protestant reformers inspired by the activist Christianity of the Social Gospel, the era's most important progressive reform movement.

But reformist arguments about social responsibility and collective action belie their originators' conception of individual responsibility. Calls for state involvement were premised on the belief that individuals should, by the fruits of their own labour, take care of themselves and their dependants. Individuals were to use state assistance to enhance their self-reliance and return to some undoubtedly mythical level of absolute economic independence.[23] Nor were those in need averse to such an assessment, as is witnessed in collective labour action to secure "a family wage," or in the intentions of mothers' allowance advocates to use these benefits to encourage familial independence. The National Council of Women of Canada contended that "the fundamental important aim" in dealing with dependent women and children" should be first the prevention of such conditions by prolonging the lives and increasing the working efficiency of men."[24] By understanding the individualist ideals underlying the period's social welfare concepts, we can grasp what is behind the seeming contradiction of invoking collective responsibility while emphasizing personal responsibility.

The rhetoric of social reform became increasingly scientific in tone, reflecting ideological currents and popular attitudes that equated science with efficiency, progress, and modernity.[25] In the language of early twentieth-century reformism, to be scientific meant much more than to adopt the scientific method typified by categorization, quantification, objective analysis, and everything else that the emerging social sciences represented. But if science was much touted as the means to a better understanding of social problems and their solution, the overall aim was efficiency. Management principles more than scientific principles shaped and influenced the reform outlook and determined the direction of reform campaigns and state policy.

From the point of view of organized labour, there was "an especial interest" in the safeguarding of health and the prevention of disease for workers, because "to no part of the community" was health so important.[26] Doctors, while conceding that low wages contributed to ill health and economic dependency, nonetheless argued that "inefficiency of labour" was itself responsible for low wages.[27] This circular reasoning made labour inefficiency both the source and the outcome of mass physical deterioration. Ill health was largely due to poor choices, ignorance, incorrect behaviour – in short, to personal deficiency now labelled "inefficiency." State responsibility for public health meant emphasizing personal responsibility, in order that all might be efficient and contribute to national vigour and prosperity.

In their attempts to offset the effects of labour inefficiency, employers had to avoid adding to overall costs. But they could not, with impunity, continue to exploit workers to the point where damaged health perpetuated and even increased inefficiency. One of the easiest methods of state intervention, heartily supported by capital, was the replacement of Canadian workers by a fresh source enticed from other nations. Organized labour interpreted this approach as a denial of capital's responsibility to its own: "when modern capitalism devitalizes the physical bodies of its own national workers, it seeks foreign immigration to fill the gaps."[28] But even substitution of healthy bodies for deteriorating ones was an inefficient remedy when the goal was to increase profits by using fewer but more productive workers. Employers would do their part to achieve long-term economic goals by introducing scientific management to the workplace, while society and the state would impress its principles upon the nation's homes. Common benefit was behind the medical argument that "the highest standard of living will be reached when in the greatest interest each one should understand his own machinery and will apply the best rules of running that machinery."[29]

With respect to children, Jane Ursel has effectively shown that the state was called upon not to substitute for the parent, but to supplement and complement the essential parenting role.[30] If mothers accepted their duty to the state and became scientific managers of the household, they could run their homes like the ideal modern factory. They could minimize inefficiency and waste at their source by improving the health of their children through scientific child care methods. And once physical welfare was assured in infancy, they could manage and train their children all along the path to healthy, productive, and efficient adulthood.

Ultimately, the new role of the state arose in response to the needs of both capital and the family. In its reproductive role, the family is simultaneously an active agent of modernization and a guardian of tradition. The decline of some of its traditional functions opened new opportunities for women on the one hand, while creating new pressures on the other. Greater stress on intrafamilial relationships, and especially the role of mothers in early socialization, meant new responsibilities to family, community, and state.[31]

Physicians became the foremost proponents of the "modern" family.[32] Since traditional support networks of neighbourhood and kin were also being disrupted by the process of urbanization and the rise of mass culture, women were impelled to turn more and more to the "professionals" for guidance.[33] The impact of medical leadership in this area was a measure of their ability to make parents, particularly mothers, cognizant of their inadequacy in raising their children without the help of modern scientific instruction. In opening the door to this emergent breed of family advisers, among whom medical professionals predominated, the home again came under the scrutiny and regulation of the state.

Against this background, parental responsibility had to be defined as a matter of national importance. Reformers confronting the plight of child labourers, orphans, and neglected children were concerned to save those threatened, but also to prevent neglect, abuse, exploitation, and abandonment. The humanitarian impulse behind the child-saving discourse is apparent, but even more striking is its grounding in economic principles of cost and investment. It was reasoned that saving children would more than repay public expenditure by redoubling the prospects of turning out a productive and worthy citizenry. Parents who were unwilling or unable to acknowledge the child as a "national asset" and to carry out their duties accordingly were liabilities to state and society. The state was constrained to see all such obligations met.[34]

With respect to child welfare, the current historiographical debate centres on the issue of maternal education and its purposes. Were doctors primarily interested in controlling mothers in their crusade to save infant lives?[35] It is my view that doctors were equally intent on both objectives: neither could be attained separately any more than they can be examined in that manner. Put simply, babies could not be approached, much less saved, except through their mothers. Children are the most subordinate of all social groups. Because it was clearly impossible to make dependent infants and children responsible for their own health and upbringing, and because health was regarded as an individual responsibility, mothers had to be made responsible according to medical dictates and by means of medical regulation. The state was required to support this regulation for the child's protection. To focus on the child directly would have meant implementing the kind of extraordinary measures that the reformers labelled "bolshevism." In only one instance in Canada did the state directly substitute for the family: that of the Dionne quintuplets, whose unique experience is beyond the purview of this study.[36]

Did the child welfare reformers actualize their intentions? The campaign's inherent paradox made the mother both problem and solution. The widespread cross-class acceptance of maternalist ideology by women themselves complicates evaluation of the issue of professional "control" of women.[37] For the majority of women in this period, the essential frame of reference was still the family. Their general willingness to be instructed in modern motherhood reveals that they continued to define personal fulfilment in terms of familial welfare. Assessments of the popular impact of literature that was prescriptive in nature are obviously problematic. What is important is the historian's recognition that, despite the large doses of moral suasion by professionals, personal choice could never be entirely eliminated. Child welfare campaigners recognized, decried, and railed against this factor of individual freedom. They declared that the future of nation and race was at stake, and that personal preferences and predilections should be subordinated to these wider and infinitely more important concerns.

Analysis of the medical discourse on these issues suggests that they fretted, declaimed, and expounded as much as they did because they knew that no amount of propaganda, regulation, and surveillance, however unprecedented, was sufficient to stamp out freedom of choice. As even the campaigners realized, mothers could attend clinics faithfully, welcome nurses into their homes, accept and read the literature with seeming enthusiasm, and still do as they chose with respect to childrearing. What was truly private remained so; it was not feasible to ensure slavish compliance, even if that was clearly what reformers wanted. Judging by the views of the mothers themselves, it is likely that they incorporated into their childrearing practices those ideas that best suited them in terms of practicality, personality, and economics. Some mothers followed the advice closely, while others discarded it entirely. Their choices in childrearing were probably most influenced by the family's material conditions. More than this cannot be said with any certainty.

It is both possible and necessary, however, to give the mothers themselves an active role to play in changing systems of childrearing. They were not simply acted upon by the medical and government advisers, but took part in the struggle to save their children, conserve their health, and modernize childrearing practices. After all, as the medical rhetoric emphasized, the major work of child care devolved upon mothers. It is also worth considering that, rather than alienating mothers from traditional advisers, the new advisers may have served as necessary substitutes in a rapidly changing and urbanizing social order that saw Canadians increasingly isolated from older forms of familial and neighbourhood support.[38]

The element of social control involved in this campaign is apparent but should not be overstated. Physicians charged that ignorance was endemic among Canadian mothers, and that working-class mothers and those of immigrant origin were especially ignorant. They were determined that these "poor unfortunates" be uplifted from the mire of ignorance and outmoded custom that they saw as the root of familial and societal disarray. But, as a necessary corollary to their efforts for working-class mothers, child welfare campaigners had to persuade middle-class mothers to take a greater interest in "cultivating" their own children in order to preserve and bolster the "better stock." The efficacy of medically supervised education for motherhood was dependent on its penetration of class barriers.

Did their educational approach permit an "easy way out" for physicians and state officials unwilling to deal with the economic basis of infant and maternal mortality? Clearly the doctors' motivations were complex, deriving from medical trends, structural changes, prevailing class and gender ascriptions and current attitudes about the relationship of public and private. But why did maternal education become the campaign's sole remedy when statistical surveys indicated, and doctors admitted, the link between poverty and health? While purporting to be scientific, the medical approach to the problem was selective in its analysis. Teaching mothers was not so much an "easy" solution – in fact, it was in many respects a daunting task – as one that was consonant with its proponents' social and political views and aspirations. If the medical program was bound by the limits of contemporary science, which had to focus on prevention in the absence of any known cure, it was proscribed as much by ideological confines and material realities.

The solution the doctors idealized was at least theoretically promising. It was also professionally satisfying. But it was certainly less than satisfactory from the viewpoint of needy mothers and considered as such even by some within campaign ranks. The campaigners' dismissal of poverty as a health issue meant that the "education" of poor families in modern child welfare principles was frequently futile. Despite expressions of discontent from some doctors, politicians, labour and women's groups, and the clients themselves, neither organized medicine nor the state attempted or promoted any alternative in Ontario during the years from 1900 to 1940.

The issue is not the doctors' failure to take on the systemic inequities of capitalism. The campaign's effects were limited because its medical leadership failed to act with the knowledge it possessed at the time, and even in accordance with its own professional standards. Doctors knew that, short of eradicating poverty, the solution was essentially one of better distribution of health care. They were aware that many Canadians were suffering unnecessarily because of the conditions of their lives and because medical aid was beyond their means. Yet they persisted in advocating education because options such as state provision for health care threatened their professional and class interests. They wanted optimum health and health care for all Canadians, but they did not want to compromise their professional authority and livelihood by embracing anything approaching "state medicine."[39] As part of a society ordered by capitalistic and patriarchal ideals, and infused with a sense of Anglo-Protestant superiority, doctors held values that could not help but reflect and sustain their socio-economic position.[40]

In order to attain the aims of their movement and to justify their increasing influence and social status, the medical experts needed parents who wanted to be informed. They participated in the creation of a need and strove to become the unique source of its attenuation. As ideologues, strategists, and administrators of this campaign, the predominant medical sector was not merely performing its expected function in guarding the national health. It was leading this collection of professional and lay supporters in a deliberate effort to intervene in the process of social change.[41] After World War One in particular, there was a pervasive triumphalism about "modernity," in stark contrast, if frequently exaggerated, to prewar traditionalism. Socially conscious Canadians were caught in a tense and anxiety-provoking space between the traditional and the modern. While intent on using science and the state as cloaks of modernity, their scientific rhetoric often only thinly disguised continuities with past concepts of the ideal society. The ideal projected by the child welfare campaigners was a modernized motherhood and childhood that nonetheless left intact traditional structures and power relations.

I have imposed a number of limitations on this study. The topic is national and even international in scope, but this examination concentrates on the child welfare campaign's manifestations in early twentieth-century Ontario, and specifically on its prenatal, infant, and preschool aspects. Ontario was the first province to experience the full impact of modernizing forces: it was the industrial and cultural prototype for a modern Canada. It was the first province to establish a child welfare division as part of its Board of Health. Toronto's Hospital for Sick Children was the first of its kind in Canada. The pre-eminent Canadian paediatrician of this period and the unofficial "grandmaster" of the campaign was the hospital's Dr Alan Brown. Both the city and the province provided national leadership in the health and welfare fields and produced much of the childrearing advice literature.[42] Of necessity, the institutional framework of public health on all three levels, municipal, provincial, and federal, is outlined. While I recognize the vital contribution of such nursing organizations as the Victorian Order of Nurses and the Red Cross Society, I have focused on the work of the public health nurses employed by the municipal and provincial governments.

With respect to diseases and discoveries, I have attempted to describe their impact on the health and welfare of Ontario's children in the period and to show how theories of disease causation and therapeutics shaped medical attitudes and initiatives in the child welfare sphere. It is not possible, however, to consider the aetiology, incidence, treatment, and mortality of each of the myriad afflictions of childhood. Nor is it necessary, since doctors themselves had the broader picture of child health in mind – hence their use of the term "child welfare" to denote a medical campaign – even as individuals studied specific diseases. Canadian doctors borrowed from and contributed to medical research in Britain, Europe, and the United States and many pursued studies in those nations. They discussed scientific findings in their journals and at their academies and conferences, but the message conveyed was that people should simply trust their doctors to take care of them with the best methods known. What is important is not so much the "great discoveries" of the period as the growing medical appreciation of the role of prevention and the selling of that professional understanding to the public. The debate over the relative significance of medical innovation and environmental improvement remains inconclusive, but I lean toward the latter in explaining the health status of Canadians.

EVEN IF HISTORIANS ARE obliged to look at children largely through the eyes of adults, the way that a society defines the ideal child and the best method for its upbringing tells a great deal about the society's self-image. The concept of what a child is and should be exposes the society's self-defined shortcomings, values, and aspirations. In the eyes of child welfare advocates, the ideal child was industrious, self-disciplined, and self-motivated, healthy in mind and body, a credit to the race, and a productive member of an internationally respected industrial democracy. When doctors took up the argument that "nations are built of babies," they were pointing out the evils inherent in a consistently apathetic response to the mounting toll of infant and maternal lives.[43] A nation with as much promise as Canada appeared to be squandering its potential for greatness. They were determined that this evil be corrected. And they were equally determined that they were supremely qualified to direct the corrective measures.

CHAPTER TWO

"Guarded Against Harmful Conditions": The Campaign's Setting

Infant mortality is a symptom complex whose diverse factors – hereditary, congenital and environmental – when judiciously balanced and evaluated present a composite picture of community life of absorbing interest and practical socio-medical value. The mortalities of infancy traced to their finer ramifications reveal not only the sanitary status of a community, but its social, economic and moral aspects as well ... the infant mortality rate has come to be regarded as the most sensitive index we have of social and sanitary progress.

Dr Alan Brown[1]

AS ITS PROMOTERS RECOGNIZED, child welfare is an issue of broad socio-medical definition. Health and health care are intimately connected to structural and cultural conditions, the scientific knowledge underpinning medical theories, and the wider ideological context that influences both diagnosis and public opinion. The child welfare campaign of the early twentieth century must be viewed within the setting of international developments in medicine and social reform, medical professionalization, and the evolution of public health systems.[2] In addition, an understanding of the ailments common to Ontario children in this period, and the doctors' response to them, reveals the impact on medicine of prevalent ideas about class and gender.

Within this context, health took on implications much beyond individual well-being, and its preservation could not be a simple humanitarian impulse. With national productivity and efficiency at stake, children had to be regarded as "national assets" whose well-being was consequently the concern of the state as well as of their parents. The confluence of socio-economic transformation, medical professionalization, and attitudinal change meant that intervention in the family was not only indicated, but essential for the common good. In the process, the private sphere became increasingly open to public scrutiny, and familial roles and relationships were reconceptualized to meet the defined modern standards. State forays into this arena, while restricted, were nevertheless unprecedented. What is clear, however, is that neither the medical profession nor the policy-makers wanted more than to "fix" what in their view was undermining existing social relations.

Internationally, the turn of the century brought a new appreciation of childhood as a specialized time of life.[3] This cultural reawakening to the value of children created a sharpened awareness of the importance of childrearing methods for shaping healthy, well-rounded and productive adults.[4] The physiological and emotional traits particular to childhood had long been underplayed, to the point where children had been perceived simply as diminutive adults. Turn-of-the-century medical practitioners testified to the changes occurring in social perceptions of childhood and their effect on concepts of motherhood: "The mothers who treat their children as little men and women are ... wrong and are pursuing a course which will not result in making the best possible men and women of them ... Every child starts on his way in life with certain inherited possibilities of development, and it should be the object of every mother, guardian and teacher to build upon this foundation the best possible superstructure that it will safely sustain."[5] Doctors thus acknowledged and encouraged these emerging attitudes.[6] The potential of both child and nation could only be realized if it were commonly accepted that "it is just as important that a child's body should be developed aright and guarded against harmful conditions as that its mind should be trained and that it should be protected from evil influences."[7]

The child welfare campaign that unfolded in Ontario was part of an international movement that dated from the last quarter of the nineteenth century. Until the years immediately preceding World War One, the Canadian response to infant mortality seems to have been one of resignation, at times even Darwinistic, grounded in the notion of "survival of the fittest."[8] Within Western medical circles, however, the turn of the century brought increasing recognition that the foremost threat to child health occurred during the first year of life and was due primarily to common respiratory and intestinal disorders. The prevention of these insidious and seemingly intractable maladies became the focus of international child welfare campaigns. Doctors began in earnest to sound the cry to save infants just as social reformers in Canada were becoming aware of the gravity of the problem.

In both ideas and methods, therefore, the Canadian campaign was strongly influenced by medical and social reform trends in Great Britain, France, and the United States. In late nineteenth-century Britain and France, news of a declining birth rate, rising infant mortality, and the appalling conditions of the working class provoked anxiety in state and medical circles. Fears about the future of nation and empire reached fever pitch over the Boer War crisis, when a startled British public learned of the great number of young men classified as unfit for military service.[9]

The emergence of eugenics in this period also captured the popular and scientific imaginations. In Great Britain, biological arguments rooted in Darwinian theory and delineated by Francis Galton suggested that the process of selection could be controlled in order to breed morally and physically superior human beings.[10] In theory, the hereditarianism of the eugenicists conflicted with the environmentalism of social reformers, who stressed protective and ameliorative legislation as the key to health and progress. The purely Darwinian concept of fitness could not be countenanced, however, in view of the declining birth rate and the panic over national ill health. The result, in Britain, was a new focus on saving infants and preserving their health in order to halt the degenerative slide.[11]

In Canada, acceptance of Galtonian eugenics by reformers lent a scientific gloss to anxieties about social degeneration.[12] It seemed to many observers, particularly medical observers, that industrialization was not only undermining the physical and mental health of Canadians, but allowing the "unfit" to reproduce themselves and to perpetuate their "unfitness" at an escalating socio-economic cost. Dr Peter Bryce, chief medical officer of the federal immigration department, expressed such fears in a presentation before the Canadian Medical Association in 1919:

In the centuries preceding the last fifty years, war, famine and pestilence prevented in large measure the increase of population and were accepted as agents of evil permitted through the mysterious dispensations of providence; but today it is the man-made agencies ... and the innumerable machines of industry which have transformed civilized communities into hives of industry, have brought women from the home and field into factories, limited their maternal powers and instincts and set their intellectual and emotional faculties to do duty, replacing largely animal functions at once simple and primitive.[13]

Doctors recognized that modern industry was damaging the health of Canadians and the patriarchal basis of society: it was undermining reproduction in its every sense. Furthermore, racial attitudes of the period construed government promotion of immigration as another means of increasing the numbers of the unfit and aggravating the menace they represented. The results spelled all round deterioration for the current generation and poor prospects for future ones. Thus the marriage of eugenic theory with child welfare concerns in Canada mirrored trends in Europe as well as the United States.

Many Canadian child welfare advocates, including their medical leadership, adopted a combined approach that incorporated both environmentalism and elements of hereditarianism. Dr Helen MacMurchy, a leading Ontario public health activist, was probably the most outspoken medical eugenicist. MacMurchy strongly advocated segregation and sterilization of the "feeble-minded."[14] Other Canadian doctors supported the eugenic approach in varying degrees; however, they consistently warned against a strictly eugenic understanding of the problem of infant mortality. The *Canadian Medical Association Journal* insisted that "there is no reason to believe that babies with an outfit of potential qualities of great benefit to the race are any less resistant to disease than babies destined to be hewers of wood and drawers of water."[15] Some doctors recognized the capitalistic imperatives that required a proportion of workers to be less than mentally astute: many of the feeble-minded were "industrious, useful citizens, plodding away at monotonous occupations which the more intelligent man might not do half so well."[16] Ultimately, the characteristics of environment were seen to be "just as truly inherited as are the fundamental characteristics of racial quality."[17]

Eugenics obviously gave expression to contemporary prejudices about socio-cultural and racial differences in the language of the current scientific theory. But however repugnant from a present-day perspective, eugenics was a legitimate science in the early twentieth century. It is not surprising that the educated, particularly those with scientific training, should espouse a theory that was credible within the intellectual contours of the time. Given the state of research and knowledge in this area, to have done otherwise would have been tantamount to failure to keep abreast of scientific advances. The eugenicists may well have emphasized the limits of environmental reform in a way that led them to "blame the victims," but for them individual responsibility was the social reform objective that ultimately justified all collective and state efforts.[18] It was not simply a matter of depicting environmental reform in purely eugenic terms as exacerbating the problem of the unfit: society and the state had to make people understand that they were personally responsible for improving their own health and fitness.

More than anything, the medical eugenicists and their lay supporters contended that social degeneration had to be prevented, because prevention was more effective and less costly than were any attempts to deal with the problem after the fact. A purely eugenic argument would justify public and medical acceptance of a high infant mortality rate. "Sound economics," however, demonstrated the value of conserving infant life: it cost the city of Toronto $50 to bury each child who died from preventable causes and only $5 to save it.[19] Although sympathetic to eugenic theory, Dr Alan Brown, Canada's foremost paediatrician and Ontario's leading child welfare campaigner, argued that a high infant mortality resulted in "a sacrifice of the unfortunate not the unfit."[20] Brown and his Toronto colleague Dr George Campbell probably best expressed the combined hereditarian/environmentalist approach in declaring that "infant mortality should not be a question of the survival of the fittest, for it is our task to see that every baby is made fit."[21] By stressing the necessity of individual responsibility in matters of health and fitness, even reformers with eugenicist leanings were able to reconcile for themselves their theoretically contradictory views.

That turn-of-the-century Canada was a nation confronting the difficult process of adaptation to socio-economic transformation is a fact attested to in both contemporary analyses and considerable historical study.[22] These reveal that, as the baneful side-effects of industrial capitalism became increasingly apparent, ameliorative reform became a pervasive middle-class concern. Much of that concern derived from the Christian activism of the Social Gospel, a movement that envisioned a more equitable and just society. But the reform discourse, whether concerned with broad principles of social justice or more specific objectives such as slum clearance, factory inspection, and the protection of women and children, reveals understandable class anxieties about the ability of the nation to sustain itself in terms of health and productivity.[23] The reformers did not encourage adaptation of the family to the modern industrial order; rather, their stance was defensive and protective. The traditional family unit was vital to the welfare of Canadian society and essential to the quality of its future. Yet modern industry, by its very nature, had unleashed destructive internal forces that were undermining capitalistic and patriarchal organization. Since the self-adjusting market mechanism could no longer be counted upon, intervention was necessary to prevent the system, quite literally, from devouring its own young.

Physicians played a major role in the creation of a modern consciousness: their professionally designed and supervised childrearing system was self-consciously modern. According to them, the one true hope of race, nation, and system subsided in the child, who was more "modern" than its parents could ever hope to be. As science and technology continued to restructure the world around children, childhood had to be reformulated to reflect evolving social needs and goals.[24] A "modern" Canadian childhood had to be carefully delineated in the hope of eradicating the difficulties, both individual and social, that doctors attributed to "improper" and old-fashioned childrearing practices. "Modernity" was as they defined it, although they never did so explicitly: in general, the term connoted "better" than that which had existed to that point.

The child welfare campaign's organizational pattern was much the same in North America and Western Europe; its early years saw medical participation subsumed within a much broader reform coalition. The same was true in Canada. Initially, the movement was largely in the hands of organized womanhood and came under the aegis of general public health reform. The child welfare problem was approached by what can only be called ad hoc experimental measures borrowed from reformist ideas and practices adopted in Britain, France, and the United States.[25] On the whole, these took the form of sporadic, localized attempts to deal with specific aspects of the larger problem of childhood illness and death, such as the establishment of pure milk dispensaries and immunization clinics. The National Council of Women of Canada (1893) used its various local councils to set up well-baby clinics and milk depots, hold baby contests, and campaign for tuberculosis control, improved housing, and Mothers' Allowances. The Imperial Order of Daughters of the Empire (1900) also established and maintained well-baby clinics and collected funds for nursing services in rural areas. The branches of the Women's Institute (1903) concentrated on improved sanitation in small municipalities and rural schools, school medical services, and health education through the distribution of literature and through conferences.

In both Britain and the United States, by the beginning of the twentieth century, physicians had stepped to the front of this incipient movement, a development not imitated in Canada until the time of the Great War.[26] By 1914, Canadian doctors believed that they would have to move quickly to take the reins of a movement rightfully belonging to them, because "the average physician does not realize his responsibility in the important work of lowering infant mortality, and by this indifference he opens the portals of this most important field of preventive medicine to social workers and philanthropists."[27] With a great deal more at stake than infant lives, important though these were, there was cause for urgency.

Doctors were uncertain about the exact reasons for rising infant mortality, but professed no lack of confidence in their ability to bring about its reduction, and in their exclusive right to lead the way. Medical professionalization and specialization had been on the rise during the late nineteenth century, a trend that effectively spurred medical dominance of the child welfare issue. The professionalization of other occupations had a similar influence on many social questions of the time.[28] Professionalization is essentially an attempt by producers of services to create and control a market for their expertise; it contributes to social inequality by emphasizing both an internal hierarchy and elite status within the larger society. It involves the domination, control, and even outright exclusion of allied and competing occupations. This collective drive to enhance and maintain status requires state backing for the establishment of a monopoly of knowledge and skill. Occupational autonomy, control over services, and maintenance of status are assured by the continuing ignorance of clients and their consequent need for professional expertise. Medical dominance, therefore, involves not only the superiority of the physician in relation to other medical occupations, most notably nursing and midwifery, but also a privileged position within the class structure that is replicated in the social distance between doctor and patient.

No professionalizing occupation in early twentieth-century Canada was as successful as medicine in attaining its goals.[29] Although the Canadian Medical Association had been established in 1867, it did not increase its membership and expand its political influence until the 1920s. By 1912 Canadian doctors had obtained enough state assistance to allow for significant professional power. In that year, the Canadian Medical Association asserted that organized medicine "should use every legitimate means in its power to enable it to speak with truth and with authority on all matters pertaining to the physical well being of the people." More importantly, physicians should assume the full responsibility of leadership in public health: they must not allow either "the political demagogue or the quasi-religious fanatic to mislead the people."[30]

The power of the medical profession rests on its ability to gain public respect for the scientific basis of its knowledge and the social value of its work.[31] The social construction of health and illness is critical to its status and role. Growing public interest in health matters and faith in science provided the cultural context that was necessary for the advancement of the doctors' professional drive. Doctors appropriated moral guardianship by legitimizing their authority to define "deviance" in scientific terms. At the same time, they were able to command the operation of the new regulatory agencies that followed the emergence of preventive medicine and a state apparatus to deal with public health.[32] Note the views of key public health administrators such as Dr Helen MacMurchy, who argued that the profession's knowledge was vital "to the very existence of the race" and that medical regulation served an important function in "the program of any civilized state which wishes to preserve its power and government from century to century." Only doctors were equipped to recognize disease and defects; they alone possessed "the scientific imagination to see what these defects, if not remedied or prevented, [would] mean to the community as well as to the individual in after life."[33] Health and welfare were legitimate matters for state concern, just as the preservation of the state was a valid medical concern and a "program" that doctors could most effectively design.

Specialization was another factor that contributed to emerging medical theories about child welfare. Paediatrics was establishing itself as a legitimate specialty in the United States and Britain in the late nineteenth century. By 1914, however, there were only 2 paediatric specialists in Toronto; in 1929, there were only 48 in all of Canada.[34] It was not until 1922, when the Society for the Study of the Diseases of Children was created, that Canadian paediatrics began to acquire a more distinct professional form. The limited number of paediatricians in the country nonetheless obliged the Society to embrace all doctors interested in child health.[35] Yet paediatrics was increasingly forming an important part of general medical service to a paying middle-class clientele, as the profession relentlessly urged parents to seek regular medical advice.[36]

Despite their numerical insignificance, the paediatricians' express interest in the conservation and improvement of child life and their precise knowledge of the child's emotional and physical make-up made them natural leaders of a child welfare campaign. Dr Alan Brown stressed that paediatricians must maintain leadership in "all matters pertaining to problems of child life" and should rightfully represent "the highest authority" in this area.[37] As their society defined it, the paediatrician's most important function was "his sphere of influence on child care as a whole throughout the country." The care given by paediatricians influenced the type of care sought by friends and relatives of their patients. Public health departments at all government levels increasingly relied upon paediatric consultation. Public addresses, broadcasts, and articles in the press by paediatricians, an integral part of the educational approach to child welfare during the interwar years, were believed to foster public demand for better child care.[38]

At a time when paediatric specialization was just emerging, medical participation in voluntary and state child welfare activities helped legitimize the paediatrician's role and his share of the health care market. The bulk of the work had to be done by general practitioners and public health employees, but specialists performed an important function as the campaign's chief ideologues. While state agencies enlarged their health care role during these years, academicians remained essential to the shaping of medical theory and practice.[39] The specialists, particularly those such as Brown who were affiliated with major children's hospitals, health departments, and medical schools, wielded a much greater influence within the campaign and its related state agencies than their numbers suggest.[40] The research findings that they contributed to their professional journals and conferences, popularized in childrearing advice literature, and propagated through clinics and nurse visits, formed the basis of child welfare activities throughout the period.

Early efforts to combat infant mortality thus saw a group of concerned lay reformers and medical professionals coalesce around a series of theories and approaches that owed as much to socio-cultural currents as to the limits of contemporary medical science. Neither early twentieth-century medicine nor the child welfare campaign can be properly understood apart from the evolution of the preventive concept and the development of public health: public health is one of the essential services that ensures the functioning of the modern industrial state. The complementary environmental and microbic approaches against disease became crucial with the growth of cities and the complex social organization characteristic of industrial society.[41] These approaches suggested that the key to public health could be found in a general "cleaning up" of society. Housing inspection, sewage disposal, and water and food purification standards would go a long way toward improving health and welfare, while bacteriological advances saw stricter regulations about the reporting and quarantine of communicable diseases. The environmental approach, however, required substantial investments of time and money as well as state involvement. In order to be truly successful, it called for nothing short of the eradication of poverty. Narrowing the scope of public health reform to a bacteriological focus promised more immediate results but still presupposed the institutional mechanisms – at the least, a committed municipal board of health and the employment of sanitary inspectors – and the legislative means to enforce regulations and coerce the public to comply.[42]

An appreciation of the limits to which public health reformers could aspire, as well as the limits of legal regulations on sanitary reform and quarantine, led to the belief that "it is only through education that progress may be looked for beyond what is secured through those activities which the group rather than the individual can accomplish."[43] Social conditions – the root of ill health, disease and death – were beyond the scope of public health departments. Medicine could not heal the problem of social inequality without restructuring a system that professionals could not fault. Disease control and reduction of mortality were worthy but frustrating goals because of the practical difficulties of enforcement, and were also essentially reactive and after the fact. The spread of eugenicist ideas in the early twentieth century testifies to growing disenchantment with these approaches. As one public health activist remarked, they could offer "but little contribution to the positive side of health work which aims to secure a maximum of healthful years as a result of hygienic living."[44]

The trend toward prevention provided scientific support for the medical belief that it was essential to begin at the beginning of life in order to mount an effective attack on the multi-faceted evils of ill health and social degeneration.[45] From the economic standpoint, preventive medicine was thought to rank alongside "such great agencies of waste elimination as forest conservation, chemical research on the utilization of waste products, engineering projects to improve mechanical efficiency, modern accounting, and scientific management," and even to outrank them "in its present or potential economic value to the community at large."[46] The modern approach called for professional and public commitment to mass education. To this end, the Canadian Public Health Association was formed in 1910. Medical involvement in World War One also stimulated this new commitment to education for prevention, epitomized by the creation of the Canadian Social Hygiene Council in 1922. The council, later renamed the Health League of Canada, was a voluntary agency dedicated to the promotion of preventive medicine as a "national and economic necessity."[47] Many prominent participants in the child welfare movement were members of both organizations. That this overlap should have existed is not surprising, considering the common objectives: regular medical supervision, instruction of the public, and the erection of competent health administrations in order to secure the "optimum health" of Canadians. By its very nature, prevention is more interventionary than curative medicine, necessitating the establishment of effective state machinery to facilitate the required medical regulation of the public: the public health department became "the first line of defence of the people."[48]

The British North America Act made little specific provision for public health matters and assigned exclusive jurisdiction for health and welfare to provincial and municipal governments. Health activities of the dominion government were divided among various departments, including those responsible for agriculture, marine hospitals, fisheries, inland revenue and finance. The Commission of Conservation, established by Laurier's Liberal government in 1909, included in its expansive roster the National Council of Health, which would act in an advisory capacity to federal and provincial governments. From the time of its own inception, the Canadian Medical Association passed regular resolutions calling for the creation of a dominion health department to provide leadership and coordination.[49] Pressure by organized medicine and reform organizations went unheeded until 1919. The department established that year was intended to cooperate with the provincial, territorial and other health authorities "with a view to the coordination of the efforts proposed or made for preserving and improving the public health, the conservation of child life, and the promotion of child welfare."[50]

The federal department's apparent commitment to child health and welfare was reinforced in 1920, when a separate child welfare division was created under the direction of Dr Helen MacMurchy. The division was to assist in "cooperative activities, coordination and education," and to study problems pertinent to this field.[51] The federal department also instigated the Council on Child Welfare, with Charlotte Whitton as its executive secretary. All nationally organized agencies engaged in any aspect of child welfare work were entitled to be represented on the council, a voluntary body that received some federal funding for its educational services.[52] The Department of Health Act also provided for the establishment of the Dominion Council of Health, another advisory body comprising the chief medical officer of each province, one scientific adviser, and four lay appointments representing labour, agriculture, and rural and urban women's organizations.[53] Its purpose was to bring the provincial health officers together regularly in the hope of attaining uniformity of procedure throughout the country.[54]

The 1919 Department of Health Act theoretically allowed a considerable leadership role for federal health authorities in the public health arena, and especially in the area of child welfare. The medical profession was initially very optimistic about the potential of this federal role. Dr Peter Bryce provided the Canadian Medical Association with an extensive list of the functions "which a federal department of health may fairly be expected to perform," beginning with "aid in crystallizing the most advanced health ideas into legislation common to all provinces." With respect to child welfare, Bryce hoped that the department would adopt measures similar to those of England's Maternity Act of 1918, which paid 50 per cent of local costs for maternal and child welfare provisions "to deal adequately with the potential soldier and producer of wealth through elaborate plans for child welfare."[55]

As will be seen, few of the brilliant hopes of child welfare advocates were destined to be realized through federal action. The advisory nature of the various affiliated divisions and councils promised much, but advice could easily be discounted in the legislative process. More importantly, medical dominance of these bodies ensured that professional interests shaped any public health measures that were eventually passed. The wording of section 7 of the Act establishing the federal department of health testifies to the fact that there was no intention of giving the dominion health officers jurisdiction over provincial or municipal boards of health. The primary responsibility for public health was to remain in provincial hands, permitting the federal government to sidestep accountability for creating, maintaining or directing health care programs beyond its commitment to provide restricted lump-sum funding.[56] Meanwhile, the expanding health and welfare needs of an increasingly industrial and urban society gave rise to an imbalance between the provincial and local governments' responsibilities in this area and their ability to fund the required services.

The Ontario Public Health Act, which had established the province's Board of Health in 1882, was easily the most important piece of public health legislation passed in Canada during the nineteenth century.[57] Modelled on the British Public Health Act of 1875, it motivated the enactment of similar legislation in the other provinces and gave Ontario a pre-eminent role in providing modern state health and welfare services.[58] The decade between 1912 and 1922 saw the modernization and professionalization of public health activity in the province. The new Public Health Act that came into force in August 1912 strengthened provincial supervision over municipal health boards by ensuring that the local medical officer of health could no longer be dismissed without the approval of the provincial board. Seven district officers were appointed as full-time supervisors of public health across the province.[59]

Greater recognition given to disease prevention and child welfare in reform and medical circles led to the creation in 1916 of the Child Welfare Bureau, the first of its kind in Canada. In 1920 the province's new Division of Maternal and Child Hygiene and Public Health Nursing promised further advances for the child welfare campaign. In the same year, the Division of Health Education was also inaugurated as a separate unit devoted entirely to promotion of preventive measures through literature, exhibits, films, radio talks and special lectures. The school health services were removed from the Department of Education and incorporated into those of the Division of Maternal and Child Hygiene in 1925. Within five years of its creation, this division had taken charge of the needs of Ontario's mothers and children from conception through puberty in an explicit acknowledgment of the campaign ideal that "the first point in any scheme for public health is emphasis on intelligent maternity ... children can grow up only once."[60]

Undoubtedly, the issues of health care costs and who should rightfully pay them were major shapers of state involvement in child welfare. For the most part, medical care in this period operated as private enterprise and was funded on a fee-for-service basis. Doctors were aware that the cost of medical care was prohibitive for many families.[61] During the 1920s, the average fee for medical examination, excluding drugs and dental care, was $5, representing roughly one-quarter of a labourer's weekly earnings, or more than a day's pay. Indigents received grudging aid from the muncipality once their need was demonstrated to the satisfaction of municipal authorities. Throughout the period, organized medicine continually reiterated its willingness to provide "a certain amount of free service" for the public good, but was ever on guard for tell-tale signs of exploitation.[62] The Canadian Medical Association consistently maintained that, by comparison with other professional incomes, the average medical income was "not excessive." In reality, the 1920s represented a period of unprecedented medical affluence. An association study of two districts in Ontario served by 500 physicians reported that the physicians' average gross annual income from 1925 to 1930 was $6,262.78, which compared favourably with the $1,024 average annual salary for industrial workers.[63]

The profession was, as a whole, opposed to "state medicine," and committed to medical control of health care and any form of health insurance.[64] Even in 1939, having survived the economic strains of the Depression, the Canadian Medical Association contended that "centralization of complete control of all sickness is neither necessary nor advisable."[65] Public health doctors already on the government payroll tended to have less fear of state medicine, but with few exceptions, they shared the outlook of private practitioners that upheld professional control of health care delivery and its remuneration. Their common concern imposed serious constraints on the child welfare campaign and on any public policy formulated to address the health needs of Canadians. Such doctors were caught in a particular bind: while they were employees of the state and committed to state leadership and coordination of public health endeavours, their activities were nonethless circumscribed by professional loyalties and class positions. Moreover, if bureaucratization was essential to the achievement of public health goals, it also contained the threat of "deskilling" and breakdown of professional autonomy because of its tendency to division of labour.[66] Ultimately public health employees and private practitioners were agreed that professional autonomy had to be preserved, despite the costs to adequate health care.

It was only during the Great Depression, when the market apparatus failed doctors as much as other working Canadians, that the medical profession invoked true state responsibility for health care, and then only as an emergency relief measure.[67] Nearly three million Canadians were classified as "medically indigent" by 1935.[68] When the Conservative government of R.B. Bennett invoked the constitutional responsibility of the municipalities and provinces in this area of relief, as in all others, it was left to the provinces to institute their own medical relief measures.[69] The system implemented in Ontario in 1935 was the largest-scale organization of medical services for a particular sector of the population in Canada, serving an estimated 50,000 people per month. Although doctors were now essentially on the government payroll, organized medicine remained in control of the scheme's administration.[70] Ironically, from the clients' point of view, it was only in the depths of the Depression, and largely in response to professional pressure, that many Ontario families were able to obtain the medical care they could not enjoy in more prosperous times.

If child welfare was increasingly attracting the attention of lay reformers, medical professionals, and the state, the remedies proposed were shaped by class, professional, and political concerns that frequently obscured and impeded the ultimate objective: saving infants and improving national health and welfare. The largest obstacle to "optimum health" was the profession's own surgical expertise in excising health and health care from the socio-economic whole. Doctors consistently downplayed the role of poverty in both health and access to health care. Given the need to balance conflicting options and to work around obstacles imposed by divergent interests, it is not surprising that the child welfare campaign was forced to operate within these boundaries. For all the rhetoric of efficiency and productivity, child welfare measures in Ontario and nationally were often inefficient and less than productive.

IT IS IMPORTANT HERE to consider the actual medical causes behind the mounting interest in child welfare and the specific medical understanding of child health during this period. Historians have long been interested in the "plagues" and epidemics that afflicted great numbers, incited public anxiety, and inspired medical crusades, research, and innovation. But many more children were victims of the decidedly less glamorous but dangerous maladies that were considered typical of childhood. Before the widespread use of sulphanomides and antibiotics to control bacterial infections and mitigate the worst complications of viral infections, a medical innovation dating only from the late 1930s, the annual morbidity and mortality rates from contagious diseases such as diphtheria, scarlet fever, whooping cough, and measles were substantial.[71]

Nor were these "children's diseases" the only threats to childhood health and life. Tuberculosis, the disease "most feared by the working man," was not a primary killer of young children.[72] By the early twentieth century, however, medical research had established that it was contagious and frequently milk-borne, thereby making children particularly vulnerable to infection. Latent tuberculosis in childhood contributed to high adult incidence of the disease, which was the foremost killer of Canadians between the ages of fifteen and fifty during the entire period of this study. The anti-tuberculosis campaign organized in Canada at the turn of the century concentrated on its prevention in childhood and gave impetus to campaigns for safeguarding the milk supply.[73]

Deficiency diseases such as rickets were also common, particularly within the lower socio-economic strata. Rickets is caused by Vitamin D deficiency; it prevents bones from hardening and leads to their malformation. Contemporary medical surveys suggested that "probably no disease is encountered more frequently in infancy": its incidence in working-class children varied from 40 to 90 per cent.[74] Although rickets was not commonly a direct cause of death, it was considered an important contributory cause in a vast number of cases. The essential role of vitamins in treating the disease was understood by 1912, but as late as 1921, medical researchers had still not established its precise aetiology. It was generally accepted that the "anti-rachitic organic factor" was contained in cod-liver oil, increasingly prescribed as a dietary supplement in infancy.

Tuberculosis and rickets were clearly correlated to socio-economic status. Their prevalence testifies to the extent of poor living and working conditions. Despite this, both the medical profession and the state approached these diseases by ameliorative methods that focused on individual responsibility. The same was true for their overall approach to ill health and infant mortality. Prevention was considered to be the most effective method of vanquishing these childhood scourges. All too often, prevention was in fact the only method available because medical science had not definitively established either causation or cure. But prevention was also a satisfying doctrine in that it enlarged the profession's social role without requiring it to engage in intensive analysis of social inequalities. The medical response to these public health and child welfare issues naturally emphasized prevention through massive vaccination campaigns, public education, and environmental improvements, especially regarding the milk supply and sanitary housing.

The concern of early twentieth-century public health reformers in Ontario about communicable diseases is borne out by the statistics of those years. Between 1902 and 1911, there were more than 2,000 deaths annually from reportable diseases, a total of 25,937 for the eight-year period.[75] The annual proportion of these deaths for children under five years was approximately 10 per cent of the total. The highest death rate was in the first year of life: the total for that year was nearly double that for the second year and for the entire five-to-nine age group. In 1922, respiratory and contagious diseases together accounted for nearly 23 per cent of all deaths under one year, while diarrhaea and enteritis accounted for 18 per cent.

The incidence of disease is barely hinted at by these mortality statistics. The only statistics available are those respecting communicable diseases that local medical officers of health were then required to report.[76] Compulsory notification of diphtheria, scarlet fever, and measles was instigated in Ontario in 1901, while whooping cough was made reportable in 1905. Therefore, underreporting, or reporting of death as due to other causes, also complicates the picture. The existence of chronic health problems resulting from these and other unreported diseases was admitted by public health authorities, but their extent cannot even be estimated. It can be safely argued that the true morbidity and mortality rates were substantially higher than official reports could ever depict. However problematic the statistics, they do allow an impression of the impact of communicable diseases on the population, and the proportion of the total that comprised childhood morbidity and mortality. What is clear is that death from communicable diseases claimed at least 1 in 6 children under fourteen, and 1 in 10 children under five, in the early twentieth century.[77] Many Ontario families understood firsthand the suffering caused by ill health and early death.

The most menacing of the childhood diseases were diphtheria, whooping cough, scarlet fever, and measles. The three-pronged campaign against these diseases centred on vaccination where possible, isolation to avoid spread of infection, and public education. The latter was considered paramount. It seemed to many medical observers that the general attitude to childhood illness was too nonchalant by far, and that parents themselves were largely to blame both for the spread of disease and its often tragic results. In assessing Windsor's mortality statistics for 1915, the town's medical officer remarked on "the appalling fact that two-thirds of all these deaths were under four years of age and of the one-third who died after four and before sixty it is quite likely that their vitality was undermined by disease in childhood." A concerted campaign by the state was essential in order to impress upon parents that the only hope lay in "correct living ... that is their proper care from birth."[78] It was assumed that correct living was a choice that could be made once people were enlightened about what it entailed.

Similarly, Chatham's medical officer argued that the annual visitation of "one or more of this quartette of children's enemies" was due to parents' refusal to regard these childhood diseases seriously. He asserted that "children do not have to have these diseases at any time in life, and instead of being the usual thing it should be a very unusual occurrence."[79] The medical officer of Hamilton commented sarcastically that parents were prone to interpreting the good advice of the family physician in ways that best suited their own interests, regardless of the ultimate health effects: "parents, often on the advice of the family physician, insist on giving the patient plenty of fresh air, which too often happens to be the air of a moving picture or other well-patronized theatre." Large numbers of children thus became exposed to infection, "sometimes from ignorance on the part of mothers, sometimes from thoughtlessness, sometimes through indifference."[80] The difference between health and sickness was an issue of personal choice and individual behaviour, and, above all, parental responsibility.

Diphtheria was the primary threat to Ontario's children, responsible for 1 death in every 6 among children under fourteen between 1920 and 1925. Fully half of these deaths occurred in the first five years of life.[81] Early administration of antitoxin, ideally at the initial presentation of symptoms, was considered highly effective in preventing death and lessening the liability to serious after-effects. The provincial health department began supplying it without charge in 1916.[82] Its increasing use reduced the death rate from 42 per 100,000 in 1896, to 7 in 1926, and to .9 in 1939. By the mid-1920s, a preventive toxoid was available, and by 1930, approximately 80,000 Ontario children had been innoculated.[83] The use of the Shick test, which confirmed immunity, showed that 80 to 90 per cent of children were protected by three doses of toxoid.

Reports from local and district medical officers of health throughout the period reveal the slow struggle to persuade local medical practitioners and the general public of the value of innoculation.[84] In 1924, the Peterborough Board of Health pointed out that passive resistance through professional and parental apathy, inertia or ignorance was only one of the reasons for the slow decline of the disease. In that town, the board encountered outright opposition from the local anti-vaccination league, which presented a "very active propaganda." That compulsory vaccination was a contentious issue is evidenced in the workings of these leagues across the province.[85] Nonetheless, persistent educational and vaccination efforts tended to succeed by their success. The incidence and mortality of diphtheria decreased steadily across the province during the interwar years. This was attibuted to three factors: the increased use of antitoxin as soon as a clinical diagnosis was made, the education of parents to call their physician immediately on the appearance of sore throat in their children, and widespread immunization. Urged on by the Ontario department, many municipal health boards organized school and preschool toxoid clinics.[86] In 1923, out of a population of 3,033,266, the number immunized was only 780, or .9 per cent of the population between birth and age fourteen. By 1935, 431,311 Ontarians had been immunized. The battle against diphtheria would continue, but by the end of the interwar period, victory was in sight.[87]

Although its menace did not approach that of diphtheria, scarlet fever caused more than 150 deaths per year in Ontario in the late 1920s, more than 70 per cent of which were in children under ten years.[88] Diseases of the ear and kidney frequently followed scarlet fever and could be debilitating through adulthood. In 1924, a simple skin test, the Dick test, became available to reveal susceptibility.[89] A course of five injections of Dick antitoxin administered at weekly intervals was believed to confer immunity to the majority of those susceptible. Scarlet fever antitoxin given to susceptible individuals who had recently been exposed protected them against infection for at least two or three weeks and lessened the severity of the disease. The provincial health department began free distribution of scarlet fever antitoxin for treatment and passive immunization and scarlet fever toxin for active immunization in that year. Two years later, it was noted that scarlet fever antitoxin for treatment had proven itself "of definite worth" and had been distributed to more than 7,500 individuals. Active immunization with scarlet fever toxin was extended to 11,000 individuals.[90] Although the Dick toxin/antitoxin continued to be used with great confidence in Ontario, by the late 1930s there was some skepticism among medical researchers regarding their value.[91] Whether due to stringent quarantine regulations, improvement in the milk supply, or in whatever measure to vaccination, scarlet fever mortality also dropped significantly from the turn of the century. In the years 1900 to 1904, scarlet fever claimed a 13.74 per cent death rate; this was reduced to 1.58 by the latter half of the 1930s.[92]

The specific prevention of diphtheria and scarlet fever had "an important economic aspect" in that the cost involved to protect a large group against both diseases was considered less than in treating a single case of the former.[93] Measles and whooping cough proved more of a challenge to public health authorities. About 104 deaths annually in the late 1920s were attributable to measles, with mortality concentrated to an even greater degree in young children than was the case for scarlet fever and diphtheria. Of the deaths from measles, 73.4 per cent were under five, 62.9 per cent were three and under, and 22.4 per cent were under one year. Widespread measles epidemics occurred regularly in Ontario during the first thirty years of this century. Human convalescent serum was employed by private practitioners after 1924, when American experiments suggested its efficacy in preventing or at least modifying the disease after exposure. The serum was produced and distributed by the Connaught Laboratories in Toronto, and was advocated for infants and young children whose physical condition was such that an attack would likely lead to serious bronchial complications. But procedures for active immunization against measles eluded medical researchers throughout the period.

Whooping cough proved to be the most serious and persistent menace to child health. Medical researchers believed that no communicable disease was more prevalent or more underreported: they estimated that five times the reported cases, or 20,000–25,000 per year, was the true extent of the public health problem presented by whooping cough morbidity in Ontario in the late 1920s.[94] Health department surveys revealed that about 85 percent of all cases developed in children under five, 60 per cent in the first year. Between 1929 and 1933 alone, it caused 799 deaths in Ontario, an average of 160 per year. Again, the health department was keen to impress upon Ontarians the seriousness of the disease, usually due to bronchial complications.[95] The younger the child, the more grave the prognosis, with more than 50 per cent of all deaths occurring in children under one year. Whooping cough was particularly difficult to control because diagnosis was complicated by the fact that the early symptoms so closely resemble those of an ordinary cold, delaying medical intervention and increasing exposure. The Health

Act required notification, isolation, quarantine, and placarding. Children or teachers in the same residence could not attend school until they had received a certificate from the medical officer of health authorizing their attendance.

The seriousness of this disease is revealed by the provincial department's records covering the years 1915 to 1926, during which there were as many deaths from whooping cough as from scarlet fever, measles, and smallpox combined. By the early 1930s, whooping cough had surpassed diphtheria as the most dangerous of the common childhood diseases.[96] Control measures were directed through the usual channels of public education, isolation, and immunization. Pertussis vaccine was distributed to the physicians of the province free of charge.[97] Doctors lamented, however, that the rates of incidence and mortality showed little evidence to support the efficacy of the control measures. Despite some progress, whooping cough remained the first cause of death in the entire group of contagious diseases at the period's end. Much more difficult to diagnose than the others, and with a higher incidence of life-threatening complications for very young children, the development of more effective vaccines and the widespread use of antibiotics were required to make true inroads in its control.[98]

Overall it would appear that the progress made in combatting mortality from communicable diseases during the interwar years was significant, at least as far as the official statistics can reveal. Education certainly played a role in alerting parents to the presenting symptoms of disease and to the fact that its spread could be discouraged by vaccination and isolation. The provincial health department's aggressive immunization campaigns, and especially its provision of free vaccine, undoubtedly made a positive impact on the health of children in this period. Although whooping cough and measles continued to defy the control measures put into effect by the health department, public health analysts argued that they might well have shown an increase in the absence of any such attempts.[99] The recurrence of epidemic influenza also complicates the measurement of health improvement in these years: 1918, 1923, 1926, and 1929 were "influenza years," causing a significant rise in the general infant death rate as well as in the rates for influenza and pneumonia specifically. About 40 per cent of infant deaths from influenza between 1921 and 1931 took place in these years.[100]

Ultimately, the real problem in measuring the health status of the population lies in the aggregate nature of the statistics themselves. Improvement in mortality rates can coexist with class, occupational, and regional differentials that still explain disease and death by economic disadvantage.[101] As Charles Webster has noted, because of the wide dispersion characteristic of mortality rates, "the average understates the advances in health enjoyed by some sections of the community, and it overstates the position with respect to a substantial minority."[102] Infant death rates in particular suggest the continued existence of a "submerged mass of ill health."[103]

Doctors were especially troubled by the stubbornly intractable mortality rates in the first year of life. By the early 1900s international bacteriological research on infant death had pinpointed its three leading causes: prematurity and congenital debility, intestinal disorders, and respiratory diseases. In 1906, the United States Census Bureau published its first *Report on Infant Mortality*, and the First National Conference on Infantile Mortality was held in London that year. The Canadian medical profession kept abreast of international research in this area, and contributed its own findings.[104] The best-known and most cited Canadian survey is Dr Helen MacMurchy's series of infant mortality reports commissioned by the Ontario government and published between 1910 and 1913. Her reports were not the only attempt at statistical analysis of the nature and extent of infant mortality in Canada, but they were more accessible to a non-medical audience and consequently had a wider impact in state and reform circles.

According to MacMurchy's findings, of 52,629 births in Ontario in 1909, death had claimed 6,932 children before their first birthday. In Toronto alone, the rate was 230 deaths per 1,000 live births. She reiterated the recognized triad of primary infantile killers and emphasized the importance, and preventability, of intestinal disease within this group. The real enemy, she pointed out, was not *cholera infantum* (epidemic diarrhaea, also called "summer complaint" because of its seasonal incidence) but an infant mortality attributable to a wide range of causes, the most important of which were ignorance, poverty, and inadequate medical attention. Private philanthrophy alone was insufficient to deal with the enormity of the problem. "National action, government action, collective action, not individual action, can save the baby," was MacMurchy's ultimate conclusion.[105]

There are innumerable similar examples of medical reasoning in an ongoing debate that would increasingly fill the pages of contemporary medical and reform journals. In 1911, its first year of publication, the *Canadian Medical Association Journal* presented an examination of "infantile mortality in Canada" by Dr C.A. Hodgetts, medical adviser to the Commission of Conservation. Long a dedicated public health reformer and formerly chief health officer of

Ontario, Hodgetts summarized information contained in the national census of 1901 and the latest available vital statistics of Ontario and Quebec.[106] The 1901 census had revealed an infant death rate of 120 per 1,000 live births, identical to that of the older and theoretically more decadent Great Britain. Ontario's statistics for 1908 showed a rate of 124. Drawing extensively from British analyses of leading causes of infant death, Hodgetts pointed out that prematurity and atrophy (congenital debility) together accounted for more than one-third of the deaths, for a national total of 6,388 in 1901. He also echoed the resignation of the British authorities in stating that this number represented "what may be termed the unfits." At this time, prenatal care was not a serious consideration in lessening the risk factor of prematurity and congenital defects. The economic basis of this seemingly unpreventable wastage was also underlined: "it is quite probable that more of such infants are to be found among people of the poorer classes than among those of the well-to-do."[107]

Hodgetts noted that diseases of the respiratory system were ranked third in importance (4,564 deaths in 1901), but paid no further attention to this cause. There was simply little that doctors could do at this time to deal with many of the acute infectious diseases, and, despite the acceptance of germ theory, there was little real understanding of their aetiology. International research revealed that intestinal disorders, primarily epidemic diarrhaea, accounted for the largest number of deaths deemed preventable. Not surprisingly, then, the medical profession directed its energies to this particular cause.[108]

In considering the predisposing factors of epidemic diarrhaea, which was ranked as the second category with 5,477 deaths, Hodgetts concluded that British findings "would in the main be substantiated" for Canada.[109] British studies noted the effects of poor housing conditions, contaminated soil, seasonal heat and feeding practices, especially the use of cow's milk. Citing Dr Arthur Newsholme, Hodgetts remarked that the leading British authority had "laid down the following dicta, which cannot be impressed too strongly upon the medical profession of Canada: epidemic diarrhaea is chiefly a disease of urban life, as a fatal disease is a disease of the artisan and still more of the lower laboring classes to a prominent extent." Yet, while stressing the class basis of infant mortality, Hodgetts still denied that poverty was "so important a factor with us." Instead, it was "probably largely a question of social status *per se*, that is, it is due to neglect of infants, uncleanly storage of food, industrial occupation of mothers, *etc.*"[110]

Hodgett's assessment of the Canadian infant mortality problem reflected the social and medical considerations of the British studies on which it was based. Countless Canadian medical studies would repeat the complicated and confused logic that recognized the link between material deprivation and illness but steadfastly refused to see poverty itself as the primary cause. Drs Alan Brown and George Campbell, in an early discussion in the *Canadian Medical Association Journal*, also upheld the conclusions of British and American studies, but were ambivalent and ambiguous in attempting to pinpoint exact causation: "If improved medicine, science, more healthful living conditions, more wholesome food, better sanitary regulations, cannot explain this seeming inconsistency of an increased infant death rate, must there not be another cause to explain the anomaly?"[111] While doctors accepted on faith that this index of "modern improvements" was nationwide, and recognized no class or regional differences in its application, they traced causation to its source in behavioural traits defined in class terms.

Several aetiological factors emerged from such analysis.[112] First, statistics confirmed that the incidence of intestinal disease was by far the greatest among artificially fed infants. It was primarily an urban disease, occurring predominantly in summer, characteristics which encouraged much inconclusive theorizing about the contributory effects of heat, soil, and housing. And closely connected was the fact that infant mortality was evidently a "class mortality," taking its toll primarily from the poorly fed, clothed, and sheltered working class. Maternal employment was also strongly implicated. As MacMurchy expressed it, with characteristic bluntness, "when the mother works, the baby dies."[113]

Thus Canadian doctors saw the role of poverty in predisposing infants to illness and death, but were reluctant to make this the foremost cause. Hodgetts conceptualized these factors in relative terms and refused to believe that Canadian workers had to contend with the abject conditions of life and work that undermined the strength of their British and American counterparts. Brown and Campbell admitted that infant mortality was appropriately termed "a class mortality for it is excessive among the poor and the low." But poverty placed third in their list of causative factors, behind neglect and ignorance and so closely correlated to these two as to appear both their cause and effect: "poverty means poor health for the mother, lower intelligence, lack of energy and general inefficiency ... poverty forces mothers to work for a living, depriving their babies of breast milk and, as a consequence, these infants are unable to thrive and develop in the poverty-stricken homes into which they are born."[114] Doctors downplayed economics by insisting that material conditions had generally improved for all Canadians. If they were better off than many others, and even better off than previous generations of Canadians, they were obviously choosing not to take full advantage of their high standard of living.

The historical record shows little in the opening decades of the twentieth century to sustain this medical notion of widespread improvement in the material conditions of the mass of the populace.[115] The cost of living rose substantially from the outbreak of World War I until the unprecedented deflation of the Great Depression.[116] A survey of seven industries conducted by the Dominion Bureau of Statistics in 1918 found that approximately 46 per cent of their labour force earned less than $20 per week.[117] For a husband, wife, and three young children aged twelve, ten and six years, "a normal family at its costly period," a decent family budget would permit $94.07 in expenses per month "or for a year about the income of a $4 a day labourer working 300 days."[118] As one Ontario worker testified in 1921, all that remained of his $15 weekly pay after feeding a family of five and paying for rent and fuel was 65 cents "to buy all necessary articles for the home for a week."[119] Nearly half the Canadian labour force could not provide for the necessities of life in a period of overall national prosperity.

That these factors had serious repercussions for the health and welfare of working-class children cannot be disputed. An American study published in the Canadian *Labour Gazette* in 1924 revealed that the mortality rate of infants whose fathers earned less than $450 annually was nearly three times as high as the rate for families in which the fathers earned $1,250 or more. If mothers were gainfully employed, the mortality rate increased again.[120] The situation was certainly no better in Canada. Studies of the conditions of the Montreal and Toronto working classes found infant mortality rates to be substantially higher in the lower socio-economic strata of these cities.[121] Contemporary social critics like J.S. Woodsworth made similar correlations between want, ill health, and crime, warning that "the worst is not the effect on the individual or even on the individual family but the effect on the younger children and the coming generation. If we give less than a decent standard of living we simply mortgage the future generation."[122]

The American analysis also showed that higher working class infant mortality rates were not due to any greater prevalence of artificial feeding in the low-income groups; breastfeeding was more common in these groups than in those more favourably situated. Brown himself noted that, while breastfeeding on the whole seemed to be declining, working class and immigrant women were more likely to nurse their children than were "the flower of the land." In addition, the artificially fed infants of the well-to-do did not show higher illness and mortality rates, suggesting even to doctors that it was not bottle-feeding in and of itself that was to blame.[123]

If contemporary health surveys seemed to contraindicate an exclusive focus on mishandled feeding, why was the medical profession so intent on making this the primary issue? In addition to the doctors' obvious disinclination to situate health in its socio-economic context, part of the reason was class suspicion. The working-class family budget usually permitted medical attention for its members when health had deteriorated to the point where calling the doctor was the sole recourse. Seeing such children at their worst in terms of health encouraged doctors to believe the worst of working-class childrearing methods. The specific medical ailments to which the children were particularly vulnerable, ailments that were inarguably related to the conditions of their lives, helped shape the profession's understanding of childhood illness. The class background of these children also discouraged physicians from looking beyond the family to resolve childhood health problems.[124] Since they believed that working-class parents were dirty and negligent, they identified inadequate parenting as the source of ill health. In so doing, they also identified its potential remedy.

Because physicians discounted environmental and professional factors, the explanation for rising infant mortality could only be found on the other side of the equation: it must lie with the parents, especially the mothers. Not poverty but "class" or "social status" were the problem as Hodgetts had phrased it, and such terms implied the sort of wilful neglect or sheer ignorance that seemingly had nothing to do with money. Perhaps the poor were victimized by a system ordered by profit for the few, but were they not providing the victim's sanction by refusing to take responsibility for their own health and welfare and that of their children? And if the victims were themselves culpable, what could be done to make them responsible? That they had to be made responsible was never in question, given the serious socio-economic costs of illness, debility, and high mortality.

Ignorance of parental duties was, according to Hodgetts, "a great and growing evil, one which must be met by a better and broader education in all that relates to the child and child life."[125] MacMurchy also emphasized the need for dispensing "exact advice" to mothers.[126] Canadian doctors, in adopting and maintaining this position throughout the entire period, were again echoing the assertions of their British and American colleagues. More than a medical position, this was a view founded in the socio-economic systems of these nations. Doctors recognized the national implications of infant mortality in terms of efficiency, productivity, and power. They believed that the problem had to be addressed by interventionary means, and that its scope and nature required state involvement. They also upheld their professional ability and duty to lead this campaign. But given their own position within this apparently threatened social order and the contemporary limits of medical understanding, doctors were compelled to point to maternal ignorance as the fundamental cause of infant mortality. The alleviation of that ignorance could only be effected through education: first, education of the public in order to motivate interest and action in fighting infant mortality and second and more importantly, education of mothers in the care and feeding of their children. And this education was to be designed and conducted by physicians exclusively.

While doctors' class perspective played a vital role in determining both their diagnosis of and approach to the problem of infant mortality, it would be simplistic as well as inaccurate to argue that their campaign was only another attempt by middle-class professionals to control the ideas and practices of the working class, and of women in particular. The control element superseded class boundaries: mothers of every class were considered to be ignorant in varying degrees and all would benefit from medically supervised instruction. Feminist historians have pointed out that maternalist ideology transcended class barriers, gaining support even within leftist movements.[127] It is also clear that organized labour supported health education as a vital means of protecting those most vulnerable to both sickness and its economic repercussions. Hamilton's *Labour News* argued that better health and greater happiness depended "on the somewhat slow process of education of the whole people in what life is and how it should be lived."[128] The *Canadian Trade Unionist* considered that "ignorance can be removed and the careless stimulated to observe the ordinary laws of health" and that much was being done to instruct workers in these matters with "a corresponding increase in the health of the average person."[129] The target audience, as later chapters will reveal, was interested in and enthusiastic about learning the health principles that doctors wanted it to learn. Where working-class participants differed from medicine and the state was not over the value of education, but over their exclusive emphasis on education that dismissed or denied the significance of improvements in living and working conditions and universal access to health care.[130]

Finally, no discussion of the medical profession's attitude to infant mortality can ignore the state of contemporary medical science. As understood by physicians of the period, the nature and extent of infant mortality also made prevention appear the only viable approach. Failing that, doctors were obliged to admit that early diagnosis held out their "only hope of reducing the mortality of acute intestinal intoxication at the present time, until the aetiology of the condition is more clearly understood."[131] By the time most stricken children were evaluated by the doctor or admitted to hospital, their condition was beyond medical treatment. A 1923 study by Dr Alan Brown, then director of Toronto's Hospital for Sick Children, revealed that the mortality ranged from 48 per cent of those admitted in fair condition to 81.8 per cent of those who were moribund on admission.[132] Diarrhaea and enteritis were responsible for 1 death in 6 in 1921, and 1 in 7 a decade later.[133] Brown was forced to admit that "prophylactic treatment affords the most hopeful means of combating this disease" and emphasized "the urgency for breast feeding" or at the very least the use of sterilized cow's milk. While medicines were "of little use," doctors had by this point understood the "paramount importance" of replacing lost fluids by intravenous therapy of saline and glucose mixtures.[134] The problem was that even effective therapy could not save children who had reached the point of no return.

The cycle of causation seemed evident to doctors. Lack of knowledge of hygienic principles, whether sloppy handling of cow's milk or general uncleanliness, was causing needless suffering and death in horrific numbers of young children, especially those from working-class households. Few of these children enjoyed regular medical supervision. Even the therapeutic advances made by the 1920s could benefit only those receiving prompt medical attention. Poverty was not the real problem: knowledge and cleanliness were within reach of even the poorest households. The victims had to be made aware of their share of the blame and their duty to participate in their own salvation.

True improvement in health and welfare called for the kind of education and supervision that only medical professionals could supply. Here was an area where, led by doctors, the state could effectively intervene without obliging any redistribution of wealth. The starting point for the campaign to save infants and improve childrearing techniques in the name of national health and efficiency would be regulation of the milk supply and regulation of mothers through medical supervision. The opening decades of the twentieth century saw the evolution of a complex institutional structure designed to serve child welfare concerns and to socialize the results of medical advances. It would take the impact of the First World War, however, to enlarge the campaign's scope and organize its efforts behind the expressly qualified leadership of the medical profession.

CHAPTER THREE

"The Infant Soldier": Early Child Welfare Efforts

Once it was agreed that mortality was highest among the artificially fed infants of the working class, and that parental ignorance was the primary cause, doctors had within their grasp the starting point for their campaign against infant mortality. The role of heat, soil, housing, and maternal employment were problematic and their correlation to infant mortality, although suggestive, was difficult to establish through laboratory testing and statistical analysis. Such factors would be brought back to do duty when required, but a medical profession intent on presenting an authoritative scientific image emphasized what was most evident and appropriate for scientific study: the feeding question, and specifically the causative role of cow's milk. If doctors did not know precisely why artificially fed infants were dying from intestinal infections or how to isolate the specific organism and name it, they were firmly convinced of the link between infant feeding and infant death.[1]

The MacMurchy reports exposed the nature and extent of the wastage of infant lives in Ontario, and helped to publicize medical views on a health issue that was increasingly defined in social terms. In the aftermath of these reports, intensified public concern about infant mortality motivated organized assaults on the most readily identified enemy: impure milk. Initial attempts to clean up the milk supply, or at least to provide pure milk for the most vulnerable of the population, were local and voluntarist in nature. With the exception of those measures taken by a few aggressive municipal health boards in cities such as Toronto, Hamilton, Ottawa, and London, these child welfare efforts were sporadic and lacking in cohesion.

Following World War One, a substantial reorganization took place in the province's child welfare sphere, one that mirrored similar events in other Western countries. Growing medical interest in saving

babies sparked more active involvement on the part of health professionals. Public health officials were empowered by the restructuring
of the Ontario Board of Health and the establishment of a separate
federal health department. By the war's end, the campaign against
infant mortality was effectively out of the hands of its largely female
volunteers and in the control of medical professionals, who were
either directly employed by governments or were acting as consultants
to these public health agencies. The Great War did not create the
child welfare movement in Ontario, but it did transform a loose
coalition of reformers into a concerted campaign under professional
direction, and increasingly, state control. The lengthy catalogue of
contributory socio-economic factors was never dismissed entirely. But
the focus became maternal ignorance, the key solution, education by
health professionals, and the principal instrument, the state.

By 1914, doctors generally accepted that the immediate cause of
"acute intestinal intoxication" was bacterial infection from contaminated milk. The common housefly appeared to be the prime vector
of infection, pointing again to unsanitary handling, storage, and
environment in dairy and home.[2] The prewar reports of Ontario's
medical officers of health bear witness to the spread of these medical
theories. Brantford's medical officer argued that the largest proportion of the 84 infant deaths in that town in 1912 was directly due to
"improper and unsanitary methods of dealing with the food of the
child," most prominently "the unsanitary feeding bottles and the
improper care of the milk from which they are infected."[3] Port
Huron's medical officer claimed to have seen a "foreign" mother
fishing flies out of milk and throwing them on the floor.[4] Stressing
the efficacy of public education, the medical officer of Guelph indicated that arrangements were being made for the town "to have the
purest milk obtainable and thus wipe out as much as possible the
chief cause of infant mortality."[5]

International attention to the function of raw milk as a disease
transmitter also influenced Canadian attempts to regulate the milk
supply.[6] Germ theory had implicated milk as a major carrier of
communicable diseases such as typhoid, scarlet fever, and diphtheria.
Robert Koch's discovery of the tubercle bacillus in 1882 had sparked
campaigns in the Western world aimed at preventing this infectious
disease. More importantly from the perspective of child health, international studies confirmed by 1910 that bovine tuberculosis was
communicable to human beings. The American and Canadian International Commission on the Control of Bovine Tuberculosis (1910)
turned the attention of public health reformers in this direction.
Prevention by means of a pure milk supply, tuberculin testing of

cattle and humans, and extensive public education was the object of the anti-tuberculosis campaign.

In 1903, New York paediatricians W.L. Park and L. Emmett Holt published a report conclusively establishing the link between feeding and infant illness during hot weather, the so-called "summer complaint" or *cholera infantum*. Their efforts bolstered the incipient movement to regulate milk production and distribution as the key to vanquishing this widespread but eminently preventable disease.[7] By the decade's end, Canadian physicians were arguing that pure milk was essential to the eradication of both childhood tuberculosis and intestinal diseases. As was the case in Britain and the United States, the anti-tuberculosis campaign and the child welfare campaign united over the milk supply.[8]

The Canadian Medical Association appointed a milk commission in 1908 and devised standards for milk collection, inspection, storage, and delivery. In April 1909, K.W. McNaught, MPP for North Toronto, moved a resolution for the appointment of an equivalent provincial commission. Using the medical studies that linked impure milk and infant mortality, McNaught argued that "what we need in this province is pure milk at the same price we now pay ... pure milk should be made a matter of education."[9] The new Ontario Milk Commission made its first report in the early months of the following year, with the result that Ontario was the first province to legislate in the interests of carrying out the Canadian Medical Association's initiative.[10]

Amendments to the Municipal Act permitted municipalities to license and regulate milk vendors and inspect places where milk was produced or handled, but it was also left to the municipalities to devise and implement the standards of purity. There was considerable debate in the legislature over the efficacy of this bill, with Liberal opposition leader A.G. MacKay leading the fight to make milk regulation a provincial matter for the sake of uniformity.[11] Not until 1916 did the Hearst Conservative government pass the Dairy Standards Act to meet these concerns. Even then, the Act, which was supposed to be operative as of March 1917, was deferred a year because of opposition from organized Eastern Ontario dairy farmers. The Dairy Standards Act was a continual source of controversy for successive Ontario governments.[12]

This early legislation tightened inspection regulations and provided for the selling of "certified milk" that met certain bacteriological standards, but it stopped short of compelling local governments to enforce pasteurization. The debate over the nutritive value of pasteurized milk, the expense of establishing pasteurization plants, and the cost to supplier and consumer, all meant delay in implementing what was early recognized as a vital method of preventing disease and death.[13] In 1930, pasteurization was in effect in only 32 cities in all of Canada: in only 25 of these (20 in Ontario) did the entire milk supply have to be pasteurized.[14] Despite continued pressure by public health reformers, organized medicine, health departments, and the Canadian Council on Child and Family Welfare, it was not until 1938 that the Ontario Liberal government of Mitchell Hepburn enforced compulsory pasteurization legislation.[15] As late as 1950, only one other province had passed similar legislation.

In the view of public health reformers, the recalcitrance of governments and lack of cooperation from milk producers made public education essential to the pure milk cause. The Canadian Medical Association urged its members to accept their responsibility in this area: "there is no more important department of preventive medicine, or one in which physicians can do more effective work, than in securing for the community a clean and wholesome supply of pure milk."[16] But even compulsory pasteurization would not suffice, because pasteurized milk could be just as life-threatening if mishandled in the home. Once again, individual responsibility was called forth. Governments could only do so much to reduce death and disease transmitted by impure milk: public ignorance and carelessness also had to be remedied through education.

In the aftermath of international medical studies, reports by various milk commissions and the MacMurchy findings, local reform initiative was naturally directed at improving the milk supply through municipal regulation. In some Ontario cities, attempts were also made to provide pure milk for infants through special milk dispensaries.[17] The dispensaries were usually run by the combined voluntary efforts of women's groups and interested local doctors. The infant milk depot was a common first step in fighting infant mortality in both Europe and North America. Originating in France in the late nineteenth century with the establishment of the "Gouttes de Lait," these physician-run pure milk depots also functioned as supervisory infant clinics and schools for mothers.[18] The milk depot idea spread quickly to urban centres in the United States and Great Britain.[19] Because British organizers had difficulty attracting consistent attendance, "lady sanitary inspectors" were sent to visit depot mothers at home to see that medical instructions were carried out and an acceptable level of home hygiene was maintained.[20] This system of supervisory clinics and domiciliary visits became the established mode of operation for child welfare work both internationally and nationally throughout the first half of the twentieth century.

Canadian physicians lamented the fact that Canada lagged behind other Western nations in organization for child welfare work. In the years immediately preceding World War One, only a few efforts were in evidence; they were limited in number, carried out only in urban centres, and then usually on the initiative of community welfare organizations rather than under the medical direction that doctors argued was crucial to their success.[21] The child welfare clinics established in Toronto, Hamilton, Ottawa and London in the immediate prewar years followed the European and American pattern. Begun as pure milk depots, they were organized and staffed by local reform groups. By 1915, they had evolved into general clinics for the supervision and maintenance of the health of infants and young children.[22] It was discovered that providing certified milk for poor mothers was futile unless they were also instructed in its handling and preparation, and most importantly, in proper infant feeding. Moreover, doctors recognized that while the milk depot system had great value, it also had an inherent flaw that they believed only medical direction could overcome:

Unless properly conducted, by increasing the facilities for artificial feeding, [the milk depot] may tend to discourage maternal nursing and possibly increase infant mortality. While the distribution of clean pure milk is important, it should be realized that the instruction of the mother and continuous observation of the child play a larger part. Everything possible should be done to encourage breast feeding and to aid it. The inexperienced mother is thus guided not by the advice of ignorant and superstitious relations or friends but by an intelligent and experienced person who not only tells her what to do but how to do it.[23]

Solving the milk problem was thus important, but it could reasonably permit mothers an easy way out, and could diminish their personal obligation to nurse their infants. In their battle to save babies, doctors delineated the two sides very clearly: on the one stood the ignorant mother and the equally, if not more ignorant, traditional advisers – family and friends; on the other, the intellectually and morally superior medical profession.

Doctors also believed that demonstration was a more effective pedagogical device than advisory consultation alone. Consequently, the child welfare clinics and home nursing visits, which together became the campaign's hallmark services, were devised "to fill a want created by the great numbers among the poor who, because of overcrowding and ignorance, require advice relating to health, hygiene and manner of living."[24] Above all, the clinics were to be centres of maternal education and supervision in scientific childrearing for those who were most deprived, both materially and in terms of knowledge.

In Toronto, the original clinics were established in 1912 at Evangelia and University Settlement Houses in the heart of the city's immigrant district. In accordance with medical ideas and objectives, these clinics did not offer treatment, but instructed mothers in child care, because "the mothers of the poor need to learn a lot of things to bring children up safely through the perils that surround them through the conditions in which they are forced to live." Although they provided pure milk and medical supervision of infants, it was in maternal education that the clinics were thought to hold most promise.[25]

By 1915, Toronto had organized the separate Division of Child Hygiene under the aegis of its municipal Department of Public Health and in close connection with Dr Alan Brown and the Hospital for Sick Children. The city's child welfare clinics were turned over to Brown's direction and supervision. The division's work began with the registration of births at City Hall, whereupon a booklet on infant care and feeding was immediately mailed to the mother. The next step was a visit by a municipal public health nurse as soon as possible after birth registration. With the permission of the family physician, the nurse then arranged for the mother to attend the nearest clinic. Infants were weighed at each visit (monthly for the first year) and a card recording the weight was given to the mother, along with information and advice as required. To emphasize that the clinics were to be solely for the education of mothers and the supervision of general infant health, and to secure the cooperation of the "neighbouring physicians," notification of each new case was sent to the attending physician. These notice cards explained that the clinic would supervise the child only with the family doctor's approval, and that the child would be referred back to him, along with all pertinent records, if it should need medical attention.[26]

The Toronto clinics showed an impressive record of expansion. In 1913, the first year of their operation in the settlements, 364 clinics were held with an attendance of 3,926. By the following year, this figure had more than doubled to 830, with 10,809 babies attending. In 1917, with 22 centres functioning weekly, 1,033 clinics were held, attended by 16,849 babies.[27] When the clinics were started, the infant mortality rate in Toronto was 115 per 1,000 live births. By 1917, this rate had declined to 80 per 1,000. In this four-year period, the number of deaths from the dreaded *cholera infantum* alone was cut from 637 to 172.[28] Encouraged by the official statistics, the Division of Child Hygiene expanded its clinic network to 28 by the early 1920s. In selecting locations for new clinics, a "pin map" revealing the rate of infant deaths throughout the city was employed to ensure that they were established "where the mortality seemed greatest."[29]

The Hamilton Babies' Dispensary followed a similar pattern of development, opening in 1909 after several years of discussion by the local medical society. When the city council refused a request for funds by a deputation representing the medical society, the local board of health, and various charitable organizations, the Victorian Order of Nurses provided the necessary $1,000. A dairy farm operating under strict regulations was selected, and trained nurses were employed to fill sterilized bottles "in proper proportions" with certified milk. One depot was established in the Market Square, another in the city hospital's out-patient department; milk was also delivered to the homes of about 60 babies daily. Milk was sold at a nominal cost of one cent per bottle, a price found to be "ridiculously low," given the seven cents per quart paid to the supplier. The operating deficit was made up by public subscription. In 1910, there were five depots functioning in the city, providing for between 100 and 130 infants daily.[30]

In the same year, Hamilton depots began to make a physician available to examine babies and prescribe individual feeding formula. Again, the clinic's medical purpose was purely diagnostic. While some cases were referred by Hamilton physicians, as in Toronto the majority were reached by a "Mother's Letter" posted as births were registered. It was discovered that "not infrequently" mothers were being referred by those who had already attended and had "appreciated the benefits to their children." Physicians were urged to cooperate by registering births promptly to avoid the tragic consequences of delay. As well, they were encouraged to recommend the dispensary to their poor patients who "on account of the expense will hesitate to call in a medical man until it is too late." In this manner, the medical volunteers of the Hamilton clinics attempted to create a network of cooperation with private physicians.[31]

Follow-up care was provided in the form of home visits by public health nurses, which were considered to constitute "the outstanding feature" of child welfare work. Through such visits, the nurse was able to "establish herself in the confidence of the mother" and thereby win a convert to the cause. The visits were also an effective means of keeping the family under surveillance. Nurses were authorized to take notes regarding the financial standing of the family and the general condition of the home; these records were preserved along with the medical history of the infant patient.[32] Believing that their cause amply justified this sort of scrutiny, child welfare campaigners did not hesitate to advocate intrusion into the family's private affairs.

Ottawa's experience with infant milk depots was directly inspired by that of Hamilton. In 1910, Dr Elizabeth Smith Shortt, an active member of the National Council of Women of Canada, anti-tuberculosis campaigner and a child welfare advocate, wrote to Dr J. Heurner Mullen of the Hamilton Babies' Dispensary Guild for information and advice. The combined efforts of the local Council of Women and the city's medical officer of health led to the establishment of four depots, two operating throughout the year and two during the summer months. All were under the supervision of the city's public health nurses.[33] Certified milk was provided daily and diagnostic clinics were held weekly, with local doctors "giving their time and services gratuitously." By 1913, the nurse-superintendent of the Ottawa depots had noted that they were becoming "more and more a school for the mother instead of merely a depot to sell milk, as most of the milk that comes to the city is good and we encourage the mothers to nurse their babies and drink the milk themselves." She believed that the number of breast-fed babies had "increased remarkably" as a result of advice dispensed at the clinics and follow-up nurse visits in the homes of clinic mothers.

Child welfare clinics were also organized in London in 1915, with three clinics held weekly in public schools.[34] The London Child Welfare Association, a voluntary group that employed public health nurses out of its own funds, broke with the usual pattern by conducting a separate weekly clinic for sick children at Victoria Hospital. This treatment clinic was maintained until the early 1930s, when Depression-induced financial difficulties made it necessary for the clinic and nurse visiting to be taken over by the city. From the point of view of the campaign's administrators in the provincial department of health, the treatment clinic handicapped the movement's broader educational aims by antagonizing local physicians.[35]

Despite official disapproval and lack of participation by local physicians, the association confidently attributed the decline in London's infant deaths directly to clinic efforts. Before the clinics were opened, over 160 children between the ages of one month and five years died in London each year. By the early 1920s, this number had been reduced to 59. The greatest cause of death, intestinal infections, had been practically eliminated "by preaching mother's milk as the only safe food for infants and where this food was not possible by teaching how to safeguard against infection of the cow's milk and feeding utensils."[36]

From the very beginning, Ontario's child welfare crusaders were adamant that their major practical measures – the clinics and nurse visits – would remain entirely in the realm of education. Any deviation from this pattern, as witnessed in London, sparked opposition from local practitioners and the campaign's provincial overseers. The supervisory clinics that gradually spread across Ontario as a result of these initial efforts to dispense pure milk were meant to complement but never to replace regular attendance by the family physician. Care was taken to prevent any real threat to the livelihood and professional status of private practitioners. The clinics were generally staffed by a rotating body of physicians who volunteered a few hours out of their general practice. In some locations, they were paid a nominal fee, but only the nurses were employed directly by municipal health boards.

These tentative steps toward addressing the problem of infant mortality in Ontario adhered closely to the British and American milk depot paradigm. Although ostensibly created to encourage breastfeeding, the clinics tended to focus on general hygiene and the proper handling of artificial feeding, a natural outcome of their original role as milk dispensaries. Increasing municipal regulation of the milk supply and professional apprehension that these depots were inadvertently promoting artificial feeding led to the obsolescence of their role as dispensaries. Even more important, however, was the general realization that a great deal more was needed to reduce infant mortality than could be supplied by a few scattered milk depots functioning in the main as voluntary and charitable organizations. The pin maps appeared to illuminate the class nature of the problem, but doctors remained convinced that the solution lay in their own continuing professional direction of a campaign that would never deviate from its original, purely educational, objective. Local women's groups were encouraged to play a support role, but doctors would lead.

Just as MacMurchy had recommended in her reports, physicians began to call for more professional and state involvement in a more efficient campaign, under medical direction, and with greater community support. Toronto paediatricians Alan Brown and George Campbell, two of the most enthusiastic proponents of a systematic and professionally supervised approach, declared that "the time when individual effort can cope with this problem has passed. The present conditions call for an organized campaign in Canada, planned on scientific lines, and carried out with business-like efficiency."[37] Revealing distinct professional biases, Brown and Campbell ascribed the shortcomings of these early child welfare measures to their voluntarist and philanthropic structure. They insisted that the work must be done by physicians "properly trained for their task and paid for it," not by trained nurses or social workers, and most certainly not by volunteers.[38] Municipally funded clinics and visiting nurses should be made available for every 20,000 inhabitants. In this way, the standardization of methods, and the proper supervision and cooperation of all concerned could best be secured.

Despite such activist medical calls for state involvement, the role of the state was always defined cautiously. Governments at all levels – but mainly municipal and provincial – gradually expanded their participation in the child welfare campaign. Yet from the campaign's outset just prior to the outbreak of World War One, state involvement was restricted to administration and direction of largely educational child welfare measures. Child welfare advocates never interpreted the rhetoric of "child as national asset" to mean that the state was to have direct responsibility for the health of children. Rather, it meant that there was a new obligation to make mothers more responsible to the state. If the state was obliged to act, always on medical advice, all were reminded that "whatever we do we must not be too ready to relieve [mothers] of their responsibility."[39]

Throughout the period, the movement's medical leadership never pressed for the kind of reform that would provide a minimal standard of living or even universal health care as rights of citizenship – in short, for the kind of reform that presupposed significant state involvement. It was in the educational sphere that the state could best do its work "to see that the rights of the children are not ignored and that the mothers have the opportunity given them of learning how best to rear their children."[40] Child welfare advocates operated on the premise that ignorance and poverty were correlated, but they resigned themselves to the latter and emphasized their duty to attack the former. From its earliest days, then, the campaign's leaders were obsessed with education. Education would upgrade parenting skills while bringing mother and child under the watchful eye of the new childrearing experts. The real economic basis of infant mortality was given nodding acknowledgment, but was consistently de-emphasized in favour of locating the source in a failure of motherhood. Infant illness and death could then be interpreted as problems separate and distinct from those of housing, sanitation, or even poverty as such: it was "mainly a question of motherhood."[41]

This focus on maternal education was also influenced by the campaign's international developments. In 1906, at the first National Conference on Infantile Mortality in Britain, its president Dr John Burns had stressed that infant mortality was "in equal parts" attributable to "the mother, society and industry."[42] The medical profession believed that it was easier and more effective to target mothers rather than society and industry, and in purely practical terms, few could dispute their assessment.[43] But education was not so much the easy way as it was an approach that fitted the limitations of their social position and outlook. It allowed them greater scope for their professional authority, and very conveniently upheld the traditional concepts of feminine roles both within the family and the campaign itself. For doctors, the most efficacious approach to infant mortality consequently lay in the improvement of mothering techniques. An editorial in the *Canadian Public Health Journal* stated the case succinctly: "The problem will be solved only when the value of intelligent motherhood is placed above that of philanthropy, of hospitals, of the medical profession and of the state. Neglect and ignorance are, therefore, more important than poverty as causative factors in the cause of infant illness and death ... Intelligent motherhood alone can give to the infant that which neither wealth nor state nor yet science can offer with equal benefit to mother or child."[44]

This early commitment to motherhood training on the part of doctors dictated the direction taken by the campaign and the nature of its measures throughout its course. It also forged new relationships between doctors and parents, parents and children, and ultimately, family and state.

By the end of the Great War, doctors were intently establishing moral sanctions on the grounds of health and the national interest and denigrating traditional child care methods as negligent and dangerous. The largest number of infant deaths were explained by "lack of the proper knowledge," including "ignorance of the penalties of immorality; of the trouble enacted by defiance of sanitation and tolerance of filth; of the fatal results of carelessness and malnutrition; and of the realization of the social and economic value of the child's life."[45] Traditional sources of childrearing information were pernicious, particularly where "neighbourly advice" was concerned. Doctors decried the fact that the woman who had "buried six" was often considered an authority on the upbringing of children: "and the results are four white coffins taken in procession through the streets of the city every day."[46] Slowly but ever more forcefully, they began to dispense child care advice in ways that were not purely medical. They argued that this responsibility to educate parents was an integral part of the function that they served in the community because they possessed "the types of knowledge not likely to be had by lay groups."[47]

The early war years found medical commentators in both private practice and public health positions consistently proclaiming that mothering could no longer be considered a natural instinct. For the sake of the children, and ultimately the nation, it could be nothing less than "a profession of the highest order."[48] Employing the imagery of wartime to good effect, they depicted the mother as the "first line of defence" for the helpless "infant soldier," whose preservation depended on her "training, education and preparation."[49] By 1918, the setting was especially conducive to the physicians' acceptance of this duty.

The nation's experience at war crystallized this new interest in the child and catalysed the movement for the scientific management of childhood. The dire effects of heavy casualties on the young and sparsely populated nation were a major concern in medical and reform circles. The Great War impressed upon physicians "as never before" that they had "a patriotic duty as well as a professional one" to save infants and keep them healthy in order to replace those young men who had left empty places in Canadian society. Moreover, "the whole trend of modern child welfare work" demanded closer medical cooperation with all organizations working for the welfare of children.[50] The phrase "as never before" resounded throughout the medical discourse on child welfare in the decade following the war.[51] These few words underscored a pervasive sense of urgency about the conservation of child life. The opportunity to save children and to ensure the nation's future had presented itself unequivocally. Doctors had only to understand that they had a decisive role to play in guiding the nation and to grasp that opportunity for themselves before others outpaced them.

The war had a similar effect on non-medical supporters of child welfare issues. The innate maternalism of women's organizations was enhanced by the experience of global cataclysm. The National Council of Women's arguments echoed those of the medical profession: "Now, when so many valuable lives are being sacrificed for the cause of greater world freedom, the prevention of infant mortality becomes, more than ever, a vital necessity of national importance."[52] In order to bring about a successful postwar reconstruction, it was essential that the victory won on the battlefield be followed by "a realization of the power of consecrated motherhood."[53]

The war effort necessitated the close coordination of state and civilian endeavours. To this end, the federal government invited a deputation of 60 representatives of various women's organizations to attend a special "Women's War Conference" in 1918. A section on public health and child welfare was created, with Helen Reid as its convener. Reid had long been active in the National Council of Women of Canada, and later was child welfare representative on the Dominion Council of Health. Also on the committee was Dr Elizabeth

Smith Shortt. After discussing the need for child conservation and the related work being done in England and the United States, the committee unanimously resolved that "one of the first and most essential things needed by the country at the present time is the establishment of a Federal Department of Health." Reid argued that a federal department was necessary to "coordinate and suggest exactly the functions of the provinces" and to treat questions like infant mortality and venereal disease (the committee's principal concerns) "in a national way, through the provinces, but backed up by the Federal government."[54] The committee resolved that "whereas the conservation of child life as an asset by the state is at this time of extreme urgency and a *War Problem*" (their italics), a federal children's bureau on the American model should be created.[55]

The war years also saw significant progress in the doctors' professionalization drive, especially with the consolidation of organized medicine as the Canadian Medical Association became a truly national body. In addition to this expanding sphere of influence at home, active participation by doctors and nurses who enlisted or carried out medical duties through the international Red Cross Society was considered a valuable apprenticeship for their role in saving the nation's children. They had learned important lessons in social service and preventive medicine that would make possible "one of the best coordinated and most aggressive health campaigns planned in the history of the world," a campaign that would revolve around "the most popular thing in the world, the baby."[56] The growing sense of responsibility toward children was judged "a not unnatural side product" of the war. Canada had lost some 60,000 of the finest of her developing citizens – "finest physically and finest in the spirit of selfless idealism from which national greatness springs." In order for Canadians to retain "the position in the ranks of greatness which their blood has bought," it was necessary to ensure that those who would take the place of the fallen be given every chance to realize the full range of their "physical, mental and spiritual possibilities."[57] For the medical profession, the war's impact was double-edged. On the one hand, there was apprehension and urgency; on the other, optimism and opportunity.[58]

The doctors' apprehension, in the most obvious sense, was due to the slaughter of millions of combatants "of a class drawn from what must be considered the most valuable, so far as productivity is concerned, of the population."[59] The war naturally drew attention to the population as a biological resource. At a time of rapid technological advance, and especially in view of the existence of an industrial giant to the south, it was essential for a fledgling industrial nation such as

Canada to run its factories with hardy, efficient workers. The class that produced the majority of workers and soldiers alike was also the most vulnerable in terms of health. Consequently, one of the "good results" of the war, when "manpower was so very vital," was to make employers realize the importance of their workers' "health and effectiveness." As explained by the medical officer of the Hamilton Steel Works, employers now regarded "a man in industry as an investment which increases in value as time passes and as the man becomes more highly trained." Because loss of time through sickness was a major cause of "waste in industry," it was evident that, in health matters, "the interests of the wage earner and the wage payer are identical."[60] National economic and military survival depended on replenishing the supply by providing for the welfare of Canadian children. Dr Alan Brown declared that the country's future depended on its poor children: "If they are eventually to justify their place in the world they must be saved from ill-health, ignorance and vice."[61] The exigencies of war brought production and reproduction to the point of crisis "as never before."

The war also reaffirmed eugenicist fears about racial degeneration. It was observed that "the veto of the medical examiner has prevented many a splendid spirit from obeying the call to duty which today is sweeping our country."[62] General Sir Arthur Currie pointed out that "something like 100,000 men went overseas who were physically unfit for service and cost the country some $150,000,000." During the period of the Military Service Act, only 83,355 of the applicants for enlistment were accepted; 181,000, or 68 per cent, were rejected as unfit.[63] The ill health of these young men resulted from "our life before the war," and had to be remedied in the present generation. Similar worries surfaced in Britain and the United States, intensifying anxiety about the imminent collapse of western civilization.[64]

Linked with the fear that those who remained would not be of adequate strength to provide for and defend the nation were various other racial anxieties. That "inferior" immigrants might fill the places of the fallen, and of those who were damaged physically and emotionally by war, now appeared a very real threat. Medical, labour, and women's groups were the most vocal opponents of federal immigration policy during this period.[65] On this issue, the professional interests of the doctors overrode the social position that they shared with business. If employers appeared content to deal with the physical deterioration of their workers by importing new stock, the medical profession insisted on a long-term commitment to the health of the "native-born" because of their eugenics-inspired apocalyptic predictions for Canadian society. A commitment of this kind also had more tangible, immediate benefits: it enhanced their social role while opening new career paths in expanding state bureaucracies.

Although doctors and workers were in agreement that the nation had a duty to upgrade the health of its labour force, they came at this issue from decidedly different stands. Labour representatives saw the class prerogatives behind business-supported government immigration policies.[66] Anti-immigration arguments revealed labour's understanding of capital's tendency to bleed its human resources while attempting to avoid responsibility by simple substitution. Labour's argument for state involvement was based on an understanding of health as an unequally distributed human resource and a fundamental right of citizenship. Whatever the position, child welfare advocates of all backgrounds contended that the government should focus its energies on infant mortality rather than on bringing in "a vast army of non-English speaking people whose presence creates great national problems."[67]

In the immediate aftermath of the Great War, state support of immigration seemed particularly misguided. The wartime classification of certain immigrant groups as "enemy aliens" stirred the forces of nativism, while the Red Scare sweeping North America during the 1920s added more fuel to the fires.[68] Increased labour militancy in the immediate postwar years, culminating in the Winnipeg General Strike of 1919, seemed to unveil the horrors of incipient Bolshevism and foreign contamination of the working class.[69] In this atmosphere of xenophobia and class suspicion, the medical profession could safely proclaim that "whatever we may feel as to the desirability of encouraging immigration, we all agree that the native-born is more desirable."[70] The call went out to the state to invest its dollars more efficiently in a medically supervised crusade for child conservation, rather than importing outsiders of dubious physical, moral and mental quality.

The war also magnified the middle-class fears about race suicide that had been developing since the turn of the century. Statisticians had recently confirmed the impressions of the medical profession that the birth rate was indeed dropping within the "better stock," in both class and racial terms. Dr J.J. Heagerty of the federal Department of Health believed that the chief factor behind this falling birth rate was voluntary restriction, "the cowardly offspring of Higher Civilization." The practice of birth control that had begun with the "educated classes" was "spreading continually" throughout the entire community.[71] From 1881 to 1911, Ontario had the lowest birth rate of any province. In 1921, only that of British Columbia was lower. At the same time, infant mortality rates remained elevated despite the efforts of the prewar reformers.

There were occasional calls from feminists, particularly within the left, for family limitation as a means of upgrading living standards for all.[72] The medical profession as a whole, however, refused to consider contraception a viable approach to child welfare and interpreted it instead as part of the problem. Birth control was clear evidence of the moral failure of the "better stock" to take their proper leadership role in national progress.[73] Nor would doctors accept any economic argument for family limitation, a stand with a built-in defence against upward mobility. In their support of large families, they deprecated parental ambitions such as "the exaggerated notion of some parents who assumed that a public school and a university education were necessary for every child."[74] Doctors were determined to keep contraception within medical control and to keep it out of the hands of women. Nonetheless, all medical arguments to the contrary, Canadians were obviously limiting the number of their children.[75] The fact that family size continued to shrink added force to arguments to save mothers and infants from unnecessary death and to improve the physical and mental quality of future generations.

With motivating concerns like these, physicians constantly returned to the concept of children as "national assets." Children were easily the most deserving of all citizens insofar as attempts to improve national health and welfare were concerned, and easily the most promising investment. Battle metaphors permeated this revitalized campaign with explicitly racial and nationalistic tones. "A sound mind in a sound body" were the prerequisites for survival, and in the degree that a nation's people possessed these qualities, the nation itself would rise or fall: "That first year of life is the worst year in all life's battle. Terrible is the carnage for thousands of our Infant Soldiers perish there ... His father had ten times his chance in Flanders."[76] Medical science would provide the means and methods for ensuring that, for every life sacrificed on the battlefields of Europe, "a thousand children shall have stronger, straighter, freer bodies and stronger, straighter, freer spirits."[77] The process of modernization, accelerated by the war, had taught Canadians to question traditional methods and to strive for the greater efficiency that entailed "a scientific organization and cooperation." The reason for deficiencies in the health and welfare of Canadians lay in the fact that there existed "no program for the scientific organization of mankind, no agency to study such a program, no teaching given on the matter."[78] In the years following the outbreak of World War One, the Canadian medical profession attempted to devise and implement such a program in the sphere that held the most promise: childhood.

By the mid-1920s, most urban centres in Ontario had some system of clinics and home visits in operation.[79] For the doctors, greater involvement in local child welfare drives represented an expansion of their parameters of concern and self-imposed responsibility. From its early, intermittent and individualistic participation, medical involvement eventually became better organized, more tightly directed and profession-wide. The doctors' involvement mirrored the evolution of the campaign itself. The war drew periodic and voluntarist local drives into a concerted, physician-led, and state-sponsored movement, that, it was hoped, would become "a cooperative part of the scientifically arranged preventive and remedial elements of an advanced civilization." "System" would be added to sentiment, and "better business methods to benevolences." Child welfare concerns had previously derived from "the natural impulses of human sympathy." By the war's end, these concerns came to be seen as "part of the defensive foresight of citizens who would protect the future of the state."[80]

This shift from philanthropic motivation to state interests was reflected in the expanded slate of child welfare concerns. While their early efforts concentrated on well-baby care from birth to the first birthday, the combined effects of wartime pledges for child conservation and increasing state involvement broadened the medical platform. The child from birth to age five became the object of the child welfare campaign. It was increasingly recognized that large numbers of children, although healthy at birth, within five years became "the physically defective entrants whom the education authority is required at no small cost to restore as far as possible to their original state of health."[81] It cost less to prevent childhood disease than to contend with its results, the impaired vitality, deformity and degeneracy "plainly taking place around us in the large cities." If "damaged and weakly infants" were not cared for, they were liable to grow up into men and women "crippled in body and deficient in mind who will fill the hospitals, prisons and homes."[82] According to doctors, Canadian society was devolving into a mad dark world of nightmarish conformation. Science was used to justify a bleak prophecy and reinforce the warning: failure to heed the medical gospel would exact an inestimable social price.

Although clinics were established to supervise working-class children, physicians believed that they also promoted the benefits of regular medical involvement in the lives of all children. The clinic system had a "marked influence" in revealing to the more fortunate members of society "not only the necessity of consulting their physicians regarding the feeding of their babies in difficult cases but [also of bringing] their children regularly for inspection and advice when they know they are well."[83] The family physician was encouraged to accept the duty of "doing for his patient what the child welfare clinic aims to do for the children of the poor." On the occasion of each examination of the child, he was to take the opportunity to "give directions as to the hygiene, diet, clothing and every detail pertaining to the life and welfare of his small patient."[84]

Clinics and visiting nurse services were established by middle-class child welfare advocates to educate and elevate the working-class family to their own exacting hygienic standards. In effect, they functioned in a "watchdog" capacity. But their emphasis on education and disease prevention penetrated class barriers, providing their medical directors with a larger audience and a more significant role to play within the Canadian family. The enhanced status and community position this implied for physicians corresponded neatly with their professional aspirations. More than mere practitioners of medicine, they could now stake a claim for themselves as tutors of the masses, purveyors of scientific enlightenment, guides and overseers of the beleaguered family, rescuers of children, and ultimately saviours of Canadian society.

In Great Britain, the wartime resurgence of child welfare concerns was met by legislation that greatly expanded state provision of services for mothers and children. The Maternity and Child Welfare Act of 1918 established prenatal supervision, medical consultations for preschoolers, milk and meals for toddlers and pregnant and nursing women, and dental care for mothers and children regardless of socioeconomic status. The child and maternal welfare system structured by the 1918 Act remained essentially intact until the establishment of the National Health Service in 1948.[85] The United States passed similar legislation in the Sheppard-Towner Act of 1921, making available to the states grants of federal money for maternal and child welfare purposes if matched by equal sums by the states themselves. This led to the establishment of Bureaus of Child Hygiene in the various state health departments where they did not already exist. As was the case in Canada, however, most of the efforts of these state bureaus were devoted to promotion of child welfare through maternal education.[86] Yet for all its shortcomings (it was revoked in 1929, then incorporated into Roosevelt's Social Security Act of 1935), the Sheppard-Towner Act at least symbolized federal initiative in the child welfare sphere by means of legislated funding that went far beyond the Canadian government's limited commitment.

In Canada during the 1920s, the state was making cautious and measured forays into the home, but the rhetoric of rights of citizenship still focused more on the state's rights than on those of citizens. Expansion of state functions as a result of military exigencies did not establish any firm commitment for the postwar period.[87] Reconstruction projects were similarly inhibited by reluctance to go much further than symbolic restructuring of government departments, with a view not to redistribution of wealth and power but to their safeguarding. This was a trend that one labour critic identified with remarkable prescience:

The reconstruction period ... will be a very important one for all members of society, but especially for the capitalist class. On the issue of this period depends their class ... they will use every means in their power to make their existence secure. All social institutions will be tampered with, more or less. They will be put in new moulds, as it were, that look well. The social and institutional adjustments that will be made by the capitalist class government are of the highest importance, because if they are pleasing to the people they will form a bulwark of defence for the capitalist system for some time to come.[88]

Reconstruction projects did not aim at making real changes in social relationships or in state machinery. The "army of officials and social welfare officers" was intent on direction and control: "this governmental machine will spin long, legal fingers that will stretch out and worm themselves into and direct even the simplest social relations."[89] And of these social relations, those between parent and child were deemed most in need of direction and regulation. Intervention would take the form of expert regulation through advisory and supervisory services, a mould that "looked well" to those who wanted intervention but feared removal of individual responsibility.

The Great War had a profound impact on the child welfare campaign, nowhere as apparent as in the rise to leadership of the medical profession. Although women's organizations first became interested in infant mortality and inaugurated efforts along the lines of child welfare clinics, their pleas for state involvement were only given political expression when war turned attention to the conservation of child life. It was at this moment that the medical profession stepped in to take over the child welfare campaign and to persuade the state to direct the measures that voluntarist groups had initiated. Women's organizations continued to participate enthusiastically as volunteers, but they never matched that participation on the professional or state level.[90]

As Canada emerged from World War One a modern nation, or at least one that consciously strove to be modern, the guardians of the nation's physical and mental health clamoured for a corresponding modernization of the family, of parenthood, and of childhood. As they saw it, childrearing had become increasingly complex because society itself had become more complicated. Traditional childrearing methods were outmoded, ineffective, and even dangerous. Science held the key to salvation for the nation's children. The means would be the education of Canadian parents in modern scientific methods by those best qualified to teach them: the medical profession.

The child welfare campaign began to accelerate noticeably in the immediate postwar years. Incremental gains in the battle against infant mortality were interpreted as heartening signs of the possibilities of medically designed child welfare programs. Armed with an improved scientific appreciation of child health, the cultural ideal of childhood evolving since the turn of the century, and a sharpened sense of social obligation, doctors intervened in the parent/child relationship not only to save infant lives but also to mitigate the worst effects of "the modern strain of life."[91]

These early child welfare efforts were undoubtedly instrumental in winning victory in the first round against infant mortality due to intestinal diseases. Encouragement of breastfeeding, improvement in the quality of milk available for artificial feeding, medically prescribed infant formula for individual cases, and instruction on general child care gradually translated into infant lives saved. By providing well-baby supervision free of charge, up-to-date medical information, and early diagnosis of potential health problems to those who could not otherwise afford them, the clinics filled a definite need in the Ontario communities that gradually established them. As testimony to the benefits of preventive medicine in the field of child health, they were an example to the middle-class parents they did not serve directly.

The development of these clinics and visiting nurse programs in the major cities of Ontario during the early years of the Great War laid the foundations for the more centralized and widespread services of the interwar period. But the expansion of these services under municipal auspices and their supervision by the new provincial Division of Maternal and Child Hygiene did not bring about a significant change in their strategy, structure or function. Poverty could not be confronted without dramatic social reorganization, and so the campaign's measures, although limited, were viewed optimistically as the determinants of overall success in the crusade to save Ontario's children. As the doctors' self-designed mandate began to embrace aspects of childhood aside from the purely medical, attention was turned more specifically to the other critical side of the total child welfare picture: the fitness and health – in every sense – of Canadian motherhood.

CHAPTER FOUR

"To Glorify, Dignify and Purify": Saving Mothers

As the child welfare campaign gained momentum, medical researchers began to probe more deeply into the causes of infant death. By 1920, some improvement was being realized in the infant mortality index, but the high rate of neonatal mortality remained static. It was estimated that at least 10 per cent of all births were stillbirths, that 40 per cent of deaths during the first year of life occurred in the first month, and that one-third of that proportion occurred on the first day after birth.[1] Prematurity was the greatest single cause of death, responsible for approximately 20 per cent of all infant mortality.[2] Fifty-one per cent of stillborn babies or babies dying within one week of birth were found to have died of cerebral haemorrhage.[3] Congenital defects took second place on the list, while the most common threats to infant life, respiratory and intestinal infections, were third.

At the outset, the medical profession focused its campaign on respiratory and intestinal infections, the third largest killer of infants, because prematurity and congenital defects were still believed to result from hereditary causes outside medical control. By the early 1930s, a more sophisticated understanding of prenatal monitoring and the care and treatment of newborn infants had been developed, which led to greater optimism about the possibility of reducing the neonatal death rate. American and British examples of what could be achieved by "adequate prenatal management, a scientific delivery and scientific postpartum care" convinced Canadian physicians that "the best proof of all of the preventability of early infantile deaths is the fact that they have actually been prevented."[4]

Once pledged to the preservation of infant life, doctors naturally committed themselves to greater involvement in the physiological and emotional aspects of maternity. The plight of the expectant mother who endured a lonely nine months, only to confront possible suffering, death, or the loss of her child at confinement, was increasingly publicized during the 1920s. The child welfare campaign became synonymous with the health and well-being of both infant and mother. Its basic premise and the foremost objective of the medical profession would be "to glorify, dignify and purify motherhood by every means in our power."[5] The doctors' desire to reinforce contemporary class and gender roles, rather than any purely scientific assessment of the health problems of parturient women, necessitated that child and maternal welfare be defined as inseparable. In order to produce healthy children who would adapt readily to the modern order and ensure its effective continuation, motherhood had to be modernized.

The new interest in prenatal causes of infant illness and death led to a greater concern over maternal mortality – the other index that had remained virtually unchanged since the turn of the century. The leading cause of maternal death was puerperal infection, "almost entirely due to the introduction of infection from without," a fact that called into question the extent of obstetrical intervention in labour and pointed to the neglect of antiseptic techniques. The second cause was the toxaemias of pregnancy, whose exact aetiology was not yet understood. Toxic complications were believed to be "chiefly due to the absence of prenatal care or to lack of attention paid to the danger signs of pregnancy." Toxaemia and its related condition of eclampsia were also responsible for premature birth and therefore a large proportion of neonatal deaths.[6]

Haemorrhage remained a serious problem, "mainly due to accident, faulty diagnosis or imperfect technique in delivery."[7] Although it was conceded that haemorrhage could occur no matter how careful the prenatal supervision, British studies reported that the death rate from haemorrhage among women who did not receive such care was four times that of the women who did.[8] Medical studies in the 1930s also confirmed the role of malnutrition in predisposing mothers to such complications of pregnancy, with direct effects for both maternal and infant mortality. But haemorrhage was still perceived by doctors primarily as a medical problem rather than as evidence of an intrinsic threat to health that was related to living standards.[9] The principal causes of these life-threatening conditions, and their solution as delineated by the profession itself, implicated physician management of pregnancy and childbirth.

The postwar idealization of traditional gender and familial roles prepared a receptive audience for contemporary medical constructions of maternity. At the same time that Canadian doctors were decrying maternal ignorance and proclaiming the supremacy of their own system of motherhood training, there was a renewed glorification of the home and the woman's place in it.[10] The carnage of world war, the social stresses induced by rapid change, the decline in the birth rate, the emergence of the "flapper" who seemed more interested in pleasure and career than in marriage and family, all inspired a backlash against further change that was made the more curious because "tradition" was held in such contempt in this newly modern world.

Canadians, women as well as men, responded to the challenges presented by the attainment of female suffrage and the growing female participation in the labour force in a manner that emphasized and reinforced the notion of "separate spheres." Middle-class women's associations joined the medical profession and other social commentators in upholding motherhood as the source of national regeneration.[11] Nor was there any disavowal of maternalist ideology in working-class circles: labour women attempted to organize a federation to match that of "the women of the big interests" and called upon women's "mighty power for the uplift of womanhood, the family and the home," especially for the protection of motherhood and childhood.[12]

Physicians lent their voices to the public debate on the modern woman's place and role with the same force and conviction that underlay their nineteenth-century pronouncements on the "woman question."[13] While conceding that modernization had introduced a host of new possibilities to answer that question, their own response was necessarily formed within the ideological framework of the system that worked best for them as leading – and predominantly male – members of the dominant class. Every "realist" would have to acknowledge that "so long as the home is to remain the ideal of this civilization, woman's part in the communal life must be different from man's." The underlying premise of this modern gender construction was obviously traditional: it was asserted that the ideal civilization depended upon the existence of the ideal home. Naturally, traditional gender roles were idealized to fit: "It is the man's place to build and subsidize the home; the woman's place to rear the young in it."[14] What would prove different – "modern" – about this domestic dream was the place accorded to outsiders, in particular to medicine and the state, in an area that historically belonged to women.

If this perception of woman's destiny was traditional, child welfare campaigners, both medical and otherwise, promoted a concept of scientific motherhood that depicted mothers as thoroughly modern creations of the new industrial order. In their view, the application of scientific management principles would benefit the household just as it was benefiting the workplace.[15] Good management by women would result in safe pregnancies, healthy children, stable homes, and a vastly improved society. Training, organization, and efficiency, as taught by medical experts, would combat high rates of infant and maternal mortality, thus meeting the perceived threat of national degeneration by upgrading overall health and productivity. At bottom, maternal fitness was "the true measure of a nation's place, a true measure of its survival."[16] And the nation's place was a measure of its increasingly intertwined physical and industrial fitness.

The profession's attempts to control obstetrics predated its active involvement in child and maternal welfare campaigns, but international medical currents were again responsible for spurring Canadian medical participation in the cause of prenatal monitoring. Prenatal pathology had begun to interest the British medical world in the late nineteenth century, particularly with the work of John Ballantyne at the University of Edinburgh.[17] In 1906 the British Conference on Infantile Mortality had successfully turned the medical profession's attention to maternal welfare as the crucial corollary of child welfare work.

Signs of growing medical interest in maternal welfare and especially prenatal supervision had become evident in Canada by the early war years, a result of both the British and American example and greater public interest in infant mortality.[18] In a discussion that became intensified after the publication of Dr Helen MacMurchy's maternal mortality report in 1928, doctors outlined the chief causes of the complications of pregnancy that spelled life or death for mother and infant. Of the medical studies preceding MacMurchy's, that of Toronto obstetrician K.C. McIlwraith provides a clear example of the related issues that most concerned the profession throughout the interwar period. Speaking before the Academy of Medicine in Toronto in 1919, McIlwraith drew upon the Ontario Registrar-General's reports for the years 1909 to 1918 to reveal a total maternal mortality rate of 5.4 per 1,000 living births, with sepsis accounting for 35 per cent of these deaths.[19] His findings were very much in keeping with international statistics on maternal mortality and its causes: in 12 countries, sepsis was responsible for some 30 to 50 per cent of the total maternal death rate. Confirming McIlwraith's analysis in an official report a few years later, Dr W.J. Bell of the provincial health department suggested that these startling figures did not truly represent the extent of maternal mortality in Ontario because of the medical profession's tendency to report cause of death "as due to almost any other cause rather than ... one of the causes of maternal mortality."[20]

McIlwraith proposed that doctors take the lead by first examining themselves and particularly their questionable tendency to "meddlesome midwifery." He also charged that doctors took for granted, "laughed at or even refused" the necessary antiseptic precautions that would eliminate many of the complications of hospital births and "if called upon to reproduce these conditions in a private house, it seems likely that many of us would not know how, or would not take the trouble." His suggestions for improvement included better education of medical students and nurses and more careful government investigation of the causes of death in women of childbearing years. Most importantly, he believed that "a propaganda should be started for the better education of the public in maternity affairs, by means of literature and the establishment of maternity centres in rural districts and municipalities which patients could attend for periodical examinations ... and by home visitation by trained workers."[21] In short, his recommendations for assuring maternal welfare paralleled the medical approach to infant mortality.

As did most of his colleagues, McIlwraith argued that state involvement in maternal welfare was justified because of the national consequences of maternal deaths, but he went further than most doctors in suggesting that the best form of intervention was the use of state power to hospitalize women whose home conditions worked against healthy delivery. Drawing from his personal experiences with "the ignorance, superstition and filth" of immigrant working-class families, he asserted that "to introduce a tidy nurse and sterile dressings into such surroundings would be but lost endeavour. The state should not be required to waste its good materials there, but should have the power to order removal to the hospital."[22]

Enforced hospitalization obviously overrode the mother's choice of childbirth experience, but what counted above all was the state's right to make its citizens responsible for saving their own lives and those of future citizens. At the same time, compulsory hospitalization would increase the medical profession's exclusive hold over obstetrics and oblige those who might choose not to cooperate to place themselves in medical hands. More and more as the period progressed, doctors argued in favour of hospitalized childbirth as the most practical and efficient solution to the maternal welfare problem. McIlwraith bluntly recognized another possible side-effect of such state intervention in claiming that "in countries where the state has some such power, it has been found to be a great stimulus to home cleanliness."[23] The options were clear: state power would make Canadians responsible for their own health either by removing mothers from their homes and placing them under professional regulation or by compelling them to upgrade their living conditions on their own initiative.

What was not clear from medical studies of the period was the actual advantage of hospital births for either mother or infant.[24] An examination of Toronto General Hospital records for the five-year period from 1918 to 1922 revealed a neonatal death rate, including stillbirths, of 86.1 per 1,000 live births.[25] Comparison with Ontario's total 1921 neonatal death rate of 84.6 per 1,000, at a time when the majority of births occurred in the home, indicates that hospitalization provided no intrinsic benefits for the infant. Toronto obstetrician W.G. Cosbie's analysis of these hospital records implicated obstetric intervention as the foremost cause of injury and death among newborn infants. High forceps were applied on 36 occasions, resulting in the death of 17 babies for an appalling 50 per cent mortality rate. Cosbie stressed the value of prenatal medical supervision to combat both maternal and neonatal mortality. Yet his own evidence, supported by many medical studies of the time, lends greater significance to his closing comment that, during the course of labour, a "sane procedure" should be adopted and that "meddlesome midwifery cannot be excused on any grounds."

If hospitalization of childbirth was not significantly safer for infants, neither was it a given that it was safer for mothers. Dr W.B. Hendry, also practising out of the Burnside Lying-In Clinic of the Toronto General Hospital and later head of the Canadian Medical Association's Maternal Welfare Committee, studied maternal deaths in that clinic between 1914 and 1922. Of 6,982 expectant mothers admitted in labour, 86 died, for a mortality rate of 1.24 per cent. Although certainly lower than the provincial average, Hendry considered this rate "appallingly large."[26] Examination of the mortality cases led him to "the inevitable conclusion" that in many cases there had been "lack of supervision during gestation, careless preliminary examinations or none at all, ill-timed and meddlesome interference, imperfect technique and an unrecognized disproportion between mother and child," all pointing to the attending physician's incompetence or negligence.

Hendry emphasized the benefits of the hospital's prenatal clinics, a position he would continue to hold as he became increasingly involved in the cause of saving mothers. There were no deaths from either eclampsia or toxaemia among the women attending the regular prenatal clinics for poor mothers, where they were also instructed "in the duties and responsibilities of young motherhood." Hendry reiterated the increasingly accepted medical understanding of maternal welfare: "it entails cooperation between patient and physician, education of the expectant mother and painstaking and sympathetic supervision on the part of the doctor." If the doctor accepted his responsibility for the care of the expectant mother and her child, he would do much "toward the preservation of a healthy motherhood and the building up of a healthy nation." As a "national asset," each infant was worth "in potential earning power, some ninety dollars to its community," so that even with all salaries and all charges paid, "the transaction still remains a richly paying proposition." Nor was this utopian fantasy, because Hendry regarded it as "strictly business, and good business if it comes to that."[27] The language of capitalism so often employed in medical discussions of health and health care delivery is a striking reminder of how these are commodified by the system.

Once again, the most influential person in publicizing the cause of maternal health both within the profession and society at large was Dr Helen MacMurchy. At the first meeting of the Dominion Council of Health in 1919, MacMurchy was asked to conduct a study on the availability of prenatal care in the country. When she presented her preliminary findings in 1924 to the First Conference on Medical Services in Canada, the Canadian Medical Association asked the federal health department to instigate a complete inquiry into maternal mortality. Her 1928 *Report on Maternal Mortality in Canada* confirmed the inseparable nature of maternal and infant mortality. Stillbirths (after the twenty-eighth week of gestation) amounted to 30 per 1,000 live births and miscarriages to four times that number: 1,150 pregnancies culminated in 1,000 living births. The tragic conclusion was that "infant mortality under one month [had] never been reduced," despite some limited improvement in the rates since the turn of the century.[28]

The same was true of maternal mortality. Drawing together the findings of a survey of 1,000 physicians across the nation, MacMurchy discovered that the maternal mortality rate in the country averaged 5.5 per 1,000 live births for the first two decades of the twentieth century. Canada had the fourth highest rate of the 19 countries that could produce similar statistics, surpassed only by the United States, Scotland, and Belgium. Ontario's maternal mortality slightly exceeded the national average at 5.6 per 1,000 live births. Like Dr Bell, MacMurchy also conceded the probability that "our maternal mortality is higher than these figures indicate."[29] The report concluded that the fault lay primarily with inadequate medical attendance both in the prenatal period and at confinement. The difficulty was that "nothing substantial" had been proposed or accomplished to deal with the problem.[30] MacMurchy's major concern was to reinforce the idea that the mother was the vital defensive instrument in the battle to save the nation's infants: "Take better care of the mother – antenatally, intranatally, and postnatally – until she has regained her strength, and neonatal mortality will grow less and less until we reach the irreducible minimum."[31] In making Canada safe for mothers, she reasoned, "we shall make it safe for the Baby."[32]

MacMurchy's examination of complicating factors in 795 of these maternal deaths revealed that almost 10 per cent of the women were "poor, even to the point of destitution." Nearly 20 per cent had suffered from "general poor health." A further 15 per cent of deaths was ascribed to other complications, that were not purely medical, such as "exhaustion due to domestic chores." In keeping with the pattern established in her own and the general medical assessment of infant mortality, MacMurchy simply noted the statistical implications of economic hardship and emphasized the by-now established medical dictum: what was required were medical supervision and education of women.[33] With respect to maternal mortality, as with infant mortality, most physicians contented themselves with passing reference to the notion of better conditions for "the underfed and over-worked poor."[34] And many argued, as before, that careful study had found no definite causal relationship between environmental conditions and maternal mortality.[35]

MacMurchy's reluctance to discuss the impact of abortion on maternal mortality is evident.[36] Studies of abortion in Canada in the first half of the twentieth century suggest that the slowly decreasing maternal mortality rates were accompanied by a concomitant increase in abortion deaths. The general underreporting of abortion-related deaths across the nation downplayed the need for legal abortions by obscuring both the numbers of women actively seeking them, and the numbers whose attempts to do so ended in death.[37] It was not that doctors were unaware of the significance of abortion-related deaths as a proportion of total maternal mortality.[38] Part of the problem of knowing the actual abortion rate lies with the category itself, which could encompass statistics for spontaneous abortion (miscarriage) as well as induced abortion; frequently, the two were not differentiated. Spontaneous abortion could lead to haemorrhage, with the cause of death listed under either category. Induced abortions, however, were most likely to result in death due to post-abortal sepsis.[39] A 1935 study by the federal Division of Maternal and Child

Hygiene estimated that from 1 in 5 to 1 in 7 of all pregnancies were being terminated.[40] Studies conducted from 1933 to the decade's end by Ontario's Division of Maternal and Child Hygiene revealed that abortion consistently accounted for about 20 per cent of maternal deaths in the province, and was the third greatest cause of all maternal deaths. Eighteen per cent of these deaths in 1934 were in single women.[41] Medical attention to abortion deaths would have forced assessment of the socio-economic motivations behind abortion, a discussion doctors preferred to avoid.[42]

Only toward the end of the interwar period did a few obstetricians admit bluntly that abortion was a major factor in the maternal death rate. In 1940, Dr W.G. Cosbie ascribed its rising incidence, which appeared "to be universal," to the unstable social conditions that had developed since the Great War. Because a conservative estimate suggested that two-thirds of the deaths from abortion followed criminal interference, Cosbie believed it was unfair that "the physician or institution taking charge of such a case when either sepsis or haemorrhage may have already determined the fatal outcome should accept the responsibility for these deaths." Cosbie's sense of injustice points to another reason for the underreporting of abortion deaths beyond the obvious matter of illegality. They were hidden under sepsis and haemorrhage statistics because doctors clearly did not feel they should be held accountable for deaths due to bungled criminal abortions. Cosbie estimated the margin of error in such statistics as close to 20 per cent because, "as might be expected the incorrect diagnoses were most numerous when death was due to abortion or septicaemia." He concluded that considerably more women died each year in Canada from abortion than from puerperal haemorrhage that was not abortion-induced. Two-thirds of these deaths would not have occurred if "care had been proper in all respects." The solution lay in the education of the public to the dangers of criminal abortion.[43]

A large part of the explanation for this professional reticence can be attributed to the physicians' ongoing drive to upgrade their scientific image and disassociate themselves from "back-room abortionists" and slovenly untrained midwives. The illegality of abortion and the moral implications of interrupting pregnancy for those who depicted themselves as "givers of life" are also self-evident as motivating factors.[44] The federal health department's deputy minister, Dr R.E. Wodehouse, referred obliquely to abortion in his plea to the profession "to discourage the people and themselves in associating the profession with measures which interfere with pregnancy before the fetus is viable." Wodehouse believed that "only a few of our profession do it," but more importantly that these few "cause most of our trouble" and "are popularly known to the laity on account of this type of conduct."[45] Finally, it must be considered that, at a time when doctors were among the foremost proponents of a maternalist ideology that was essentially pro-natalist, it was important to depict motherhood in its most positive light. Some doctors even feared that public education about the "dangers" of maternity might have an effect opposite to that intended, and cautioned that "the pathological aspect of midwifery should not be over-emphasized."[46] To focus on those women who deliberately chose to avoid giving birth, whether by means of contraception or abortion, might shatter the unquestioning acceptance of maternity that doctors wanted women to believe was their only "normal," legitimate, and acceptable response. Within this ideological context, they could neither sanction reform of abortion laws while arguing forcefully for saving babies and promoting motherhood, nor accept any responsibility for the lives of these clearly amoral women who symbolized the antithesis of what doctors wanted women to be.[47]

Doctors could reasonably have used abortion-death figures to their own purpose as evidence of what lay in store for women who refused maternity.[48] That they generally chose not to do so suggests recognition of the fact that a significant number of women were actively seeking abortion, as well as fear that undue publicity of this fact might provoke more questioning of the norm as they defined it. Since they were determined to take a leading role in all aspects of reproduction, they were wary of "grey areas" over which they had no control: illegal medical areas such as abortion and contraception, and "amoral" radical notions such as women's rights over their own bodies. As active spokesmen for a patriarchal class society based on the twin pillars of the family and the law, their response could hardly be otherwise.[49]

In an era when the "scientific" was held in great popular esteem, the publication of careful statistical surveys was an effective stimulus to social reform.[50] Although MacMurchy's report was in fact more impressionistic than scientific, it opened up an internal medical debate to public participation, the requisite first step in any reformist movement. "Maternal life is held in too light esteem!" proclaimed the editors of *Chatelaine* in response to the report.[51] And the *Canadian Home Journal* assured its largely female readership that "all is well when Mother and Child are guarded by knowledge, doctor and nurse."[52] Just as had her earlier infant mortality reports, MacMurchy's maternal mortality studies inspired greater professional, official and popular concern. Their release led to agitation for adequate prenatal medical attention for as many women as possible, but even more importantly from the campaigners' viewpoint, to active promotion of the need for this medically supervised care.

The Canadian Medical Association immediately placed the MacMurchy report on the program of its annual meeting. A special committee on maternal welfare was appointed with the objective of "arousing the medical profession to a clearer sense of its responsibilities in the matter." The association also succeeded in getting "cordial support" from every provincial medical association: provincial, district, and county medical societies promised to arrange for the discussion of preventive obstetrics and methods to improve the general efficiency of obstetric practice.[53] The Canadian Nurses' Association began to explore the possibilities of obstetrical training for nurses, and the Red Cross Society pledged to expand its services in this area.[54]

Outside the profession, women's organizations responded with particular enthusiasm.[55] When MacMurchy's report was sent to every Women's Institute in Ontario in 1928, the slogan "Make Maternity Safe in Ontario" was adopted immediately by their Health and Child Welfare Committee. The chair of the Women's Institute, Dr Margaret Patterson, regretted that prenatal care was the only omission in the organization's "whole program of caring for the child."[56] By the following year, Women's Institute members had set up prenatal clinics in some localities and a special study of the care and feeding of children had been undertaken. Several branches called on every woman in their section and distributed the federal health department's childrearing manual, MacMurchy's own *Canadian Mother's Book*. With the adoption of this maternal welfare platform, Patterson believed that the Institute was making "great progress" in this long-neglected area of reform.[57]

The National Council of Women of Canada made the MacMurchy report the focus of its annual meeting in Ottawa in 1928. The council requested a popular edition, and the deputy minister of health agreed to issue "one for men and one for women."[58] A special committee on maternal welfare was also established by the National Council, and its local branches were instructed to generate community interest. In Hamilton, a "Drama on Motherhood" held by the Local Council of Women in 1930 drew 800 people on opening night, and was believed to have spurred intense popular interest: "the effect was seen by the officials of the Public Library, as they said they had never had such a demand for books on these subjects." The closing scene depicted "Progress, Science and Humanity renewing their pledges to fight for mothers."[59]

In Toronto, special Mother's Day activities were carried out through a joint committee formed by the Local Council of Women and the city's Child Welfare Council. To climax their promotional campaign, the committee members held a mass public meeting at Eaton Auditorium on Mother's Day, 5 May 1931. Leading government officials and medical representatives addressed the audience on maternal welfare. With the cooperation of the clergy, press, radio, moving picture theatres, and various business firms assisting in publicity, about 900 listeners heard the message. The audience endorsed a resolution that Mother's Day be evermore connected with maternal welfare, and that the Toronto Board of Health direct a study of existing maternal care programs in the city.[60] The Joint Committee declared its intention of continuing the educational campaign on the premise that "the mother does not exist for the municipality, the medical profession, or the nurse; they exist for her and they must remember it."[61]

The Ontario Division of Maternal and Child Hygiene and Public Health Nursing also gave much greater attention to maternal mortality in the province during the 1930s. In 1930 its director, Dr John T. Phair, addressed the "public belief" that official health agencies were "not sufficiently seized of their responsibility" in the matter of maternal deaths. Without wanting to justify "any unwarranted inactivity" on the part of health departments, Phair argued that the whole question was one of adequate prenatal medical supervision and "the maximum of obstetrical service during labour." No health department could do more than urge that the two concerned parties, expectant mother and attending physician, "should establish a professional contact at the earliest possible moment," and "to place before the profession their responsibilities in terms of the maximum of obstetrical care."[62] The role of official health agencies in this matter was to inform and educate mothers and medical practitioners of their joint responsibility for bringing about safe deliveries of healthy infants.

The federal health department, for its part, was also content to continue MacMurchy's emphasis on promotion and education.[63] When Ontario MP Agnes Macphail asked whether the government was taking any action on MacMurchy's report, the Liberal minister of health replied that its action would consist of consultation and support for all voluntary and provincial endeavours. Macphail feared that working with existing child welfare organizations would not materially affect maternal mortality, and urged that the government consider "a special appropriation to cover the very great need." The minister responded, three times, that the work was provincial or municipal and "really out of our field." Although Macphail argued that "from a national point of view we cannot just sit still and say that this is the work of the provinces," the subject was very quickly changed.[64] But the federal government's position remained unaltered throughout the period.

Within a short time of her report's publication, MacMurchy was confident that public education had been greatly advanced by the efforts of the Women's Institutes, the National Council of Women of Canada, and other women's organizations.[65] The Canadian Medical Association's Committee on Maternal Welfare "reported with satisfaction" the educational efforts of these groups and their effect in awakening public interest in maternal welfare, while cautioning that the work of the "female laity" must also have "the wholehearted support of the doctor."[66] With medical and public interest in the maternal welfare question evidently aroused, the profession's attention turned to the best methods for ameliorating the situation. The central question actually predated MacMurchy's report: would improved obstetrical technique or maternal education provide the most effective remedy?

Throughout the interwar period, the profession's stand on the best means of reducing maternal morbidity and mortality was tenuous and contingent, the issue being one of accountability. Who was more responsible: doctors or mothers themselves? As first chairman of the Canadian Medical Association's Committee on Maternal Welfare, Dr W.B. Hendry consistently argued that the avoidable factors in maternal mortality were largely in the hands of the profession itself.[67] In his report for Toronto's Joint Committee on Maternal Welfare, the city's medical officer of health also contended that "bad obstetrical judgments" were an important contributing factor to Toronto's high maternal death rate. Although he supported the need for more hospitalization, he concluded that, up to that point, home confinements had proved safer.[68] Similarly, public health activist Dr Grant Fleming told the Dominion Council of Health in 1933 that the answer was "adequate care by the physician throughout the whole prenatal, intranatal and postnatal cycle."[69] The physicians' inability to decide this issue conclusively inspired a continuous and circular internal debate, resulting in confusion over goals and means. As if to avoid overstating professional culpability, the Canadian Medical Association's 1935 report argued that many tragedies could have been prevented had pregnant women "assured themselves of proper prenatal care."[70] But the central fact that many women were unable to do so, either because of the expense or unavailability of medical help, was not confronted.

The Ontario Health Department's stand was revealed in a review of the MacMurchy report by Phair and Dr H.E. Young.[71] Although Young and Phair generally concurred with MacMurchy's recommendation for expanded prenatal care, they were skeptical about charges of undue cost and inaccessibility. They believed that the expense of obstetrical care should not in itself prove a serious deterrent, since women "in less fortunate circumstances" could be served through local health authorities, free clinics and voluntary associations. They were concerned, nonetheless, that prenatal care did increase "very materially" the cost of medical attention for those families whose social position precluded free clinic care.

Worries about the plight of the middle-class family faced with the need for expensive medical attention were a common refrain within medical circles. In an early discussion on maternal mortality by the Dominion Council of Health, it was agreed that middle-class mothers who did not qualify for clinic services, but could not comfortably afford private attention, were "those who suffer most."[72] Doctors were clearly in a quandary about providing improved medical supervision to all mothers. They believed that the diffidence of working-class mothers regarding prenatal care was a major obstacle in the battle against maternal mortality; the campaign's attention should rightly focus on this class of mothers. On the other hand, it appeared that, ironically, mothers of the lower-middle and middle class, in perhaps even greater need of their help than the others, were being excluded by the thrust of medical efforts.

One possibility for providing cheaper and more accessible medical attendance was the use of trained and licensed midwives, an important component of the maternal welfare campaign in Great Britain.[73] In the United States, the 1921 Sheppard-Towner Maternity and Infancy Protection Act also permitted the training and licensing of midwives; 31 states established midwife training programs.[74] Despite the fact that the majority of births in Canada before the Second World War took place at home, and despite estimates that as many as 40 per cent of these were unattended by trained medical professionals, Canadian physicians were firmly opposed to the licensing of midwives.[75] And, unlike their American and British colleagues, they were successful in preventing enabling legislation.

Despite their increasing domination of the obstetrical field, doctors recognized that childbirth was an area still largely controlled by "traditional" community healers such as untrained midwives.[76] In a nation of sparse and isolated settlement, these non-professional birth attendants were difficult to displace. Moreover, the concurrent early twentieth-century drive for professionalization of nursing actually aided doctors in their own objectives. Nurses sought to disassociate themselves from the unscientific, uneducated, and traditionalistic role represented by midwifery. In so doing, they cooperated in the medicalization of childbirth, even though the process reinforced and institutionalized their own subordination to the medical profession.[77]

Although the practice of midwifery had been outlawed in Ontario as early as 1865, the evidence shows that midwives continued to deliver babies in rural and isolated areas of the province in the early twentieth century.[78] The medical debate over the midwifery issue reveals that this alternative for providing medical attention to mothers, like so many others that did not appeal to doctors, made midwives part of the problem. Hendry described midwives most graphically as "those untrained, unkempt, gin-soaked harridans, unfit for the work they were supposed to do and a menace to the health of any women they might attend."[79] MacMurchy skirted the issue in her advice to rural and outpost mothers by insisting, ludicrously, that they try to settle within reach of medical and nursing aid. She was obliged to admit that where this was not possible "there is some woman in Canada who would be a help to you and would come." But she always referred obliquely to "neighbours" in attendance and never to midwives.[80] Although she supported trained and licensed midwives in her prewar infant mortality reports, MacMurchy's discussions of maternal mortality suggest that she subsequently adopted the professional line. The "midwife problem" was so contentious, and so close to the heart of medical autonomy and authority issues, that few doctors in private practice – and even fewer in public positions – dared to do otherwise.

While the women's organizations ultimately followed suit in deferring to the medical profession on this issue, they did attempt again and again to lobby for trained midwives.[81] They were aware of the need and tried to make their views heard despite guaranteed medical opposition. When the Imperial Order of Daughters of the Empire passed a resolution in 1922 that trained midwives be sent to sparsely settled areas of Ontario, doctors expressed their vehement disapproval. Dr H. Amyot of the Dominion Council of Health argued that "on account of the difficulty of controlling midwives it is one of those things one could not encourage at all. Midwives are pretty dangerous individuals and owing to their fixed ideas it is pretty hard to train them."[82] Medical dominance of the council outweighed the views of its representatives from women's, labour, and rural organizations, effectively silencing all pleas for alternative health care in the face of obvious need. The "female laity" was useful to doctors, but no one spoke for women in political circles unless their requests meshed with other special interests.

The National Council of Women of Canada, following the lead of the Canadian Nurses Association, with which it retained an active connection, consequently gave up its early promotion of midwives. Dr Elizabeth Smith Shortt, in a report on "Maternity Nursing and Trained Midwives" prepared for the council in the mid-1920s, revealed the tenuousness of her own position as both council member and medical doctor. On one hand, she argued that "if we are truly concerned in the saving of the human infant ... then perforce we are deeply interested in having some sort of trained service at the time of birth." But she also commented on "the insurmountable difficulty" of securing adequate training and pay. If midwives received sufficiently large fees to ensure a good income and justify the expense of training, the majority of those denied trained service at confinement could still not afford it. Furthermore, although entire families had been born in isolated places in the prairies and in northern Ontario "with no other accoucheur than the husband," most of these outpost homes "even if accessible" could not make accommodation for a travelling midwife.

For all the reasons stated, and doubtless many unstated ones related to professional concerns, Shortt decided that the trained midwife did not seem a "possible solution." It would be more efficient and less costly to extend Red Cross outpost hospitals in isolated districts. Likewise, in the cities, the amount of trained service could be increased by the extension of free maternity wards or hospitals. Shortt ended her examination for the National Council of Women with "the dismal conclusion that the ideal of trained service for all will be long in coming and it may be that it will only eventually be achieved by compulsory hospital care."[83] When the midwife question rose again in 1930, the council decided, after consultation with the Canadian Medical Association, to defer to its ruling.[84] But the manner in which this issue continued to come up before the women's groups reveals that there was questioning of, and resistance to, medical hegemony. It was not so much a case of women's innate deference to male professionals, although this may have been a factor, as it was a contest that women simply could not win. Their political impotence made them especially vulnerable to medical dominance, even on issues such as childbirth that were central to the lives of most women.

The growing professional attention paid to the improvement of obstetrical technique meant a measure of medical support for a compromise in the form of the trained obstetrical nurse.[85] The graduate nurse could perform much of the drudgery of the "careful watching and waiting" required in labour, and perhaps prevent the unnecessary intervention that resulted from the impatience of doctors and the allegedly greater impatience of ignorant family members and friends.[86] She could assist the attending physician capably and remain under his direction and control. An editorial in the *Canadian Medical Association Journal* supporting the idea of trained obstetrical nurses quoted a British practitioner who, by relying on the assistance of two or three "trained and registered midwives," reduced his forceps deliveries from 30 per cent to 3 per cent. He now had leisure for reading and attending society meetings.

Nurses, just as eager as doctors to distinguish themselves from traditional midwives, urged that they be allowed to play a larger role in confinements. They pointed to the exemplary record of the Victorian Order of Nurses (VON), which had been established in 1897 and had been active in child and maternal welfare across the nation from its earliest days. The VON was responsible for between 6 and 10 per cent of all Canadian births, and boasted the lowest infant and maternal mortality figures in the country.[87] On the issue of trained obstetrical nurses, as on virtually every other in the sphere of maternal welfare, the profession's position was inconsistent. The Canadian Medical Association wavered between support of trained nurses, never called midwives, and arguments that "there are still some, uncritical in their acceptance of statistics, who attribute better results to the midwife than to the medical obstetrician."[88] The deputy minister of pensions and national health defended the doctors' poor showing relative to that of the trained nurses' organizations by insisting that the nurses' services dealt in the main with full-term pregnancies. In Ontario, he argued, only one-half of the deliveries ending in death were full term, and one-third of such deaths occurred during the first and second trimester. Curiously, he also suggested that the nursing services dealt "mostly with mothers wishing to have the best possible done for themselves and having hope for a living child." This argument was supposed to cast blame on feckless and ignorant mothers, but reads as scant praise for doctors. The minister concluded that statistical comparison of official maternal death rates and those of the nursing services was "unfair and casts a wrong reflection on the medical or obstetrical care in Canada."[89]

In the end, no attempt was made to train and license midwives. Although trained obstetrical nurses were employed by the provincial health department in its Division of Maternal and Child Hygiene and Public Health Nursing, their work was cautiously defined as educational and they attended confinements only in emergencies.

Even the "trained obstetrical nurse" was never allowed to realize the full use of her skills because of the perceived threat to medical control. State backing through legislation consolidated the medical monopoly over obstetrics and reinforced the profession's exclusionary powers, despite the fact that doctors could not meet the needs of many mothers and were well aware of the situation.

In their examinations of conscience about which class of mothers was neediest in economic and medical terms, doctors again over-looked the crucial factor of socio-economic inequality. Of the 140,000 women between the ages of fifteen and fifty listed as gainfully employed in Ontario in 1921, nearly 80 per cent of those who had reached the age of twenty were married. The vast majority of these married women, present and future mothers, were employed in working-class occupations.[90] A survey on married women workers conducted by the National Council of Women discovered that, "owing to home conditions, the married woman was very often obliged to contribute to the income."[91]

The problem of safeguarding the female worker's health was par-ticularly challenging "by simple reason of her womanhood." As labour representatives argued, the "womanpower" of Canadian fac-tories had to be regarded as both "servants of the nation" and "poten-tially mothers of the race." Their conditions of work, the strain of long hours and "unhealthy or unsuitable tasks" affected not only their own health, but also "the physique and intelligence of the children to be born to them."[92] Protective legislation for working women was one of the earliest examples of state intervention in the social reproduction process, but this legislation gave no special con-sideration to maternity.[93]

Contemporary studies indicated that working mothers had a higher percentage of stillbirths. The babies of mothers gainfully employed during the year preceding birth had a mortality rate of 199.2 per 1,000 live births compared to 133.9 for the infants of unemployed mothers. The rate for babies of mothers gainfully employed at home was 149.8; for mothers who worked away from home, it was an astounding 227.5.[94] It had not been "sufficiently demonstrated" whether the employment of the mother during some part of the year following childbirth was an independent factor in the infant mortality rate. In a sample of 679 employed mothers, however, 150 deaths of infants under the age of one year were recorded. The mortality rate among these babies was 220.9 compared with a rate of 122 for babies whose mothers did not return to work during any part of the year following childbirth. The younger the baby, the more marked the effect: 33 of the 119 babies whose mothers worked away from the home before the baby was four months old died in their first year.

The report's inevitable conclusion was that "children born of women gainfully employed are of a low physical and mental standard."[95] MacMurchy had expressed the problem even more succinctly in her prewar infant mortality reports when she argued that any occupation that prevented a mother from nursing her child was "a direct cause of infant mortality," because "nothing can replace maternal care."[96] It is hardly necessary to point out the patriarchal "male breadwinner ideal" that underlies these statements. But beyond their express desire to keep women in the home, these medical assessments at least recognized the reality of the hard working and living conditions that faced women who had no choice but to work, and the influence that such conditions had on the health of women and children. What was seemingly beyond their grasp was any recognition that poverty and inadequate substitute child care were more significant factors in infant mortality than was the absence of mothers due to outside employment.

Labour representatives, also predominantly male, supported the view that mothers needed special consideration because of the national implications of childbearing: "woman, being the mother of the race, should have laws enacted to protect her ... As a mother is supposed to give her children the heritage of good health, and to nurse them, care for them, doctor them and train them to be useful citizens, the framing of our laws to that end is absolutely necessary." The regulation of working hours was vital in order to prevent exhaustion. "As the health of mothers is essential to vigorous offspring," they argued, "the physical well-being of women becomes an object of public interest and care in order to preserve the strength and vigour of the race."[97]

For working women, prenatal care had to comprise more than medical supervision during pregnancy. The state had to recognize the value of improving overall working conditions as a preventive measure: "No one would minimize the importance of any phase of child welfare work, but it would seem that if the highest type is to be realized the wisest statesmanship is that which concerns itself with the young women who are the potential mothers of the race."[98] Once again, the evidence suggests that patriarchal ideology in its myriad formulations found support within the working class.[99] More importantly, these labour views illuminate an aspect of social policy formation that is often overlooked: the active participation of the would-be clients in urging state involvement for the common welfare. More than simply "regulating the poor," health and welfare programs, however limited, were actively sought by the poor to mediate crises in the sphere of social reproduction that were beyond the coping capacity of both family and capital.[100]

Maternity benefits were another possibility for helping working-class women through a safe pregnancy and the birth of a healthy child. In her prewar infant mortality reports, MacMurchy supported "mothers' pensions" to enable working women to stay home and nurse and care for their infants. She cautioned, however, that such legislative reform would take a long time to devise and implement.[101] While the medical profession seems to have approved of maternity benefits in principle, it was never more than mildly enthusiastic about state involvement that presupposed redistribution of wealth: most doctors opposed state health insurance. Dr J.T. Phair observed warily that state aid in maternity had been tried in several countries, with mixed results.[102] Yet he believed that maternity benefits merited serious consideration, as did Dr W.B. Hendry in introducing the subject to the Canadian Medical Association. On the whole, however, doctors were deeply troubled by the moral and professional implications of "state obstetrics":

As the insured contributes to the fund, her right to cash benefits cannot be denied, but I am opposed to cash benefit by the state. I remember once being met by an indignant husband who objected to his wife being moved to a hospital. When my wife, said he, was known to be sick, people were sorry for us, and gave us things; but now you are going to take her to hospital and what am I going to do for a living? Why should public money be spent in supporting such a man? The best thing the state could have done would have been to have administered Cromwellian discipline and "knocked him on the head."[103]

The concept of economic individualism would die hard in Canada, as the Great Depression confirmed. Enthusiasts for maternity benefits and health insurance were perceived as carrying the idea of state intervention to extremes of the kind that would "lead directly to bolshevism."[104]

Thus, even those doctors who favoured such benefits were leery of too strong a role for the state, fearing not only pauperization of the masses and the evils of bolshevism but especially encroachments on their own livelihood and professional authority.[105] Dr J.W.S. McCullough of the Ontario Department of Health probably captured the most favourable professional opinion in declaring that such an allowance would be "a good thing from the doctor's point of view because many times the doctor would not be paid and he suffers perhaps the most of any."[106] This argument would reach the height of its popularity during the Depression, when more and more doctors became convinced that they were unfairly carrying the load of medical relief.

From the perspective of labour, the concept of maternity benefits, or at least some type of state health insurance, merited more than just consideration. The Ontario Medical Society was addressed in 1918 by a Labour party representative who declared that "more particularly in obstetrics, labour felt itself at the disadvantage of being unable to secure for the wives of their class those advantages that wealth could command" and that "government should adjust this inequality."[107] On this issue, the state was no more responsive than was organized medicine to labour demands for legislative action. In 1921, under the United Farmers' government of E.C. Drury, a Labour member moved the second reading of a "Bill for the Protection of Women During Confinement" that included maternity benefits for working women. Drury's minister of health, Walter Rollo, expressed his view that "the principle behind the bill is a good one" but suggested only that it be referred to the government's Labour committee.[108]

During the ensuing debate, the Labour member for Parry Sound argued the soundness of "beginning at the other end" by improving the working conditions of the father "so that he may give the mother of his children the best possible conditions under which to live." Although espousing more fundamental reform than was being offered, his argument underlines the cross-class idealization of the traditional family supported by the male breadwinner, as does Drury's response: "in most Canadian homes where the father is worthy of the name "Canadian," the utmost would be done for the protection of the mother."[109] This familial form was probably more mythical than real for most working-class families, but the "family wage" and the stay-at-home wife were idealized nonetheless.[110] Most Ontario legislators must have agreed with the premier that such protection was a paternal responsibility and "beyond the realm of practical politics," because the bill never moved beyond its second reading.

Maternity benefits and "state obstetrics" received wholehearted support only from the most radical of doctors, like J.E. Hett of Kitchener, who published a tract in 1920 on the "nationalization of the medical profession." A former mayor of Kitchener and a practising physician for thirty years, Hett had supported himself through medical school by working as a carpenter. He maintained active involvement in the labour cause through the Labour Educational Association of Ontario. Hett advocated free medical attendance, free hospital service, and maternity benefits among a host of other state-funded health and welfare innovations, including the establishment of a "Ministry of Motherhood" and a "Ministry of Sex."

However radical and far-ranging his proposals for state intervention, Dr Hett clearly ascribed to the prevalent medical view of feminine ignorance and negligence: "under this ministry [of motherhood], special scientific training should be given to girls to fit them for the great responsibility of motherhood, and believe me they need it." Hett also proposed the establishment of free maternity homes for "special training and aid given to women before childbirth and care for them afterwards." In addition, mothers should be given a bonus "for their great devotion." These programs could be funded by confiscating estates over $100,000 because "it is a crime to be rich."[111] Not surprisingly, despite the avid support of the Trades and Labour Congress and the Labour Educational Association, both government and organized medicine seem to have met Hett's proposals with complete silence. Within the context of contemporary medical ideology, they must have appeared the rantings of a bolshevistic madman and traitor to the profession.

Support for state aid to maternity was also evident in the first convention of the United Women's Educational Federation of Ontario, the women's component of the Labour Educational Association, held in Preston in May 1921. The labour women resolved that, "whereas the child is the foundation of the future status of the nation both morally and physically; whereas it is necessary that the natal and antenatal period of the child be surrounded with every care and consideration," the federal government should provide state medical attention for all maternity cases, "the fees for such cases to be fixed by state decree and paid by the state out of current revenue, all practising physicians to be subject to such a decree."[112] They also petitioned for state provision of hospital accommodation where necessary, to be supplemented by adequate convalescent accomodations both before and after childbirth.[113] The United Farm Women of Ontario passed a similar resolution in 1928.[114] That year, immediately after publication of the MacMurchy report, the Trades and Labour Congress also resolved to inquire into maternity allowances in all countries with a view to their potential adoption in Canada. Bert Merson, Congress leader and labour member of the Dominion Council of Health, asserted that "If this country can afford and is spending the money it is on immigration, then surely we should protect those who are being born within our borders."[115] There is no indication of serious consideration given to these petitions by the provincial or federal governments or by organized medicine.

Despite this organized pressure, legislation ensuring maternal and child welfare as rights of all Canadians did not come into being during the interwar period. The only exception to this policy of government non-commitment was some support for mothers and children deemed especially deserving by virtue of being deprived of their male breadwinner. Mothers' allowances were implemented in Ontario in 1920. The legislation's medical supporters recognized that "while called the Mothers' Allowance Act, it is in reality an Act to provide home life and home care for fatherless children."[116] The National Council of Women argued that it was payment "for service to be rendered," and initially wanted allowances limited to women and children "at the point of greatest danger" – the infant's first year – and on the understanding that the mother nursed the child.[117] In the view of organized labour, mothers' allowances also "enlarged the opportunity of work for others and made somewhat easier the maintenance of higher standards of working conditions" by removing these women and children from the labour force. In addition to the benefits for male workers, the legislation would ensure that the future generation would be "healthier and more virile."[118] Thus the United Farmers' government moved to protect the health and welfare of a limited number of needy women and children, substituting the state for absent husbands, lessening female labour force competition and strengthening the traditional family ethic. For women who had husbands and who were simply poor, it was left to their husbands to provide for them in the traditional manner.

Working-class mothers were predisposed to complications in pregnancy and childbirth because they were more likely to be undernourished and overworked than their middle-class sisters. Yet there were doctors who argued against assured maternity leave under insurance protection, as instituted in Great Britain, because "many women would be compelled to stop work who might have continued without detriment."[119] By the mid-1930s, doctors had also recognized the impact for mother and infant of nutritional deficiencies during pregnancy, but no medical argument was made for supplementary food and milk for poor women.[120]

While physicians recognized the special needs of working-class mothers, they also believed that existing protective legislation and health services were already serving them adequately. In Toronto, the death rate for mothers in the public ward of hospitals was only

.4 per cent, half that of unsupervised private cases. Stillbirths among mothers who had been supervised through clinics and visiting nurses amounted to 1 per cent as opposed to 4 per cent in unsupervised private cases. The profession interpreted such statistics as evidence that "even in comparatively well-to-do patients who had some private care the rate was higher than in the rough and tumble ward cases."[121] The problem of the working-class mother was one that the profession considered especially amenable to education. Because these mothers were particularly ignorant, they would benefit most from any instruction and supervision that the medical profession could offer. The material sources of their ignorance and general ill health were not medical concerns.

Within a remarkably short time of MacMurchy's call for better medical care, it was believed that this was an accomplished fact, at least according to the profession's own definition of what such progress entailed.[122] By the early 1930s, doctors were declaring it "a matter of satisfaction" that the practice of obstetrics was being carried out much more effectively than only a decade before.[123] However, the impressive improvements detected in the practice of obstetric medicine were not borne out by mortality statistics. In 1933, the Ontario Division of Maternal and Child Hygiene instigated compulsory reporting of information pertinent to maternal deaths in hospitals and requested the cooperation of private practitioners in supplying details about unhospitalized cases. The findings were published regularly by the division commencing in 1934, and gave no cause for medical celebration.[124]

By this time, the toxaemias of pregnancy had displaced sepsis as the first cause of death, and deaths from haemorrhage had also declined.[125] The division's director was pleased that Ontario's maternal death rate of 4.94 per 1000 living births in 1934 was the lowest recorded since 1919. But he cautioned against medical and public complacency because this was not a significant reduction from the rate of 5.5 that had prevailed during the 1920s. Nor was the neonatal mortality rate improving greatly: in only 47 percent of the maternal deaths was the outcome a live birth.[126] Medical optimism about the extent of obstetrical improvements came from the profession's unwillingness to admit culpability, to push for more widely accessible medical care, or to concede that deteriorating living standards were causing health problems made acutely visible in maternal and neonatal mortality statistics. Federal and provincial health department reports during the Depression remained positive about the nation's health outlook because they did not probe too deeply into the class and regional differentials behind the numbers. To have done so would have reflected badly on state policies for dealing with the crisis.[127]

If, as the doctors maintained, obstetric medicine was not wholly the cause, and if such remedial action as was warranted had been effected, why were the maternal morbidity and mortality indices not showing signs of improvement? For doctors, the answer lay not with the medical profession or the state, but with the expectant mothers themselves. As in the infant mortality campaign, doctors believed that maternal ignorance and die-hard traditional notions were the basis of the problem, not economic inequalities or medical incompetence. Even as the interwar period drew to a close, physicians were still proclaiming that "you cannot blame the medical profession. [Maternal mortality] is something all our efforts will not prevent, unless some drastic means are taken. It is particularly through ignorance of the women that these things occur."[128] Physicians had come to view infant and maternal mortality as inseparable, and their solution was to be found in a common objective: maternal education. Attainment of improved prenatal care was being confounded by those who stood to benefit most, due to "ignorance; a rigid adherence to ultraconservative ideas; peculiar diffidence which all women associate with the pregnant state; and the apparently inherent desire to conceal their condition as long as humanly possible from even those most intimately associated with them."[129]

Superstition, "old wives' tales," unprogressive and uninformed views about pregnancy, traditional concepts of feminine modesty: these all pointed to a desperate need for feminine enlightenment by means of modern medical science. Doctors were eager to supply effective medical attention. Municipal and provincial governments were willing to make this service available to those who could not otherwise afford it, at least in its supervisory aspects. It was apparent to doctors, therefore, that the frustratingly static quality of the maternal mortality indices was due primarily to the recalcitrance of the women affected.[130] If greater effort had to be expended by medicine and the state in the interests of saving maternal and infant lives, mothers were also obliged to participate more willingly and wholeheartedly.

The movement toward direct physician management of pregnancy and childbirth, which had commenced with the late nineteenth-century specialization in obstetrics, accelerated as a result of this interwar campaign. Yet, as indicated earlier, physicians and health officials were by no means universally convinced of the merits of hospitalization. Some conceded that "hospitalization has not proved

as satisfactory a solution of this problem as its proponents antici-
pated."[131] Nonetheless, there were many arguments in its favour;
certainly the Canadian Medical Association recognized the hospitalization of childbirth as a coming trend. The association's Committee
on Maternal Welfare devised a guide establishing minimal standards
for hospital obstetrical facilities and rules governing hospital
maternal services, which was presented to the Canadian Hospitals
Council in 1937.[132] Since an increasing number of obstetrical patients
were being hospitalized, hospitals needed to upgrade their standards
according to the association's directives.

There is no doubt that more babies were being born in hospitals
as the 1930s progressed. The trend was nationwide, with British
Columbia leading the way.[133] More than just a manifestation of physician concern over maternal and infant death rates, this was partly
the outcome of increased medical sophistication and professionalization.[134] Antibiotic therapy, blood transfusions, oxygen and incubators for infants at risk were coming into greater use by the late 1930s.
Thus, medical discussions of neonatal and maternal mortality at the
close of the period increasingly advised hospitalization, because hospitals had the new technology close at hand.[135] These developments
correspond with the 1938 turning point for hospitalization of childbirth in Ontario.[136] Hospitalization became more convenient and
"professional" than physician attendance at home births, a view that
greater numbers of middle-class women began to adopt as well.
Notwithstanding medical advances in spurring hospitalization of
childbirth, then, even more significant were changing attitudes that
made hospitalization the method of choice. Institutional births gradually gained in favour because they appeared more scientific,
modern, and safe to both mothers and doctors, even if their medical
superiority over home confinements was not substantiated by contemporary records.[137]

In the end, despite the internal wrangling, and the external pressures placed on medicine and the state to consider other possibilities,
the educational aspects of the maternal welfare campaign received
the greater part of the profession's attention.[138] Doctors were agreed
above all on the social, professional, and medical value of "a campaign
of education in which the women and their husbands are taught that
it is their right and their duty to demand reasonable care during
pregnancy and at the time of labour."[139] On the eve of the Second
World War, the medical argument had changed little. The chief
causes of maternal deaths in Canada had remained largely the same
since 1900, despite an overall decrease in the rate of mortality during
this span of forty years. The major contributory factors, according

to medical analysts, included injudicious obstetrical intervention, frequently called "meddlesome midwifery," improper attention to antiseptic procedure, lack of prenatal medical supervision, lack of medical attendance in childbirth, poor obstetrical training and lack of supervised experience for doctors and nurses, maternal ignorance and irresponsibility, and poverty. The list devised by doctors themselves suggests that, with respect to mortality rates for women who did receive medical attention, professional culpability was the paramount reason. For those who lacked medical attention, poverty or inaccessibility to professional care because of geographic isolation were the foremost predisposing causes of death or injury to mother, child, or both.

If there was seeming agreement on the reasons for high and unchanging rates of neonatal and maternal mortality, physicians were anything but agreed on the weight that should be ascribed to the respective professional and social factors. As a result, the question as to the ideal nature of maternal welfare efforts in Ontario remained unresolved throughout the period. Even those who argued that the problem was mainly due to medical incompetence or the unavailability of medical care were undecided about the best remedy. Most favoured a combined approach involving improved medical education, publicly funded prenatal clinics, and hospitalization during childbirth. This strategy would address the factors of professional incompetence, unaffordability, and inaccessibility. Most importantly, however, it would keep squarely in the hands of doctors the control and authority over medical practice, remuneration, and the entire spectrum of obstetrics from prenatal to postnatal stages. It also permitted the extension of the child welfare campaign to the prenatal period without altering its scope and function. Medical supervision and education for motherhood would solve the problem of unnecessary maternal and neonatal death just as it would remedy the "improper" child care habits behind so much of the ill health and mortality of infants and children.

The doctors' ambivalence about the extent of their own responsibility for maternal mortality, combined with their inclination to the all-encompassing "maternal ignorance" explanation, meant that the prenatal aspects of the child welfare campaign were easily the least organized and developed. While attempts were made to improve obstetrical training and practice and to provide prenatal supervision, education remained the panacea.[140] It was reasoned, in 1940, that there were still too many Canadian mothers who simply did not "know the advisability of early and regular medical and nursing supervision ... our task of creating an informed citizenship which will help to solve the health problems of all Canadians is only just begun."[141] For many of the campaigners, close to two decades of activity in this field had shaken neither their belief in the general ignorance of Canadian mothers nor their dedication to the educational solution.

There was no general commitment to the notion that better obstetrics in itself would lower the maternal mortality rate. The need for improved medical technique that was often invoked as essential to the cause does not seem to have been considered a monumental task. On the whole, the profession appeared satisfied that more uniform standards and better-regulated procedures were required, rather than any radical overhaul of obstetric practices or universal accessibility to medical care. Certainly Canadian physicians were never willing to consider licensed midwives as a viable alternative to inadequate or inaccessible medical attendance, any more than they were agreed on the improvements in maternal and child health entailed by state subscription. What they did agree upon was the expansion of their educational campaign to include the subject of maternal welfare. They would make the public, particularly the expectant mother, aware of the need for prenatal medical supervision, and they would teach expectant mothers the science of modern motherhood.

Once the indivisibility of the spheres of child and maternal welfare was accepted by the reformers, education became doubly important. If women could be taught the need for medical supervision of pregnancy, childbirth, and childhood, the prenatal period could be further utilized in preparing women for "healthy motherhood" in the fullest sense of the word.[142] It was no longer sufficient to attract these mothers in the first year of their children's lives; the training period had to be pushed back even further. This expanded conception of child welfare fitted well with the prevalent medical belief in prevention through regulation. If doctors could persuade Canadians that "perfect parents" were made by medical decree, then they could easily justify the medicalization of maternity in all its aspects.

CHAPTER FIVE

"We Want Perfect Parents": Mothers, Medicine, and the State

The medical definition of the ideal mother and the ideal child had at its base the regulation of familial relationships for goals more ambitious than improved health. Doctors were intent on saving children, but they were equally intent on adjusting maternal behaviour to fit their analysis of what ailed Canadian society in this period. Given their ambivalence about the role of the state in child welfare endeavours, it is not surprising that the most important function they would ascribe to it was that of the major disseminator of their ideas. The medical profession's avowed intent to position its members within the family circle as maternal tutors was furthered by official and popularized child care information aimed directly at mothers.

Through the medium of printed information, the medical profession articulated its views on the ideal doctor/mother and mother/child relationship and formulated an ideology of scientific motherhood. Information literature was produced apace by medical professionals and official health agencies at the federal, provincial, and municipal levels, and popularized by lay advisers in mass-circulation magazines and newspapers. Its immediate purpose was to promote improved health and hygienic standards. Far from being purely informative, however, the advice literature served as propaganda for the experts' cause. It strove to establish the physician as maternal mentor and child saviour, to associate child welfare with national interest, and to define anew the experiences of childhood and motherhood.

To make a place for themselves within the modern family, doctors had to construct a relationship with mothers that was premised on explicit recognition of their superior knowledge. They alone possessed the scientific facts about infant mortality and child health, and they alone could interpret those facts to fit each particular

childrearing situation. Around this axis of knowledge and its interpretation revolved the new doctor/mother relationship. Knowledge
itself could be attained by those outside the professional circle, even
by ignorant mothers; indeed, dissemination of such knowledge was
the doctors' chief objective. But in order for doctors to maintain and
uphold their professional power, they had to impress upon their
clients that only they held the interpretive skills to allow application
of that knowledge through the mother/child relationship. While
mothers could become better educated themselves – a step that would
enhance maternal authority – they still had to make doctors an
integral part of their family circle. Simply acquiring the facts would
not in itself alleviate their basic inability to raise children without
medical supervision. Between knowledge and interpretation existed
a social space wherein both medical dominance and the power relations subordinating women – by virtue of gender, and doubly by
virtue of class – found reinforcement.[1]

The goal of motherhood training was to unite the two mutually
interested groups, mothers and child care experts, in a "close and
vital relationship" that would serve both child and nation.[2] In the
modern scheme of things, raising a family was an "exceedingly complex job," while the sort of training needed for the task was itself
becoming complicated.[3] The social conditions of the time made the
new experts' advisory role acceptable and even welcome. The repercussions of urbanization for intergenerational and neighbourhood
ties caused young parents to become isolated from traditional advisers. As well, such urbanization, along with immigration and industrialization, fostered closer contact between members of different
ethnic backgrounds and social classes with contrasting customs of
child care.[4] The professionalization and specialization taking place
in the medical field meant that information about the body and the
fundamental human activity of child nurture also became specialized
and removed from the stock of "folk knowledge."[5] Changes in the
composition and structure of Canadian society in the early twentieth
century had created an information vacuum that professionals
attempted to fill.

The new scientific lexicon of child care could be shared with
parents through popularized childrearing advice literature. But the
traditional parent/child relationship would have to open up to
embrace the physician in a childrearing partnership: "The professional mother of the advanced type stands to the physician in a
relation akin to that of the nurse, not asserting personal opinions
opposed to his more extensive knowledge, but trained so thoroughly
that she can work in harmony with him."[6] Despite the emphasis on

professionalism for both mothers and nurses, neither was to expect or enjoy a partnership of equals with doctors, either in intention or in fact.

The maternal education movement did not arise solely in response to professional ambitions or even to mothers' needs for new sources of information. The foundation of this campaign was the growing medical belief that there was a great need for better ways to rear children than those prescribed by tradition.[7] Research in child development, both physical and psychological, commenced in earnest in North America and Western Europe in the late nineteenth century.[8] The combined forces of scientific progress and socio-economic change meant that the intelligent and conscientious parent felt "an imperative need" for a new understanding of children. Children were being born into a world that was changing so rapidly that "each day is as new to the adult as it is to the child." The traditional precepts that had served the purpose of "guideposts" for child nurture had been swept away.[9] Here was the justification for medical management of all aspects of maternity and childhood. The crisis of modernization had opened a leadership vacuum that was manifesting itself in the homes of the nation, where the old values had become outmoded and meaningless. Mothers and children were suffering and dying in great numbers, while those who survived were dragging down national productivity. But sickness and death were fostered by an ignorance that could be vanquished by science.

The early twentieth century thus witnessed a period of profound social optimism about science and technology: they not only promised improvements for the earth but also for its inhabitants.[10] The high morbidity and mortality rates for infants and mothers seemed to disprove the efficacy of traditional methods. It was now simply beyond the capacity of the individual parent, no matter how conscientious, to train a child to adapt to the intricate and interwoven socio-economic system that was evolving. Canadian mothers, then, were confronted with the crumbling of the traditional childrearing culture and urged to embrace scientific methods at a time when there was a pervasive faith in science. Under those circumstances, they could reasonably be expected to look to the new authorities for guidance rather than to take on the burden of raising children by "going it alone."[11] By advising mothers from the prenatal stage onward, doctors were forging "a definite bond of trust and confidence." Babies born to women under their supervision were "logical patients of theirs, already bound to them in a very definite way, theirs permanently for the exertion of a little effort."[12]

The production of childrearing information was by no means new to the 1920s and 1930s. What was different about the advice of this period was the fact that it was predominantly medical in authorship and that the various levels of government took increasingly active part in producing and distributing it.[13] To reach the broadest sector of Canadian society, the information that was directed specifically at the middle class, such as childrearing manuals and family-oriented magazines, had to be supplemented by mass distribution of free advisory publications. In no other area of the campaign to save the nation's mothers and children did the medical call for state intervention receive such enthusiastic professional and government support. Science and state together lent their authority to social constructions depicting the ideal mother, the ideal child, and the ideal family relationships. Because the medical understanding of the child welfare problem pointed to the mother as both primary cause and remedy, the information was directed at her even when it purported to address both parents.

The medicalization of social problems thus created newly activist roles for doctors and the state in the private sphere. Because such state activity was still regarded with misgiving, even by those who tended to favour it, and because the medical profession jealously guarded its own autonomy and authority, intervention in a purely advisory manner was seen as the best form of state mediation in the interests of the family. The wartime resurgence of concern about child health, and the establishment of a federal health department and various provincial divisions with stated commitments to child welfare, facilitated both state and popular acceptance of this attempt to fortify parental responsibility. In essence, state agencies became the campaign's nerve-centre.

At the meeting of the Dominion Council of Health in May 1920, a unanimous request was made for "original Canadian publications of a national character" on maternal and child welfare. The new Division of Child Welfare, under the leadership of Helen Mac-Murchy, gave immediate attention to the production of fifteen such publications, popularly known as the "Little Blue Books." The division reported enthusiastically that requests for them were arriving in large numbers from every province and from the territories.[14] The most important and influential of this federal advisory series was MacMurchy's own *The Canadian Mother's Book*, with a total issue of 150,000 by 1923. The federal division encouraged distribution by sending a "card for the baby's mother" to district registrars, to be forwarded to mothers upon registration of birth. The book was also actively promoted by the Canadian Government Films News Service in advertisements included in the newsreels that typically preceded feature films at theatres throughout the country.[15]

In producing this advice literature, the federal division stressed its cooperation with provincial officials and authorities and its responsiveness to their numerous requests for information "concerning a great variety of subjects within the scope of child and maternal welfare and home interests." The division also sought cooperation with voluntary societies engaged in child welfare work.[16] To this end, the Council on Child Welfare (later the Council on Child and Family Welfare) was created as a clearing house for child welfare endeavours. As a volunteer agency, the council would work closely with Mac-Murchy's official division. Its secretary was Charlotte Whitton, formerly with the Social Service Council, which had strongly advocated a children's bureau for Canada like that established in the United States in 1912.

Under Whitton, who became full-time executive officer in 1926 (until 1941), the council was transformed into the most influential social service tribunal in Canada.[17] The federal government agreed to set aside an annual grant of between $5,000 and $10,000 for the council's educational purposes. The Canadian Life Insurance Officers' Association also provided an annual grant to allow the consolidation and expansion of the council's services, which would now be directed by its own full-time staff.[18] The substantial range of the council's literature distribution gives the impression that the Canadian public was fairly inundated with state-produced maternal and child welfare information throughout this period.[19]

From the time of its founding in 1920, the Council on Child Welfare held a broad mandate to plan, compile, and distribute informative health literature. This literature was intended to spread the sort of interesting and straightforward advice that, it was hoped, would be relevant and applicable to all ranks of mothers across the nation. "The Child Welfare Council is mentor to thousands of mothers the Dominion over" proclaimed one enthusiastic magazine headline: "The value to Canadian families can scarcely be overestimated. With it goes a sense of national pride that at last there is an all-Canadian service, applicable over the whole Dominion, developed with the Canadian background and with a constant eye to Canadian conditions."[20]

The advice was only "Canadian" in the sense that it was compiled by Canadian doctors and published by the Canadian government. Nor was it "national" in any real sense. Following closely upon the example set by such childrearing information in Great Britain and the United States, the publications also reflected a decidedly urban and middle-class bias. Aside from this, they stressed the international medical preoccupation with correct feeding and strict habit training that grew out of the common socio-economic concerns of the Western industrial democracies and their common focus on infant and maternal mortality as social problems with disastrous potential.

In the late 1920s, the council initiated its immensely popular pre-natal and postnatal "letter series," which were circulated by direct subscription. A large number of private practitioners regularly pro-vided patient lists, and distribution was extended through church organizations and women's clubs, hospital superintendants, visiting nurses, and well-baby and prenatal clinics.[21] Five magazines – *The Canadian Home Journal*, *The Farmers' Advocate*, *Le Droit*, *La Revue Moderne*, and *La Bonne Fermière* – also featured the council's educa-tional services in every issue and referred all mothers who inquired to its letter service. Other mass-circulation magazines, in particular *Chatelaine* and *Maclean's*, as well as the many daily and weekly news-papers, ran regular childrearing advice columns that frequently cited the council's literature.[22] The council also sponsored conferences, produced films and radio broadcasts, and sent exhibits and special speakers to a wide area across Canada. In his address to the council's annual meeting in 1934, Dr John Puddicombe, its consulting obste-trician, observed "with justifiable pride" that the prenatal and post-natal letters alone had reached one-quarter of all Canadian mothers during that year. The letters kept before the expectant and new mother the necessity of frequent contact with the physician, and were "constant reminders of the doctor's advice."[23]

Direct letters of advice and guidance were also sent by the council's consulting staff, Puddicombe and paediatrician Lionel MacHaffie, in answer to queries about individual difficulties in child care and chil-drearing. This special correspondence was maintained "for the ben-efit particularly of those poor unfortunates who are living in remote districts where no medical man is available."[24] Although this service provided a desperate lifeline of medical information, it was a tenuous source at best. Responding to these letters was an arduous task for the two specialists. It was difficult, if not impossible, to diagnose symptoms, suggest treatment, and generally offer advice for condi-tions described only by letter. They were concerned as well that their "advice-by-letter" service might infringe on the rights of private prac-titioners, or interfere with established clinic services.[25] From the point of view of the "poor unfortunates" themselves, medical consultation in this manner was certainly less than satisfactory. But if the com-mitment to education was to be maintained, this method, albeit limited, was the best available for decreasing infant and maternal mortality: "If we can get the cooperation of those mothers to seek and demand prenatal care which the medical profession is willing and anxious to give, we shall go far towards obtaining that end."[26] The onus was on Canadian mothers to tap these resources, first to be educated to recognize their need for expert advice, and then to apply it.

In 1934, the council took over the activities of the official Division on Maternal and Child Welfare following the retirement of Mac-Murchy as chief of the division. MacMurchy's retirement provided the Depression-wracked Bennett government with an opportunity to save money by streamlining federal child welfare obligations in this area. It was reasoned that since the division's work was designated "educational and cooperative or liaison," and since the voluntary (and therefore less expensive) council had carried on a significant proportion of this work, "the change in this regard is a matter of reduction of one Dominion-wide effort by two offices to one." This was, in fact, Charlotte Whitton's own argument for absorbing the medical division.[27]

The Child Hygiene Division of the council would now be directed by a graduate nurse specially trained in public health and social service and "possessing approach to all women's organizations and field nursing services." The nurse could be paid less than an experienced public health doctor, a fact that organized medicine interpreted as equivalent to the "cheap labour" threat. The two medical specialists were retained, however, and would make daily visits to the office and advise in all correspondence requiring their expertise. They would also assist in the preparation of articles for publication in both popular and professional journals. The federal health department stressed that all matters of policy, the conduct of the council's Child Hygiene Division, and the preparation of literature would be "discussed and formulated and finally approved from a medical point of view." The final argument was that "an advantage should accrue to the child hygiene and maternal care work in Canada."[28]

Notwithstanding all reassurances to the medical profession that this rationalization of state child welfare efforts still involved a large measure of medical participation, doctors were vehemently opposed to this takeover. Dr J.J. Heagerty, MacMurchy's chief executive assistant, informed the minister of pensions and national health that "The suggestion that [the Division] be turned over to the Council on Child and Family Welfare should not be seriously considered. [The latter's] child welfare work is now confined almost exclusively to the distribution of literature and is apparently occupying an increasingly small part in the activities of this organization owing to the added demands that are being made on it for assistance in relief and family welfare."[29]

Heagerty was unjustifiably pessimistic about the council's "increasingly small" involvement in the health aspects of child and maternal welfare, since it continually revised, redistributed and expanded its existing literature in this area. But his primary concern was that, "in this highly specialized medical and public health field, it is essential that there should be a full-time medical director," possessing "a good foundation" in both paediatrics and public health.[30]

Heagerty's belief that "the substitution of a lay director [Whitton] for a medical director would be a mistake" was upheld by the Canadian Medical Association.[31] At its annual meeting of 1934, the association's Committee on Public Health placed its opposition to the transfer on record: "medical problems" such as maternal and child welfare should rightly be administered by an organization "under general and immediate medical direction." The association also reiterated its belief that the dominion government should provide "inspiration and leadership" in the field of public health. To reinforce this issue of medical authority in state health activities, the association argued that departments of health, both national and provincial, should "constantly endeavour to engage in closer cooperation with the medical associations of Canada with a view to promoting health interests in Canada."[32]

Organized medicine felt threatened more by what was perceived as a loss of control over state initiatives in child welfare than by the abdication of federal responsibility for leadership. The expanded role of the council was, in practice, no different from that of MacMurchy's official division. Dr Robert Wodehouse, deputy minister of the department of pensions and national health, felt called upon to point out the misconceptions behind the objections of the Canadian Medical Association. He absolved the federal health department for the establishment or maintenance of an official child welfare division, something that had never been promised and was not a federal obligation to begin with.[33] Wodehouse also emphasized the continuing medical involvement in the administration of the council's own child hygiene division, and in the production and distribution of publications. The association's criticism was unjustified: "the participation in child welfare now exercised by the department is technically better, clinically more expert, and the service rendered the public more effectual than heretofore." As official medical apologist for the federal government, Wodehouse employed an argument that, in varying forms, was the major justification for the government's consistent dismissal of any liability for health and welfare provisions throughout this period. By maintaining that it had no constitutional obligation to lead in these areas, and that it was compelled neither to promise nor to deliver such initiatives, the federal government was able to stand firmly on the sidelines of what it was determined would be a provincial game.

This clash between organized medicine and public health administrators was not over ends but means, and particularly the means of control. Education was the foremost solution to the child welfare problem – but only if it remained in the medical profession's own sure hands and only if the state bowed to medical authority in this area. Just as doctors were determined to subordinate mothers in a relationship hinging on their exclusive ability to interpret medical knowledge, they were also determined to make the state acknowledge and uphold their professional power.

Charlotte Whitton's own social work perspective, with its emphasis on individual responsibility, closely resembled that of the medical profession.[34] But doctors did not want to share their inclusive and closely guarded territory with other professionals, despite any commonality of outlook. Whitton was so sensitive to medical disapproval after the transfer that she sent the council's secretary as an "ambassador of good will" to Dr J.T. Phair at the Ontario health department "in the hope that he would seek a favourable opinion of the Council to supplement negative ones."[35] Doctors regarded the direction of public health education as a medical prerogative. No amount of argument by public health administrators, even if they too were medical professionals, could modify this view. The public health bureaucracies and their various departments had to remain in professional control to offset the potential "deskilling" of medicine by division of labour and diminution of professional authority.[36]

Within four years of this contentious transfer, the federal maternal and child welfare division was returned to separate status and medical directorship. The council found "insistent demand" for its educational services an ever-increasing strain on staff and financial resources. In direct contrast to Heagerty's ominous predictions, the volume of maternal and child welfare publications trebled between 1934 and 1938. In 1938, the council's federal grant was substantially reduced, once again because of Depression-induced cost-cutting. The King Liberal government then decided to re-establish an official maternal and child hygiene division in an effort to appear more efficient, active, and responsive in the welfare arena than had its Conservative predecessor, all the while biding for time until federal and provincial responsibilities could be clarified.[37] Dr Ernest Couture was appointed chief of this reconstituted division, while Whitton remained in charge of the council, whose child hygiene section reverted to the supplementary status it had previously held.[38]

This time, it was Whitton and lay child welfare supporters such as the National Council of Women who protested. Using much the same argument as had the Canadian Medical Association regarding the division's 1934 abolition, Whitton and the "female laity" feared that reintegration of this work within the Department of Health, subject as it was to political and budgetary constraints, would mean a lower priority for child and maternal welfare efforts.[39] The struggle for control, however, had been a pyrrhic victory for the child welfare "laity," and one that did not lead to any redirection of the campaign or reconceptualization of the problem itself.

The newly reconstituted Maternal and Child Hygiene Division appeared to promise the medical profession a more specialized role on the state side of the cause. Two scientific advisory committees, one on maternal welfare and one on child hygiene, were immediately created and staffed by "outstanding members of the medical profession" in order to "make available a knowledge of the most modern developments in these sciences." The committees would make recommendations to the Dominion Council of Health for "consideration and appropriate action when practicable."[40] The federal health department's approach now appeared more coherent, more "scientific," and more professional, but this was to prove illusory. These committees did not actually constitute new departures. The aim was to expand the division's capacity as an "information bureau," rather than as a policy-making body. The Dominion Council of Health was left firmly in charge of policy directives, which were to be decided at its own discretion. Moreover, these various bodies were all purely advisory; not only did they duplicate each others' roles, but they had little practical effect from the point of view of improving the health and welfare of mothers and children.

The fact that the advisory committees and the Dominion Council were overwhelmingly composed of medical professionals suggests that the federal role was not only limited but self-limiting: doctors regarded "dominion leadership" in public health as political acknowledgment of their authority to educate the public. Legislative intervention in this area was not desired by the profession and so doctors did not advise the government to take such action. The new committees' mandate, then, was to provide "expert advice," for the reason that the government and the people were in need of it. The medical profession was undoubtedly gratified by this official recognition for which it had so long campaigned. However, the committees' actual power to make effectual changes in the health portfolio of the federal

government was never realized, largely because its medical membership had other goals. Doctors enjoyed significant representation in
Parliament itself: physicians and surgeons constituted slightly more
then ten per cent of the federal MPs between 1930 and 1935. Ontario
led the way with 14 doctors among its 82 federal members.[41]

Because of the essentially conservative aims of medicine and the
state, this seemingly progressive step by the federal government did
not inspire new initiatives on the part of its medical participants
either. At its first meeting in April 1938, the Scientific Advisory
Committee on Maternal Welfare outlined the standard medical recommendations regarding the promotion of "a higher standard of
maternal hygiene" through public education, proposed in the face of
statistical evidence that nearly twenty years of such efforts had
brought about little improvement in maternal and neonatal mortality
indices.[42] As was true of its sister committee, the Scientific Advisory
Committee on Child Hygiene also remained dedicated to the profession's aims of medical leadership and control, and public education.[43]
Even with respect to specific projects, the committee's major under-
takings were "traditional." In 1939, it completed a new childrearing
manual, *The Canadian Mother and Child*, to replace *The Canadian
Mother's Book* and it conducted a national survey of infant, neonatal,
and maternal mortality, whose findings became available in 1941.
Both were published under Couture's name.[44]

If the medical profession fought for and received a more active
role within the state, it is clear that in the process neither party
envisioned anything more substantial than health promotion and
education. Although both were battered by the Depression, each
seemed determined to hold off welfarism as long as possible. Doctors
feared relinquishing autonomy and control, and the federal government feared assuming any health and welfare responsibilities that it
could argue belonged to the provinces. For the child and maternal
welfare campaign, the result was stalemate. During the Second World
War, the federal health department continued to carry out even the
educational aspects of child welfare work in a more limited way than
it had since its original commitment in 1920. The Division of
Maternal and Child Hygiene was suspended for the first year of the
war due to government reorganization for the war effort.[45]

Despite its internal problems, the council was the campaign's central information house during the interwar period. It not only produced and distributed educational material in quantity, but it also
influenced the material that became available through other sources.
On the provincial level, wartime exigencies pre-empted the publication efforts begun by Ontario's Bureau of Child Welfare, established
by the Hearst Conservative government in 1916.[46] The creation of

the provincial Division of Maternal and Child Hygiene and the Division of Public Health Education in 1920 (under the administration of E.C. Drury and the United Farmers of Ontario) resulted in expanded activity in publication and dissemination of advice literature of both provincial and federal origins.[47] Much of the initial effort in formulating the division's program was ascribed to its paediatric consultant, Dr Alan Brown, who trained its nurses and other officers. The Ontario division immediately began publication of its childrearing booklet, *The Care of the Baby*, which also acknowledged Brown's input and direction. The booklet was sent to the parents of every baby upon registration of birth, along with an invitation to attend any existing local clinics. An estimated 40,000 copies were distributed annually.[48]

Health exhibits and the distribution of "sound literature" were the core of the Ontario department's child and maternal welfare work during the interwar years. Like the Council, the division relied not only on direct mailing to new mothers and distribution to physicians, but disseminated information through schools, the Women's Institute, and other interested voluntary agencies. The literature was advertised in local newspapers, sometimes alongside "health columns" that were also provided by the division. The creation of the separate Division of Public Health Education under the direction of a "competent physician," Dr J.J. Middleton, testified that the province, too, was firmly committed to medically supervised public education. Middleton's role was to supplement the advisory efforts of the Division of Maternal and Child Hygiene and to promote all public health concerns by providing material for discussion groups, exhibits, and the "health columns" that appeared in 220 weekly newspapers by 1921.[49]

Like their federal counterparts, the various provincial divisions charged with the work of disseminating health information also frequently duplicated each other's efforts, thereby providing a service that was never as efficient or as cost-effective as its proponents hoped and claimed. Yet the enthusiastic public response to these information services confirmed the government's belief in their value and efficacy, as did the medical profession's view of their absolute necessity.[50] It is not surprising that Ontarians were eager to know how best to take care of themselves and their children. But for many of them, it appears that their interest was contingent more upon the fact that their medical advisers were beyond financial or geographical reach than by any innate value in the literature itself.

Throughout the interwar decades, the provincial health department took a more active lead than its federal counterpart: it not only produced literature but sent its doctors and nurses into the field to demonstrate child welfare work. It also kept close surveillance over local health officers and municipal boards. If its activities went further than those of the federal department, however, they still did not go beyond supervision, demonstration work, and public education. Successive governments, from Drury's labour/farm coalition through those of the mainstream parties, were unable to shake traditionalistic notions about the relationship of family and state, and that of state and society. Nor were they able to overcome the problems posed by finances and jurisdiction. Drury believed strongly in the preservation of the family, and was not averse to using legislation to protect women and children. But his views, and his government's record, reveal the inspiration of a Social-Gospel inspired Christian paternalism more than any spirit of collectivism.[51] Elected in June 1923 and reigning to the end of prosperity in 1929, the Conservative government of G. Howard Ferguson took a "laissez faire" view of the state's role in health and welfare, and was staunchly committed to the principles of individualism and local responsibility.[52] Ferguson's successor, Liberal premier Mitchell Hepburn, utilized traditional cost-cutting and belt-tightening measures to ride out the Depression crisis – all the while crossing swords with his arch-nemesis in Ottawa, Mackenzie King, over jurisdictional issues.[53]

In theory, the provincial government had a wider scope for public health work because of its jurisdictional control of this sphere. Its officials and public health workers – doctors and nurses both, but especially the latter – were often acutely aware of the shortcomings of an exclusively educational campaign. The province was obviously subject to current professional and popular attitudes about state intervention, and especially about taxation. But it also had to face serious financial limitations. Without a promise of shared funding by the federal government, the province could no more carry the weight of "state medicine" – health insurance, maternity benefits, widespread permanent prenatal and postnatal clinics, and assured medical attendance for mothers and children – than it could deal with the Depression's unemployment crisis on its own. Like the federal health department, therefore, the provincial department's efforts in this area were most enthusiastic and measurable in the great quantity of information literature that it produced and distributed. Alongside the federal contribution and that of the larger city health boards, it is clear that few Ontario homes in this period escaped delivery of some version of medical advice for childrearing.

The literature itself, in its official and popular versions, hints at the wider concerns behind the medical message delivered to Ontario mothers. By the end of the 1920s, and especially in response to MacMurchy's maternal mortality report, physicians came to believe that medically regulated pregnancy and motherhood training in the crucial prenatal period would be more fruitful on all counts. In combination, the two could reasonably prevent, catch, and remedy potential problems in child health and childrearing even before the moment of birth. In a scientific, rational, orderly, and efficient manner, imperfections in these areas would be spotted and corrected on the production line to avoid the wastage, in both human and economic terms, of repairing a defective final product. Pregnancy was simply the best time to establish the ideal tutor/pupil relationship. From the doctors' perspective, this approach was effective as preventive medicine, public education, and social welfare – as well as good scientific management. And doctors would continue to hold the top management position.

For much of the 1920s, the main concern for the expectant mother's health and the focus of the campaign to encourage prenatal care were the infant during gestation and for the first month of life.[54] "Improper care" thus signified lack of medical supervision. Despite all evidence that many mothers could not afford or were not within ready access of such care, doctors were convinced that mothers simply chose not to avail themselves of it, a failure that was tantamount to negligence. Even a temperate lifestyle dictated by common sense and supplemented by the "good intentions" of traditional advisers was not an adequate substitute for professional supervision, as various government publications pointed out: "Neighbours and relatives may tell you much gossip in regard to the bearing of children which will tend to alarm you or misguide you. While in most cases, the intention is good, the advice or alarming story is generally quite unsafe to follow or believe. Follow the advice of your physician and it will save you much worry."[55] In its most valuable form, therefore, the advice literature emphasized that prenatal care would comprise "care before the baby is born together with advice and instruction which fit [women] to assume motherhood safely and successfully."[56]

From the initial concern with its repercussions for infant health, the growing interest in prenatal care shifted toward the health of the mother herself.[57] If infant and maternal lives were to be saved, all pregnancies had to be regarded as potentially life-threatening and all pregnant women had to be kept under medical surveillance. The medical trend to view pregnancy in this manner had been evolving gradually since the late nineteenth century. However, even in the 1920s, the medical definition of pregnancy was ambivalent and contingent:

We fully recognize that normal pregnancy is a physiological condition, and that if the expectant mother is in good physical condition and her mode of living a healthy one, there is no necessity to suggest many alterations during her pregnancy. At the same time, we have come to fully realize that the various organs of the body are subjected to an increased strain during pregnancy, and therefore the expectant mother may be properly given advice on various matters with a view to increasing her comforts and decreasing the chance of a breakdown.[58]

On one hand, doctors characterized pregnancy as a normal physio-logical state and reassured pregnant women that they could and should continue their lives in much the usual manner. On the other, they made it clear that maternity demanded a scientific approach and medical regulation because of the very real possibility of a "breakdown" – itself a mechanical term. Once a "natural process" regarded as "identical in the countess and in the cow," maternity was now portrayed as "a hazardous occupation."[59]

There was a large element of anxiety intrinsic to this medical advice. Childbearing was said to be fraught with danger "to those who fail to appreciate the importance of the occasion" – put simply, to those who refused to seek or accept the physician's advice. The duties of childbearing were tremendous: "Every woman owes it to herself, to her family and to her country to take the best possible care of herself during pregnancy with the reasonable expectation that confinement will be normal and a healthy baby result."[60] This appeal to women to seek prenatal care did help to secure the health of mother and child, as it was intended to do. But placing the responsibility on mothers clearly did nothing to bring this care within reach of the majority of those who needed it. At the same time, the tone of the advice literature must have fed on and heightened the expectant mother's natural anxieties. She had ample reason for fear in view of the statistical indications across the nation, a fear that only medical management of pregnancy could alleviate. The physician alone appeared to hold the key to both physical health and peace of mind. It is not surprising, therefore, that the Council on Child and Family Welfare's prenatal information series insisted that "our first and most important instruction to you is that you will at once place yourself under the care of your family physician for regular advice and supervision."[61]

The goal of maternal education was not so much to teach women to understand and cope with the physical changes wrought by child-bearing as to direct them to leave this subject to the experts. Women were to trust doctors implicitly and to follow their instructions explic-itly: "When a women becomes pregnant, she is starting on a period of considerable strain, a period when skilled advice is required."[62]

From the doctors' point of view, maternal ignorance could best be dispelled through faith in medical expertise rather than through personal understanding. Such methods, however, with their insistence on blind faith and compliance, could not alleviate to any appreciable degree the feminine ignorance they so passionately decried.

Medical ambivalence about the true nature of pregnancy was rationalized by reference to the "unnatural" stresses and strains of modern living and their ramifications for what had once been a natural function: "When we tell you that pregnancy and labour or confinement are natural physiological processes, you naturally ask us, if that is so, why do so many women experience so much discomfort when they become pregnant ... This is for the most part due to the fact that as a result of our modern methods of living having departed so from nature and nature's laws, we have developed such sensitive nerves that we cannot quickly accommodate ourselves to sudden changes."[63] This view of the pregnant woman and her "sensitive nerves" was not far removed from the Victorian concept of the "neurasthenic" female. This was a modernized version, however, in that the new explanation was societal rather than biological.[64] Socioeconomic change and its ill effects for life and health had transformed childbearing into a health "pitfall" which made the intervention of modern medicine imperative. According to doctors, the medicalization of pregnancy was the result of both obstetrical advances and the greatly accelerated pace of modern life.[65] They would "furnish every mother during pregnancy with intelligent oversight" in order to protect her from the "dangers incident to industrialization, and render childbirth reasonably safe."[66] For, as Dr Alan Brown asked, "Can a function ... that kills thousands of women annually, that cripples many more, and that is responsible for a very large infant mortality, be called safe?"[67]

By the close of the 1920s, as maternal mortality was increasingly publicized, every aspect of the pregnant woman's life during those critical nine months was portrayed as needing meticulous regulation. Adequate prenatal care required that "no stone be left unturned" to ensure the birth of a normal healthy infant and the mother's safety. This meant the early selection of an attending physician, prudent restriction of "all other than ordinary" activities, the avoidance of worry and excitement, and a simple nutritious diet with rest, fresh air, and exercise "in prescribed amounts."[68] The notion that "there is no reason to suggest many alterations during pregnancy" gave way to a much more strictly ordered and all-encompassing idea of how a pregnancy should properly be managed by physician and conducted by patient. Many Ontario mothers, however, saw doctors only at the time of delivery, if even then. Because the doctors explained this in individualistic and behavioural terms, they continued to give advice that was irrelevant to many women.

As the medical sphere gradually widened to take in maternal welfare in all its aspects, the idea of preparing women for childrearing even in advance of childbirth gained in popularity. The concept of prenatal motherhood training progressed logically from that of greater medical control of pregnancy. The untutored and unsupervised woman was more inclined to neglect her own health as well as that of her unborn child. If both survived childbirth, her ignorance would lead her to ineffective, outmoded, and "dangerous" childrearing practices.

At the same time, expanding opportunities for women seemed to be shaking the social order at its very foundation, and doctors were especially worried that, as a result, women of their own class were failing in their principal duty as mothers. The modern young woman was portrayed as a classic example of feminine disillusionment, frustration, and resentment, all of which was due to society's failure to provide her with preparation for motherhood on a level comparable to professional career training.[69] This deficiency in the education of middle-class girls for their ultimate role left them with little recourse but to trust in "magic" for the mastery of their new profession. It was of the first importance, therefore, that the training of young women should always be directed "wisely, tacitly, with no fuss or protestation" toward this "one great fact."[70] The medical theory about maternal ignorance did not respect class barriers, thereby providing doctors with a potentially unlimited audience of women who needed their instruction simply because they were women.

In addition to the constant refrain of ignorance and irresponsibility, there were various other charges brought to bear against the modern mother. Dr Woods Hutchinson, a frequent contributor to *Maclean's* on family issues, catalogued the alleged defects of the young woman of the period:

First, that she is physically incompetent for the tasks and strains of maternity; second, that she is selfish in that she prefers her own comfort and good looks and success in life to either the number or the health of her children; third, that she has become so ambitious for independence and public recognition that she is neglecting the duties of her home. Fourth, that the management of her children is remarkably injudicious, that she has no idea of discipline and that they are spoiled and pampered and allowed to grow up without any respect for their elders; fifth, that partly by the weakness of her own nerves and partly by the unnatural and unwholesome conditions of food, housing, dress and social habits, under which she permits her children to grow up, she is impairing the stamina of the race and undermining the future.[71]

Women of the "better stock" were roundly accused of not providing leadership and setting appropriate examples. Yet Hutchinson upheld the modern Canadian mother, albeit in an idealized version, as an example of the best to which mothers could aspire because she was "modern" in the most progressive and impressive ways. He argued that, while everything possible was being done to increase the productivity of workers in business and industry, "we throw up our hands in horror at all proposals to increase the intelligence and individuality of the workers in our greatest, most vital and most profoundly important productive industry, for fear that it will make them less efficient."[72] Saving lives was an important first step, but in order to realize true progress, improvements in health and vitality had to be matched by the "modernization" of outlook encapsulated by the term "efficiency."

Thus the modern mother was as much superior to the "old-fashioned, rule-of-thumb, wash-day, baking-day grandmother" type as "a steam engine is to a stage coach" – if she were willing to embrace specialized training by expert tutors. Only by means of such training could this dichotomized image of the modern mother – on the one hand, inept, irresponsible, and overwhelmed, and on the other, vastly superior to her traditional forebears – become fused in the unique end product: a prototype of the modern manager directing thoroughly modern citizens who would in their turn become models of efficiency and productivity at whatever rank their destinies held for them. The modern mother that Hutchinson defended did not yet exist except in his imagination and that of many other doctors of the time. Like the advice literature in general, this model was a prescription and not a description, leaving tremendous opportunity for doctors to guide, teach, and regulate.

Whatever its publishing origins or means of dissemination, both the intent of advice literature and its medical foundations remained constant. Canadian parents may have been deluged by information on how to raise their children, but they were unlikely to have found themselves confused by conflicting opinions. Federal childrearing pamphlets such as MacMurchy's and later Couture's, the council's letter series, the province's *How to Take Care of the Baby*, Dr Alan Brown's own manual, *The Normal Child* (1923), and countless magazine and newspaper columns all derived their authority from medical science. They argued unanimously for the production and rearing of physically improved, mentally and emotionally "fit," and socially responsible Canadians through expert supervision and guidance.

Society and science demanded the parent's cooperation. Advice offered in *Chatelaine* typified this view: "Wise parenthood requires not only a desire to do what is best, more than any other profession, it demands an infinite understanding, grounded on the studies of experts, and in addition, ability to keep up with the increasing mass of child lore, as well as with the growth of particular children."[73] A mother's job was a "stupendous undertaking," argued the *Canadian Magazine's* resident expert. She urged mothers to participate in the magazine's childrearing forum by drawing on the glorious symbol of modernity: "if a man builds a motor car he consults with engineers, studies, examines patents and others' suggestions. Isn't the moulding of human life of more importance than a motor car?"[74] Scientific childrearing meant parental objectivity, which would allow mothers to make every effort to achieve "perfect health and perfect training." Health and proper socialization went hand in hand to inspire "new hope for the generations to come."[75]

The prerequisites considered essential for healthy parenthood closely resembled the advisers' definition of an ideal modern childhood: "The father has been a healthy, naturally fed infant with a good constitution throughout childhood, puberty and adolescence. He is a good athlete, with a sound constitution including good teeth; is mentally, morally and physically free from disease; has made a success in life and is a good husband. The mother is a healthy, naturally-fed infant grown to womanhood. She is free from disease, has had proper prenatal care, has a happy home and companionship and a healthy outlook on life."[76] This idealization of contemporary parenthood was a projection of what they believed would be the rightful outcome for the current generation of children if their system was implemented. It was obvious that the parents of their time could not fit this ideal, but they would be spared the label of "bad parents" if they cooperated fully to ensure that their own children became future "perfect parents."

Bad parents were simply those who made no attempt to improve deficient parenting techniques. Advisers took great pains to explain that good parenting was possible in all social ranks and that good children could be reared in the most inauspicious surroundings. This emphasis on attitude seems to contradict the medical profession's assessment of the wilful irresponsibility and negligence of working-class mothers, but it was conveniently reconciled with their larger social objectives and their own professional goals. By insisting that it was not material circumstances that counted, but attitude and receptivity to expert instruction, doctors could again sidestep the contributing factor of socio-economic inequality. They had to reassure mothers, however poor and ignorant, that their children would thrive and prosper if they allowed themselves to be informed by medical experts.

Furthermore, their aims for the nation and their own aspirations for social leadership meant that doctors had to persuade all mothers of the value of their cause. Lest middle-class mothers regard advice as necessary only for the economically deprived, they were compelled to argue that that these mothers, too, must "progress in the knowledge of that most wonderful of human possessions, the human body." Medical supervision of childrearing was a wise economic investment, in that "five dollars of preventive advice is worth perhaps hundreds of dollars of curative advice – besides all the heartbreaks and distress which follow fatalities."[77] Despite their own arguments, then, child care advisers aimed to dispel any notion that only working-class parents needed expert assistance.

Advisers were quick to point out that the modern parent/child relationship was much better than that which had preceded it for generations. "Under the old idea," they argued, children were regarded as "plastic material to be moulded into what shape the parents desired." The new idea defined the chief duty of parents, after providing the fundamentals of life, as surrounding their children with "loving and sympathetic guidance while their development proceeds as nature intended."[78] Although they insisted that parenting was not a "natural" but a scientific process, their use of the nature metaphor also corresponded closely to their overall aims.

That the "natural" and the "scientific" were not necessarily conflicting terms in doctors' vocabulary can be seen in their assessment of the physical and mental capabilities of the newborn infant. It was commonly believed in this period that a newborn was little more than a vegetable – unseeing, unhearing, and essentially unfeeling. In the context of contemporary medical science, the baby at birth was curiously subhuman: "The face of a very young baby when awake has an expression of wondering surprise. The look of intelligence which is there is only an apparent one. It is a pity, perhaps, to shatter a mother's fancy that her child notices what is going on, recognizes her and expresses pleasure at her approach; still, the truth is that the baby at birth is about as intelligent as the sensitive plant, the leaves of which customarily close when touched."[79]

Yet if the newborn baby were a plant- or vegetable-like creature, did this not underscore the necessity for the sort of careful nurturing that doctors prescribed? The late nineteenth-century views of

Friedrich Froebel that depicted the child as a "seedling" were not entirely abandoned even as the mechanical ideal came increasingly into vogue.[80] The older, romantic concept of the child had, in common with the emergent behaviourist one, a focus on the home environment and the importance of correct parenting. Thus the best sort of helping hand that science could provide for nature took the form of the medical expert. The physician was as fundamental to the child's healthful development as were food, clothing, and shelter.[81] But such support was not without its price. The mother was obliged to relinquish her autonomy in playing her parental role. The medical ideal required that "every detail of the child's daily life should be under the oversight of the physician, and if he is to do his full duty he must give a certain amount of voluntary unsought advice."

Nor was this medical supervision to lapse once the child had safely passed the much-dreaded second summer.[82] Just as the child welfare crusade's original focus on the infant had been pushed back to the prenatal period, it now gradually shifted to include the entire pre-school stage. By the late 1920s, the "no man's land of childhood" between the first birthday and school entrance became a matter of intense interest to the medical profession. As the period progressed, child welfare crusaders were making greater strides toward lowering infant mortality and getting mothers under their preventive medicine banner. Medical inspection of school children was an accomplished fact even prior to the launching of the infant mortality campaign itself.[83] Consequently, crusaders were eager to appropriate any over-looked area of child health and welfare.[84]

In the late 1920s and early 1930s, popular writers on child care matters were noting that "the study of the problems of the two-to-six-year-olds is still new."[85] Taking their cue from the medical profession, the popular advisers believed that "in many, many homes, the preschool child practically goes it alone." This "positive neglect" of the young child was by no means a condition confined solely to the poorer homes, for "children from well-to-do homes are often badly nourished." Children of preschool age needed as careful attention to their health as did infants. It was in the important years from two to six that "definite lessons" in health were to be given systematically and health habits begun in infancy firmly established.[86]

The medical school inspectors were instrumental in expanding the campaign's focus to include preschoolers. They had discovered that a large percentage of children entering primary school – with esti-mates ranging from 30 per cent to a remarkable 70 per cent – were marred by physical defects.[87] Because they paid little attention to the class differences behind these averages, it was apparent to inspectors and advisers alike that the problem was the parental ignorance that led to inadequate medical supervision of children beyond the second birthday. The entire period of childhood commencing with conception was slowly redefined as "critical." No opportunity was to be squandered to educate misinformed or simply uninformed parents. By the mid-1930s, medical management of childhood was coming full circle to encompass the entire range of health and welfare needs of the child from conception through puberty, but the social problems underlying inadequate health care were again confronted largely by educational means.[88]

Parents needed to learn that careful health habits for children had to be taught and maintained from infancy onwards: "Apathy, indifference and ignorance, a triad of prime causes of ill health in the runabout child, must be conquered ... It is the attitude of "laissez-faire" which, when adopted in child care, is responsible for much ill health and future expense and suffering, for the health of the child determines the health of the adult, and the child of today is the citizen of tomorrow." Doctors thus recognized the negative health repercussions of "laissez-faire" parenting while generally ignoring those of "laissez-faire" medical politics and state approaches to social welfare.

Optimistic interpretations of the downward trend in infant mortality rates by the end of the 1920s may have inspired the new arguments for an extension of infant welfare activities to the preschool stage.[89] The statistics were frequently touted as proof of the campaign's efficacy and could therefore be used to justify closer medical supervision of children of all ages. But, once out of the grasp of the medical overseer, doctors warned, the seemingly healthy infant could quickly deteriorate to become the physically and mentally defective school child. More than anything, their examinations of school children actually revealed the limitations of the medical approach. Saved infant lives did not necessarily mean better child health, because problems such as malnutrition continued to predispose children to other health problems that many parents could not afford to have corrected.

In 1934, the Council on Child and Family Welfare dutifully expanded its information "letter" services to produce "preschool letters" that covered four-month intervals for the period of childhood from fifteen months to six years. The letters stressed that parents were to be vigilant in noting all aspects of the child's development, physical, mental, and social, and in reporting regularly to the physician: "Be sure to tell him all that you have observed and to follow his instructions minutely. Avoid the advice of neighbours and relatives and accept that which you pay for getting."[90] The seemingly hardier preschooler was no less endangered than the fragile infant by ignorant or misinformed parents.

What is clear from this discussion of the production and dissemination of childrearing literature is that it was sanctioned by both medicine and the state as the best form of cooperation in the interests of national health and welfare. Although not without controversy, as is witnessed in the various professional attempts to ensure not only consultation but control of the federal government's information services, it was easily the least threatening method of state support for the medical campaign. The doctors wanted that support, but feared excesses that would infringe on their income, social authority, and professional autonomy, and that might even endanger the very system they were struggling to reinforce.

Meanwhile, the various levels of government had to respond to professional and public pressure for state action in child and maternal welfare. But they were crippled by the dominant class's antipathy to statism, by the immaturity of the state apparatus in a young nation whose institutions were struggling to adapt to rapid modernization, and by constitutional confusion that both hampered federal initiative and provided a ready excuse for shunting responsibility onto provincial and local governments. In turn, the latter's treasuries and bureaucracies could not effectively cope with burgeoning health and welfare needs.

The child care instructions tendered by the medical advisers and their popular imitators were uniformly prescriptive in nature and intent. Analysis of the literature reveals much about the sort of familial relationships that they idealized, and equally about the ideal medical role. Few within the ranks of either parents or experts could dispute the worthy objective of improving child health and preserving child life. There was universal agreement among the experts that parental ignorance was endemic, that traditional patterns of child nurture were outdated and harmful, and that they alone were armed by science to lead the battle against infant morbidity and mortality. As such, the literature also suggests the sort of relationship that they envisioned between medicine and the modern family, especially between doctors and mothers, and mothers and children. Doctors would be overseers, training, regulating, and supervising mothers so that they in turn could manage their children in the correct "modern" manner. Even in the area of physical care, "training" and "management" became the key concepts.

More than any other service in the interests of mothers and children in Ontario and across the nation, doctors and governments designed, produced, and handed out information. Once parents had been educated and had started on the correct path by implementing the requisite standards of care and feeding under medical supervision, they could be taught to construct on this solid foundation an infinitely more far-reaching program of habit training. The result would be a truly modern, healthy, admirable Canadian citizen.

CHAPTER SIX

"A Healthy Programme for Life": The Management of Childhood

The childrearing advice of the interwar period was clearly prescriptive. It aimed to inculcate a certain set of standards and values that the advisers believed was woefully lacking in Canadian homes. Their self-imposed obligation to set parents on a path enlightened by modern science suggests that this advice reflected an ideology in the making rather than an established value system.[1]

Determined to take direct action to mitigate the crisis they perceived within the nation's families, doctors used advice literature not only in the interests of health but, just as importantly, in the interests of "management." The advisers of the interwar period were inspired both by medical developments and the emergence of what can only be called a modern industrial ethos. Interventionary efforts could not stop at saving lives and improving health: modern industrial capitalism demanded increased labour efficiency.[2]

What replaced "outmoded practices" in the childrearing advice literature of the 1920s and 1930s was the concept of scientific management. Frederick Winslow Taylor's *Principles of Scientific Management* was translated into the language of every industrial nation by 1913. Against the background of industrial consolidation and technological innovation, the early twentieth century witnessed increasing professionalization of management and an all-out campaign for the systematization of the industrial setting.[3] The efficient use of labour with an eye to raising productivity and profits was the foremost objective of the science of production. But the application of science to industry had ideological implications far surpassing the original intentions of its advocates. The term "efficiency" was not to be confined to "the mere speeding up of production." "By efficiency," proclaimed one expert, "we mean an understanding working knowledge of human nature and how to put it to the best use."[4] The concept of scientific management imbued the professional ethos and, through its advocates, gradually made its way into the private sphere.[5] The concomitant expansion of the bureaucratic state actually placed physicians in an ideal mediatory position between the social and the scientific. Involvement in new state health and welfare schemes gave them official sanction to prepare a scientific blueprint for a much-improved Canada.[6]

The new medical orthodoxy was infused with the spirit of industrial production, with its unrelenting demands for regularity, repetition, and scheduling. Mothers had to submit to the same kind of systematization and discipline in the handling of their children that was required of factory workers on the production line.[7] Modern industry stood for nothing less than order and efficiency, and this was, after all, the world that these children would inherit. In order for Canada to keep up in the industrial race, Canadian children must surpass their parents in both health and productivity.

While the infant began its existence as an unresponsive little "vegetable," effective early training would quickly transform it into a "little machine."[8] Modern technology has not simply modified the human environment: it can be seen to have penetrated "the deepest recesses of the human being."[9] The machine came to represent the most evolved human type, the very best that modern parents could want their children to be. The emphasis on ingrained discipline, clockwork regularity, and mechanical efficiency made parents responsible more for engineering and managing children than for nurturing them. The experts again justified their claims that they followed the laws of nature and common sense by arguing that nature had been perverted by the forces of modernization. If people still lived under the conditions "that Nature first intended mothers to have," all would be well, but "civilization, or the results of civilization," made it necessary for science "to help these conditions and prove that Nature's methods are the best."[10] Yet, for all their professed admiration of nature, the period's advisers were obsessed by hard and fast rules and stringent regulation. Their regimen was not based on the natural response of parents to their children's natural needs and desires, but on the rule of the clock; it was, in short, more mechanical than natural.

The advisers unanimously upheld strict regulation and timetabling for the infant's every activity. Baby's bath, playtime, sleep, handling, hours of fresh air and sunshine, and above all, feeding, were to be carefully scheduled and the schedule adhered to without deviation.[11] The needs of individual infants and their mothers' instinctive responses were to be surrendered to the dictates of the clock, which was depicted as the indispensable tool of modern childrearing.[12] The normal infant was expected to do little more than sleep for the better part of the first year, with conscientious fuelling and maintenance, like a perfect little machine.

Interaction between mother and child in the infant stage of development was limited severely by the schedule, which allowed for only about one and one-half hours of mother/child activity each day outside of feeding. The advice literature suggested that an emotional and physical distancing of mother from baby would ensure infant health and well-being.[13] This emphasis on leaving babies alone as much as possible contraposes the very concept of child "nurture" as commonly defined and understood. Parental love was to be expressed exclusively by careful attention to proper childrearing methods and not by effusive displays of affection: "You cannot love your baby too much. But it is possible to be very unwise in just how you show your affection. By your gentleness, the tone of your voice, and the many necessary services you perform for him day in and out, you may express in the very best way the great love you have for him. These are much better than exposing him to the danger of infection by kissing him or allowing others to do so."[14] Dr Alan Brown suggested that a quick kiss on the forehead or top of the head would minimize the potential damage if the urge for intimacy became overwhelming.[15] In the first few months of life, an infant wanted "nothing more in the world than to be left alone." Parents had to remember that the infant was not born "solely for his relatives' pride and amusement. He is beginning a very important career of his own."[16]

These regulations about the physical handling of the infant were integral to "habit training" programs. By the mid-1930s, doctors were charging that the mental hygiene aspects of medicine had been "grossly neglected." Just as maternal ignorance caused untold suffering and unnecessary mortality, the mother's indifference to this element of child health, and her own "lack of emotional control" were responsible for "more warped mental lives in the world today than any other single factor."[17] Nervous ailments brought on during infancy and early childhood due to overhandling and misguided displays of affection, the experts contended, were seldom completely overcome, and "many a grown-up neurotic can trace his trouble to an unquiet babyhood."[18] Yet advisers did not strive to minimize handling and affection only to encourage independence and self-control in parent and child, though these were valued goals. Their first concern was the child's exposure to potentially dangerous disease. Because of children's particular vulnerability to communicable afflictions, advisers preferred to err on the side of caution, although their vehement justifications for "a good deal of letting alone" suggest that they never considered the possibility of being mistaken. While isolating the child meant that parents had to deny themselves "many things you would otherwise enjoy doing," the child's health and emotional welfare were worth the price.[19] Truly loving parents placed their children's healthy development first and proved their love by following doctor's orders.

The modern mother's greatest concern for children of all ages was feeding; it was, in fact, her foremost duty, and one that connoted much more than physical nourishment, for all its importance. The feeding issue first had motivated doctors to campaign actively against infant mortality, providing them an entry into home and state. The basis of the entire medical program continued to be feeding. Every advisory source and professional journal of the period included lengthy discussions on the necessity of breastfeeding, or at the least, of physician management of artificial feeding, the caution required by the process of weaning, and the handling of "food fussiness" in infants and preschoolers.[20] By 1920, Toronto's Hospital for Sick Children had opened a special nutritional clinic, which held daily sessions for mothers in the proper feeding of infants and children.[21] The importance of nutrition for pregnant and lactating mothers was also a matter of medical concern by the 1930s, and again served to confirm the value of prenatal medical supervision.[22]

Much of the published advice and most of that delivered in clinics and by visiting nurses concerned feeding. A baby who "failed to thrive" for whatever reason was usually first diagnosed as a "feeding case." Only when the adjustments in feeding outlined by the physician did not produce the desired results were other steps at diagnosis and treatment taken.[23] The medical emphasis on feeding meant that some women went to considerable lengths to find suitable methods of nourishing their infants. One middle-class mother, in an anxious letter to Dr Elizabeth Smith Shortt, recounted how her doctor had advised a wet nurse when she was unable to breastfeed her son. After some difficulty, a local mother was found, but then the baby was exposed to chicken pox in her home on his second day there. She expressed tremendous gratitude and relief when Shortt prescribed a modified cow's milk formula, and felt that the baby was "much happier and more contented."[24]

In a pamphlet produced by the Ontario Department of Health to promote breastfeeding, Dr J.J. Middleton argued that no system of artificial feeding "however scientific" could compare in value to maternal nursing: "Every mother in the province should become an active apostle both by example and advice of this most important stepping-stone to a healthier childhood." The campaigners' aim of improving the prospects of coming generations rested upon the feeding question, which deserved "a foremost place in the minds and hearts of all."[25] The progress of child welfare work in Ontario depended largely on "how this unnatural practice can be counteracted."[26] As some doctors feared, however, the clinics tended to foster the very bottle-feeding they decried because much more energy was expended on teaching proper handling of artificial feeding than on the tedious process of establishing and maintaining breastfeeding, a process not in the realm of personal experience for most doctors. They also devoted themselves to modifying cow's milk to make it resemble human milk as much as possible. Infant feeding was the basis of paediatric practice in this time, at the very least "a high and complex art" properly left to the qualified medical practitioner, whether specialized or not.[27]

Doctors worked diligently to come up with new and better infant formula and to maintain their exclusive hold on the management of artificial infant feeding. Protein milk, introduced at the Hospital for Sick Children in 1914 and widely prescribed for ailing infants across Canada, was one of Alan Brown's earliest contributions to the infant mortality campaign; its use was considered to reduce dramatically the duration of gastrointestinal infections in children.[28] For infants who were failing to thrive due to difficulties in digesting milk, Brown recommended the use of lactic acid milk, a predigested and more readily tolerated feeding.[29] By the beginning of the Second World War, a number of commercial formula companies were producing both varieties and they were more generally prescribed in the treatment of "feeding cases."

Despite the medical attention paid to artificial feeding, however, all the advisers tried to convince mothers of the irreplaceable quality of breast milk as the best insurance for the infant's health.[30] Very early in the campaign, maternal nursing acquired the patriotic and imperialistic overtones essential to the campaign's premise that "nations are built of babies." As Helen MacMurchy contended in 1913, "The greatest safeguard for the little Baby's life is nursing at the Mother's breast ... If fed any other way, the chances are great that you will bury your Baby. The fact should be known to every voter in Canada. We cannot rear an Imperial race on the bottle. When a Canadian sees the mother of his child nursing that child at her breast, he sees her doing something of Imperial importance."[31]

Feeding was clearly a life-or-death issue for both infant and nation. Maternal nursing was at once a question of national import and an ethical issue at the very heart of motherhood. The mother who did not nurse her child was depicted as "sub-letting her duty to a cow."[32] She was the "worst kind of thief for she steals from the baby something that cannot be replaced by any modification of cow's milk."[33] She deprived her infant of its "natural right to its natural food." Dr Alan Brown was particularly disturbed by his impression that "women seem very often not to be oppressed by their failure in this that is act and pact of true motherhood."[34] The healthy bottle-fed baby was "merely a brilliant exception to the well-established rule that mother's milk is the one and only proper food for mother's baby."[35] While acknowledging "all the successes" in decreasing the dangers of artificial feeding, the editor of the *Canadian Public Health Journal* declared that he had "no hesitation in advocating breast-feeding even under surroundings which appear to be unfavourable."[36]

Whatever the reasons cited – the employment of mothers outside the home, maternal ignorance, physician indifference, advances in artificial feeding, ruthless advertising tactics at a time when advertising was increasingly important in the marketplace – the advisers' impression that more mothers were resorting to bottle-feeding was realistic. They ardently promoted breastfeeding because it was not common practice.[37] Surveys conducted by Dr Alan Brown in Toronto in 1918 and by the Child Welfare Association in Montreal in 1930 revealed that fewer mothers were nursing their infants than had done so at the turn of the century.[38] Brown believed, typically, that the infrequency of nursing was explained chiefly by the ignorance of the laity, but he also blamed the indifference of the physician.

One of the principal reasons for the decrease in the proportion of breastfed babies was seen to be the employment of married women, largely from the working class, to the point where MacMurchy argued that any occupation that prevented or impeded nursing was "a direct cause of infant mortality."[39] Breastfeeding necessarily kept women tied to home and family. The issue prompted some of the more progressive child welfare campaigners to urge the adoption of maternity allowances so that working-class mothers could stay home with their infants. On the whole, however, they preferred to castigate these mothers for their negligence rather than finding ways to make up the lost wages that they needed. But Brown also pointed out that "the poorest mothers are not those who commonly find difficulty in breastfeeding," and so other reasons besides the ignorance and negligence of working-class mothers had to be found to explain the Canadian mother's reluctance to take up this sacred duty.[40]

Also contributing to the decline in breastfeeding were the "exaggerated claims" supporting artificial feeding and the "popular delusion" that "their adaptation to the physiologic needs of each infant is so simple that the process can be safely entrusted to little mothers."[41] Neither the manufacturers of canned milk who advertised the benefits of their products for infants nor the mothers who bought them were qualified judges of proper feeding.[42] Rima Apple's comprehensive analysis of the shift to bottle-feeding in early twentieth-century America suggests that, with respect to advertising and medical expertise as relative influences on modes of infant feeding, no one factor clearly dominated. As artificial feeding became less complex for physicians and mothers alike, and as the profession gained control over the dissemination of infant feeding information, the bottle came into more common use. Some physicians actually admitted their part in encouraging artificial feeding, which they had taken up "with the best intentions if mistakenly."[43] Dr Frederick Tisdall agreed that "the present-day success in the artificial feeding of young infants" was behind the "erroneous belief" entertained by many young mothers that cow's milk preparations would adequately substitute for their infant's natural food.[44]

For all their espousal of breastfeeding, it is clear that doctors also supported bottle feeding as a healthy alternative if it was carried out under their direction. Although analyses of infant mortality implicated artificial feeding as the primary cause of deaths due to intestinal infection, doctors were convinced that it was not bottle-feeding in and of itself that was to blame, but "improper" bottle-feeding resulting from maternal ignorance. Moreover, despite the fact that medical studies of the time demonstrated the relevance of economic conditions as a significant variable in deaths among bottle-fed infants, doctors continued to maintain that carelessness was the uppermost problem.[45] Brown, and many of his colleagues, believed that medically supervised artificial feeding was a viable alternative to breast-feeding: "methods of artificially feeding the normal infant today are simple and productive of most satisfactory results."[46] The physician should familiarize himself with scientific infant feeding and then see to it that mothers applied his advice in carrying it out.

The experts were consistently unwilling to sacrifice their scientific and social prestige to either lax commercial companies or unqualified practitioners and nurses. Thus, mothers were advised that, "if the baby must be bottle-fed, do not let anyone persuade you to use any of the patent foods, many of which are of very little value ... Ask your doctor to make out a proper formula."[47] Mothers were also cautioned never to experiment with the preparation or formula of modified milk for the baby. The profession was so concerned about the potential for misuse and abuse of artificial formula that the

Canadian Public Health Association wanted artificial foods and "so-called milk substitutes" for infant feeding controlled by law so that only physicians could prescribe them. Such a law, it was argued, would greatly reduce infant mortality. Undoubtedly, it would also provide legal protection for the physicians' monopoly over feeding that was now medical treatment.[48]

Advice on feeding increased the burden of maternal guilt: if babies were not gaining according to the medical yardstick, mothers were obviously doing something wrong, perhaps even dangerously wrong. The result of a medical diagnosis of "failure to thrive" based primarily on slow weight gain may actually have prompted mothers to resort to artificial feeding, since cow's milk has a higher caloric content and results in faster weight gain. One public health nurse visiting Espanola encouraged the mother of an underweight two-month-old infant to continue despite her frustrations with breastfeeding. The baby started to gain, "however, the gain was slow and it required some persuasion to induce the mother to continue ... Neighbours' babies were getting fat on Eagle Brand," a popular condensed milk with a high sugar and fat content.[49] Infant weight was so important that many clinics became largely "weighing stations" rather than centres for well-baby supervision and health teaching, as they were intended to be. As well, the "pounds race" fostered maternal competitiveness, perhaps to the detriment of the baby's health: babies of "ideal weight" were regularly awarded prizes at baby shows and exhibits sponsored by various child welfare agencies.[50]

Doctors were thus caught in a professional bind concerning natural versus artificial feeding. They extolled the virtues of breastfeeding and rebuked mothers who did not nurse as irresponsible, unpatriotic, unwomanly failures. They also invested time and effort in studying and developing the science of artificial feeding, advising mothers, prescribing formula, and defending their professional rights in this sphere. Paediatric specialists received a substantial proportion of their income from this particular activity: doctors who advertised themselves as specialists in infant feeding "were always busy."[51] The root of this feeding dilemma was the scientific motherhood they so eagerly promoted, based as it was on the denigration of "traditional" methods. Not surprisingly, then, mothers tended to associate bottle-feeding with modern scientific methods, especially since considerably more professional energy was directed towards the refinement and regulation of artificial feeding than the encouragement of breast-feeding. Even Brown was forced to conclude that "breastfeeding, in consequence, has not gained in public estimation, and many who would have breastfed have not dared persevere under the implication that this is an ordinary way of infant nurture and that babies must not be deprived of anything scientific or good merely to save the instinct of the mother to nourish and care for them herself."[52] The ideal, responsible, modern mother was supposed to be scientific, not merely instinctive, but science actually seemed to be making some mothers less than ideal and responsible, according to the doctors' own views. In waging war against tradition, doctors lost this battle, ironically because they were so successful in promoting their larger ends. If women were unwilling to nurse their infants, doctors simply had to protect their professional authority and economic position by taking over the direction of artificial feeding, however much they opposed it in principle.

Contemporary medical knowledge and therapeutics placed every detail of the child's diet under the rubric of medical treatment. By the late 1920s, the parental task was simplified considerably when Brown, in conjunction with paediatricians Frederick Tisdall and Theodore Drake, developed Pablum. This food was acclaimed internationally as an excellent cereal addition to the infant's diet, and remains a staple in present-day infant feeding. In 1931 Brown arranged for the Mead Johnson Company to produce it commercially with all patent royalties for the first twenty-five years turned over to the Hospital for Sick Children. The team also developed and marketed Sunwheat Biscuits, made from whole wheat and fortified with bone meal, as a nutritional supplement for toddlers and young children.[53] Thus not only the feeding process but food itself became "scientific."

Physical care remained central to the advice literature, but as child welfare advocates began to take heart in declining infant mortality rates and pride in the slowly expanding network of clinics, other facets of child development attracted their interest. Changes in the nature and content of this advice from the 1920s to the 1930s demonstrate that the "modern" concept of childrearing was more than a product of emerging medical and psychological theories and any corresponding therapeutic innovations. It was an evolving system of values grounded in existing class relations and the new social realities of post-World War I Canada.

From the medical perspective, infancy and early childhood represented an unparalleled opportunity for both observation of normal growth and personality building. Child behaviour – a subject not purely "medical" – began to establish itself as a legitimate area of medical investigation just as child psychology was also emerging as a specialized field. At this formative stage, the subject was never entirely relinquished to the psychologists. Some enthusiasts even argued that no physician could treat his young patients adequately without a psychological diagnosis, which was just as vital to child health as was medical examination.[54] Physicians and psychologists alike believed that parental management of the child's physical nurture was so closely intertwined with its training for emotional and social "fitness" that the two were inseparable: "Assuming that the young parents understand the proper hygiene of their child's physical development and are carefully carrying this out under the guidance of a physician, they are almost unconsciously laying the foundation for certain definite habits that tend to law, order and obedience. Bath, meals and sleep at certain intervals and in regular order reduce nervous fatigue to the minimum."[55] The establishment of proper health habits in the first year of life would help the infant acquire "obedience, truthfulness, cheerfulness and perseverance as they apply to these simple but necessary activities," even in the absence of explicit parental intent to impart these traits.[56]

This intimate connection between physical care and habit training justifed the doctors' interest in mental hygiene and their own merits as childrearing advisers on matters other than purely medical. Interprofessional borrowing was common during this period. Child psychologists acknowledged their debt to the medical experts, while the latter were clearly influenced by contemporary theories of child development.[57] Physicians interested in mental hygiene used much the same arguments as those interested in the prevention of infant mortality to support their involvement in this aspect of child nurture: "There is a growing consciousness that the conservation of human material is at least as necessary to civilization as the development and preservation of our natural resources. The most substantial promise for alleviation of at least some of the misery, unhappiness and failure of adult life lies in a more intelligent management of the period of childhood."[58]

The advice on habit training produced by both groups of experts is so generally interchangeable that it is difficult to assess the professional origins of some of the information. Both were agreed that what was needed was an overall theory of child management, parents who were educated in the application of the new methods, and children who were trained from birth. Effective motherhood training began with the teaching of the fundamentals of physical care, especially feeding, and then progressed to the correct ways of cultivating obedience, honesty, and courtesy as well as coping with fears and anger. Mothers also had to learn to foster intellectual development, independence, and good work habits. The ideal mother/child relationship would bring forth a generation of ideal modern Canadians.

Discipline was integral to the new childrearing techniques, but it was a modern concept far removed from the old-fashioned maxim of "spare the rod and spoil the child." This was a built-in discipline in the form of regulation. The goal was not to exact the child's blind obedience, for all that this was required of mothers in their new relationship to doctors. Instead, by following doctors' orders, mothers were to lead their children to an intelligent understanding of correct behaviour. The child trained in this manner would "know no other way" to behave. Inspiring such childrearing notions was a theory of productivity based on mutuality of interests.[59] Just as labour productivity depended on the workers' comprehension of its value to themselves as well as to their employers, "productive" children had to understand that carrying out their parents' requests would benefit all concerned.

Because children were initially ruled by instinct, proper training from birth would transform infantile instincts into correct habits. Careless or incorrect parental management would see the instinctive behaviour of the child deteriorate into "bad" habits:

It is with instincts as a basis that habits are formed, and the sum total of our particular habits we call our characters. Since instincts are most prominent in early life, it is the training then given that makes or mars children ... Since the child is normally in the home with the parents as teachers, chiefly the mother, the responsiblity of parents for the formation of the characters of their children is overwhelmingly great. Practically the whole of the law and the prophets in regard to child training can be summed up in this one word, habit.[60]

The "good" child was well trained from birth. The "bad" child was the heir of inadequate parents who had indulged its bad habits. Prevention, as usual, was much easier and more effective than cure: "To let a baby have its own way for the first few weeks or even the first few months and then be forced either to acknowledge baby as tyrant or else to start the severe parent business is kind neither to yourself nor to the little being you have brought into the world."[61] Habit training benefited both sides of the parent/child equation. It was also to the benefit of society, the state, and the experts' themselves, since its application affirmed their wisdom and power, and carried on their particular vision for the nation. Habit training became the cure-all for an expansive catalogue of individual, familial, and social problems.

By the experts' definition, the best kind of habit training consisted of "an intelligent and scientific correlation of each individual's potential assets to develop them to the utmost, and at the same time bending every effort to eliminate liabilities."[62] The balance sheet was easily calculated. Bad habits were non-conformist behaviour traits, or at least those that did not conform to the advisers' prescriptions. Aspects of child development such as nail-biting, thumb-sucking, crying for attention, bed-wetting, mouth-breathing (an "unhygienic" habit that was believed to make the child more vulnerable to disease of the tonsils and adenoids), and masturbation, were obvious examples of bad habits to be eradicated by maternal diligence.

Good behaviour in the child from day to day ensured good character in the adult, and the smooth functioning of society. Children had to learn to conform to society's expectations, mothers to see that the lesson was learned through careful direction and regulation: "The parent's main duty is to direct the life of the child so that he will fit into our social life with as little confusion as possible to himself and others."[63] The only "truly constructive principles upon which to build the future successes or failures of an individual" were to be found in a child-training program that controlled habit formation.[64] And on this manner of individual success rested the ultimate triumph of the modern order.

The growing emphasis on habit training and personality building reflected the broadening sphere of medical management of childhood and regulation of motherhood. Ill-behaved children were simply conditioned that way by ill-trained, irresponsible mothers: "The familiar sight of a woman dragging a screaming, squalling three-year-old along the street by the arm is public testimony that there is much to be desired in the qualifications of that woman in her efforts in home training."[65] Modern training for motherhood meant changes in the method of childrearing and much of its content:

We have come to interpret health as a whole state of being, involving not only the physical but the mental, emotional and social aspects of the individual. Teaching regarding the physical care of the baby has become impregnated with these new ideas and we do not merely say to Mrs. White, "give the baby cereal", but we teach her how to start this new food so that she may develop within the child an attitude of acceptance. The mother is taught ... that habit training is a learning process in which the attitude of the parents plays a very large part, that the starting point of all habit training is the education of the parents in the knowledge and methods of dealing with behaviour problems.[66]

Changes such as these were hailed by child welfare advocates as evidence of their own progressive outlook. The more subtle changes in the mother/child relationship that were "side-effects" of their prescriptions went unnoticed or at least unremarked. While arguing continually for the modernization of the family, advisers conceptualized its emotional and psychological dimensions within the narrow structure of the traditional mother/child relationship, and neglected to consider the impact of their prescriptions on mothers.[67]

In the advice literature of the interwar period, particularly during the 1930s, there was a substantial expansion of the duties connected with childrearing. The scheduling of baby's day appeared to allow mothers some free time. In effect, however, by charging them with new responsibility for the child's cognitive growth, emotional adjustment, and future civic worth as well as its health, experts were devising a system that made childrearing an ever more time-consuming and stressful process.[68] Given the possibilities for harm, mistakes could not be countenanced: "The thousands of unfortunate results of a trial and error method of rearing helpless children can be seen in many of the physically and mentally warped and twisted lives we see around us."[69]

Children were increasingly viewed as morally neutral and passive in their ability to influence their own lives. Just as the infant was physically and mentally little more than a vegetable, it entered the world in a condition of moral *tabula rasa* that effectively rendered it a "vital bundle of potentialities."[70] This image of the child actually allowed for greater parental influence in its development, and consequently greater medical influence on parents in determining the nature of that development. At the same time, parents – especially mothers – became the source of all blame should their children "turn out" badly: "Remember that it is what you do, day after day, and your personality that will largely determine the sort of child your baby will be."[71] Regulation of mothers by experts in turn promoted and sustained the regulation of children.[72] The process, however, had to be instigated at birth, because then it was easy to make the child conform to a routine schedule, "but just as easy for him to learn to accept a haphazard existence."[73] Any hint of the haphazard was anathema in a modern industrial society ordered by the watchwords of efficiency and productivity. The alternatives presented to parents were to fit the child to the modern order or to ruin its prospects for life, while contributing to the downfall of the system itself. Which parent could consciously make the latter choice?

Both the medical childrearing advice and its popularized versions reflected a transfer of allegiance from the hereditarian notions underlying the eugenicist ideas prevalent at the turn of the century.[74] This was not an abrupt ideological shift: there are various instances in the advice literature, particularly in the early 1920s, that reveal remnants of hereditarian attitudes alongside emergent environmentalist ideas.[75] By the end of the 1920s, however, the notion that variations in individual personality were primarily inherited had been largely overtaken by the opposite viewpoint. It was argued that differences in character derived from differences in experience. This emergent theory drew its strength from conditioning and learning experiments in psychology and from research in cultural anthropology that demonstrated that personality differences could be correlated to cultural variations.[76]

The new rigidly environmentalist viewpoint reached its extreme in the late 1920s in the work of John B. Watson, the American originator of behaviourist psychology. Watson and his behaviourist school absolutely discounted all but environmental factors in character development. "Give me a dozen healthy infants and my own world to bring them up in," he proclaimed, "and I will guarantee to train any one of them to become any kind of specialist I might select – doctor, lawyer, artist, merchant, chief, and even beggarman or thief."[77] Behaviourism adapted the infant to fit the world into which it was born by means of "conditioning." Behaviourist child training was premised on parental manipulation, called "management," according to predictable patterns of stimulus and response.[78]

Outside the area of intelligence, very little scientific research was actually performed to establish the comparative influence of heredity versus environment. The debate over the plasticity and malleability of human nature has veered from one extreme to another throughout the course of the twentieth century. The "nature/nurture" debate continues to this day: the relative effects of parental behaviour on the child's character have yet to be established conclusively. It is significant, however, that the major thrust for parent education manifested itself when environmental determinism was at its highest point in North American research circles during the first half of this century.[79]

The psychogenic hypothesis, which postulated that early life experiences were causally related to later life disorders – physical, mental and "social" – was also integral to North American psychiatric theory at this time.[80] At any age, all and any "bad" characteristics displayed by the child or adult could be traced directly to earlier parental error or negligence. Environmental and psychogenic theories, supported by science, led to the conclusion that one of the "most cheering things that science has done for parents of late has been to prove pretty conclusively that our children do not come into the world handicapped from the start by all our faults and foibles of disposition and temperament ... It is now generally agreed that personality and character are shaped more largely by the child's environment than by any other factor; which means that the youngster's home can either make or mar him."[81] This was "a very happy fact" because it suggested that "we can make our children what we wish them to be" by proper training.[82]

On the other hand, by discounting "that bogey heredity," which was simply "the lazy parent's excuse for her own shortcomings," such theories greatly magnified the mother's responsibility.[83] Parents were naturally inclined to take credit for their children's good behaviour, while there was "always a tendency to blame the defenceless ancestor" for negative character traits.[84] Advisers insisted that their views were scientifically based, but it was actually the absence of firm evidence proving the durable effects of early childhood experience that permitted their attempted regulation of parental behaviour. Environmentalist ideas corresponded to their own aspirations, and so they were eager to propagate them. Their adoption of this particular theory of behaviour reveals the enmeshing of cultural trends and contemporary ideals with scientific evolution.

The Great War brought an end to the easy optimism that had seen human perfectability as a simple biological problem. In the aftermath of the war's destruction, and in the context of the new order that was evolving, the solution seemed to lie in some sort of human engineering. A "method" or "program" was needed in order to bring destructive human traits under social control – and especially under professional regulation – so that the fabric of civilization might be mended, reinforced, and scientifically improved. Other forms of regeneration no longer held out hope. Behaviourist ideas were consonant with the social temper of the times: "Will not these children, in turn, with their better ways of living and thinking, replace us as society and bring up their children in a still more scientific way until the world finally becomes a place fit for human habitation?"[85]

In the prewar childrearing advice literature, and occasionally in that of the 1920s, psychological differences between children were handled in a relatively humane and pragmatic fashion, whatever the rigidities of scheduling. Dr Alan Brown urged that parents learn to empathize and identify with their individual offspring in order to see through their own eyes that particular child's view of the world.[86] Brown contended that the ideal child raised in an ideal manner would become "a little machine," but he did allow for individual differences in psychological make-up. In contrast, the psychologists who made such on impact on the medical experts during the 1930s proposed to eliminate these differences, just as doctors tended to ignore differential physical development in children. Canadian psychologists William Blatz and Helen Bott allowed for no deviation from the path of parental control:

If we were asked what was the keynote of a practical and common sense parental attitude in respect to child training, we should sum the matter up in one word, discipline. By discipline we mean the reasonable regulation and supervision of the habits of a child throughout all stages of development and a consistent plan for having a child observe those rules that are laid down ... Consistent adherence to a few simple rules without any deviation whatever will permit the child to learn to make adequate social adjustments.[87]

Every child was to be "conditioned" to respond in the appropriate manner to parental requests. All the advisers – medical, psychological, and popular – insisted on the centrality of discipline to any modern habit training program.

The consensus was that regulation or scheduling – much the same thing – were the most efficacious methods for inculcating good behaviour in children.[88] The new discipline was to be a much broader, more encompassing, omniscient parental control. It would be imposed from the moment of birth and used to order every aspect of the child's development. It would seek to regulate the child's inner life in a manner that corresponded to the mechanical rhythms of its outer world – modern industrial society. The child would not need to be told what to do repeatedly, because it would intuitively know how to act as a result of this management.[89]

Parents were thus required to perform a considerable juggling act: they were both to retain their authority over the child as "the fountainheads of wisdom and help" and to encourage it to follow their counsel "because he knows his father and mother are his best friends and not because he is compelled by fear."[90] While parents were to be consistently firm and authoritative, they were not to expect "enforced and rigid obedience" to their commands. Such an expectation, the advisers cautioned, was "almost certain" to incite outright disobedience or deceit. Obedience "viewed merely as an abstract virtue" was not necessarily virtuous: "Some of the most obedient children have some of the least moral responsibility and are easily led into wrongdoing by others, because the habit of unquestioning and unreasoning acceptance of superior authority has been so thoroughly fixed in them in childhood."[91]

This view of the darker side of obedience was reiterated more and more as the world witnessed the suppression of individual rights and the enforcement of dictatorial rule in the fascist states of Europe.[92] European studies published in the mid-1930s suggested strong links between patriarchal authoritarianism and the development of personalities prone to totalitarianism.[93] Thus, the goal was not to exact "slavish, unintelligent obedience," but to develop self-control in the child.[94] Modern parents asked only that the child should "learn to obey his own wishes to fit into society, to consider others, to make his own way, to use his own judgment."[95]

Mothers were advised to distinguish between "deliberately bad behaviour and that which is quite innocent of such intentions, however annoying it may be in its results." If a child strayed in any way, its behaviour was to be looked upon "as a mistake and not as a crime." The whole situation was to be examined "as carefully as the State examines such cases in court," and mothers were to be as fair and just.[96] While insisting on the development of this maternal sixth sense, advisers did not provide guidelines on fostering such a discriminatory talent. The young child who could not verbalize its motives would not be much help; the child who could explain the "reasons why" would conceivably be inclined to deny any ill-intention. Since the experts generally laid the burden of guilt on maternal shoulders, mothers who failed to make the distinction correctly would have to blame themselves once again.

Punishment was a key issue in discussions on discipline and the general management of children. Corporal punishment was condemned as the least intelligent parental response to unacceptable behaviour. It was not only irrational, but gave the child a strong sense of injustice. It was the least effective means of child training, in that spanking "seldom makes a child want to be better."[97] As Dr Tisdall argued,

There is no place in the bringing up of children for corporal punishment. This statement is made only after a careful investigation of the results of such treatment ... Corporal punishment is usually administered in anger. The use of corporal punishment always means emphasizing "what not to do". The better method is to stress "what to do" so that the discipline of the child begins at birth. It can best be described as "regulation" ... In this way, the child learns what is expected of him and has a chance to fit into the family picture.[98]

Physical punishment not only failed to accomplish its only legitimate object, "namely to make the child sorry for what he has done and to give him a desire to do better," it also permanently weakened the parent/child relationship.[99] Moreover, the implementation of an internal form of discipline through regulation was thought to make old-fashioned punishment virtually obsolete.[100] Mothers who were prepared with the proper attitude and training would gently but firmly impress their expectations, and those of society, upon the child. The best approach was to "help the child to meet his obligations to society, himself and his parents. He should and can be educated to derive no satisfaction from repeated offences against the standards of the community." Parents had to trace the wrong-doing to its source and deal with the motive, not the result.[101] This enlightened method would go far towards eliminating "what we regard as the need for corporal punishment."

While corporal punishment was regarded askance, there was a subtle change in the advisers' arguments both against it and for the new system of internalized discipline. During the 1920s, they used "social benefit" arguments but promoted the new methods largely on their benefits to parents: their child would know better than to misbehave and would thrive and pose them no difficulties.[102] While this selling point was also recognized by the advisers of the 1930s, they were more inclined to emphasize the wider social implications. Bad behaviour in a child was not primarily an offence against its own parents, but against the standards of the community as they defined them. The child who repeatedly misbehaved was deviant in a larger sense. The regulation of child life was essential not only for peace and stability in the household, but because it meant that behaviour could be "adjusted to social customs and practices." Advisers argued that the child should not be trained to any "rigid code of behaviour." This might conceivably allow parents too much freedom to decide which behavioural traits the child should possess in keeping with their personal preferences. Rather, the child was to be taught to "fit in with his fellows."[103] Standards of child behaviour would be defined by society to reflect broader social concerns and aspirations rather than individual or familial goals. In reality, of course, society's goals were those of the medical experts and their supporters.

The campaigners' constant and unwavering objective was national regeneration through the training of model citizens by means of professional intervention in the process of social reproduction. Their arguments acquired a new urgency, however, during the 1930s. While the experience of the Great War profoundly influenced the child welfare campaign, its impact was primarily ideological. The war drew attention to the depletion of the population as a human resource, not only through battle casualties but through the negative health repercussions of modern industrial society. It spurred medical intervention largely on the basis of prevention of future ills. Although some 60,000 Canadians had sacrificed their lives overseas, the day-to-day devastation and deprivation were confined to Europe; the vast majority of Canadians had had no direct encounter with the social upheaval wrought by war.

The Great Depression, on the other hand, was an immediate, personal source of anxiety for all Canadians, and none more so than the dominant class. No ready network of social benefits existed to deal with the widespread hardship. Moreover, a vehement defence of capitalism when it was clearly faltering was not altogether convincing as a promotional tool. Productivity and efficiency remained important concerns because enough middle-class faith survived to make these appear not only worthy goals, but instruments of economic recovery and future prosperity. The emphasis now switched to support of social stability, which at that moment appeared to be collapsing, where previously it had only threatened to do so. From the point of view of reformers, the crisis, once impending, had now arrived.

If doctors had earlier perceived the need for their active involvement in social reproduction, the unprecedented distress of the Depression years confirmed and strengthened their views. At the level of childrearing, "arbitrary methods" employed by disheartened parents could introduce dissonant values to a new generation. More than ever before, social conformity was promoted as the ultimate end of modern childrearing. The modern, scientific, and rational training system had to do away with "arbitrary" traditional methods because the latter were "totally at variance with modern ideas of pacifism and equal rights." Corporal punishment engendered "ideas of violence that rationalize wars, strikes, riots and crime."[104] Modern ideas were those espoused by the progressive class, with which doctors associated, while arbitrary and possibly violent notions were ascribed to the benighted masses. The holders of power feared what the masses might be capable of perpetrating in a volatile environment. "Unquestioning obedience," on the other hand, was contrary to democratic ideals and liberal notions of individualism. Scientific methods of child training provided the only viable alternative, the one final hope.

Advisers reasoned that parent education would at least console economically distressed families by allowing the parents to focus on the intangible benefits that could be derived from a "good home environment" instead of their inability to supply material goods for their children.[105] It would also help parents to prevent the insecurity that might afflict their children as a result of the family's financial worries: "Let us beware that, at all costs, we protect our children from such a feeling. Young ones, like young plants, cannot flourish if they are not firmly rooted ... Let us see that they find [a sense of security] where they look for it – in their parents." The mother's "irritability and preoccupation" and the father's "loss of grip and sense of futility" would react badly on the child and "it will not be surprising if [he] grows thin and nervy."[106] Rationalizations such as these also attempted to militate against popular discontent and the threat of social conflict arising from destitution and hopelessness. Those with nothing left to lose were to be feared, particularly in the face of state unresponsiveness to their suffering. By arguing that the destitute still had their families to consider, and by urging that they place their children's immediate emotional welfare ahead of their own resentment of the system's failure, society's representatives hoped to contain festering social protest. In particular, they could make mothers responsible for keeping it all together by holding their children hostage to the future.

If their rationale changed slightly from the 1920s to the 1930s, professional and popular advisers universally supported the notion of preventing personal failure and social deviance through a "healthy programme for life." Their scheme was intended to put an early stop to those "various attention-getting devices" that were bad habits in the making. Inevitably, getting baby into good habits and used to the prescribed routine involved a great deal of crying, probably the single worst habit that an infant could acquire during the first days of its life. Any amount of effort expended in the early weeks was worthwhile if it avoided the horror of the crying baby. Advisers believed, not without cause, that "nothing breaks up the happy home" like this curse: "it robs mother of her looks and father of his temper so that he often goes cursing from the house, leaving both wife and baby crying together."[107] Familial contentment and even marital relations hinged on the mother's ability to manage her children properly.

It was the mother's duty to teach her baby that injudicious whining was to no avail. In answering the vital question as to what knowledge an "intelligent infant" was to acquire during the first year, one expert asserted "for one thing, not to cry without cause." This lesson would be learned very quickly "if all those about him see to it that, his needs attended to, he is left to amuse himself."[108] The baby who was picked up every time it cried would soon become an utter nuisance: "It takes only one or two days of this for the baby to cry *to be picked up* and for no other reason."[109] Should the baby stop crying promptly upon being held, it was considered that "he will have given his secret away and all sensible adults who actually have his interest at heart will read the warning and act accordingly." Those innately passive little beings were capable of turning into conniving creatures when the purpose suited them, but more importantly, when they were assured of their mother's foolish cooperation. In order to disabuse the baby of any such notion, mothers were to permit baby to cry "as long as he wishes." Despite the acknowledged hardship for parents and neighbours, advisers insisted that there was no alternative. Giving in was unconscionable: "it is quite plain that they are training the child to realize that the best way of getting what he wants is to be angry, and this lesson is very easily and quickly learned."[110] It was considered that "one good battle – and the earlier the better" – would teach the baby that the parent was not to be swayed without sufficient reason.[111]

The 1933 edition of the Ontario government's manual, *The Baby*, suggested that, should the baby pick up the corresponding habit of breath-holding while crying, "it would be well to speak to a physician."[112] In the 1940 edition, the situation was not permitted to deteriorate to this point and the mother was advised to consult her doctor about crying in itself.[113] The earlier advice to ignore the baby's crying gave way to yet another reason for calling the doctor. Advisers may have changed their counsel on this point because they suspected that many mothers (and fathers) did not have the requisite nerves of steel and strength of character to endure relentless crying. It was better by far to seek a professional diagnosis than to ruin the child by excessive attention. Medical intervention in this regard also strengthened the possibility of regulating mothers of weak moral character. Because the experts dismissed or disregarded the infant's emotional need for human contact and affection, "crying to be held" was not a legitimate infantile urge but a deviation from the "little machine" ideal. If not stamped out firmly, crying would become a "bad habit," reflecting negatively on the mother's abilities and earning her offspring the "spoiled" label, the worst possible indictment for the conscientious modern parent.

The training of children to manage themselves in mind and body was not only the chief duty of mothers, but a fundamental part of social reproduction. By learning "self-management," children are integrated into the wider social structure.[114] Although experts feared that infants could be spoiled within days of birth, they regarded the postinfant, preschool age as the "preventive period in mental hygiene," at the same time as the most fruitful opportunity for habit training in its myriad forms and the most perilous for "spoiling."[115] The mobile, active, articulate preschooler posed difficulties that were not amenable to simple scheduling: "They learn to demand what they want, and if indulged, become of the teasing, whining or tyranical type ... and in a little while, we have a vain, conceited or offensive small person who is a sort of smart Alec." Mothers who yielded to their child's every whim, whether out of ignorance or some deeper moral flaw, were establishing "false expectations of what life will give." Even the youngest member of the family had to "learn to pay the price in some way."[116]

The tell-tale symptoms of the spoiled child were many and varied. Aside from crying for attention, however, none perturbed the advisers as much as "food fussiness." Training a young child to eat three proper meals daily took on much more than nutritional significance.[117] Mothers were again counselled to remain detached and emotionally distant in what could prove to be a very tense situation, especially if they took to heart the innumerable medical warnings about malnutrition and failure to thrive. The management of the youngster's diet and eating habits was vital not only for its physical development but also as proof of maternal control. If followed expressly, such advice could easily transform the traditional family dinner into a battle of wills.

Advisers believed strongly in the curative strategy of withholding food. In very short time, they insisted, the child would come to a conscious, rational decision to eat what was prepared.[118] One popular adviser recounted the story of how she had overcome her three-year-old daughter's sudden unreasoning aversion to applesauce by serving her nothing but the offending portion for three days until the child, undoubtedly hungry and suitably chastened, had finally relented.[119] Although this mother-adviser understood that going without food would not harm the child as much as "forming a foolish distaste which would later be inconvenient and difficult to overcome," her personal observations about this struggle reveal the emotional conflict between strict adherence to "science" and maternal instinct: "When I tucked her in bed for the night and kissed the little face that to my over-anxious mother's eye already seemed thinner and more pale, my heart sank and I went to bed only to dream of her, lifeless and thin, floating on a raft in a sea of applesauce. I wakened prepared to give her almost anything for breakfast, but with the morning sunshine came a return of my common sense, and again Barbara faced a breakfast of but one thing – applesauce."

The tragicomic potential of this tale may appear intentional, but this adviser was earnestly applying her own advice and that of the medical masters. What mattered infinitely more than the child's momentary deprivation and the parent's inner turmoil in every facet of habit training was the ultimate victory of the "system": "Our battle was won, for never since that day has she shown any signs of refusing or objecting to any food that is placed before her."[120] Applesauce now symbolized the mother's personal competence. Giving in to the child at feeding time would establish a precedent for "giving in all along the line," and a mere child was not to be allowed "to take the reins of management into his inexperienced little fingers."[121]

None of the experts, popular or professional, went quite as far as the dean of childrearing advice, Alan Brown, in advocating a sort of psychological game-playing to "cure" poor appetite or food fussiness. He advised placing the child in bed under the care of one person "as though he were very ill," the object being "to prevent his getting food other than what is ordered." The patient/victim was then offered four ounces of plain chicken broth or mutton broth every three hours the first day, six to eight ounces at the same interval on the second day. By the third day, the child was usually ravenously hungry and could safely be provided with three or four good meals. To reinforce the point of the exercise, any food item that the child especially disliked was to be included in the first regular meal.

Brown was confident about the efficacy of this strategy, although he realized that "some mothers will not be a party to such heartless treatment, as they are inclined to call it."[122] He was probably correct in predicting the average mother's unwillingness to participate in the systematic starvation of her child. He was equally correct, however, in denying that "heartlessness" played any part in this medical ploy. The root of this advice was the same notion of universal applicability – the fallacy of "everybaby" – that inspired all the period's childrearing information. The experts did not acknowledge that children, like adults, have different food preferences, varying appetites, or diverse tastes of any kind. All properly trained children had to eat all their properly prepared meals at proper intervals. In this, they were not simply being taught to eat the right foods for nutritional benefit; they were learning "obedience and how to submit to someone who knows better," a vital lesson in power relations.[123] Through management and parental example, the child would learn to be "happy and contented, rather than discontented, energetic instead of lazy, thorough instead of careless."[124] Again, food was a moral issue.

Childrearing experts, from physicians through popular columnists, frequently addressed themselves to "parents" in the course of their educational efforts. It is evident, however, that they were speaking almost exclusively to mothers. While the mother's part in childrearing was elevated to the point of sanctification, the father was correspondingly confined to an accessory role. Advice directed specifically at fathers was rare and was generally as restricted as the part they were obviously intended to play in their children's lives. They could become involved in playful activities, in providing moral support for their wives, and as masculine role models. The Council on Child and Family Welfare's "Postnatal Letters" encouraged fathers to "Begin *now* [baby's second month] to show your little child a certain amount of attention each day ... It is true that you must be away most of Baby's waking hours, and when you come home at night you want recreation and quiet. But it is part of your responsibility as a father to have a certain amount of fellowship with your children."[125]

The father's sacrifice in playing when he preferred to relax after an arduous work day was appreciated. For the most part, it was also assumed that fathers would not be around while their children were awake, at least if the children were well-trained to sleep to schedule. Despite the predominance of men in the leadership ranks of the child welfare campaign, fathers were given far less responsibility for their children than were mothers, and fewer opportunities for companionship with them. They were not active partners with their wives in raising their own children, a role coveted by the experts. As they prescribed his modern role, the traditional patriarch was now little more than a figurehead, symbolically important, but lacking in real authority. The father's part was almost purely biological and economic, since the model the experts promoted made him the primary breadwinner and official head of the family.

Some commentators on the new childrearing trends questioned this omission of specific fathering advice in the abundant literature for parents. As early as 1919, the *Family Herald*'s resident adviser voiced such a view:

A good beginning has been made in the instruction of mothers, but what of the fathers? How many men clearly understand and recognize the responsibility of fatherhood? Their number today is certainly less than the number of women who possess a modicum of knowledge in respect to motherhood. It is clearly the duty of each man to possess sufficient information to permit of his discharging the duties of this important and sacred trust. How should this information be obtained? What is required is the specialist qualified in physiology, medicine and hygiene, who will, by tactful handling, in a practical manner, impart to the fathers and to the young men the facts they should know and the duties they must meet, and should discharge, in cooperation with the mother, in all that relates to the birth and upbringing of their offspring.[126]

She was not simply calling for greater paternal participation in childrearing, but for an expansion of the medical expert's duty to extend his knowledge to the father as well as to the mother.

Nearly a decade later, *Maclean's* advice columnist Mabel Crews Ringland posed the same question. Ringland contended that, just as advisers wanted middle-class mothers to apply their premarital business training to childrearing, so fathers should utilize business techniques in this all-important area. Because they had "more complete experience" in the working world, fathers were actually better suited than mothers to this task:

A father today is expected to bring to bear on his relations with his children a little of the same skill and efficiency and understanding that he uses in his business, the idea being that a child may perhaps be a very vital factor in society and of sufficient importance to merit some study, even by busy men. It has taken us a long time to realize that a badly reared child is of more potential danger to society than a poorly driven automobile, a badly run business or an inefficiently operated or antiquated machine. And if human nature is ever going to advance in proportion to the improvements in industry, science and business methods in general, it will be because the fathers, as well as the mothers, regard their job of parenthood as a science for which some intelligent preparation is required, just as it is for any other skilled occupation.[127]

In Ringland's view, if the vastly improved future order that the advisers envisioned were ever to be realized, fathers had to be rescued from the sidelines, trained properly, and put to effective use in the drive to turn children into efficient, modern machines. Since the thrust of her argument was exactly the same as that which advisers had presented to mothers, their exclusion of fathers is striking. "Management" was the core concept informing their prescriptions, and management in this time was an almost uniquely masculine endeavour. Due to their familiarity with managerial activities in the working world, fathers could reasonably have had the advantage over mothers in enforcing schedules, regulating their children's lives, and imposing efficient training methods.

The contemporary celebration of maternalism, fortified as it was by medical views, suggests the key to this puzzle. The enhanced social implications of childrearing as a service to the state created a veritable cult of motherhood. The child welfare campaigners were intent on modernizing parenting techniques without challenging traditional gender roles. While the techniques of mothering were deficient and needed to be improved by science, the role definition itself remained within the traditional bounds. As always, mothers were seen as the primary influence in their children's lives, while "mothering" was to be professionalized in the modern fashion. If mothers were inclined to believe that their authority and status were expanding, it was made clear to them that advancement of position was possible only through subordination to the male-dominated medical profession, and within the context of patriarchal social relations.

The council's advice package did acknowledge that "in the average home the fathers contribute too little to the family life, the mothers too much." This was not, in their view, "a healthy or desirable arrangement" for the family.[128] Fathers were encouraged to accept their "necessary contribution" to their children's emotional and physical development and to formulate "conscientious plans" to do their share. By including a few lines of advice addressed directly to fathers, the council deviated from the general pattern without suggesting any radical departure from traditional parenting roles. The prescribed solution to this problem put the onus on the already hard-pressed mother. She was to use her well-honed mothering talents to draw in the potentially reluctant father: "Try to remember to tell your husband of all the very interesting experiences you have day by day with your baby, of what a delight it is to see her grow mentally and physically ... Never dwell upon the day's vexations, worries and work. Then your husband will get the idea that this job of bringing up your baby is a mighty interesting experience and will be looking for chances of being with and doing for his child."[129] The woman's nurturing role was paramount. In order to be a well-trained modern mother and to interest her husband in parenting, she had to "mother" him as well by shielding him from the day-to-day realities of the hard work of raising baby. Her role, in the family as in society, was to serve and to smooth the way.

Men supported this socially and medically sanctioned concept of mothers as the principal influence of childhood, but some resented their newly prescribed accessory roles in their families. "It must have been worthwhile being a father in the good old days," argued one disgruntled "modern" father, "when a frown from the paternal brow plunged the entire household into abysmal gloom!" Modern childrearing methods burdened the mother with weighty responsibility, but she was at least rewarded with a correspondingly enhanced social and familial position. Father's role as "household head" seems to have simultaneously diminished to the point where he was considered little more than primary breadwinner.[130]

Some men evidently felt that modern scientific motherhood contained the seeds of decline for patriarchal authority and undermined traditional masculine gender roles and images. It cannot be denied that, for many men, adherence to the experts' prescriptions for modern childrearing must have amounted to a negation of their personal value as parents and a rejection of their best efforts for their children. As families became more "mother-centred," fathers were increasingly left out of their children's lives and hearts: "Hang it all, fathers ought to count too!"[131] If men were, by definition, little more than the source of the family's material welfare, while women were the source of all nurture, how could fathers expect affection and a strong emotional bond with their offspring? It could well be that fathers were disheartened by the new expectations of them. If they heeded the experts' advice and became thoroughly modern in accordance, they had to accept a position somewhere in the margins of their children's lives. The intervention of professionals and the state was supposed to reinforce familial patriarchy. But for individual fathers, the psychic costs may have been high.

Another surprising omission in the advice literature on early childhood is any significant attention to gender differences; Freudian theory seems to have had little effect in Canadian medical/psychological circles during the interwar years.[132] Advisers, both medical and popular, always referred in standard manner to "he" when discussing children, and rarely differentiated between the handling of boys and girls in the preschool years. For all their insistence on habit training from birth as the key to the future assumption of prescribed roles, they did not emphasize sex-role socialization. Part of the reason lies in their profound conviction about the universal applicability of their precepts. Proper childhood management could not help but result in the assumption of proper adult roles for both sexes, since deviation from the professionally constructed norm was eliminated in the process of habit training. Conceivably, their intent to regulate mothers, also with the objective of preventing deviation from the womanly ideal, was considered sufficient to ensure the development of traditional gender ascriptions in children. Since children learned proper behaviour by imitating their "perfect parents," the mere application of modern childrearing methods would successfully bequeath prescribed roles to succeeding generations.

Ultimately, such childrearing information reveals far more about its authors than it does about their audience. The period's child care advisers, whether medical professionals or popular writers inspired by trends in medicine and psychology, were disheartened by the social order they inhabited. The modern Canada whose emergence they were witnessing was remote from the modern Canada they envisioned. Yet this was a nation with an abundance of resources and territory, a nation that had survived the cataclysm of global war, had matured politically, and had made great strides in its socio-economic organization despite the problems that modernization posed. The nation held promise, a promise embodied in its children. By insisting on and creating a new role for themselves in the care and upbringing of Canadian children, doctors would not only reach their professional goals but would also help to attain that national promise.

The advisers of the interwar period refused to depict children in the outmoded manner as "little adults" but constantly and relentlessly discussed their upbringing in terms of character building or personality development. Children, as the doctors and psychologists regarded them, were not only "adults in the making" on an obvious level, but also in the sense that they were the inheritors of modern Canada. To unite the promise of childhood with that of science was the unique vision of the childrearing experts. They believed fervently that they could effect their aim by using the best that modern medical science could offer. And they were determined to use every means in their power to do so.

CHAPTER SEVEN

"By Every Means In Our Power": Child and Maternal Welfare Services

As in other Western nations, the child welfare campaign in Canada depended on three types of service to further its goal of maternal education: advice literature, diagnostic clinics, and domiciliary nurse visits. All three drew on the participation of official public health agencies as well as private practitioners and voluntary organizations. Attempts were made by state agencies to answer the medical profession's call for the establishment of clinical and visiting services without overstepping the boundaries that doctors held sacrosanct. Nevertheless, clashes did arise between public and private health care, doctors and nurses, competing child welfare groups, and provincial and municipal governments that had important repercussions for the campaign's practical measures.

As evident in the previous discussion of federal/provincial production of advice literature, the medical profession was uncertain about the extent and nature of state involvement. In turn, economic, ideological, political, and even geographic constraints caused trepidation on the part of the various levels of government. The historical bugbear of jurisdiction meant that the federal government, all rhetoric to the contrary, consistently failed to provide the leadership that would allow for a coherent and well-organized national network of child and maternal welfare services. It was left entirely to provincial governments to establish and coordinate these services. The Ontario government, for its part, concentrated on demonstration work to promote public awareness and the hiring of municipal public health nurses.

An examination of some of the child and maternal welfare efforts of the provincial and local boards suggests the degree to which the child welfare campaign's ideals were transformed into practice. No matter how fervently these ideals were shared within and across government levels, their attempted realization by means of practical programs frequently fell short of the mark. Professional rivalries, ideological limitations, economic restraints, and geographic realities prevented the campaigners from achieving their own goals.

In particular, professional concerns often impeded progress. The major share of the task of disseminating information and providing the necessary, and many times the only, medical supervision for mothers and infants belonged to provincial and municipal nurses. The nurses were the essential foot-soldiers of the crusade, a fact that physicians recognized and commended. However, the doctors' determination to keep control of the nurses, who were to operate within the limits doctors set, frequently obscured the broader aim of promoting child and maternal health. The doctor/nurse relationship, with its inherent potential for conflict, was prevented from becoming dysfunctional by the nurses' traditional deference and by shared ideals.[1] For the nurses, this relationship entailed the acceptance of their subordinate position, as well as the realization that they were not doing all they could for their clients. The vital role of the nurses and its circumscription by doctors is a recurrent theme in the history of the child welfare campaign, and one that effectively demonstrates the disparity between rhetoric and actual practice.

Analysis of the campaign's services also reveals that, in practice as in theory, health officials at every level avoided treating poverty directly. Even in the depths of the Great Depression, when a few timid voices expressed fear of the long-term effects of widespread hardship, the health services devised were largely of a short-term, stopgap nature. Education, self-help, and moral responsibility were supposed to solve the problem. The century's greatest crisis of capitalism confirmed their views about the family besieged, but destitution in itself did not spark immediate legislative response.[2] Individualist ideas and strained budgets upheld the campaign's educational focus, even when it became evident that, however helpful, education alone was not the answer.

During this period, resolutions by organized medicine, voluntarist groups, and individual politicians urging greater dominion leadership and financial support were consistently turned aside. Most critics charged that federal health department expenditures were wasteful and inefficient, with money going largely to departmental salaries while "absolutely nothing" was being done for the public health.[3] It was argued that the federal government should "lessen the cost of the machine here and increase the efficiency of the work done" by granting more money to the provinces.[4]

Inefficiency of administration, lack of initiative, and an unfair burden placed on the lower levels of government were charges repeated with force throughout the period. In 1929, one parliamentary critic wondered "what might be accomplished if we had a real, live Department of Health" that would confront the "terrible wastage" due to preventable illness and death by a "properly organized effort."[5] The federal government was spending 7.5 cents per capita when an appropriate standard of public health required an expenditure of $2.50 per capita. The total expenditure of all three levels of government came to the "magnificent sum" of 37.5 cents. The critic recommended that the country be divided into health sections directed by full-time health officers paid equally by federal, provincial, and municipal governments.[6] In response, Liberal minister of pensions and national health J.H. King pointed to section 7, the "escape clause" in the 1919 Department of Health Act, which prohibited any federal jurisdiction or control over provincial or municipal health boards. King asserted his confidence in the Dominion Council of Health and its ability to bring about cooperation with the provinces.[7]

Disavowal of federal responsibility was also the answer to a similar resolution presented in 1930.[8] The minister admitted to receiving petitions requesting that the dominion contribute one-third of the amount required to fund full-time health units; these came from various organizations, including the Canadian Nurses' Association, the Women's Institutes, and several provincial governments. Stressing the importance of local control, he quoted Prime Minister Mackenzie King's statement that the principle was "vicious" because it amounted to "interference with provincial health matters."[9] Opposition leader R.B. Bennett countered that Parliament could appropriate money for any purpose: "it is no more a vicious principle to grant money to a province in order to ensure the health of the Canadian people, surely, than to grant money to a federal commission for the beautification of this city of Ottawa."[10]

Bennett was making political hay out of this subject of inappropriate Liberal spending; his own government's later responses to health and welfare questions also hinged on the crucial matters of jurisdiction and funding. Resolutions in 1934 and 1935 that the federal government adopt "a definite health policy which could be carried on in cooperation with the provincial governments" were preempted subject to "investigations being proceeded with."[11] Bennett's "deathbed conversion," represented by his 1935 "New Deal" package promising comprehensive health and welfare measures, was jettisoned on jurisdictional grounds. For his part, Mackenzie King appointed the Royal Commission on Dominion-Provincial Relations in 1937, thereby postponing until the 1940s any further federal consideration of the matter. For the entire period, public health, and child welfare specifically, were problems for the province and its municipalities.

The Ontario government's establishment of a Bureau of Child Welfare in 1916 was hailed as an inaugural attempt to demonstrate state responsibility in this vital area of public health. Forced to operate within wartime budgetary restraints, the bureau limited its work entirely to sending one nurse across the province on its "Child Welfare Special," an exhibit clinic on wheels.[12] In these early years, demonstration work was performed largely in the hope of impressing upon resident medical practitioners the value of their own involvement in establishing local clinics.

As part of the government's postwar reconstruction plans, the Ontario Board of Health was restructured in 1920.[13] Public health nurses specially trained in maternal and child welfare were sent in pairs to carry the campaign to the furthest reaches of the province. While "no hard and fast plan" was decided on, the goal was to have the nurses provide three months' demonstration in each locality. These temporary excursions into the smaller communities and more isolated areas were intended to awaken a sense of need that could then be addressed by the hiring of a municipal public health nurse.[14] The Division of Public Health Nursing was incorporated with that of Maternal and Child Hygiene in 1921, in the belief that the campaign's goals could best be attained through an intensive and coordinated system of public health nursing that would focus on "teaching health in homes, clinics and schools."[15] If beneficial within these confines, Ontario's child and maternal welfare services ultimately excluded a significant number of the families that needed them most.

By the end of the interwar period, the publicity campaign waged by succeeding Ontario governments had persuaded a number of municipalities to take up this work on a permanent basis, but its effects were generally disappointing. In 1921, the first year of organized provincial demonstration work, 24 municipalities had public health nurses and child welfare clinics; by 1938, the number had increased only to 36. Not included in the latter figure were the 28 clinics boasted by the city of Toronto alone.[16] Many more municipalities than not declared their approval of child welfare projects but declined participation because of budgetary considerations.[17]

The diagnostic services offered by province and municipality consisted of well baby clinics, occasional preschool clinics, a few prenatal clinics in larger centres, and home visits by nurses. Both clinics and home visits were, by strict definition, instructional and supervisory. The Ontario health department defined child welfare as "an essentially public health activity" and endeavoured to disassociate this work from the treatment of sick or "potentially sick" infants. This stress on prevention and education necessitated precise guidelines for clinics and nurse visits, in order to avoid any conflict of interest with private practitioners. Only well babies were allowed to attend clinics, so that their mothers could benefit from such health instruction as the public health nurse "may properly give." Well babies were those gaining steadily and not exhibiting fever or "any gross sign of illness."[18] The clinic physician, usually a local volunteer, conducted a complete physical examination on the first visit. Any child who showed evidence of a physical defect was referred to its own family physician. Due to the critical importance ascribed to the preschool years "upon which hang the future health and the physical and mental standard of the school child and the adult," these clinics were viewed as the campaign's key component.[19]

On the municipal level, no city in the province or the nation could match Toronto's efforts to promote child and maternal welfare.[20] The city's Hospital for Sick Children played a far-reaching role in the provincial campaign, thanks largely to its physician-in-chief, the indomitable Alan Brown.[21] Brown was appointed director of Toronto's Department of Child Hygiene in 1914. When he became chief of the hospital in 1919, it was a simple matter to link clinic work throughout the city with the Hospital for Sick Children. All doctors and nurses staffing the 28 clinics established by the period's end were trained and directed from the children's hospital, "so that the instruction and the work in these clinics is uniform and kept constantly up-to-date."[22] Beginning in 1919, the nurseries of every hospital maternity ward in the city were also directed from the Hospital for Sick Children. The local Children's Aid Society and the various children's homes were staffed by hospital-trained personnel. By the early 1920s, Brown was child health consultant to the School of Hygiene at the University of Toronto and to the dominion and provincial health departments, "thus enabling practically all phases of children's work and problems to be guided from the children's hospital."

The Hospital for Sick Children served an essential function for the campaign in its administrative, research and service capacities. In addition to his renowned administrative skill, Brown's professional reputation made the hospital a vital therapeutic and research centre for paediatrics internationally. Through the hospital laboratories and the university's medical school, much of the important Canadian research on infant mortality and child health was conducted under Brown's direction and frequently with his participation. The hospital also set an important example by incorporating the campaign creed into its everyday functioning and trumpeting its message to the community. Brown believed wholeheartedly that a children's hospital should not be "just an institution for treating sick children." It should be above all an educational institution established for the benefit of all the community's children.[23]

The hospital's postwar commitment to community service and preventive child welfare work was reflected in the rapid expansion of its own educational services: "[The hospital's] method for the prevention of serious illness among Ontario children is to convince the mothers and fathers of the wisdom of early diagnosis and to offer them counsel from experts." In 1921, the hospital's outpatient department saw 57,574 children, more than twice the number of the previous year. Since the department's purpose was to treat minor ailments and injuries, its expansion suggests that it filled a definite need in many families lacking the requisite "family physician." But the hospital's directors insisted that its efforts concentrate "more particularly" on the education of parents "in order to minimize sickness and otherwise to help in raising healthy families."[24]

Toronto undoubtedly provided the best prenatal supervision in the province as well. The city's general hospitals were operating prenatal clinics in the early 1920s, in advance of the MacMurchy report on maternal mortality. In 1922, four neighbourhood clinics were established by the city, "to meet the need created by distances, and the fact that some women do not like a hospital."[25] In the first year of their operation, 170 women attended. It was hoped that these neighbourhood clinics would be centres for maternal education and would spread to the women "the truth of the necessity of proper prenatal care." The municipal Board of Health also sent its nurses on home visits to expectant mothers, a service assisted by the Victorian Order of Nurses and St Elizabeth nurses. Widely considered the prototype for modern child welfare work in the country, Toronto's efforts were unrivalled. Where prenatal medical supervision was concerned, in spite of intense moral support by organized medicine and interested women's groups, little was accomplished in Ontario outside of its capital city.[26] In this more than any other, the campaign's vision was destined to remain unrealized.

The nurses were the medium through which the medical gospel of maternal and child welfare was conveyed. While doctors insisted that mothers consult regularly with private practitioners, mothers were reached through nurses in clinics and in their own homes. In 1918, Toronto's Division of Child Hygiene trained 20 public health nurses for the specific purpose of disseminating advice and information to expectant and new mothers.[27] By the end of the period, the Toronto Board of Health employed 96 nurses.[28] The city nurses believed that the ideal approach to motherhood education was a personal one that allowed them access to the homes of their patients while permitting them to develop an understanding of individual childrearing problems: "the nurse's duty has come to mean she must find a way of presenting her teaching which will make the mother realize this teaching applies to her and to her baby."[29]

It was standard practice for visiting nurses in Toronto to have mothers record their problems as they occurred and to note their procedures for dealing with them. The use of a "recognized baby book" was considered essential to effective teaching in the general care of the baby and "for definite instruction in habit training."[30] The nurses were also careful to note home conditions "found in relation to the objective planned with the family and the action taken to correct what seems unsatisfactory." Their approach was very much the one idealized by the medical leadership: strictly ordered, scientific, and based on the use of charts, notes, manuals, and planned routines. As they were trained to do, the nurses were teaching mothers how to impose order and efficiency in the home. Even the profusion of advice literature that penetrated Ontario homes could not surpass the didactic benefits of these visits, where the nurses actively demonstrated feeding and handling routines and repeated the lessons until they were convinced that mothers had grasped them.[31]

From the point of view of the campaign's medical leaders, the nurse was the essential liaison between mother and profession.[32] Most of all, however, nurses were expected to carry out doctors' orders and see that these orders were obeyed by mothers.[33] The "Mothercraft controversy" that erupted in Toronto during the early 1930s and continued unabated through the Second World War illustrates the nature of this relationship. Founded in Toronto by businessman-philanthropist I.E. Robinson in 1931, the Mothercraft Society was directed by his wife, Barbara. Barbara Robinson had practised nursing in New Zealand and was trained in the Mothercraft methods originated by Dr Frederick Truby King, an international leader in child and maternal welfare.[34] The Toronto Mothercraft Centre was staffed entirely by Truby King nurses who counselled interested mothers in strict adherence to his methods. The centre operated six child welfare clinics, called "Advice Rooms"; mothers attended by appointment and paid a fee commensurate with family income. Mothercraft nurses also visited homes upon request.

The controversy that arose in connection with the Mothercraft Centre was essentially one of control. Mothercraft nurses followed the Truby King regimen exclusively, prescribing infant feedings for individual cases when all attempts at breastfeeding had failed. While this was accepted practice in the Truby King strongholds of New Zealand and England, North American physicians held steadfastly to their professional right to prescribe infant formula and to their authority to dictate to nurses the information they wanted conveyed to mothers.[35] Most adamantly opposed to the Mothercraft nurses was Alan Brown. As foremost paediatric expert in Canada, Brown was not inclined to allow nurses trained in "foreign methods" to undermine his position of supreme authority. Moreover, his personal conviction that his own system was the most effective did not permit him to consider the possible benefits of Truby King methods, for all that the two were similar in many respects.[36] Robinson also defined "cooperation" as the department's adoption of "every smallest item" of Mothercraft teaching. The division could not sanction any form of cooperation for two "official" reasons: Dr Brown was "very definite in his disapproval of them" and "Mothercraft nurses prescribe[d] feedings."[37] These two reasons were, in effect, a single one. Brown's disapproval was inspired by the Mothercraft nurses' role in prescribing for their infant patients, a role that held serious portents for physicians involved in child welfare. As chief adviser of Toronto's Division of Maternal and Child Hygiene, his ruling on the matter held the force of law.

There was also the potential for conflict inherent in competition between two agencies attempting to further the interests of the city's mothers and children. From the perspective of the "established" side, the aim of providing a rationalized, centralized, well-ordered, and physician-directed system of medical supervision was in jeopardy. As director of Toronto's public health nurses, Eunice Dyke's response to the Mothercraft controversy revealed the official stance: "I would say that Canadian nurses must resent the substitution of long-distance medical research and direction of Canadian baby feedings or the nominal responsibility of Canadian physicians who are introduced to New Zealand medical research by nurses. We must distrust, also, any health insight, no matter how valuable, which refuses to strengthen existing organizations where they are weak, and insists upon setting up parallel organizations."[38] Dyke expressed her "individual" opinion that public health departments, private practitioners and hospitals would provide "all Canada needs in the way of health organizations." She was confident that Canadian physicians would delegate as much responsibility to nurses "as it is wise for us to accept." But she asserted, tellingly, "of course, I think we can do more for healthy babies even now than you expect of us."[39] The nurses' duties were restricted more because doctors wanted it that way than because of their inability to perform certain functions.

Because of Brown's hearty disapproval of the Mothercraft Society and of the impossibility of compromise, the Toronto Division of Maternal and Child Hygiene maintained a straightforward policy of refuting its rival. The University of Toronto's Department of Paediatrics, the Academy of Medicine, and the Hospital for Sick Children also denounced the organization and refused any cooperation with it. The view of the established order was that there were "very few, if any" problems in the area of maternal and infant care that it could not handle on its own.[40] The opposing sides were united in their goal of transforming "the art of motherhood" into "the science of mothercraft." But this was to be a mothercraft devised by the legitimate, recognized authorities in the field and not by an upstart nursing society with "foreign" roots, no matter what its name implied or how similar its methods.

Nor was the "Mothercraft controversy" an isolated example of this attitude. From the campaign's beginnings, the nurses involved in maternal and child welfare confronted this issue of role definition repeatedly. And, as was the case in Toronto, the feeding question was the source of the problem. Although they believed fervently in the value of clinics, so fearful were campaign supporters of any possible infringement on the practising rights of physicians that the provincial health department restricted even feeding instruction to mothers of infants who were entirely breastfed. Artificial feeding belonged to the realm of specialized knowledge, which only properly trained doctors possessed: "artificial feeding in the first year of life must be accepted as medical treatment. Infants wholly or partly artificially fed should in every instance be referred to the family physician for the formula and directions."[41]

Given that mothers were increasingly taking up bottle-feeding, and that many of them received no regular medical supervision beyond clinics and nurse visits, doctors feared that nurses would overstep their bounds in this area. As a result of this professional anxiety, many Ontario doctors turned against them. The Division of Maternal and Child Hygiene grasped every opportunity to reassure the medical profession that the scope and function of the public health nurse was carefully defined and supervised by the department itself. Nursing director Mary Power realized nonetheless that, "In spite of the fact that both workers, public health nurses and practising physicians, are seeking the same goal by parallel roads, there exists in some places a lack of sympathy between the two groups which I am convinced is based on misunderstanding. Doctors who are not thoroughly familiar with the ways of public health nurses may fear that these nurses are in the habit of diagnosing, prescribing drugs, giving treatments and of committing various other ethical transgressions."[42] Power admitted that some nurses were occasionally guilty as charged, and warned that the nurses themselves had to understand the dangers inherent in any takeover of the doctor's legitimate role: "Surely [the nurse] cannot attempt to do these things without the certainty that sooner or later she will blunder and cause harm."

If Alan Brown felt threatened by the incursion of a child welfare agency outside his sphere of authority, the average small-town general practitioner reacted just as negatively to any suggestion that these "modern" child welfare nurses with their "modern" teachings and clinics might interfere with his livelihood and community status. The fact that the provincial health department was sponsoring the touring nurses may have persuaded some physicians to participate in clinic demonstrations as requested, if only to avoid unfavourable publicity. On the whole, the responses of these doctors ranged from a polite interest, through indifference, to outright hostility.

The demonstration clinics held in Galt in 1920 were judged successful because of the enthusiasm of the townspeople. The participation of local doctors was lukewarm at best. As the visiting nurse observed, they all performed only the most superficial examination of the babies. After one session, the nurse brought in a basin of water for the attending doctor to wash his hands. His response was, "Oh, I need not wash my hands, I didn't touch any of them"; he had examined 13 infants "by the touchless method."[43] In Hawkesbury in 1921, the visiting nurse reported that "the people have taken very kindly to the work" but the doctors "as usual" knew nothing about the department's work. More surprisingly, the medical officer of health claimed that "he had never even heard of [child welfare demonstrations]."[44] When the visiting nurse in Little Current complained about local medical indifference, her supervisor replied, with a mixture of stoicism and resignation, "I believe from your account and my knowledge of the situation in Little Current that any results we may obtain will be due to our own efforts and lack of antagonism of the physicians, rather than from any active cooperation on their part. However, as this seems to be the prevailing condition throughout the province, we cannot hope for more at present. I do feel, however, that we are receiving much more cooperation and consideration now [in 1926] than when the work began, so we cannot feel exactly discouraged."[45]

As the stalwart foot-soldiers of the crusade, it seemed to the nurses that many of their victories would be won in spite of the physicians, not with their assistance. Nurses felt themselves to be "angels without wings" who were subjected to undue criticism, "often captious," for all their efforts.[46]

Although the campaign's official agencies at the provincial and federal levels waged an intensive publicity campaign, this kind of medical apathy seems to have been common within the rank and file. At times indifference turned to outright opposition. In Bowmanville, the visiting nurse discovered that "the doctor with the longest and largest practice is the biggest knocker." She believed that he was doing the cause considerable damage, and lamented that his wife was also the president of the local Canadian Club: "their influence goes a long way."[47] Similarly, the situation in Bracebridge was declared "very peculiar." The medical officer of health was "absolutely dead set against public health work of any kind" and his colleagues were "quite as determined" in their opposition. The nurse was obliged to conclude "I do not think a clinic would ever be a success here with the attitude of the medical men such as it is at present."[48]

These professional suspicions proved enduring. A 1938 visit to St Thomas found the chairman of the local board of health, a doctor, agreeing that there was plenty of work available for a full-time public health nurse in the town. Yet he did not approve of free immunization nor of clinics of any kind. A clinic had been held there fifteen years previously and the nurse had apparently changed feedings that had been ordered by family physicians, "although he admits he did not come to St Thomas until after this was reported to have occurred." Because of these prejudices on the part of highly placed doctors, "the program has been at a standstill for many years and is likely to be for many more."[49] Just as in Toronto, the physicians who felt most threatened were frequently those who held the most power in their communities. If their worst fears about the deterioration of their authority were ever realized, such doctors had the most to lose.

The foremost question for avid child welfare supporters and the "uncovered" alike was how much could be done in clinics without hurting the family physician. Doctors were generally more favourable to the hiring of municipal nurses than to the establishment of public clinics. As a nurse visiting Barrie observed, "the kind of thing that happens at a clinic is this – a mother who is interested and has perhaps come a long way at much inconvenience is asked by the doctor, 'Why don't you go to your own doctor?' ... The doctors think that the clinic, because of the feeling that is sure to arise among the medical men if their patients are interfered with, is going to spoil the chances of the nurse being a success."[50] Similar medical responses met the demonstration clinics in other Ontario towns, to the point where one small-town medical officer openly admitted that "he would prefer to have this phase of the programme neglected" rather than worry local practitioners.[51]

Attitudes such as these on the part of local doctors obliged many municipalities with clinic and nursing programs to request physician permission before allowing mothers to participate. For example, Chatham physicians were so critical of the clinic that all mothers attending were asked to bring a note of permission from their family physician.[52] When contacted by prospective prenatal patients, the municipal nurse in St Mary's requested that they call their doctor first "and ask him to give her the necessary orders." Much to her dismay, in many instances she "heard no more about it."[53] Because of the "considerable objection" voiced by Hamilton physicians to the proposal that all registered babies receive a nurse visit, a compromise was reached permitting a call to every home "when medical supervision by the family physician would be urged and a baby book left." Cases attending clinics had to be referred by family physicians.[54]

This fear of both state and nurse "interference" in the realm of private practice invoked "considerable discussion" across the province from the campaign's beginning. In 1921, Beryl Knox, associate director of the province's public health nurses, cited what she believed were the strongest arguments against this negative view: "that since the clinics are for well children only, the family physician would never be called upon to attend [these children]. That no treatment is given in the clinic but only advice. All cases needing remedial work are referred to the family physician. Therefore instead of interfering with him or his practice we are increasing his work ... We are primarily preventing disease and not curing it."[55] The problem was larger than that of appropriate doctor/nurse relationships. It was rooted as much in a clash between private practice and public health services, and between medical autonomy and state encroachment. Dr Grant Fleming, in a 1934 address to the Canadian Medical Association, remarked upon the increasing medical opposition to clinical services that were interpreted as a public invasion of private practice. Fleming argued that it was the disinterest and inaccessibility of private practitioners that necessitated state efforts in child welfare in the first place. Prior to the establishment of well baby clinics, the number of babies under regular physician supervision was negligible. Prenatal care remained "practically untouched" by public health services but the number of expectant mothers receiving regular physician supervision was "comparatively small."[56]

The best solution was not to "weaken the standing of the family physician" but to integrate the medical profession more closely within public health organization so that private practitioners would have "a definite place in organized community work." Those who could afford private physicians should be encouraged to continue to use them.[57] As long as doctors held a ruling position within the health care sector, they supported state health care activities. Whenever they felt that their rigidly defined boundaries were threatened, they were quick to voice opposition, resist encroachment, and pressure the state to uphold their professional monopoly, despite their humanitarian rhetoric.

In the end, physicians at all levels opposed prescription and treatment by nurses. The child welfare campaign's official agencies also opposed them, not only in policy but by keeping a close watch over any such indiscretion.[58] While the provincial nurses seem to have shied away from prescribing formula, local nurses were not as timorous. In many instances, this practice was necessitated by the parents' economic need or the local practitioners' indifference. During the Depression, when a Cochrane nurse advised a mother whose baby was doing poorly that she should see her family physician, the mother replied that she knew the doctor would put the baby on a special formula that she could not afford. The nurse gave her a simple-to-prepare prescription for an improved cow's milk formula.[59] The East York nurse also prescribed formula and changed feedings, using Alan Brown's instructions. Very few of the infants attending her clinic were under a physician's supervision. Because 60 per cent of these families were on relief, the nurse did not think well babies should have to see a doctor just to have a normal formula made out. The Strathroy nurse did the same for her poor clients.[60]

Even though provincial policy expressly forbade nurses to do more than advise, doctors felt that there was a very fine distinction between advice and the kind of service that only they were entitled to give. The maintenance of professional privilege required continued domination over allied and competing occupations. Since subordinate positions such as nursing and midwifery were also feminine by definition, the power relationships involved were all the more forceful because they derived from both professional and gender inequality.

Medical authority necessitated inequality between expert and client – knowledgeable doctor and ignorant mother – but also between doctor and nurse.[61] The parallels between mothering and nursing have often been noted, as has the patriarchal structure of nursing. Feminist theorists contend that nursing exemplifies the subordination of female labour and the exploitation of women because of ideas that assert their innate biological aptitude for certain jobs.[62] The predominance of women in nursing also illustrates the persistent use of female labour to cheapen costs. Women as mothers and nurses have historically contributed to the production and reproduction of human labour at the lowest possible market price.

The campaign's medical leadership needed nurses to perform the decidedly unglamorous field work, but just as doctors stressed their superiority to mothers, they also constantly asserted their superiority to nurses. Nurses were "valuable aids" in the campaign; their role was "not only great and important but indispensable." The physicians-in-command, however, were adamant that nurses' value depended on their ability to work under close supervision with "their activities and limitations clearly defined."[63] It was never to be forgotten that "the most potent force in reducing morbidity and mortality in newly born infants and mothers is the physician well-trained in obstetrics and paediatrics."[64] By definition, the nurses' position would always be subordinate to the doctors, whose role was to provide the "wisdom and leadership" for the campaign.[65]

The provincial and municipal nurses understood physicians' fears and generally trod very carefully in order to avoid antagonizing them. At the same time, they often resented this enforced submissiveness because they believed that they were offering parents a service of value. "The amount of good done by the doctor at the clinic can be done by the nurse in her visit to the home," argued one nurse; typically, she felt compelled to add that, "where needed the nurse can advise seeing the family physician."[66] The tragic irony of this situation is inescapable: the campaign's noble objectives were hindered more by the doctors' professional insecurities than by the alleged errors of nurses who overstepped their prerogatives.

In addition to professional politics, the all-important cost factor limited the number of mothers and children who could be assisted. Despite the pleas of public health activists that "to spend money on public health is true economy," the Depression witnessed a curtailment of essential funds for many health programs.[67] In 1932, greater use of Toronto clinics by families who were increasingly unable to afford private medical attention caused an appointment system to be introduced. The result was a noticeably decreased attendance.[68] By the mid-1930s, although the policy of notifying the public health nurses of all registered births in the city continued, it became necessary to establish guidelines for rationalizing this service. Only first-time mothers were visited routinely. Also removed from the rolls were those whose circumstances "as shown by the birth registration slips or by other sources of information" suggested that "it is likely that a paediatrician will be in charge of the baby."[69] Finances obliged the Board of Health to narrow its goal of educating all mothers in favour of providing basic instruction to those believed most in need, although even its selection criteria were questionable.

Just as hard times were making these services important to a much larger number of mothers across a broader social spectrum, governments were forced to cut them back. Visiting nurses were acutely aware of the physical deprivation and emotional stress that the Depression had brought in its wake. The deteriorating conditions of life were undermining maternal and child health: "We have found in the past few years situations of poverty and of mental distress caused by unemployment, worry and discouragement. This all reacts on the mother's attitude and on her ability to care for her baby."[70] Economic difficulties also prevented parents from obtaining the necessary "corrections" for health defects detected in their children. A survey of 12 Ontario cities by the provincial Department of Health in 1930 revealed that there was a delay of a year or more in securing the necessary medical attention in 45.5 per cent of cases. The reason cited for delay in more than half these cases was inability to pay for treatment.[71]

The length and severity of the Great Depression provided irrefutable evidence of the relationship between poverty and health. As early as 1931, it was estimated that one-half million families were forced to live on an income lower than the $950 considered the subsistence level.[72] By 1934, there was evidence that the rate of illness had increased among the unemployed, "especially where social relief has been unequal to the situation," as it was in most cases.[73] The infant and maternal mortality figures for 1933 also proved discouraging to the nation's child welfare advocates. There was an increase of 421 infant deaths under the age of one year, representing a rise from 70.8 to 73.6 deaths per 1,000 live births. It was feared that this increase was "an indication of the results for which we have been watching with some anxiety, of changed standards of living."[74] The Council on Child and Family Welfare drew attention to the long-term health and economic repercussions of mass deprivation, but argued at the same time that previous educational efforts and general prosperity had placed the population in "a fair condition in which to stand a siege." The council cautioned that, despite its optimism, "the effects of need, uncertainty and strain within a home are essentially cumulative and it is probable that Canada will begin to pay these costs of economic pressure in the years immediately before us and may continue to pay them for many years to come."[75]

These fears were borne out by the vital statistics for 1937. The general mortality rate, which averaged 9.7 (per 100,000) from 1931 to 1935, rose to 10.2 in 1937. The heavy increase in the infant mortality rate was partially responsible for this upward movement.[76] From an all-time low of 66 per 1,000 live births in 1936, that rate moved up to 76 per 1,000 due to a sharp increase in three diseases – pneumonia, enteritis, and influenza – all aggravated by poor nutrition and inadequate living conditions. Although maternal mortality

edged downward from 5.1 to 4.9 in 1937, the rate remained one of
the highest in the world. Childbirth was still responsible for the death
of more Canadian women between the ages of fifteen and forty-nine
than any other cause except cancer and tuberculosis. The Depression
underscored the binding ties between maternal and child welfare:
neglect of the mother resulted in adverse effects for the health of
children.

As was true of state efforts to deal with mass unemployment,
attempts to provide adequate maternal and child welfare services
under such conditions were piecemeal and temporary. Because the
problem of the "medically indigent" was of particular concern during
the Depression years, "state medicine" became more relevant than
ever before from the viewpoint of profession and public alike. It was
estimated that nearly 3 million Canadians were medically indigent
by 1935.[77] Resolutions placed before the federal government in 1931
and 1932 to provide a measure of federal support for medical relief
met with "sympathetic consideration" by the 19 speakers in the
debate, with the notable exception of Prime Minister Bennett and
his minister of health.[78] Debates over "state medicine" in 1935, just
before Bennett's electoral downfall, were also inconclusive. Several
speakers argued that doctors had to be given first consideration in
any such system of health care provision: "any nation-wide health
policy which would not recognize the medical man in his relation to
the home as the key of the whole situation would be a failure before
it was well started."[79] The minister of health believed that the matter
had to be approached very gradually "because the medical profession
have to go along with it," and advised waiting for the Canadian
Medical Association's proposal on the subject.[80] The only speaker in
this debate who objected strongly to medical dominance of any such
project was Agnes Macphail, who believed that it was the government's responsibility to develop health policy and that this initiative
should not be left to the medical profession. In the end, the medical
relief plan adopted by the Ontario government was both designed
and administered by organized medicine.[81]

One of the earliest medical relief programs under municipal auspices was Toronto's Maternal Welfare Service for indigent mothers,
instigated in September 1933.[82] Conceding that the maternal welfare
problem was "partly economic," the city took on financial responsibility for the home confinement of indigent patients as it had for
their hospitalization. Women wishing assistance had to register and
be examined at a prenatal clinic. Investigations of the home's suit-
ability and the patient's financial eligibility were directed by the
Department of Public Welfare. The decision was then made by

committee.[83] Once the lengthy and complicated investigative process was completed and the patient was accepted into the program, the physician of her choice was notified. He could then elect to provide personal care or to have the patient attend a clinic, an option available without application to the program. At a time when home confinements were the norm, it is to be expected that the "indigent" patients preferred to deliver their children at home. While the plan provided a desired and much-needed service, the extent of bureaucratic scrutiny involved, at a time when "relief" carried a definite social stigma, probably had a deterrent effect. But the choices that remained to poor women were themselves largely unappealing: an unsupervised home confinement; payment for a physician's attendance despite the hardship; reliance on outright charity; or perhaps, as the least of these evils, hospital confinement on city orders. The service was itself threatened periodically by budget cut-backs: local women's groups had to exert pressure on the municipal government to secure continued annual appropriations.[84]

According to the campaigners, mothers were performing a duty of national importance by giving birth to healthy children and raising them in the medically prescribed manner. However, access to services such as the one implemented in Toronto were based not on their right as valued members of the community, but on financial need. It was the client's responsibility to declare herself needy, and that of the various municipal departments to judge whether her need was sufficient. Obviously the economic exigencies of the time necessitated a careful administration of sorely stretched municipal finances. But while the medical profession and health officials publicized the mother's duty to the state to produce a healthy child that would be a "national asset," their duty to the mother was not as readily converted from the ideal to the practical. The plan's seemingly half-hearted measures and wholehearted regulations may have eliminated, either through personal decision or "ineligibility," a good proportion of the women designated as its prime beneficiaries.[85]

The investigative committee had acknowledged that the basis for this service was at least "partly economic." Given that the number of applicants diminished considerably as better economic times returned, and given the stringent requirements, it is apparent that the need was entirely economic (see Table 1). By the decade's end, of 4,500 patients treated under this program since its inception, only seven deaths had occurred. The maternal mortality rate was 1.6 in comparison to the national average of 5.4 per 1,000 live births for the same period. Alice Thomson, the city's director of public health nursing, judged that the plan had not only prevented unnecessary

Table 1
Toronto Maternal Welfare Service

	Total cases accepted	Number of applications for care	Percentage rejected
1941	301	432	30.3
1940	396	501	21.0
1939	419	527	20.5
1938	637	770	17.3
1937	624	775	19.5
1936	772	899	14.3
1935	972	1,152	15.6
1934	957	1,222	22.0

Source: City of Toronto Archives, RG 11, Box 4, File 1, A. Thomson, "City of Toronto Maternal Welfare Service," October 1940.

deaths, but had ensured "a certain mental peace" for women faced with the prospect of asking for charity or delivering their child without trained assistants.[86] Yet this was a benefit attained by a comparatively small number of needy women at the relatively large cost of personal privacy and dignity.

The practical efforts inspired by the child welfare ideal were strongly weighted on the side of making the mother accept her personal responsibility, while downplaying the state's reciprocal obligation. During this period, therefore, the struggle usually veered to the side of limited state intervention. The benefits for Ontario residents were correspondingly restricted. Nowhere was this more apparent than in the province's rural and outpost districts. The problems of transportation and communication in a difficult climate were aggravated by the primitive outpost conditions in northern frontier communities, the "New Ontario." Even the rural areas of the industrialized south only benefited from medical programs to the degree of their proximity to an urban centre. The province established a skeleton framework of public health services for its sparsely populated regions, but only 10 municipalities in all Ontario in 1936 had a full-time medical officer of health. Out of a population of 3.6 million, only one-third lived in areas where public health services had adequate direction.[87]

The scarcity and cost of medical care and the problems incidental to less-developed areas impeded the establishment of a clinic and visiting nurse network where the need was greatest.[88] In addition to distance and cost factors, there was little municipal organization in much of New Ontario; existing municipal governments were unable to finance child welfare efforts; and federal and provincial governments were at an impasse on this subject as they were whenever funding was at issue. Families outside the province's cities and larger towns were assigned to the outermost fringes of a campaign that was supposed to be dedicated to the service of the mothers and children most in need. For such families, health care proved to be the scarcest resource of all.

Proportionately greater numbers of nurses and physicians were situated in the more settled areas. By the mid-1930s, 28 per cent of Canadians resided in the 20 cities with a population of 30,000 or more. Yet these city-dwellers were served by 45 per cent of the physicians, 48 per cent of the nurses and 49 per cent of the dentists.[89] Specialists in particular were drawn to the larger towns and cities where their expertise would find the sort of clientele that guaranteed them a livelihood. The Canadian Medical Association was so concerned about the scarcity of physicians in rural districts that it repeatedly urged provincial governments to place and maintain recent medical graduates in these outlying areas.[90] The association's pleas went unheeded.

The federal health department also worried about the special difficulties of outpost settlers, and declared that their situation was one of national importance: "Even in the oldest settled provinces we have information of homes from fifteen to twenty miles away from doctor or nurse." Beyond conferring with provincial health officials, encouraging discussion by the Dominion Council of Health, and publishing a special supplement to MacMurchy's *The Canadian Mother's Book*, no federal action was taken.[91] Sparsely populated sectors of Ontario were not left entirely without medical assistance. However, if density of population can be taken as a reasonable index where the application of health services was concerned, the larger the centre, the more adequate the health program.[92]

By 1926 the provincial health department had decided that the advantages of "such service as is available" should first be extended to the districts of Northern Ontario that had difficulty supplying it for themselves.[93] Diagnostic clinics for infants and preschool children were held either at the request of local medical practitioners, or in conjunction with the nurses' regular field work.[94] These nursing services could not begin to cover the population's needs, and were often restricted to school inspection. Throughout the interwar period, at least half the province did not enjoy the health protection offered by a public health nursing program.[95] The division was frustrated by what was interpreted as the unwarranted obstinance of local governments in refusing to hire municipal nurses and establish their own child welfare services. By 1929, its director had to conclude that three years of intensive demonstration work in Northern Ontario had revealed only the futility of proving "the practicability of a well-rounded out, full time, public health nursing service" to the target municipalities. It seemed that "unreasoning opposition" more than offset any community interest.[96] As far as provincial administrators were concerned, the opposition was primarily founded on "a pronounced disinclination to spend even the minimum of money upon anything as intangible as health."

For all its efforts at persuasion, the provincial health department could not compel the municipalities to accept their responsibility for the health of their people. The administrators explained municipal reluctance in terms of popular ignorance and "false economy," but the reports of local medical officers of health repeatedly pointed to financial constraints as the true source of non-compliance. And, as typified by federal-provincial conflicts over fiscal responsibility for health and welfare, the senior level was determined to allocate blame to its benighted local counterparts rather than taking on more of the burden itself.

With respect to health care, inequalities of distribution were structural as well as regional, and were contingent as much on population distribution and the local tax base as on individual socio-economic status. The smaller towns, and especially the northern outposts of Ontario, were definitely "have nots" where public health and child welfare were concerned. Voluntary organizations attempted to fill the void where official agencies were unwilling or unable to provide medical services. The Red Cross "Hospital on Wheels" operated in Northern Ontario's most isolated districts. The first of these outpost centres was opened at Wilberforce in 1921. By 1940, there were 29 centres operating in the province.[97] Red Cross nurses also provided prenatal supervision and attended confinements in areas where no physician was available. In 1931, for example, 110 babies were delivered by Red Cross nurses alone, without the loss of a single mother or infant.[98] In spite of these valiant efforts, the Red Cross Society's program was also restricted by economic considerations and the extent of the need encountered.[99] As the Dominion Council of Health reported in 1933, no effective technique had yet been developed whereby a satisfactory prenatal service could be provided for women in rural and outpost areas. At the same time, "the problem of inducing private practitioners in rural areas to give adequate prenatal care to their private patients, with or without assistance from the provincial health department, would seem to be unsolved."[100]

From the start of provincial demonstration work in these areas, the program's administrators argued that the problem lay in undeveloped local health administration outside the cities. The part-time medical officer of health who ran local efforts was clearly a failure.[101] In 1921, the 8 Ontario municipalities (of 904) with a full-time service averaged $1.25 per capita in public health expenditures, while the remaining extensive area averaged only $.23 per capita. According to an investigation made by the provincial department in 1919, 38 of 54 rural counties spent only $.10 per capita on public health work. The report recommended $.71 per capita as the minimum required for a reasonable public health service.[102]

In addition to the limited tax base that impeded major municipal investments in public health, one of the chief obstacles in these municipalities was a lack of community organization. Even for those clients who could pay, distance between patient and physician precluded regular supervision, while the absence of medical specialists deterred prompt correction of many childhood defects and disabilities. Exacerbating such problems were poverty and the lack of even minimal social welfare provisions: "Isolation makes for slothful travelling of the health gospel, limited income lessens municipal expenditures for so-called innovations ... No free clinics or service clubs exist here. The further one goes, the worse it gets, until one reaches the geographical fringes of the province where difficulties of transportation and climatic conditions make even adequate nutrition a problem, and medical and dental service is obtained only after real sacrifice."[103]

It was frequently difficult to reach the neediest mothers because of their isolation, the adverse conditions of their daily lives, and the burden of work they had to bear. In her summary of conditions found in the Thunder Bay district in 1922, a provincial nurse reported that young women were typically in poor physical condition, with equally sorry results for their children's health. Referring specifically to the "entire lack of obstetrical care" in the area, she pointed out that these women were unable to procure any medical assistance before or at confinement due to distance and poverty: "There have been many who have had six or seven children without proper care and are beginning to realize that many of their ailments and suffering have been caused by their lack."[104]

This situation was encountered repeatedly. The district health officer for North Bay reported that home visiting, such as it was, had not been satisfactory because of the poverty that prevented mothers from making the necessary expenditures to put into practice the nurse's recommendations.[105] Due to conditions peculiar to the less-settled areas, nurses, as "messengers of mercy," were even more vital to the campaign's ends in rural settlements, villages, and resource communities than in the province's larger towns and cities.[106] But as the provincial nurses quickly discovered, lack of publicity about the services that were available, and problems of distance, transportation, and precious time away from the homestead prevented many women from making the pilgrimage in search of medical guidance. Despite the fact that campaigners insisted on the unquestionable value of nurse visits and child welfare clinics, such benefits remained rare in the lives of these mothers.

As a result, child health, already undermined by poor living conditions, suffered all the more due to late diagnosis of ailments and the inability of parents to pay for correction. A 1925 health survey of 1,392 children in Dundas Region found that one-third were 7 per cent or more under normal weight, and had diseased primary teeth and lymphatic gland enlargement, among various other defects.[107] Agnes Macphail, arguing before the House of Commons in 1930, asserted that "farm men, women and children suffer greatly because they are afraid to call the doctor in, fearing that they cannot pay his bill; and so they keep on being sick, far below the standard that should be their rightful standard of life." Children were simply "allowed to continue" with health problems, with the result that "the whole outlook, indeed the success in life of that child, is adversely affected."[108]

Their discussions of the health problems affecting rural and outpost families reveal the doctors' larger anxieties about racial degeneration and the adverse impact of modernization on the population's reproductive capacities. One of the "most appalling revelations" of the immediate postwar years, declared Alan Brown, was that the rural children of the nation were on the average less healthy than were urban children, "including all the children of the slums."[109] It was not the unhealthy environment, then, but the absence of medical regulation and supervision that accounted for the discrepancy in the health status between city and country children. In Brown's estimation, the nation's agrarian traditions and future glory were also betrayed by the government's shortsightedness in neglecting rural medical needs: "If rural Canada is to continue to be a satisfactory nursery for human life for the Dominion, it must provide conditions favourable for the cultivation of the best possible human material."[110] Brown's eugenicist inclinations led him to romanticize the countryside as the seed-bed of racial superiority, but the thrust of his argument is clear: rural mothers and children were essentially beyond the pale of medical intervention.

These eugenic concerns, redoubled by continuing popular belief in a "rural myth" and the ambivalence of contemporary reformers toward modernization, led the medical profession to take a firmer than usual stand on state health care delivery in isolated areas. In 1925, organized medicine asserted that "our profession should insist that every rural child in every county should have equal privileges with the city child" and that the improved sanitary organization of rural districts should be brought to the attention of politicians as "one of the most important subjects to be discussed."[111] The Confederated Women's Institutes of Canada placed before the House of Commons a resolution that county health units be established as "the most satisfactory method of securing results in rural and small urban areas."[112] The influence of ongoing medical lobbying was evident in the 1930 proposal that the dominion government subsidize the establishment and permanent maintenance of full-time health units to the extent of one-third of their cost.[113] Not until 1944 would this forward step be accomplished, despite continual pressure on the federal government from organized medicine, the province, and other interested groups. Even then, it was the Ontario government that provided the requisite funding.[114]

The reports of the provincial nurses who travelled the Ontario countryside confirm the doctors' assessment of dismal, and deteriorating, health conditions. The first point of demonstration in eastern Ontario in 1921 was Rockland, which had a population of 3,000. As the nurses observed, this town was greatly in need of general public health reform: "The town was in an unsanitary condition, there being no sewage system, no water filtration, no clean or adequate milk supply, no paved streets, no street lighting. Public health teachings were unknown and under these conditions there could be little else than sickness, distress and high death rates. Employment was provided for the majority of the men in the town by the lumber mills but the families in all homes were so large that one wage earner had difficulty in providing proper food and clothes for the children."[115] Poor living conditions meant that 75 of the 160 children born in 1920 had perished during their first year of life, along with another 10 under the age of five years. The financial state of the town was such that there was no possibility of appointing a permanent nurse to carry on maternal and child welfare work. At the end of their three-month stay, the provincial nurses withdrew, believing all the while that "the mothers being young and interested, had profited by the help of the nurses and the results could be seen even upon a second visit to the home."

The nurses recognized the odds they were battling in delivering the child welfare message to these poor and isolated communities. Conditions in some sparsely settled areas were so pitiable that there was little hope of improving health by means of the vaunted educational methods. In North Hastings County in 1925, a nurse noted that "stagnation of industry, lack of education, bad housing, overcrowding, immorality, intermarrying and the many evils which follow in its train are some of the most outstanding problems of the district and are the direct result of isolation and poverty." Coupled with this was "the daily struggle for a mere existence on land so rocky that in some localities farming is practically impossible." Bad housing and overcrowding were another problem, "not only from the physical and health standpoint but from the moral as well."[116]

The nurses' moral sensibilities were undoubtedly offended by what they encountered, but they were sensitive to the desperation of these people and the magnitude of their daily struggle for survival. They understood that destitution did not provide fertile ground for health education. More importantly, diagnosis of health problems and recommendations for treatment meant nothing without the ways and means to provide for remedial action. In such situations, the nurses believed that, unless arrangements could be made for having the work done, there was not "much use in going back." Lessons in healthful living were best concentrated on "the small number who might be taught and helped."[117] More than any of the campaign's other participants, the nurses who took its precepts directly to the people of Ontario were forced to confront its limitations. At times their most concerted evangelical efforts were to no avail because their concepts were irrelevant within the context of the people's lives. Within the context of the campaign itself, the visiting nurses were empowered to do little more than offer sympathy. For "the small number who might be taught," they hoped at least to impress upon them the rudiments of modern preventive hygiene.

What was required to uplift such families to the reformers' standards of health, hygiene, and family living was not education alone, but the means to alleviate their poverty. Unlike doctors, whose social distance from their patients permitted them to conceptualize ill health as the result of some individual failing, nurses witnessed the persistence of parents trying to do the best for their families, despite the incredible odds imposed by poverty. In the lumber town of Hawkesbury, the visiting nurse was appalled by conditions at "the Sneigh," a slum surrounding the Hawkesbury Lumber Company:

The first family we called on was a houseful of twelve and they all have scabies. Have had it for a year. In the next was one child deformed since birth for whom nothing has been done, and who was also a decided mouth breather with huge diseased tonsils. In the same house was a three-year-old with discharging ears. In the next house was a very sick baby with tonsillitis. The fourth was a family of eight, three of whom had scabies and two very bad throats. In the fifth house was a widow with nine children, six under fourteen for whom she gets a mother's pension ... There are about ten to feed on $50 per month ... The heads of all these families make perhaps $12 per week ... There are just dozens of families like those I have mentioned and they have absolutely no money for doctors' bills and if the doctors attempted to do it all for nothing they would all be kept busy just attending the needs of "the Sneigh."[118]

Modern health teachings were meaningless for families justifiably preoccupied with subsistence. The so-called "essentials" of preventive health care – cleanliness, adequate clothing, nutritious food – were unattainable luxuries. Moreover, the burden of extra work that stringent hygienic principles entailed for poor women was tremendous: "If we can clear up a family of twelve with the scabies, who have only one set of clothes to wear and absolutely no facilities for taking baths, I think we will apply for medals; not for ourselves but for the mother and old grandmother who are putting the children to bed and washing their clothes each day."[119] Difficulties of transportation and communication magnified the hardship of many rural and outpost settlers, particularly in instances of acute medical need. Roads during the winter and spring were at times almost impassable, and a trip for the doctor could mean 24 to 48 hours travelling. In the Bruce Peninsula, for example, the doctor was called only in "extreme cases," and "a good deal of hardship" was endured by pregnant women: "The nearest practical nurse available for Tobermory lives at Dyer's Bay 15 to 20 miles distant – an old lady who can neither read nor write, but as the doctor says, does as she is told and providence does the rest."[120]

Inaccessibility greatly increased the vulnerability of pregnant women and families with young children. Parents went to considerable lengths to protect their children, as illustrated in the case of a family stricken with diphtheria in Sterling Township, sixty miles from Fort William, on a homestead isolated even from the main road by three miles of swamp and very rough country. The father started across the swamp at four o'clock in the morning carrying his ailing six-year-old son on his back six miles to the train. On reaching the city four hours later, and learning that his child had diphtheria, he left the boy in the hospital and accompanied a nurse back by car and across the trail on foot to get his younger son. As the nurse reported, "We arrived at Hurkett by supper time as the road after twenty miles was not the best and it was dusk when we started back through the trail, [the father] carrying the four-year-old boy on his back. We reached the car by ten o'clock and the hospital by two."[121] That both boys survived was due in no small measure to the courage and will of their father. Evidence of this nature effectively counters the suspicions of the medical profession that poor parents were especially indifferent and negligent about their children's health. Time after time, the nurses were impressed by the way that they strove and endured within the inflexible confines of available resources. And even in the primitive surroundings of backwoods Ontario, parents appeared grateful for any assistance, however meagre.[122]

There is little reason to believe that reports of the isolation of rural mothers and the eagerness with which they accepted medical help of any kind were exaggerated to justify and promote the cause. Letters to the Council on Child and Family Welfare permit a firsthand glimpse of the kind of hardship confronted by women that would make the slightest assistance appreciated. In one instance, the writer was eighteen years old and "settled among strangers" in an unnamed rural Ontario community. She had given birth in April, "just when seed grain and machinery had to be bought." There was no money for baby clothes, a bath, a nurse, or other helper, although enough had been set aside to provide for a doctor to attend the confinement. A neighbour was relied upon for two days' assistance, and then the young mother was left to her own devices. She bathed the baby in a borrowed basin, a two-hour process; six days after the birth, she scrubbed the baby's laundry on a board, a task that took the better part of a day because of her weakened postpartum condition. This young woman seems to have borne her lot with a courage that makes it all the more pathetic, since it is apparent that she had no recourse: "Of course, I must not give the impression that I was not cared for, as my husband came in from the field every hour or two to see if we were all right. He also helped with meals what he could."[123]

The problem resulted directly from the absence of relevant educational efforts and more especially, of practical medical services. Women outside urban areas were doubly hindered in taking care of themselves and their children because both instruction in modern health principles and medical care were out of their reach. In 1928, the United Farm Women of Ontario attempted to politicize the issue of medical care for women and children in rural and outpost areas by petitioning the federal and provincial governments. They stressed, contrary to prevailing medical views, that "the chief cause of our appalling death rate of mothers at childbirth is economic, the remedy of which is slow." To address "this calamity," they outlined a comprehensive approach to the problem of maternal and child welfare in non-urban areas. They called for public education based on "scientific knowledge," and improvement in medical training and obstetrical practice, as well as state-funded research in these areas, maternity insurance, and state placement and subsidization of doctors.[124]

The only request on behalf of rural mothers and children that was answered by the state was a wholehearted commitment to the dissemination of health information. While the various government publications on prenatal, postnatal, and child health were distributed by mail to rural women, their urban bias frequently made the advice they offered irrelevant or simply inapplicable to rural conditions. Middle-class city women were more likely to have household appliances, such amenities as indoor bathrooms, and access to services such as laundries. Expectant and new mothers in the province's larger centres also had help in the form of nearby doctors, visiting nurses, clinics, and hospitals. They might well profit from the medical advice that suggested that they should continue their lives "much as before," just as long as they remained under a doctor's supervision.

For pregnant farm women whose daily workload was far more onerous, such advice could conceivably prove life-threatening, given the physical strain involved in their housekeeping and farm chores.[125] Typical rural conditions made some helpful suggestions – such as the one that the mother's room be situated near the bathroom – difficult to put into practice. An attempt to make advice literature more relevant to rural and outpost mothers actually confirmed both the extent of their need and the federal government's incapacity to meet that need adequately. The supplement to *The Canadian Mothers' Book*, written by Helen MacMurchy and published in 1923, proposed to advise these women on "what to do if baby arrives before the doctor does." Written in MacMurchy's customary simple style, it detailed the process of childbirth while giving discreet acknowledgment to the fact that most women in isolated communities had to rely on midwives, who were often untrained neighbours. MacMurchy never referred directly to midwives and insisted that neither the supplement nor the neighbour should substitute for the doctor, but were intended to help only "until the Doctor comes."[126] Lest the supplement be seen by the medical profession as promotion of midwifery, it was not circulated upon request but published "for distribution by doctors and nurses only."

It must have been small consolation to anxious expectant mothers for whom the impending arrival of the doctor was little more than fantasy. For the settlers of Bergland, in the Rainy River district, the distance from a physician meant that "the people are dependent on one another" for help during illness or "on a few elderly women who act as midwives for confinements." Reliance on untrained midwives was a worrisome prospect for expectant mothers, but there were no ready alternatives:

One lively Scandinavian midwife of 64, speaking broken English, told us she used no eye-drops for newborn babies; that she had no instruments, but in difficult cases "she knew tricks with her hands" and used a nail to bring down the head. She would not explain but we had been told some vague tales by others of her having used "a nail" or "a needle" or "scissors" and some had lost confidence in her ... She told us that every now and then she is in the position where the mother's life is in danger and something has to be done; and there is and can be no doctor to act. The distance is 26 miles to Rainy River Town alone and the patient may be any distance beyond that, with no road broken or an impassable one, and weather below zero.[127]

The conditions discovered in this region were commonplace in rural and northern districts.[128] The nurses also found, to their horror, that newly delivered mothers were obliged to maintain supervision over household and family "although in bed," and that many took up their normal labours, including field work, much too soon after confinement. In contrast to the ideals of the child welfare campaigners, the rural mother's maternity experience was typically defined by the exigencies of farm and frontier life.

Rural and outpost women shared with their poorer urban sisters the fundamental problem of paying for medical care even when it was otherwise available. The few physicians settled in these districts were at times leery of attending to poor families, especially during the Depression when their own incomes were declining. Before the adoption of the Ontario Medical Relief Plan in 1935, no relief program covered the near-indigent farmer, and as long as farmers could produce enough to feed their families, they were not officially considered indigent. Doctors were asked to accept all kinds of produce in lieu of cash. One general practitioner in Ayr received over 20 chickens, several ducks, geese, a turkey, potatoes, and wood on account in the winter of 1933. Because rural farm families slipped between the cracks of even the minimal welfare provisions available, they were worse off in terms of health care than were those on direct relief.[129] The provisions of the Ontario Medical Relief plan did not apply to unorganized rural municipalities. Meanwhile, the country doctors argued that they were having trouble "collecting sufficient to purchase the bare necessities of life."

In a letter written from Wawbewawa to the minister of health in 1935, "A Worried Expectant Mother" revealed that physicians in her area demanded assurance of full payment for attending confinements before they would agree to do so. The young woman felt that "as a pure Canadian mother," she had every right to bring her complaint to the attention of the department. She asserted that hers was not a letter begging relief: "I am in need true to say of both clothes and food as it goes, but not so much as the thing weighing most heavy on my mind." This burden consisted of her inability to pay the $25 confinement fee requested by the nearest doctor, who lived twelve miles from her homestead. Nor was the approaching delivery the only one she had faced without any prospect of medical attention:

In January 1933 I was in a family way and took sick on the 26th January, although I had not expected till February 15. My husband was to be paid for some work he had done on February 5th, but as it happened, I took sick sooner than expected and not a cent in the house. My husband went two miles on snowshoes to the nearest phone and called the doctors. They wanted to know if we had $25 to give them ... a kind neighbour, poor as we, but who by a miracle had five dollars on hand, told my husband if the doctor would come for that, he'd lend it to us. My husband hurried back that distance and over the phone offered five dollars, but they refused to come. And all that time I was suffering agonies impossible to describe. In one last desperate plea to the doctors to come, they told my husband to bring me to the hospital. Imagine a poor soul suffering the agonies of hell being taken out in below zero winter weather and driven in an open sleigh twelve miles to a hospital! It was impossible.[130]

The woman was in labour for two days with only the help of "a poor little woman" and her husband. She gave birth to twin boys and was so weak for the following month that she "could not speak or raise a hand." One of the babies was "nearly dead" at birth: "for an hour my husband rubbed and the woman worked with the infant until it acted alive."

The writer justifiably concluded that "it's a perfect disgrace to this Canada that the mothers of the land must suffer without only a part even of the care necessary at that time."[131] She had since produced a daughter, again without medical assistance and for the same reasons. A similar bitter experience confronted her sister-in-law, settled a mile away; although she offered $10, the doctors would not come for less than $25. The result was that "she came through alive, but who knows how near she was to passing away too. She is only 17 years old. The one attending her was nearly desperate before the worst was over."[132]

At the time of her writing, this "worried expectant mother" was awaiting the birth of her fifth child at the age of twenty-three. The letter must have struck a responsive chord in the Council on Child and Family Welfare, testifying as it did to the tremendous courage of young mothers across the nation who were struggling to keep their families intact during the trying Depression years.[133] Charlotte Whitton immediately sent out prenatal and postnatal information packages and investigated the services available in the woman's district. Her efforts turned up little more than what the "worried expectant mother" had herself described. There were no public health or bedside nursing services in her area. The Ontario Department of Health could suggest only that the woman should go to the hospital at Englehart, twelve miles from her homestead, where the municipality would cover the costs of her confinement.[134] Whitton also intimated that there was perhaps a "question of ethics involved which might be inquired into by the Ontario Medical Association." However, she felt that the council, as an advisory family welfare agency, had performed its duty by providing the literature and checking on available health services.

The council's response must have proved disheartening to the "worried expectant mother," and many others like her whose private ordeals went unrecorded. Rarely were state efforts on their behalf sufficient to make a real difference in their lives and in the well-being of their families. It was apparent even to public health employees that, much more than advice, these mothers needed actual medical care and treatment.[135] The nurses understood the real needs of the people they served, and consequently the campaign's real limitations. In 1922, after two years of participating in travelling child welfare demonstrations, one nurse boldly recommended that, "if what money we have to spend ... could be devoted to GIVING A SERVICE, even a minimum one ... we might get more valuable returns in the long run, and the Department would not only be filling a great need, but would be highly commended by the public." She rightly sensed that, contrary to the provincial department's ultimate aim, the municipalities were generally unwilling or unable to appoint public health nurses. It would take several years to cover all municipalities, "and meantime those not served are without any public health education, the outlying people get little in the way of magazines and have no time to read as a general thing."[136]

The campaign's directors were well aware of the gap between their aspirations and the practical efforts conceived to attain these. In 1932, the Ontario government's public health field staff conducted a survey of the effectiveness of child health services in the province.

The proportion of parents "sufficiently interested in the well-being of their children" was not only high but "fairly constant" in every location visited.[137] It appeared that the ignorance and fecklessness of mothers were not major factors in preventing the campaign's success. The problem was that these programs frequently failed to meet their prospective clients' real needs, or even their own stated goals.

Publications, clinics, and nursing visits were reaching, at least in some measure, an increasing number of Ontario mothers and their children. In qualitative terms, however, such services remained seriously deficient. The 1932 survey pointed out that the problem of providing all women with the maximum amount of prenatal and postnatal care was still "a long way from solution." In addition, in spite of myriad attempts to establish municipal clinics, there was still "no satisfactory health programme in operation which is appropriate to the needs of the preschool age group."[138] In many Ontario towns, nothing was carried out on a systematic basis for children of any age.

Even some of the campaign's directors recognized that, rhetoric aside, not enough was being done to help Ontario mothers and their children. Their critique exposed the contradictions at the base of their program. On the one hand, they saw that education was insufficient and that increased medical assistance and physician cooperation were essential. The relationship between the medical profession and the official health services, they argued, was "not as intimate as might be desired, having in mind our ultimate objective." Certainly the experience of nurses across the province sustains this assessment. On the other hand, the program's critics also believed that "the local staffs are bending too much of their effort toward increasing the attendance at the official operating clinic instead of urging that all children receive regular supervision by the medical men of the community."[139] The implication was that local child welfare efforts were inadequate, largely because they were promoting community care of mothers and children instead of impressing upon parents their own responsibility to seek regular, private medical guidance. This was a line of reasoning that was definitely endorsed by most of the province's doctors. The major impediment to the campaign's practical services was exposed by the views of its policy-makers: it was very much a case of public versus private effort.

Conflict between state and private initiative was always an underlying current in social welfare schemes during this period.[140] For all that child welfare supporters adamantly professed their modernity and called for state involvement in the care and training of the child as a "national asset," ideological restrictions as much as purely economic concerns held them back. When it appeared, during the Depression emergency, that increased state involvement was inevitable, they were genuinely afraid of the possible ill effects for the Canadian family: "If the care of the child is thus no longer the privilege of the home ... and if his material needs also be supplied without parental intervention, it is imperative to consider what part remains for parents to play. Must we not fear that the family of the unemployed, thus shorn of its prerogatives and functions, may lose all significance for the child and be doomed to decay? The outlook is serious and calls for close attention ... Whatever the difficulties to be overcome, all welfare work should aim at supplying the child's needs through the parents."[141]

Child welfare advocates wanted an active interventionary role for the medical profession in the mother/child relationship and called for state support in realizing it. But just as many private practitioners who endorsed child welfare work still feared its threat to their practices, the directors' ambivalence regarding methods belies a similar apprehension. If they were committed to improving the lives of Canadian mothers and children, they dreaded the implications for the current order of drawing in the state. As an increasingly important element of the dominant class, doctors were particularly resistant to any incursions on their professional autonomy and control of their clientele.

Not until 1935 did the provincial government act to provide a permanent public health service, with emphasis on child and maternal welfare work, for an impoverished area of eastern Ontario. The first rural health unit in Ontario was established for the eastern counties of Stormont, Glengarry, Prescott, and Russell.[142] Two-thirds of the necessary funds for the Eastern Ontario Health Unit were contributed by the municipalities involved, and one-third by the provincial government. Its headquarters were in Alexandria, with public health nurses, two to a county, situated at Cornwall, Finch, Alexandria, Lancaster, Hawkesbury, Plantagenet, Rockland, and Casselman. It was directed by a physician with special public health qualifications.

The importance of such a service to the area had long been apparent, above all to the nurses visiting there. For every 1,000 infants born in the unit area between 1930 and 1934, 97 died before their first birthday.[143] The unit's nurses found that their difficulties in contacting expectant mothers and persuading them to see their doctors persisted despite the new organization. A year after the unit was founded, it was discovered that very few of the district's pregnant women reported for medical attention before the time of delivery.

This was believed to be due partly to economic reasons and partly to the fact that "the medical profession do not encourage maternity patients to visit them at regular intervals for care and a postpartum examination is rarely given."[144] It was decided that the nurses would secure the attendant physician's permission and then visit these mothers "as often as necessary." The unit's staff nurses also conducted well-baby clinics in five centres, with far more encouraging results. The provincial supervisor noted that, during their first year, no deaths had occurred among infants attending the child health conference conducted by the unit each month.[145] Following the pattern for child welfare work in urban centres, the nurses also made home visits "to a great many more infants who cannot come to the conferences."[146]

The establishment of a permanent health unit represented significant progress by comparison to the temporary, periodic demonstration work that had preceded it. Nonetheless, the educational solution retained its primacy. The unit simply institutionalized child and maternal welfare work for the counties it served, without expanding the scope or changing the nature of that work. The problems recognized by the provincial nurses in the early 1920s continued. The unit's directors were obliged to admit, as had the nurses before them, that many of the client families' health problems were so aggravated by social and economic difficulties that their efforts were largely fruitless.[147] Yet the doctors in charge remained convinced that the only worthwhile solution was to change the living habits of the entire area served by the unit: "The people are very willing to have toxoid administered, tonsils and adenoids removed and defective teeth corrected at the expense of the state, but the changing of their living habits is a slow process and best accomplished by an attempt to establish the relationship between cause and effect through the home. The medical profession in the area has not considered this to be their responsibility and talks to general audiences are ineffective ... therefore we have not pushed this phase of the work."[148]

Unmistakeable evidence of the material basis of the district's health problems did not challenge the medical paradigm upholding a cultural and behavioural explanation. Local doctors were also culpable in this respect, in that they had failed to carry out their duties regarding the regulation of "living habits" according to medical standards. While realizing that state provision for medical treatment was effective, they interpreted its efficacy as evidence of a general moral lassitude that encouraged exploitation of public funds, and not as proof of the population's inability to otherwise obtain these services. Because ill health and destitution were viewed in individualistic and moralistic terms, even in the depths of the Great Depression, few state initiatives could be justified.[149]

For many parents, the assistance delivered by the child welfare campaign was simply too little, too late. However thankful she may have been, one young expectant mother paid the price of society's neglect and professional self-interest through the loss of two daughters within one week. As a visiting nurse recounted:

They lived in a very small shack which was very clean but very little room ... The child was lying on the bed fully dressed and burning up with fever. She had not had the doctor as she cannot afford it ... I went several times a day to help her. The child improved but took a relapse and died. It seemed very hard losing the two children so near together. It was a pathetic sight to see the little body wrapped in a sheet lying on a wooden bench in the corner with a lamp burning at the head and a piece of new patched quilt on the wall to improve the place and the mother's thanks for the help that we had been to her was very touching.[150]

Nowhere was the impact of economic deprivation and maldistribution of wealth and social services as apparent as in the rural and outpost areas of the province. The campaign's participants could always console themselves that they were doing their best for these mothers and their children. Within the contours of contemporary medical and political ideology and its related theories of economic individualism, they undoubtedly were.

Despite the tragedies that occurred, child welfare advocates did not stress education only because education seemed the easiest remedy for perceived parental ignorance. As these stories demonstrate, providing education was in itself far from easy. But education was an essential component of modern science and technology, inspiring medical support as the foundations of the profession's knowledge and power, and popular faith in an age of technological advance. Education also corresponded to middle-class aspirations for reforming Canadian families; it enhanced specific professional status concerns while protecting the system. The focus on education fitted well with the social welfare philosophy prevailing in government circles and the determination of the federal government to make the municipalities and provinces accept their responsibilities in this area. The comparatively low cost of educational efforts speaks for itself as a motivating factor; certainly the cost-effectiveness of social welfare programs grew in importance during the Depression.

The efficacy of these child welfare demonstrations is difficult to measure. It is likely that they spurred the hiring of municipal nurses

Well Baby Clinic, Hamilton, 1930 (AO 1349). The photograph shows a doctor in attendance, but the clinics were more commonly staffed entirely by nurses.

Visiting Nurse from the Ontario Division of Public Health Nursing and Maternal and Child Hygiene, Lakehead District, 1924 (AO 1351). The nurses who were sent to carry the campaign to isolated northern districts encountered much poverty and hardship.

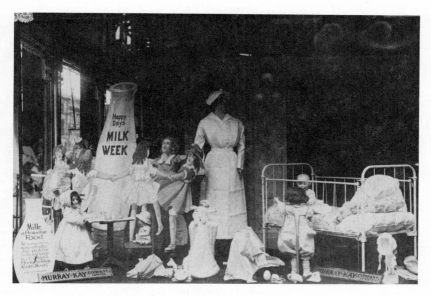

"Milk Week" Window Display, Murray Kay Company, Toronto, 1921 (AO 1348).
Eaton's and Simpson's also joined the pure milk/child welfare cause with window
displays, free milk for children under ten years, and weigh-in clinics staffed
by nurses.

Prenatal Clinic, Hamilton, 1930 (AO 1350). The prenatal aspects of the campaign
were the least developed.

and the establishment of local clinics only where the interest existed and the financing was already available. In the northern parts of the province, temporary annual visits by provincial public health nurses constituted the only child and maternal welfare services that these mothers would know throughout the period. In the end, despite good intentions, issues of authority, control, and responsibility limited the effectiveness of the campaign's hallmark services and suggested to some of its participants that the emphasis on education was an inappropriate and ineffective solution to the child welfare problem.

There were many indications that parents shared the aims of the nurses and doctors who carried the child welfare message across Ontario. Many accepted their need for instruction in modern child care and home hygiene and wanted to learn the best and most up-to-date methods of caring for their children. Yet the child welfare workers' enthusiasm for education and propaganda may have raised parental expectations for further state aid that never materialized. For many Ontario families, the result may have been greater alienation and frustration in the face of an uncaring, negligent state, distant in every sense. Advice, along with irregular medical supervision, emergency medical services and nurse assistance, and other piecemeal attempts to improve the lives of mothers and children all represented a meagre beginning to a campaign of national significance. Whatever the campaigners could muster in the form of instruction in modern methods could not compensate for the real health needs of these Ontario families.

CHAPTER EIGHT

"Ninety-Nine Percent Child Study Conscious": The Public Response

If child welfare advocates were determined to elevate "the masses" to their standards for family life, they could not simply impose their beliefs on an unwilling audience. The element of social control inherent in this campaign is apparent to the extent that its participants were largely middle-class professionals, and that their definition of the "healthy" Canadian family was based on middle-class ideals and experience. But however much they urged parents to adopt their ideas and practices, the parents themselves made the decision as to whether they would do so.

There is no evidence to suggest that parents who did not cooperate were policed, harrassed, or otherwise threatened merely for refusing to be enlightened. The medical profession did play a part in obliging some parents to comply with their standards: visiting nurses were used to monitor families who were receiving mothers' allowances and those who were on the Children's Aid Society's "suspect" list. For the most part, however, the child welfare campaigners had no direct means of forcing most parents to study the information given to them, to apply it, or to attend their clinics. Parents may have felt a certain psychological pressure to comply with the standards that were being established by a socially and politically influential group.[1] But it was only when the family fell under surveillance for other reasons, such as poverty due to a father's death, disability or desertion, or suspicion of child neglect or abuse, that the state could enforce parental cooperation at the risk of loss of benefits or of the children themselves.[2]

However ignorant and irresponsible the campaigners considered mothers to be, they still believed that children fared best when raised by their own parents. The Council on Child and Family Welfare promoted this all-encompassing faith in the family and in motherhood as twin pillars of state and society: "If, believing in the innate dignity and sanctity of human life, the chief purpose of the state be the common good, then the community must regard the home and family as fundamental ... the place and preservation of the mother in the family [is] essential to the growth and greatness of the state itself."[3] Their aim was to ensure social reproduction according to their standards, to be achieved by professional intervention through the regulation of motherhood.

Doubtless the medical profession attained social dominance because state and society, in some measure, accepted and upheld its claims to knowledge, power, and authority. Since health is a universal concern, and a resource that, like labour power, cannot be produced in the marketplace, there is little reason to believe that working-class mothers found the campaign's objectives inimical to their own hopes for their families. But if medical dominance was an integral component of the increasing rationalization of modern society, even dominance of this nature does not necessarily preclude resistance nor render opposition ineffectual. Medical ideals could create an impact on the way that women regarded their maternal duties without making them the passive and submissive "patients" that doctors wanted them to be. Far from simply taking in the entire modern childrearing package as presented by the new experts, mothers themselves recognized the limits of "scientific motherhood." They appreciated instruction and clinical supervision, but they also wanted tangible help in the form of affordable medical assistance for themselves and their families. And they believed that such assistance was owed to them by the state as a right of citizenship.

Any historical discussion of the popular acceptance of ideas and their behavioural effects is fraught with difficulties of assessment. Obviously, the number of parents who incorporated these ideas into their daily practices cannot be determined precisely. It is possible, however, to gain an impression of their overall awareness of and receptivity to the new methods by studying sources that reveal their views. While such material is rare, letters to the Council on Child and Family Welfare from parents across Ontario, supported by the observations and official reports of the provincial public health nurses, do permit at least a glimpse into the private lives of these families.

Child welfare workers believed that their educational efforts were making a definite impact on their target audience. Not only were increasing numbers of mothers being reached through clinics, nurse visits, and literature, but there were hopeful signs that maternal attitudes were being influenced in the right direction. The nurses, in the best position to assess the situation due to their closer personal contact with mothers, had a sense that popular ideas about childrearing were changing. By the close of the Depression decade, they were discovering that "we are dependent upon a public which is becoming increasingly more interested and better informed. The education which is being constantly carried on through newspaper and magazine articles, radio talks, lectures, extension courses and personal contacts is creating in the public a sense of need. This is naturally followed by a demand for a type of service which will meet this need." It appeared to them that mothers' perceptions of the new medical relationship with the family had undergone "a very radical change."[4] The campaigners were confident that, in a relatively short time, they had succeeded in making mothers aware both of their own need for instruction and supervision, and of the campaigners' ability to fill that need.

To those intent on shaping a new ideology of motherhood and a modernized childhood, it seemed that the relevant concepts were asserting themselves in the behaviour of mothers. The visiting nurses were finding the mother "better prepared to discuss her problems ... She is more aware that there is a routine to follow and that she must have a plan, a plan which will not only be of value in training her baby but will aid her in establishing a system whereby she can follow this routine and get sufficient rest and recreation to keep herself fit for the many duties which confront her."[5] The language used in generalizing about these "radical changes" in childrearing patterns was once again that of scientific management – words such as preparation, training, plan, routine, system – all of which added up to "fitness" in every sense of the word. The public health nurse was finding herself more and more a welcome visitor in the home, "a friend and a member of the community." The general perception in medical circles was that there was a growing acceptance not only of the ideas of the child care experts, but of their new supervisory role within the formerly self-enclosed family circle.

One paediatrician formulated a "cod-liver oil" analogy to describe the penetration of the medical regimen into the home, as well as its possibilities. He noted that 99 of 100 mothers attending the clinic at Sick Children's Hospital in Toronto reported giving cod-liver oil to their children, a recent medical innovation urged on mothers as a precaution against the development of rickets. To doctors, adoption of this practice held significance beyond the fact that the majority of clinic mothers accepted the medical dictum and claimed to be conscientiously applying it. First of all, it demonstrated the "spread effect" of ideas. It did not matter why a particular precept was being put into practice, nor whether the reasons, even if known, were fully understood by those implementing it. What mattered most was that once the idea was accepted by some mothers, their example sparked its widespread acceptance and the requisite modification of behaviour: "No matter how ignorant they might be of other factors in diet, they knew that their babies should have cod-liver oil. All their friends gave it to their children – it was done, therefore they did it. Cod-liver oil will build healthier bodies for our children, even though the mothers do not know the vitamin content."[6] The cod-liver oil analogy hints at the process whereby scientific concepts are popularized. Most importantly for this contemporary medical observer and the historian alike, the process of mass acceptance suggested the prospects for assimilation of the weightier ideas behind the new childrearing trends. Once parents knew "the right answers" to questions regarding discipline and habit training, they were likely to try out their new-found knowledge: "even when they do not know why they act as they do surely something at least will be gained. We must, therefore, make our parents 99 percent 'child study conscious.'[7] Enlightened parent-hood was not a matter of full comprehension of the experts' ideas, but of enhanced parental consciousness, and above all, of popular faith in professional expertise. What counted most was acquiescence to the superior knowledge of the doctor.

It is naturally in the best interest of visionaries to claim that their ideas are gaining popular acceptance. Ideologues are peculiarly and necessarily attuned to any evidence, however incidental, that their system of thought is influencing attitudes and behaviour. Since popular acceptance is their cardinal objective, they consciously seek out corroboration, and frequently locate it through their own diligence. But they have more to gain from these declarations of influence than mere self-gratification and self-justification. As the cod-liver oil story suggests, the simple perception that an idea is widely embraced may be sufficient to cause its further dissemination, and the corresponding spread of the practice. Doctors argued that, if a mother could be convinced that all intelligent mothers were performing a particular duty, she too would willingly and eagerly comply. They recognized that the force of popular opinion is self-generating. It is not only the object, but the vehicle in any campaign of public education.

The role of advertising, both in fostering the modern ideology of scientific motherhood and as a measure of the campaign's acceptance, cannot be overlooked. Advertisers had a practised eye for trends, and were quick to sense the postwar generation's desire for modernity. The media were very effective in popularizing the new child care ideas. Through radio, magazines, and newspapers, ideas about scientific childrearing entered countless homes in a way that doctors and nurses could not.[8] Always uneasy about its ability to resolve the problems drummed into its consciousness, the public is usually willing to grasp a solution that appears reasonable, especially if the solution is also relentlessly pushed. In this manner, ideology becomes popular opinion.[9]

The new child-centredness of modern life was sold to the masses through advertisements depicting the importance of a particular product or service in any truly modern childrearing system. The majority of these advertisements promoted specialized child care products such as soap, cereal, canned milk and patent medicines. Portraying a modern, well-adjusted child glowing with health and self-confidence was also a popular sales technique for goods not specifically linked to child health and welfare. In such advertisements, which involved items like refrigerators and furnaces, the connection was made clear for the potential consumer. Parents who put their child's well-being first recognized the value of this investment.

Some advertisers went beyond incorporating "modern parent/ modern child" imagery into their copy and borrowed the childrearing experts' vocabulary. Advertisements for Castoria, a "special children's laxative," repeatedly pitted the modern mother against the forces of outmoded tradition and misinformation in the guise of the campaigners' prototypical bogeys, the mother-in-law, the neighbour, the elderly aunt, the unprogressive father. The modern mother always emerged victorious in these battles, because she had the modern doctor and the special, scientific child care product on her side.

No advertising campaign better exemplified this trend than that of Parke, Davis and Company (Walkerville, Ontario), "the World's Largest Makers of Pharmaceutical and Biological Products." Parke, Davis and Company produced a line of baby care goods, but none of their advertisements name or illustrate these goods, nor do they even refer to them. Their full-page advertisements in various popular magazines read as though written by the campaign's medical ideologues. Except for the fact that the company's name appears at the bottom of each one, the advertisements seem to be promoting only the noble cause of child welfare. More than anything else, they urged parents to take advantage of modern medical expertise.

These advertisements posed the critical question: "Are affection, the determination to give children every advantage and parental devotion enough?" The answer was taken straight out of the campaigners' mouths: "No, frankly, they are not. The two pairs of hands of even the most conscientious parents are not enough to guide a

"Let's duck...here comes that nosey pest again!"

*How Esther raised
her baby the modern way . . .
in spite of a snoopy neighbor*

1. NEIGHBOR: Well, well, well . . . if it isn't our new mother . . . Did you take my advice about your baby, dear-r-r-R-R?
ESTHER: No, I didn't. I thought it was too old-fashioned.
BOB: (Under his breath) Atta girl!

2. NEIGHBOR: Why . . . what do you MEAN! I know *something* about children. I raised five of them, didn't I?
ESTHER: Yes, and you certainly made it hard for yourself. Me . . . I'm following *modern* methods.

Castoria, the "modern" laxative especially for children, promoted "modern" childrearing – and advertised its products – in the popular "photo-novella" style of the period: from *Maclean's*, 15 September 1939.

3. NEIGHBOR: Modern methods? What kind of bosh is that?

ESTHER: It's not bosh. It's common sense. My doctor tells me that babies should get *special* care . . . all the way from *special* baby food to a *special* baby laxative.

4. NEIGHBOR: *Special* laxative? My dear! That's putting it on!

ESTHER: It is *not!* It stands to reason that if a baby's system is too delicate for adult foods . . . it can also be too delicate for an adult laxative. Yes, even in small doses.

5. ESTHER: That's why the doctor told me to buy CASTORIA. It's made *especially* and ONLY for children. There isn't a harmful ingredient in it. It won't upset a baby's stomach, and it works mostly in the lower bowel. It's gentle and SAFE!

6. BOB: Oh boy! . . . you sure told off that old snoop about Castoria . . . but why didn't you tell her how *swell* it tastes, too?

ESTHER: I should have! I wish she were here to see how the baby goes for it . . . the old buttinsky!

CASTORIA

The modern—SAFE—laxative made especially and ONLY for children

During those first vital years

ROSY cheeks, sparkling eyes, good disposition, steady gains in weight, these are characteristics of a healthy baby who sleeps all night and is happy all day. Such a child is a joy to himself and to his parents today, and he is building a rugged constitution that will be a splendid asset to him in later years.

He must have the right food now, properly prepared. You cannot do better than to select for this important cooking the safe, efficient, hygienic, "Wear-Ever" Aluminum Utensils used every day by the leading Canadian hospitals for the preparation of infants' food.

The kitchen of the *modern* home is completely equipped with

"Wear-Ever"
Aluminum Kitchen Utensils

ALUMINUM COMPANY OF CANADA

"Modern" products, a "modern" home, and a "modern" mother – in her "traditional" domain – ensured a healthy modern child: from *Maclean's*, 1 February 1928.

Even the makers of malted milk employed the military imagery that was commonly used to describe the "battle" to save the "infant soldier": from *Maclean's*, 15 July 1937.

Are two pairs of hands enough?

Parke-Davis, a pharmaceutical company, ran full-page ads urging parents to keep up regular medical supervision for their children: from *Maclean's*, 15 September 1937.

child safely past the hazards that confront her. A third parent should be added to the family circle ... the doctor. He, too, should have hold of her little hand, guiding her along the road of health that is every child's right."[10] Such advertisements were clearly meant to touch a sensitive chord in parental hearts, and to convey the message that childrearing was fraught with hidden terrors that only the medical experts could exorcise. Parents, and especially mothers, might have to surrender some of their own authority and autonomy in order to embrace that of the better-qualified "third parent," but this was assuredly a small price to pay for the benefit of their child.

On the most obvious level, these advertisements publicized the child welfare campaign's goals and promoted the worthy ends of preventive medicine, improved familial and social health, and conscientious parenting. Did readers also realize that they were being sent to the doctor in hopes of increasing sales for the company's products, as the doctor's scientific image became more and more a promotional tool for any number of the increasingly desirable modern consumer goods? More important is the fact that advertising not only reflected the period's socio-cultural currents, but contributed in no small way to their assimilation by the public. The childrearing information produced by the new experts reflected an ideology in the making. The advertisements that were aimed at "modern parents" helped to create that ideology at a time when consumerism was hitting new strides in mass culture.[11]

The impression that mothers were yielding to modern childrearing methods was not restricted only to those in the front ranks of the campaign. Isobel Ecclestone Mackay, writing for the *Canadian Magazine* in 1918, wryly noted the effects on parents of the "special articles, pathetic stories, plays upon the stage and lectures upon the platform" that comprised the subtle but penetrating process of public education. The modern mother was becoming increasingly "self-conscious," both in her personal view of what motherhood entailed and in how best to go about the complex task of mothering. From the very beginning of the educational campaign, the line was carefully drawn between modern scientific motherhood and old-fashioned, traditionalist "motherly ignorance":

Appalling the ignorance of that olden time! It used to be that mothers did not know a thing about babies except what they learned incidentally from bringing up eight or ten of them. These women had never read a book in their lives on "Care and Management of Children," "What To Do Before Baby Comes," on "How Can I Make My Child a Personality," on "Baby's Diet for the First Three Months" ... When Baby cried, mother went and picked it up to see what was wrong with it. If she couldn't find out, she sent for grandma, who probably knew. If grandma failed, she sent for the family doctor. The family doctor always said he knew, whether he did nor not. In time, Baby stopped crying. It sounds incredibly simple. But slack, terribly slack.[12]

In a clearly tongue-in-cheek manner, the writer pointed out a crucial change in the perceptions of motherhood resulting from the emergence of the experts and the growing trend toward maternal education. Developments that had been unfolding gradually since the turn of the century had accelerated perceptibly by the war's end. Motherhood training was taking mothers further and further away from time-honoured, usually harmless but always "terribly slack" methods toward stringently taught and applied scientific techniques.

The writer used exaggeration for literary effect in her satire of the new breed of mothers, babies, and experts alike. She was amused by various elements of the modern childrearing regimen, but her comments on the new-found talents of contemporary mothers in such areas as "distinguishing between cries" could have been lifted directly from any serious source of advice in this period: "The modern mother knows that baby's howls are really comparatively few in kind, definite in degree and easily classifiable ... It is her duty to study these cries, to distinguish between them, and to act as advised on page 128, paragraph 14."[13] If she exaggerated the extent of change, she had a definite sense that change was occurring. These new ideas about motherhood training were beginning to make themselves felt, at least within the book-reading, lecture-attending educated middle class. And it was precisely these mothers that the medical profession hoped would lead those most in need to enlightenment.

While expressing a certain awed admiration for such careful, cautious, well-read and well-schooled modern mothers, Mackay was not altogether convinced that the new methods were truly superior, nor that the modern child and the modern mother stood to benefit greatly from their adoption. She warned that, in the sphere of childrearing, "in spite of all our enlightenment and all the earnestness with which we attack the subject," even careful adherence to all the rules would not necessarily result in a "model" child.[14] Childrearing under any name was unpredictable, and the way a child "turned out" was contingent upon many factors in addition to the book or system used by its parents.

Other observers revealed a similar skepticism about modern parenting as the campaign intensified.[15] Focusing on the habit-training aspects of scientific childrearing, "An Average Mother" contended that "psychology does not always work." This particular mother was obviously well-versed in the current advice literature. From her vantage point as one who had read, absorbed, and apparently tried to apply the precepts, she was able to point readily to the "fly in the ointment." While mothers were expected to control both themselves and their children at all times and in all circumstances, the children could not always be counted upon to respond according to the advisers' dictates: "According to the books, the average mother is a most undesirable creature ... she must never lose her temper, never demand blind obedience ... her child must never be snubbed or repressed, and ... on no account must she use the word 'don't'. In short, she is to be an angel from heaven, while her child gets less like one everyday ... A psychologist bringing up a child in theory is not a weary mother trying to be housemaid, cook, nurse and psychologist rolled into one and expected to be her husband's ray of sunshine in the evening."[16] This mother was commenting on a point that is immediately evident in any reading of the period's advice literature. Maternal responsibilities were overwhelming and ever on the increase. If modern technology promised women some respite from servitude to kitchen and household, new childrearing duties had filled those precious moments with increasing numbers of, and certainly more emotionally taxing, obligations. Just as socio-economic changes were opening up new possibilities for women, experts in medicine and psychology were modernizing motherhood in a way that actually harkened back to the Victorian concept of "angel in the home," even if the modern angel had electrically powered wings.

The ideas may have been soundly based in logic and scientific knowledge of child development, but their consistent application required a superhuman effort from women who were already overworked. It may be expected that, while such ideas were read, understood, and even accepted in principle, they were frequently abandoned in everyday moments of stress.[17] What the medical and psychological advisers overlooked in their single-minded obsession with creating the "little machine," was that both mothers and their children are human. Unlike machines, they possess human whims, flaws, and foibles. This "average mother" was trying neither to prove the experts wrong nor to exonerate mothers of her kind, "only, when she fails to make psychology work, give her a little sympathy, for it is one thing to bring up a child on paper, and quite another to bring him up in reality."[18]

This maternal reaction against the "lofty ideals" of the childrearing experts was echoed in the observations of Enid Griffis, a regular contributor to the *National Home Monthly*. Unlike the "average mother," Griffis was speaking from the more detached point of view of the journalist, but her sentiments were similar:

It is enough to wring tears from the eyes of the tender-hearted to observe, through a casual perusal of columns devoted to the rearing of children, the thousands of harassed mothers who are daily being bullied into nervous breakdowns and early graves by babies of four years and under ... Babies are notorious bullies. Before they are out of their swaddling clothes the majority of them have acquired an accurate estimate of their parents' disciplinary powers, and have developed a species of low cunning with which their emotionally involved elders are ill-equipped to cope. The parent who fails to grasp this fact and to meet the infant on its own ground is, to use a common expression, licked before she starts.[19]

Leaving aside the humour, this view of the baby's potential for trickery was not unlike that of the advisers themselves. The difference lies in the fact that Griffis attributed this "species of low cunning" to the child's innate ability to assess its mother's likely responses, giving it the upper hand in the relationship. Experts argued that children simply responded to stimuli provided by their parents, and were thereby conditioned to act according to these cues. The mainstay of their system was the parental upper hand. Like Mackay and the "Average Mother," this commentator understood that the theory was somewhat simplistic within the context of the regular give-and-take of mother/child relationships. If mothers took to analysing all childrearing situations according to the books, they might miss the point that children are frequently capable of manipulating a situation and their parents to their own liking.

As Griffis defined the crux of the problem, the new childrearing system, while "excellent" in principle, was simply "much too new:" "Nobody knows yet whether it actually works or for how long." In very short order, Canadian parents were expected to do away precipitously with traditional modes of childrearing, as well as ignoring the old reliable sources of advice. They were asked, even commanded, to accept the notion that "the future is now." Customary patterns of family living were to be eradicated in favour of the new. At the same time, if ideas, attitudes, approaches, and methods were to be revolutionized – if the family were to change radically from within – it was still to maintain the form, appearance, and function of the traditional family. The mother was in charge of the home, the father was the breadwinner, the children were dutiful. It is not surprising that intelligent and informed Canadians were confused by what was being asked of "modern" parents, regardless of the consistency of the advice and its sources.

Parents are initially exposed to parenting skills through the example of their own parents and the nature of their own upbringing. Exposure to childrearing information, whether actively sought to meet a particular need or ingested as a contemporary fad, may produce increments in parental knowledge and changes in parental behaviour. Over time it may produce change in cultural patterns, but the process is slow and evolutionary, and involves reshaping and resistance as well as acceptance and adaptation. While the experts urged a revolution in childrearing, this cultural cataclysm was unlikely to take place with the sort of urgency that would satisfy them. The ideas were "simply too new." The entire blueprint for the production of the ideal human being had not yet been designed.[20] Exposure to the new system, public interest in scientific childrearing, and even the establishment of the necessary mechanisms for providing expert supervision, were not in themselves sufficient to bring about the "radical change" that the campaigners desired and believed they were witnessing.

Mothers needed time to assimilate the new ideas, to become comfortable with them, to "try out" these modern precepts on their children, to discuss them within their particular social circles, and to discover what other parents were doing. Undoubtedly, changes were taking place. However, these were very subtle alterations in childrearing patterns that pointed to a perceptible, but nonetheless slow, "enlightenment" rather than to the desired revolution. The professionals also failed to recognize that mothers could accept the principle of child management without swallowing the entire text. After some consideration and perhaps experimentation, mothers could adopt the principles that they found appealing and applicable, discard the rest, and retain the traditional concepts that they found effective.[21]

Some critics believed that the changes sought by men of science in the parent/child relationship undermined parental authority and encouraged disrespect. This obsessive child-centredness, with its basis in scientific theory, was fraying the old familial bonds of deference and mutual consideration:

In China, where everything is opposite, the children bow to their parents and worship their ancestors. In Canada, many parents bow to their children, whose general opinion of their ancestors is that they must have been a pretty poor lot. We make an awful fuss over our offspring. Scientists and pseudo-scientists propound academic hypotheses concerning child psychology for the bewilderment of young parents. Clergymen and educators, publicists, statesmen and the overlords of Hollywood are all of a dither about the Younger Generation; and the Younger Generation grows cocky and fat with ego, because of the spectacular attention forced upon it ... There is so much instruction, it is so vehement and so diverse that the job of bringing up a family, which seemed simple enough in the old days, has become a problem involved with theories and weighed down with suppositions.[22]

Commentators in popular magazines occasionally registered their grievances against modern experts and their methods, but these magazines, on the whole, promoted them vigorously through their features, advice columns and advertisements. Judging by the attention given to professional expertise, the need for medical supervision, and the importance of maternal education, mass-circulation magazines oriented to women and family interests were active agents for new childrearing ideals.

The labour press reveals a certain sharing of these ideals, as well as a skepticism shaped by particular class concerns. The *Canadian Congress Journal*, the official organ of the Trades and Labour Congress and one of the rare labour publications that discussed contemporary childrearing concerns in any detail, hints at a more pervasive working-class disenchantment with the scientific, manual-obsessed regimen, and especially with its focus on conformity. "Follow the baby, not the book, and you will save yourself much misery," argued an anonymous mother's adviser in 1927:

According to the books, or most of them, all babies are moulded to one pattern, all can be treated alike, all can be trained alike. And in your heart you know all the time, by the vagaries of your own small family, that it isn't true. You know very well, though the book never says so, that every baby born is different, and that you can never treat two of them alike ... And what rubbish it all is! Because John allowed himself to be brought up to pattern, must Dickie conform too? Probably he won't ... Dear little mothers, do be sensible! By all means, try to have the "book baby," but when you find your baby just won't be a book baby, then study his individuality because a happy baby is a healthy one.[23]

The journal's advisers consistently encouraged mothers to rely more on maternal instinct than on strict scientific precepts, precisely what the ideologues of modern childrearing were earnestly battling. Although they supported the campaign's general aims, working-class advisers stressed a more relaxed attitude towards childrearing. They tended to see parental response to the individual child's needs as the touchstone of effective parenting.

Sociological surveys of the period uncovered systematic class differences in childrearing, suggesting that middle-class parents tended to be more exacting in their expectations of their children, while those of the working class were somewhat more inclined to be lenient.[24] The working-class adviser was more likely to argue that "keeping baby contented often requires sympathy and imagination as well as a regular routine." In a tale "About Barbara's Baby" that was probably entirely fictional but intended both to satirize modern methods and to urge mothers to respond affectionately to their children, the advice exemplifies these class differences in childrearing. Barbara was a young, educated, well-informed, middle-class woman pledged to raising her infant son "by the book." Her baby was having a particularly fretful day, but she was determined to adhere to the rules and let him "cry it out" in his crib. Salvation arrived for both of them in the form of the cleaning woman, Mrs Smith. The latter had five children and "didn't hold with new-fangled notions." Wisely detecting "a little quiver of distress" in Barbara's voice, she convinced the young mother that her baby craved attention and amusement, and that these were as important to his well-being as were regulation and discipline:

Barbara thought a good deal over what Mrs Smith had said. Of course babies had to be trained properly – it was all wrong to spoil them – and a certain amount of crying was quite good for them, everyone said so. But wasn't it possible to make modern methods your masters instead of your servants? So Barbara came to the conclusion we all come to when we have real live babies and not text-book models to deal with: that firmness must be tempered with a great deal of imagination and sympathy. Babies have feelings that should be respected; and a little occasional variation from one's set programme doesn't mean (as mothers often fear) that we shall have to repeat that variation every day afterwards.[25]

The sensible and practical Mrs Smith, champion of the heart and voice of untutored reason, urged the young mother to enjoy her baby instead of just managing it. If mothers paid attention to their children only when they were being troublesome, "stands to reason they get the idea they'll have to give trouble before anyone'll notice they're still alive." In a curious, if unintentional, twist on the nature metaphor much beloved by the experts, Mrs Smith demonstrated the homey wisdom that sustained her childrearing views: "Treat a baby like a vegetable, I always say, and don't be surprised if it grows up with no more brains than a mashed potato!"[26]

There was a real sense in the popular press that parenthood and childhood were in transition.[27] Modern parenting and a thoroughly modern childhood, despite the claims and longings of its advocates, medical and otherwise, had not yet truly arrived. They were well on their way, however. For some observers, the changes were not altogether positive, even from the child's point of view. There was a feeling that childhood had already changed to such an extent that "most children nowadays ... never are children at all."[28] They passed their childhood in rigorous training for greater things than simple play would allow. They seemed to be forfeiting their innocence and freedom to the expectations and aims of those who held social power. Just as motherhood was being "professionalized" according to the experts' regulations, so childhood was becoming an intensely specialized and managed event.

No other children in Ontario were raised as meticulously "by the book" as were the Dionne quintuplets. Kept in their own special "Quintland" under the constant surveillance of doctors, nurses, psychologists, and countless tourists, the quints' early childhood was very much of the idealized "little machine" variety. When they were ultimately returned to their parents, the latter were unable, and more importantly, unwilling to modify their childrearing values and objectives, which were rooted in rural French Canadian and Catholic tradition. The result was the quints' tragic alienation from their parents, the emotional difficulties they encountered as adults, and the sorrow and public humiliation of the elder Dionnes. The pitiable destiny of the Dionne sisters indicates how "scientific motherhood," in this case taken to extremes thankfully beyond the possibilities of most parents, could end in the objectification of children themselves.[29]

The new managers, intent as they were on performing unprecedented feats of human engineering, overlooked one important detail. Even if their methods could ever succeed in creating "little machines" of babies, at best a dubious proposition, it was quite unlikely that mothers would ever become the automatons they needed to be to raise those little machines. The advisers' persistent inability to recognize the factor of human individuality and its effects on parent/child interaction only served to increase the burden of stress in a relationship that was already innately stressful. Ironically, individualism pointed the way to both salvation and downfall.

While the childrearing experts demanded of parents an immediate and complete acceptance of their regimen, parents typically change their behaviour through a process of accommodation.[30] As the visiting nurses observed repeatedly in their forays to poorer districts, the most effective approach was a gradual one. It was essential to teach mothers the fundamentals of healthy living first – cleanliness, careful preparation of food and milk, nutritional requirements, the importance of fresh air – and to train them in those aspects of child care that they were most likely and most able to carry out. For poor parents, the finer points of personality training did not constitute a vital lesson. What use were instructions on handling food fussiness or toy fetishes to people whose choices were severely restricted by poverty? Their priorities were keeping their children alive and reasonably free of physical suffering, which far surpassed the importance of turning them into model citizens.

In fact, class consciousness made some labour commentators particularly resistant to the notion that their children should be raised to meet the needs of an exploitative system and its prime beneficiaries. At one extreme of hopelessness was a writer who argued that, since this was "a day of sham and an age of graft," it would "in millions of cases be more merciful to sacrifice childhood to the old Moloch than to doom it to the horrors of our modern industrial life."[31] Although few went this far, most labour writers on issues of health and child welfare agreed that the systemic inequalities of industrial capitalism had to be confronted before a healthy existence could be ensured for all.

Moreover, the damage and wastage would not be vanquished by the plans and programs of the dominant class, designed to reinforce the system and their own power, but by worker solidarity and action that would address health problems from their material basis. A poem published in the *Industrial Banner* in 1920, tellingly entitled "Denied a Chance," bore witness to the superficiality of these programs from the point of view of those they were supposed to serve. The editor commented that the writer drew from personal experience, and that "the verses speak for themselves and point out the inhuman results of money-god worship." The poem tells the story of a widowed mother standing watch over her dying child. The mother explains how she had to work and leave her child in another's care, how her husband's death had deprived them of the few material comforts they had enjoyed, and how the deprivation had affected the health, and was now claiming the life, of her only child. The poet concludes, with justified bitterness and cynicism:

They build their institutions to have the child well born,
Their clinics and their welfare leagues galore;

Yet they seem to miss the multitude and seem to treat with scorn
The great enduring efforts of the poor ...
This mother's burning statement that her child had not a chance
Shows us that there is something very wrong
The system needs revising from the church pew to the manse,
And the weak not trampled under by the strong.[32]

That the system needed fundamental revision was always adamantly denied by the vast majority of the period's social reformers. Yet the inability of the medical campaigners to reach "the multitudes" because of their narrow focus and their evident scorn for the poor "ignorant" mothers whom they blamed instead, meant that the sacrifice of the weak was perpetuated.[33]

Jean Farrant, writing in the *Canadian Trade Unionist* in 1932, considered that "although we of the working class are very fully occupied with the daily struggle to live, there is another ever present worry for those of us who are parents. What will become of our children?" With the system struggling under the weight of the Depression, even the limited options of previous years were obliterated. Yet under "a properly organized social system," children "with bodies ruined by lack of food and attention" would not exist. Parents would welcome their children, not dread additional mouths to feed. Life itself was being ruthlessly wasted, "all in the sacred cause of Profit." Farrant urged that the worker "look at the deaths which are preventable and yet go on, and ask yourself is it worth wearing out the only life you have in bolstering up a thoroughly rotten system, which exists for the benefit of the few?" Only by realizing their own power and standing together could workers "forever abolish the spectre of dread which now haunts every working-class mother."[34]

Canadian historians are uncovering the details about informal working-class support networks, but we still know little about provisions made for the care of the sick.[35] Reports of the "Maple Leaf Auxilliary," composed of the wives of Toronto machinists who belonged to the International Association of Machinists, show that these women went into members' homes "when sickness and distress were dwellers there, and with their comfort and cheer – often of a very tangible nature – left a ray of sunshine behind."[36] The auxilliaries were especially interested in "anything that will better the conditions and pave the way better for children."[37] The Maple Leaf Auxilliary also provided $200 insurance for the cost of a membership fee of $2.00 and $.25 in monthly dues.[38]

In the early twentieth century, a growing number of benevolent schemes were initiated to provide selected medical services to those who could not afford the private fee-for-service practice that doctors insisted upon.[39] Whether established through fraternal and ethnic lodges, the workplace, unions, or auxilliaries, these were never more than a minor annoyance to the medical profession and had little impact on its market strength. Dr Peter Bryce scoffed at the Friendly Societies in Ontario, which in 1917 spent barely one-tenth of their insurance budget of $811,774 to care for 33,468 sick members. According to Bryce, this showed that there was either "little real sickness" or that the insured members went elsewhere for treatment "on the ground that the quality of the services so poorly paid would be about in proportion to their cost."[40] The "friendly societies" may have provided a measure of comfort to their members, but they posed little threat to the free-enterprise health care system. Doctors had no reason to believe that state health insurance would offer a better option for themselves than these benevolent systems, nor did the systems operate as a viable structure upon which to construct a state-run program.[41] The "welfare capitalist" schemes introduced at the workplace in the early twentieth century often included some measure of medical care, but this provision was extended only to the employee and not to his or her family.[42]

Attempts at consumer activism were not entirely pre-empted by the medical profession's state-supported hold on remuneration for service. As previous chapters have shown, delegations of farm, labour, and women's groups repeatedly applied political pressure in attempts to motivate state action on maternal and child welfare concerns. A 1920 Industrial Banner editorial, "The Value of Motherhood," voiced support for legislative measures such as those enacted in England and France to make maternal and child welfare universal rights. Maternity benefits were singled out as a clear indication of "the need for the public protection of motherhood and babyhood on a basis which would make proper care available to every mother."[43] The Canadian Trade Unionist also called for increased public health expenditure and committed local, provincial, and dominion leadership in this area.[44]

Women's labour groups were particularly active in lobbying for improvements in health care delivery. In 1932, the Women's Canadian Labour Council passed the following resolution:

Whereas the serious depression in the economic life of the country and the consequent unemployment and reduced incomes have created a health problem unprecedented in the history of the country ... and whereas much suffering and death have been caused under the present system due to delayed treatment, and delayed hospital services on account of high fees and the inability of the patient to pay, especially in maternity cases and surgical operations; be it therefore resolved that we, the Women's Canadian Labour Council ... hereby express our full support of the principle and practice of state medicine.[45]

The United Women's Educational Federation of Ontario and the United Farm Women passed similar resolutions and sent delegations to petition municipal and provincial governments to "get measures through in the interests of women and children."[46] Efforts on the part of these groups failed to bring about either specific changes in the child welfare campaign's direction and focus, or to achieve the greater goals of universal access to health care and redistributive legislation. But their failure does not negate the fact that they actively pursued the kind of state intervention in health and welfare matters that best addressed their needs. The unresponsiveness of the state demonstrates the extent of its support for the medical profession, as well as the strength of medical dominance in state circles.

Health care is fundamentally an issue of citizenship. Just as is the case for access to better housing, education, and other welfare benefits, the rights to health are the outcome of class organization, political action, and ultimately, democratic representation. Both labour and women's groups organized and applied political pressure for better health care as for so many other issues relevant to them. Yet the particular interests of these groups were not sufficiently represented in the political process to make a real difference, especially by comparison to those of the medical profession.

Workers and farmers also noted the hypocrisy of medical professionals and their middle-class supporters who employed humanitarian arguments and displays of moral superiority to further their cause without considering the repercussions for those whom they professed to help. Often the very help proffered was not only unproductive, but counterproductive. In 1931, the National Labour Council made formal protest to the Board of Governors of the University of Toronto and its paediatric department, against "the unethical and profit-making spirit shown by these two recipients of public funds in granting an exclusive right to manufacture a substance containing Vitamin D for use in the making of bread, to an American bread corporation. And further that we request these bodies to show a true scientific spirit and grant the same right to any Canadian bread manufacturer, without license, fee, or profit charges, in the interest of public health."[47] The resolution passed unanimously. As the *Canadian Trade Unionist* argued, this nutritional supplement should not be "the property of one concern – and that a foreign one."

Its use should be freely available to any baker, "in order that its health-giving properties may be obtained by the poorest of our children in their daily bread." The editors urged protest to the Ontario government from every union and every father, to secure "justice for our master bakers and health for our children."[48] Clearly, organized labour felt its own material interests compromised by this development. But it is equally evident that workers believed that health should not be commodified, and that science should be used in the public interest for collective benefit and not for private profit.

Similarly, a "farmer of Nepean" wrote to Dr Elizabeth Smith Shortt in 1918 to protest the Ottawa Local Council of Women's drive for Sunday milk delivery so that infants could secure fresh milk seven days a week. In several letters to the *Ottawa Citizen*, Shortt had charged local dairymen with immorality, irresponsibility, and lack of concern for the poor, who did not have ice boxes to keep milk from spoiling over summer weekends. As this farmer responded to her accusations: "Bet you are one of the hypocrites like the rest of the swelled heads of your class. I am a dairy man and I want Sunday to rest my horses also. But it is the like of dam fools like you thats advocates these things ... My own brother delivered you enough coal last fall to keep half a dozen families from freezing but you like to ack the hog. Try and not ack the hypocrite in the future."[49] Responses like these indicate that class suspicion did not operate solely from the top down. If medical professionals charged their social inferiors with ignorance and irresponsibility, the lower classes were not taken in by humanitarian pleas, no matter how sincerely phrased. If their own economic interests were threatened, they too fought to maintain control, and revealed in so doing that they understood the element of self-interest behind reformist rhetoric.

Opposition, resistance, and calls for changes in policy and campaign tactics are important elements in understanding the process of socio-cultural adaptation, but they do not preclude the possibility of shared ideals. The subject that seems to have met with the greatest acceptance among middle-class and working-class commentators alike was also that which nurses found most welcomed by mothers – child hygiene. The decline in infant death and disease due to preventable causes suggests that the concepts of better hygiene and increased medical supervision, wherever attainable and affordable, were influencing the attitudes of many parents. Despite middle-class suspicions, dirt and poverty did not necessarily correlate. The results of better health and hygiene habits were more immediate, tangible, and gratifying, because they were evident in decreasing rates of illness in the family. There were many other factors involved, but the point is that improved child hygiene was not mere esoteric theory. It was proving its value in saving babies and keeping them healthy, something every parent could appreciate. The *Canadian Congress Journal* pointed out:

There are still some people who look upon all that is modern in Baby's routine as so much fuss ... They say, "Oh there wasn't all this set-out over managing a baby when we were young; we hadn't the time for it – but I can't see that our babies fared any the worse." Well, the fact remains that in the last twenty five years there has been a great increase in the number of children who come safely through the first year of life. And this increase is most noticeable in the districts where there are infant welfare centres and where the mothers are best able to look after their babies ... It seems as though we shall be rash in giving the name of "fussiness" to any up-to-date teaching which helps to reduce the death rate, once so pitiful amongst tiny children.[50]

If anything approaching a public consensus could be found on the new scientific regimen, it was in this area of physical care. Here, modern means were often acknowledged as superior.[51] All mothers could appreciate that advances in science and medicine were improving their children's prospects for life and health. If poor mothers had far fewer choices with respect to good food, clothing, shelter, and health care, they could at least understand the principles of disease prevention that were embodied in better sanitation, isolation of carriers, and careful handling of food and milk.

That mothers in Ontario were interested in, actively sought, and sincerely appreciated educational efforts is demonstrated by their response to the major sources of childrearing advice. Mothers across the nation were grateful for the services provided by the Council on Child and Family Welfare, the central agency for childrearing information in this period. Judging from the letters to the council that have survived, many mothers felt motivated to express their views on the value of the letter packages that they received during pregnancy and their children's preschool years.[52] The packaging of this information was ingenious. Each letter appeared to be just that, a personal missive addressed to "dear madam," providing clear, simply worded advice and interesting details about every stage of pregnancy and child development. Firmly but kindly, in a "for your own good" manner, the letters set down guidelines for the management of each period. Except for the extent of detail supplied, they could easily have been written by a wise old aunt or experienced friend rather than by a government agency. And the women who received them responded in kind. They did not merely send the appropriate thanks, but gave information on their home conditions, their personal health, and that of their children. Frequently they sent photographs of their children to express their pride in what they believed was a job well done, due to their careful adherence to the valuable advice they had received from the council.

Many of these letters indicate that mothers were indeed attempting to apply the precepts of modern childrearing described in the literature. The information was particularly appreciated in first pregnancies. One young mother was so taken with the advice package lent to her by a friend that she wrote for her own set: "We have a baby boy two months old, and I find myself confronted with many problems which are answered here."[53] Some parents who wrote to the council felt that the provision of this service demonstrated the government's interest in the welfare of their young families. Fathers also appeared grateful for the service, suggesting that they were perhaps more involved in childrearing than the experts believed or even prescribed. One father wrote to thank the council "for your very helpful and informative letters that preceded the baby's coming." He then asked for the postnatal series, commenting that he and his wife would find these "a great asset especially since this is the first baby." He closed by informing the council, "You'll be happy to know that the baby boy is a perfect baby weighing at birth exactly eight pounds and is continuing to gain daily. Your helpful interest has been deeply appreciated."[54]

A letter from Toronto revealed that the information was used as intended, to supplement and complement the advice provided by a private physician: "Their timely information was a great help because it is impossible to receive all the small details from a busy doctor."[55] The fact that mothers were using the advice in this manner must have pleased the campaign's leaders immensely, since their goal in establishing advisory services was to educate mothers without infringing on the physician's livelihood and professional status. A letter from an Oakville mother requesting the postnatal series and describing her own situation must also have been reassuring in this sense: "Our first daughter came five weeks prematurely and was every month to a paediatrician and is quite a healthy little two year old. However, our last baby came only a week too soon and is progressing quite well, so will be taken to a general practitioner every month. I would greatly appreciate the postnatal letters for they might contain some important facts that would be overlooked."[56] The kind of monthly physician supervision she described was beyond most family budgets, especially in regard to the specialist's services. But this mother had obviously learned the lesson well. Although her children were certainly not suffering from lack of medical attention, she still felt herself in need of advice for fear of having "overlooked" something. Her anxiety and eagerness to learn made her just the type of mother sought by the campaigners, since this "ideal mother" would conform to medical regulation.

Especially grateful for this free information service were mothers in isolated rural and outpost communities who simply did not have the same access that city mothers did to infant welfare clinics, visiting nurses, or private physicians. For many of them, cut off from kin and neighbours, the council may have constituted their only source of medical advice: "It means a whole lot to rural mothers to have such a splendid advice and assistance offered to us free and from a reliable source."[57] A mother from Kapuskasing, writing to request the new preschool series in 1935, described happily the impact that she felt the prenatal and postnatal series had made in her life: "I had a very comfortable pregnancy and confinement and was rewarded with twin daughters ... We followed suggestions as to diets, schedules and habits and our babies are healthy and happy."[58] She was obviously delighted to share the credit for her own health and that of her daughters with the council.

For women who placed their faith in the literature and applied its precepts successfully, this "modern" source of information must have fulfilled all the glowing attributes that the campaigners ascribed to it. A young mother could want no more for her children than their health, comfort, and contentment: "I had a fine strong 7½ pound boy on October 21st. This is my first birth without all the trimmings such as hospital, gas, *etc.* Believe me, I shall never ask for an anaesthetic again, even though I might like to have someone to help me next time ... As it was, I was quite alone except for two sleeping children, and was able to wash and dress sonny myself, not to mention lighting the fire, getting hot water, *etc.* Surely God helps those who help themselves."[59] Mothers like these obviously turned to the council's information services to fill the loss of traditional sources of advice – their own mothers, neighbours, and friends. In their circumstances, even modern medical help in the form of physicians and nurses was not always readily available.

Many of these mothers were also recent immigrants, who undoubtedly felt especially alone and in need of assistance and encouragement: "I should be very glad of your advice, this being my first little one and all my people are in the old country – for I want to do all I can for my bairn. Would you suggest anything for me – I have had rather a trying time, my husband having been very sick and as we live on a farm and no help, I am afraid I have been running about so much and do not feel at all well. I cannot afford to go away as things are so hard on the farm and we are trying so hard to keep up our payments."[60] The difficulty of their everyday lives made a lifeline of the council's services. The council took on the role of mother's helper and personal friend for many of them, and gave them a measure of moral support along with scientific advice.

Many of these isolated women were sincere in ascribing to this educational program a contributory role in the success of their own childrearing efforts:

I have received your series of letters for the expectant mother and now I have the twelve postnatal letters. This morning I wish to express my deepest appreciation for the help you have given me. I brought my baby from the hospital to a homestead miles from a telephone and many more miles from a doctor or any dependable person of whom I could ask advice. But your letters overcame my difficulties even before I found them. They have been just like letters from a very dear and trusted friend and I miss looking forward to their arrival. My little Beth is 8 months old now and has never had a sick day and I think her health and sunny disposition is a direct result of your advice.[61]

Similar views were expressed in a letter from Ayr describing the arrival of a daughter "perfect in every way" and telling how these young parents "used to look for [the letters] and both feel now we have our baby that they helped us such a lot."[62] As one rural mother put it succinctly: "there was so much in them that is especially helpful to me as we are on a farm and it is not just as convenient to get advice as in the city."[63]

Whether the advice really played a role as crucial as these mothers believed is not as important as their perception that it did. They willingly placed their faith in the efficacy of the modern knowledge that the medical profession was so intent on imparting. Their faith in itself probably contributed to the success of these methods. Just as the campaign's ideologues contended, this information filled the gaps in their personal understanding of prenatal care and childrearing. Paradoxically, it may have increased pressure on them to perform to new and exacting specifications even while bolstering their confidence as mothers. Some mothers, as doctors hoped, became evangelists for the cause, enthusiastically passing on to other mothers the gospel of modern childrearing: "I know of other expectant mothers in this district ... I will tell them how they can be helped through their period of waiting."[64] Similar letters from American women to their Children's Bureau reveal that women of all classes actively sought and followed expert childrearing advice. Inevitably, however, their economic circumstances more than anything else determined the way that they raised their children.[65]

On the whole, the reports of the Ontario government's travelling nurses convey the impression that mothers everywhere were responsive and willing to learn, even the "foreigners" who were feared to be impervious. British immigrants who did not have to face the language problem seemed to feel their exile from family and friends less keenly when the nurses showed interest in their prospects. A young Englishwoman in Lindsay, expecting her first baby, felt anxious and alone until a nurse called to talk to her, provided her with knitting instructions and patterns for a baby outfit, and advised her to consult a physician. On the nurse's return, "the little mother was in much better spirits, having followed all the instructions and was enjoying the best of health, everything pointing to a happy termination of the case."[66]

The true "foreigners," those recently arrived from Southern and Eastern Europe, needed help not so much because of their "aloneness" as because of their perceived ignorance: "Upon visiting an Italian family the youngest child nine months old was found rolling on the floor with a nursing bottle containing a brown mixture which he had been drinking. When questioned as to what it was the mother delightedly replied, "O, tea, everybody drink da tea over here so I thought it must be good for da babby." When its harmful effect upon children was explained to her, she promised that he should have no more of it."[67] In Galt, a visiting nurse taught an Armenian mother the names of everything used in the preparation of her baby's food, the names of kitchen articles, and a few sentences in English. On her second visit, the mother showed her a public school primer she had bought and said "See baby, English nice," her way of requesting an English lesson whenever the nurse called to see the baby. The nurse was reportedly happy to oblige.[68]

These mothers at least appeared willing to learn and amenable to making suggested changes once shown the error of their ways. In other cases, where ignorance and superstition apparently reigned supreme, the nurses were less optimistic about the possibility of enlightening the parents. In Penetang, a nurse was sent by the local doctor to visit an eight-month-old "foreign" baby suffering from pneumonia. She found the child with a bag of chopped raw onions tied to each foot and "a heap on its back and chest." She removed these and set the baby on the table to bathe it, whereupon she was told that this was a "very bad omen," while "the bath itself was unheard of for a sick baby in the winter." After three visits and three baths the baby appeared on the mend. The nurse hoped that the improvement would continue, "Otherwise I fear Dr Nettleton and I may as well leave town."[69]

Although this nurse was horrified to find unscientific health practices still in operation, and explained their persistence by the superstitious ignorance thought peculiar to immigrant parents, traditional remedies derived from cultural custom and folk medicine were common. The women's pages of western farm journals in the early twentieth century reveal that women frequently traded health care advice based on home remedies devised from experimentation or handed down through the generations.[70] Doctors were also aware of the vast catalogue of myths and quasi-truths that persisted despite scientific advances and their own determined efforts. In 1934, for example, Toronto paediatrician Edward Morgan presented a scholarly discussion of several of these "time-honoured beliefs," inherited from "ignorant progenitors," which were nonetheless "so implicitly accepted by a large percentage of the lay population and by a surprisingly large percentage of the medical world that they are almost impossible to eradicate."[71] Even if mothers increasingly adopted new scientific trends in child care, childrearing culture, like the broader culture of which it is a vital part, exhibits strains that are both residual and emergent.[72]

Realizing this, the nurses were ever aware of the importance of a sensitive and wary approach in an area as private and sacrosanct as that of childrearing: "It is felt that the only way to reach the people is to give them something they can understand ... Although there is a great deal of ignorance on child welfare matters, there is a great conservatism and objection to learning anything new – in fact, quite a little open opposition amongst the most ignorant – the very ones we want to reach. So I think the only way to break down the prejudice is to go slowly until the people are more alive to their needs."[73] The nurses believed fervently in the value of modern methods. But they acknowledged that the conversion process was slow, tentative and best handled cautiously and diplomatically. Traditional beliefs and methods could not simply be jettisoned, no matter what the campaign leadership preached.

In spite of the simple gratitude that such instances portray, some mothers harboured justifiable grievances about the campaign's exclusive focus on education. In particular, they resented the limited scope and nature of the state's involvement. Education alone would not benefit families suffering the lashes of poverty. The most evocative testimony is found in the letter to the minister of health from the "worried expectant mother" from Wawbewawa. It is worth quoting again for the starkness with which it shows what it meant to be young, poor, and female in 1930s Ontario, in some respects a world without pity: "If I were strong I would try and face the next [delivery] as brave ... but I fear I have not the strength nor the proper nourishment to enable me to stand it without some aid ... Too many of we poor young mothers are too brave and face too much and that is why it is just taken for granted that we are made for this purpose and so must tough it out the best we can ... Canada should have a better law for the pregnant mother. If we are aided in bringing strong healthy babies into this world we will have a strong healthy nation."[74] Like the campaigners themselves, this woman recognized the indivisibility of child and maternal welfare and their national implications. Her personal experience of poverty, isolation, and state and medical indifference to the plight of pregnant women made her realize that not nearly enough was being done.

As efforts to subsume the Division of Child and Maternal Welfare within the Department of Health commenced in the late 1930s, even the information services were threatened. One northern Ontario woman vented her bitterness at what she termed the government's callous disregard of the nation's mothers and children. Not only was health care in many communities limited and expensive, but now mothers were to be deprived of the major free source of reliable information they had known. She believed that the information was helpful, but stressed that what mothers really needed was affordable and accessible medical services: "Having children should be taken out of the luxury department and put within the reach of every aspiring soul who desires a home." As she saw it, the child welfare campaign was confounding itself because of the discrepancy between its broad-ranging ideals and its grudging measures. The state, in particular, was failing in its obligations:

If you don't mind me suggesting it, a government is a poor blind and horribly ignorant affair that is too busy with the petty details of its today to think of the nation of tomorrow. As a mother of a four month old baby I am actually astounded at the casual "by guess and by damn" method that is used with the future's men ... We have no baby clinic in Sudbury ... We pay $40 to have a baby and then another $5 if we want an examination afterwards ... If you were a bunch of real statesmen and nation-builders rather than a scraggly bunch of cheap politicians you would be thinking of building the nation some backbone for its future.[75]

Again, the argument for greater state involvement in child and maternal welfare was precisely that used by doctors: the nation's future depended on national recognition of the child's value. But this writer, like so many others who voiced dissatisfaction, felt strongly that these ideals could not be attained by current measures, and most assuredly not by the sort of state intervention that the doctors wanted. Echoing Agnes Macphail in her courageous attacks on medical dominance of health care politics, she believed that the federal government's duty lay in asserting its leadership and breaking through that power barrier in the interests of national health and welfare: "Do the doctors boss you or do you boss the doctors? Isn't it possible for you to pass a law saying that every doctor must examine every maternity patient before they are paid by them? You are in a position to allow healthy clever young people to have healthy clever babies and a foundation for a grand new nation. What are you going to do about it?"[76]

The great array of childrearing information which became available in Ontario during the interwar period through publications, clinics, and visiting nurses was relatively accessible to parents. However, it is difficult to ascertain precisely how it was used. The motivating factors that lead a parent to reach out for this information, or to be highly receptive if exposed to it, cannot be readily defined. The individual parent may be ready for information relevant to specific concerns that arise as a result of a particular childrearing problem. That information can produce an increment in knowledge, a change in perspective, or perhaps a shift in general attitude. The ultimate result of this process may be a change in childrearing practices.[77]

Social scientists have discovered that the desire to obtain and utilize this information is unequally distributed within any large group of identifiable parents.[78] Therefore, general statements as to the class status, level of education, ethnic origins, and rural or urban location of those Ontario parents who actively sought or embraced this information must remain speculative. The advisers' own description of their audience is impressionistic and probably serves more as self-justification than as an accurate evaluation of the people they were reaching. The standards and values they prescribed were those generally attributed to the middle class. The paediatricians' manuals and the popular magazines also claimed a largely middle-class readership. The information produced by the various health departments penetrated a wider proportion of working-class and farm families; it was distributed primarily by mail, and through clinics and visiting nurse services created to provide well-baby supervision for those who could not otherwise afford it. However, because of the middle-class outlook conveyed by the literature, the applicability of much of its advice to the working-class family is questionable. The urban slant of the advice also placed limitations on its value to rural and outpost mothers.

It is apparent nonetheless that Ontario parents were interested in improving the health and welfare of their children. However limited the campaigners' efforts, they found appreciation in even the poorest households. But despite the medical profession's high hopes, no sudden revolution in childrearing occurred. As could be expected, most parents accepted those tenets of the new system which they believed to be valuable, and which they were capable of implementing, given their material circumstances, their individual needs and character traits, and those of their children. Those which they found impractical, personally repugnant, or inapplicable to their situation they probably ignored or discarded. There is little reason to believe that mothers, in particular, became slaves to modern methods or modern medicine.

If there was no revolution in the true sense of the word, new trends in childrearing were definitely making themselves felt in Ontario during the interwar period. Even small changes in childrearing behaviour that are introduced slowly over time can lead to a significant alteration in cultural patterns if the changes are accomplished on a widespread basis.[79] The modernization of the parent/child relationship was mediated by the retention of those cultural patterns that parents found personally significant. What is clear is that if mothers of all classes shared common concerns for their children's health and common interest in learning better methods to ensure that health, those most vulnerable according to the doctors' own definition were also the least satisfied with the means undertaken to improve their families' welfare.

CHAPTER NINE

"Despite the Best Efforts": The Campaign's Effects

By 1940, the incremental improvements in the mortality indices served the campaigners as evidence of the positive results of their twenty-year effort. Public health officials in Ottawa and Toronto were generally optimistic about the progress made in maternal and child welfare, which they ascribed to the combined effect of medical advances and public education. The occasional upward jags in mortality rates during the Depression were interpreted as momentary setbacks. Health department reports at both levels made only passing reference to the widespread deprivation of the 1930s. When hard times were mentioned, it was usually in the context of gratitude that they had seemingly made little impact on the health of the people. Confidence was expressed that, on the whole, the efforts put forward by medicine and the state had benefited all Canadians and particularly mothers and children.

The statistical record, at least with respect to mortality, confirms the positive assessments of health officials. The numbers indicate that maternal and neonatal mortality were edging down. Infant mortality in the post-neonatal period was almost half its turn-of-the-century rate in 1940, and the mortality of children under five due to "childhood diseases," especially diphtheria, was declining as well.[1] To judge by the official health reports, it would be difficult to call the campaign anything but an overall success.

However, the problem of reliability presents itself in using these statistical averages as evidence of health improvement. Historians have tended to accept official statistics at face value, and to adopt the belief of their reporters that they represent objective evidence of material reality. As discussed in previous chapters, problems of underreporting, which are especially evident in morbidity statistics where a limited number of diseases are classified reportable at any given time, raise questions about the extent and nature of disease and ill health. Health department administrators often expressed fears that local medical officers were failing to report disease-related deaths, or were reporting them carelessly. Changing classifications of disease and causes of mortality also distort the picture.[2]

In addition, public health officials were inclined to interpret the statistics in very general terms: any downward trend was hailed as unqualified progress and a telling measure of their own success. They emphasized decreasing numbers without paying much attention to the proportion of decrease, nor did they analyse categories where improvement was particularly slow. Public health workers and private practitioners alike accepted that there was an intimate connection between the level of infant mortality and the community's general standard of health.[3] Improvement in infant survival rates meant a rosier health picture for all Canadians. Those concerned about child and maternal welfare took heart at the steady downward trend, and rarely attempted to penetrate the statistical surface. When they did recognize the hesitant decline for particular categories of figures, their attempts to analyse the causes were perfunctory and often amounted to little more than reiteration of the standard medical interpretation: ignorance caused people to make poor health choices, and especially to refuse medical advice and medical assistance. By way of suggestions or recommendations, they typically called for more medical investigation, intensified public education, and greater reliance on recent medical innovations.

In addition to the usual medical logic, public health officials had obvious political motivations for prompting dismissal of any more ominous statistical indications. As employees of governments that were coping with the Depression by means of piecemeal, temporary, emergency, and largely ineffectual measures, it would be indeed surprising if they emphasized the contribution of material deprivation to the deaths of women and children. Because of an unsurpassed crisis that seriously undermined both production and reproduction, state recalcitrance about welfare policy, and the financial exigencies that plagued provincial and municipal governments, they were compelled to interpret public health and welfare in the most favourable light.[4]

Finally, the manner in which they compiled statistics made it as difficult for health officials then as it does for historians now to grasp fully the class and regional differences in morbidity and mortality rates. The statistics are aggregates that were not broken down by class, occupation, or region, nor do they distinguish the employed from the unemployed. For all these reasons, then, the numbers cannot be taken as their reporters themselves understood them. We must look to flesh out these sweeping health department reports by re-examining them in light of the economic realities of the period, its medical knowledge, more particularistic medical studies, and regional health surveys. While the end result of such an exercise will remain impressionistic, it will at least assist us toward a more balanced assessment of the campaign's impact on the health and welfare of Ontario mothers and children.

In 1942, the federal health department issued its most detailed statistical survey to that point on the extent and nature of maternal, infant, and neonatal mortality in Canada. The report covered the years from 1926, when national statistics first became available, to 1940.[5] From a peak of 5.8 per 1,000 live births in 1930, the maternal mortality rate a decade later was 4.0 per 1,000, the lowest it had ever been in Canada. Dr Ernest Couture, chief of the federal Division of Maternal and Child Hygiene, cited the reasons for this improvement: the educational campaign carried on by child welfare agencies, the multiplication of prenatal services, better hospital facilities, the increase in hospital births, and better obstetrical techniques. Since these were the campaign's key objectives, their apparent realization signalled a major victory for child and maternal welfare.

Couture recognized that the historical figure for 1940 still did not signify attainment of the ultimate goal of reducing maternal mortality to "the irreducible minimum." Moreover, the predominant causes of death remained all too familiar: 72.6 per cent of maternal deaths, or 702 of 967, were still attributable to puerperal sepsis, toxaemia, and haemorrhage. Puerperal sepsis was again the foremost cause of maternal death in 1940, with a mortality rate of 11.5 per 1,000 live births. Couture was heartened by evidence that the use of sulphonamides since 1936 was gradually reducing its incidence. But he made no mention of the fact that gains in this category seemed more readily explained by increasing therapeutic efficacy than by progress in eliminating its cause. The persistence of puerperal sepsis calls into question Couture's optimistic judgments about improved obstetrical techniques and the superiority of hospital delivery, while simultaneously suggesting that many mothers continued to give birth in conditions that were not conducive to good health, and with less than adequate assistance.

After an encouraging drop in the toxaemia rate in 1932, there was a steady rise until the end of 1936. Couture decided that "this reaction might bear out the contention that poor nutrition or a general lack of prenatal care during the economic crisis" were responsible. This was as much as he would comment on the Depression's

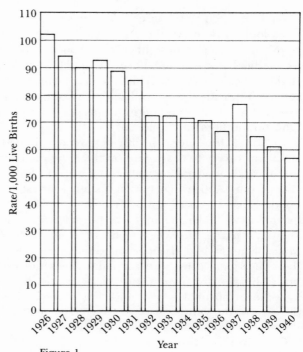

Figure 1
Infant Mortality in Canada, 1926–40
Source: Federal Division of Maternal and Child Hygiene, *A Study on Maternal, Neonatal and Infant Mortality* (Ottawa 1942)

effects for maternal health and mortality. Since the rise in toxaemia deaths coincided with the worst years of the Depression, his tentative references to poor nutrition and lack of medical care carry much more weight than he was willing to ascribe to them. Couture explained the subsequent reduction in such deaths after 1937 in terms of expanded state efforts: he surmised that "perhaps this is the result of better organized relief in necessitous cases, and the establishment of a greater number and variety of services." The state's efforts, however, were neither improved nor expanded. The painfully slow rise in employment during these years between 1936 and the Second World War was probably a more important causative factor, in that it brought some families at least a few steps out of the abyss.[6] In 1940, deaths from toxaemias of pregnancy numbered 234 or 23.9 per cent of total maternal deaths.

There had been only minimal improvement since 1931 in maternal mortality from haemorrhage, the third major cause of death. Public health investigators were able to find "little satisfactory explanation" for the sudden advance in the rates for specific years. A pregnancy survey conducted in Manitoba by the federal division brought out the fact that transfusions were underused, and recommended that blood banks be established especially for emergency maternity cases.[7] Couture admitted again that nutrition surveys showed how the incidence of haemorrhage could be reduced through adequate diet during the prenatal period, suggesting that the "satisfactory explanation" for the upward jags in the haemorrhage rate was not as elusive as "investigators" contended. In 1940, maternal deaths from haemorrhage numbered 138 or 14.1 per cent of all such deaths.[8]

The federal study revealed the same general downward trend in infant mortality rates. Since 1926, infant mortality had declined sharply, dropping by 45.1 per cent and signifying 11,100 infant lives saved. With the exception of 1937, the improvement was constant. Diarrhaea and enteritis deaths, the original focus of attack, had been cut by more than one-third in the decade since 1930.[9] The rates for congenital debility, long a source of anxiety about racial degeneration, had also improved steadily. The chief cause of infant deaths remained prematurity: in 1940, 3,194 babies born before full term were lost. Incubator services for care at home and transportation to hospital had proven their worth in saving some babies born prematurely at home, but it appeared to doctors that hospitalization with its attendant medical technology was the only completely reliable solution.

Neonatal mortality, which had first inspired interest in maternal welfare in the 1920s, was still a serious concern. In 1940, of the total deaths that occurred in the first year of life, 52.6 per cent were in the first month. A staggering 74.5 per cent of infants died during the first week, which accounted for 39.2 per cent of the total infant deaths during the first year.[10] British studies had recently revealed that maternal malnutrition was the most important factor in causing stillbirths and neonatal mortality.[11] Couture offered no further comment on this issue.

Ontario's director, Dr J.T. Phair, took a more realistic view of the campaign's provincial results for the interwar period. Phair conceded that failure on the part of the public to appreciate the significance of pregnancy and childbirth was not the major cause of high maternal mortality rates. Despite "the best efforts of the department and other agencies," he found little to celebrate in the record for the years 1924 to 1937. Ontario's maternal mortality rate for 1924 was 5.8; in 1937 it was 5.2.[12] The rate for puerperal sepsis in 1938 was 18.1, by comparison to the average of 20.7 between 1933 and 1937. Like Couture, Phair believed that this decline was indicative of "the

efficacy as well as the more general use of the newer chemotherapy."
The mortality rate for the toxaemias of pregnancy had also changed
little, from 24.2 (1933–37) to 21.5 in 1938.[13] Haemorrhage deaths,
meanwhile, had declined at a similar rate, from 11.4 to 8.8. As early
as 1931, the federal Division had suggested that "perhaps maternal
mortality is now a more reliable index to the health and welfare of a
nation than infant mortality."[14] If this was the case, it is difficult to
support an optimistic assessment of health in this period.

As was true nationally, Ontario's infant mortality figures were much
more encouraging. At the beginning of the campaign, the figure of
50 per 1,000 was considered "an approach to the irreducible minimum." The rate for 1938 was 49.6, by comparison to 75.8 in 1924.[15]
Diarrhaea and enteritis now ranked fourth, behind pneumonia, as
causes of death: the combined categories of respiratory and intestinal
disease accounted for 20 per cent of total deaths under one year in
1938. Phair commented that the leading causes of infant death were
taking on "new significance" as the emphasis shifted from infectious,
intestinal, and respiratory diseases to prematurity and birth injury.
The problem of conserving infant lives had become a problem of
ensuring the delivery of a healthy, full-term foetus: "the hazards of
the postnatal period are now less than those associated with intrauterine stay and the dangers of delivery." In contrast to the general
decline in infant deaths, deaths from prematurity were actually
rising. In 1925, prematurity was behind 26.4 per cent of infant
deaths; in 1939, the rate was 31.5. Deaths from birth injury almost
doubled, rising from 4.9 to 8.7 per cent, again casting doubt on the
perceived improvements in obstetrical and hospital technique.

Neither Couture nor Phair gave much thought to the slowing of
the decline during the 1930s. Nationally, between 1926 and 1932,
infant mortality fell from 101 to 73 per 1,000 live births, a drop of
about 38 per cent. The 1933 rate, however, was still 73. Until 1936,
the rate declined by only 1 each year, rising to a high of 76 in 1937,
and then dropping more rapidly to 61 in 1939. For the years 1933
to 1939 the rate of decline was roughly 16 per cent. The overall
picture of neonatal mortality in Canada shows a similar pattern of
faltering decline. The rate dropped from 48 in 1926 to 35 in 1932,
a reduction of 27 per cent. Between 1932 and 1938, it remained
virtually static in the mid-30s. Stillbirths in 1926 showed a rate of
3.0, rising slightly in 1930 to 3.1 and remaining between 2.8 and 3
throughout the Depression; only in 1939 did these figures edge
downward to 2.7 per 1,000 live births.[16]

The provincial story shows maternal mortality during the Depression dropping 19 per cent from a high of 6.2 in 1930 to a low of

5.0 in 1938. But most of that decline took place after 1937; the rate never fluctuated by more than a few percentage points yearly during the first seven years of the decade. The same was true of infant mortality in Ontario: infant mortality rates for 1934 and 1935 were roughly the same, in the mid-50 range, as they were for 1936 and 1937.[17] Although a decline was definitely taking place, its overall rate and the narrowness of fluctuations in yearly rates shows that, much as Charles Webster argues for Great Britain in this period, "the 1930s emerge as a drag in the downward trend."[18]

Narrowing the focus to a smaller area of the province permits a closer look at the relationship between health and poverty and the Depression's impact on the well-being of certain sectors of the population. The reports of the Eastern Ontario Health Unit that was established in 1935 to serve the counties of Stormont, Glengarry, Prescott, and Russell, reveal much the same medical and political considerations as those of the provincial division. The unit's director, a public health doctor, certainly shared his superiors' outlook on public ignorance, but gave enough attention to the area's economic conditions to allow an impression of their impact on health.

The area's total population in 1935 was about 93,200, of which 30 per cent was urban. It had two centres of industrial activity that year: Cornwall, the largest town in the area with 12,000 residents (in Stormont county in the south), and Hawkesbury (in Prescott county on the Ottawa River). Pre-Depression conditions in Hawkesbury were already so bad that they drew continual comment from the nurses visiting there.[19] In these two towns, the pulp and paper industry was the chief employer. Cornwall had a more diversified industrial economy, with a large artificial silk manufacturing plant, a textile mill and a chemical works. Before the Depression, there were active woodworking plants in Alexandria (Glengarry) and Rockland (Russell), each employing 300 to 400 workers. These plants were wiped out early in the 1930s, and the families affected had since been on relief.[20]

Timber and dairying predominated in the region. In the area's centre (a strip about fifteen miles wide that cut across the northern counties of Prescott and Russell in particular) the poor quality of the soil made grazing and the cultivation of fodder crops so difficult that, "at the best of times," farming was "a continual struggle for a bare subsistence." The northern and southern sections had better land and were taken up by mixed farming, but again dairying predominated. In 1935, Cornwall was the sole "bright spot" in the region's economy. By the mid-1930s, markets for dairy products and other farm produce had been curtailed, taxes were unpaid, and mounting relief costs had brought many municipalities to bankruptcy, or perilously close. The director commented that, with the exception of Cornwall, living conditions in the area had been "very difficult" since the start of the Depression, although many of the area's workers and farmers had not known markedly better conditions even during more prosperous times. For families in these circumstances, medical care was frequently delayed until too late: "the family not on relief but too poor to pay their physician suffers severely in this respect and there is urgent need for some type of medical service for this group."[21]

The area's health statistics, according to the unit's director, barely revealed the true extent of morbidity and mortality because only a few local registrars complied with his request for complete records of births and deaths. Maternal mortality was given only passing mention in his reports, probably due to this fact and also because, as he acknowledged, very few women saw doctors during their pregnancy or even at confinement. The visiting nurses (two to a county) managed to reach only about 5 per cent of all expectant mothers in the entire area.[22] The statistics are obviously problematic, even from the point of view of their reporter. The glimpse they allow of the condition of these Ontario families, however shadowy, lends credence to the theory of a "submerged mass of ill health" that morbidity and mortality figures alone cannot uncover.[23]

In January 1935, the health unit reported a higher tuberculosis death rate in the four counties served than in any other comparably sized sector of the population in the province.[24] Next to the so-called "disease of the working man," the problem of infant mortality in the four counties was "of chief importance from a public health standpoint." One of the principal reasons for the unit's creation was its very high infant mortality rate. In 1925, the area's overall rate was 104 per 1,000 live births, by comparison to the provincial rate of 78.9. In 1931, it was still 99; by 1934, when the provincial rate was 56.6, it had risen again to 103, and thereafter began to decline slowly. Looking more closely at the individual counties, we see that the two poorest, Prescott and Russell, had the area's highest rates in 1925 at 112 and 102 respectively. Infant mortality actually rose steadily in these counties between 1931 and 1935: in both, the 1934 rate (119 and 107) was higher than that of 1925 (see Figure 2). No explanation for the regional differentials was given in the director's report, except for a comment that the best rate of decline was in Glengarry county, where, at the time of the report, three monthly child health conferences had been operating for a year and a half. Russell had two child welfare clinics and Prescott had one, both of which had opened a

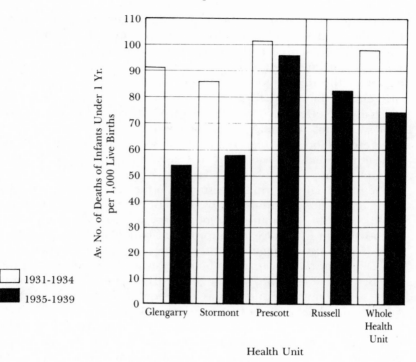

Figure 2
Effect of Child Welfare Work of Health Unit on
Infant Mortality Rates
Source: PAO, RG 10, 30-A-1, Box 1, File 17, "Report on the
Effect of the Child Welfare Work of the Eastern Ontario
Health Unit," 1939

few months prior to this report. The only death among all clinic
attendants was accidental.

The reduction in the area's infant mortality rate between 1935 and
1939 – to 74 per 1,000 from 98 per 1,000 in the 1931–34 years –
was celebrated by the unit's public health workers. Glengarry's figure
was almost halved: it fell from an average of 91 to 55, indicating a
39.5 per cent rate of decline. Stormont's rate also declined significantly, from 88 to 58, or 34 per cent. The poorer counties saw
decreases as well: Russell's infant mortality dropped from 110 to 82,
while in Prescott, the rate moved down much more slowly from 102
to about 96. The rate of decline in Russell was 25 per cent by
comparison to a reduction of only 6 per cent in Prescott.

This cursory analysis of the area's infant mortality is meant to bring into sharper relief some of the aspects of health and health care that are obscured by the provincial and national statistics and their official interpretation. Most apparent, although unacknowledged in the unit's reports, are the regional and socio-economic differentials that influence general health and mortality patterns, especially the effects of unemployment. With few exceptions, significant sectors of the area's population were economically disadvantaged even before the Depression and consequently had few reserves of health or wealth to withstand the crisis that hit with full force by the mid-1930s.

The provincial government's attempt to meet the extensive health needs of the area's population by establishing the Eastern Ontario Health Unit did contribute to some improvement in its health status, at least insofar as this can be appreciated by looking at infant mortality. The statistics suggest that the clinics and visiting nurses were beneficial. But the fact that this benefit was most pronounced in the counties that were comparatively better off economically also points to the outer limits of education as a method of health improvement. At the same time, the fact that the slowest decline occurred in Prescott, the poorest county with the fewest services, suggests that inaccessibility of medical attention was also part of the problem, exacerbating the economic factors behind infant mortality. As a test case for the relationship between poverty, ill health, and infant death, the Eastern Ontario Health unit establishes above all the fallacies inherent in taking official statistical averages and health reports at their word.

It stands to reason that the advantages that accrued to residents through expanded public health services were more fully realized by those who were in a relatively better economic position to begin with, and were slightest for those who suffered most in material terms and in terms of health care delivery. As one parliamentary health critic described the situation in 1939, "the number of deaths from tuberculosis and the number of maternal deaths vary widely not only from one municipal centre to another but from one province to another and this ... clearly indicates the unfair handicap that we place upon the low wage earner or the indigent, and their families, by depriving them of the medical counsel and services so necessary for the maintenance of health and life."[25] Dr Norman Bethune, whose well-known "radical" proclivities distanced him from the majority of his medical colleagues, declared that the crisis in medicine was identical to that occurring in capitalism during the 1930s: "poverty of health in the midst of scientific abundance of knowledge of disease."[26]

The survey of existing public health services compiled for the Royal Commission on Dominion-Provincial Relations (1939) also discovered that provision for maternal and child welfare was "hit-and-miss" throughout Canada.[27] Little wonder that the report found "many instances of poor organization, lack of cooperation, lack of planning, lack of knowledge, lack of adequate funds at any time, lack of adequate funds at the right time, and consequent waste." The commission noted that, quite apart from the human factors involved, there were "impressive calculations of the economic loss resulting from preventable sickness and death."

By the end of the interwar period, other social surveys and medical studies confirmed that the declining statistical indications emphasized overall improvement while masking the persistence of health problems in a significant minority. Studies conducted in Montreal and Toronto in 1937 showed that the families of the unemployed suffered from higher rates of inadequate nutrition, unhealthy teeth and gums, tuberculosis, defective vision, deafness, infected tonsils, cardiovascular defects, "and other disabilities." Of the children, only 37.6 per cent were rated "good" in comparison to 56.2 per cent of those whose parents had at least part-time employment. The surveyors concluded that, "in general, the impression that there is a direct relationship between unemployment and the nutrition of those living in the homes of the unemployed is substantially confirmed."[28] The Canadian Welfare Council's 1935 study on maternal mortality also recognized that a significant percentage of maternal deaths was due to "impaired health generally," and arose "particularly out of conditions of disease and malnourishment of the young mother in her own childhood and adolescence."[29] As Denton Massey argued in the House of Commons in 1939, "surely we cannot ignore the fact that the undernourished female child of today is to be the young mother of tomorrow; and if we fail to provide adequate nourishment for her, we are undermining the very foundation of the nation itself."[30]

By 1940, Dr Alan Brown was also arguing for closer medical attention to malnutrition as a predisposing factor in ill health, disease, and mortality. The Toronto Committee for Dietary Studies had just completed a two-year food consumption survey of 100 lower-income families, whose average weekly income was $19.92. Only three of these families secured the caloric supply recommended by the Canadian dietary standard. The average protein intake per family was only 77 per cent of the standard, while the amount of calcium secured by children was "distressingly low" at only 57 per cent. Advances in the study of iron-deficiency anaemia had shown that women need more iron than men, but women in these families received only an average of 53 per cent of their requirement. Addressing his colleagues in the Canadian Medical Association, Brown pointed out that "this is sufficient evidence for you to realize that malnutrition is an important problem."[31]

In a subsequent discussion before the association, Brown remarked that the Toronto study had exposed the effects of prenatal diet on maternal and infant health. The study found that many low-income expectant mothers were not receiving the foods necessary for their own health. In many cases their diet was "totally inadequate" for the developing foetus. One nursing mother received about one-third of the amount of protein, calcium, and iron considered satisfactory, a diet that "would not be considered sufficient for a woman living in complete idleness." The family's income was well below the average, about $12 per week. Her baby died two weeks after the survey was completed. As one investigator commented on the case, "the baby's death ... may not have been due to the wretched diet of the mother, but there is an unfortunate coincidence."[32] Complications such as haemorrhage and sepsis also appeared in greater proportion in the "more unfortunate poorly nourished women." Miscarriage, infection, and severe anaemia were more common than in women on good diets.[33]

The survey's findings suggested that the ability of the mother to nurse her baby successfully appeared "almost twice as good" in mothers with adequate prenatal diets. The implications of maternal nutrition for infant health were also apparent: babies born of mothers on poor diets did not thrive as well during the first few months of life as did those born to well-nourished mothers. The study's sample revealed no infant deaths in the latter group, while there were several deaths before six months in those born to ill-nourished mothers. Brown concluded that "the evidence suggests that the feeding of the infant begins in intrauterine life," and recognized that "these influences might possibly be the answer to some of the deaths during the first few weeks of life which have been so difficult to eliminate."[34] He declared even more forcefully that the most important contributory factors in ill health, disease, and mortality were malnutrition and secondary anaemias, which predisposed individuals to all other diseases.[35]

This was Brown's most direct statement on the medical profession's long-standing disregard of economic factors. But he was not entirely willing to surrender the equally persistent – and consistent – medical view on individual responsibility and feminine ineptitude. He still maintained that ignorance played a large part, "in that many mothers who could afford a proper diet do not know the essentials or do not take the trouble to provide it." He also contended that "one never sees a death from a nutritional disturbance now in private practice because the people of the intelligent class know the value of health supervision." Similarly, one of the members of the Toronto nutrition study felt that the survey's data could not provide "a clear-cut conclusion regarding the effect of income" on nutrition, despite the fact that only 3 of 100 families secured total amounts of food equal to the Canadian standard. He also believed that "lack of the necessary knowledge to choose foods wisely and economically" meant that many mothers were "handicapped in trying to provide proper meals."[36]

Stressing that this awareness of the necessity of good nutrition and medical supervision should be made to apply to all Canadian children, Brown was evidently oblivious to the fact that people of "the intelligent class" were also those who could purchase quality food and quality health care, both scarce commodities for a significant number of Canadians. His own findings and those of other medical researchers made him see more clearly the material basis of health, but he continued to emphasize the individual behavioural element. While making "lack of knowledge" the foremost cause of nutritional deficiency, he still went further than ever before in admitting that "there is no use in our trying to educate the people ... unless the price of these foods is within reach of their purchasing power."[37] Brown offered no suggestions as to how malnourished people who could not afford a proper diet should go about achieving one in the meantime, leaving the problem to the marketplace.

By the end of the Depression decade, there were already signs that the child welfare campaign was diminishing in intensity. The reinstatement of the Maternal and Child Hygiene Division within the federal Department of Health in 1938 effectively ended the Canadian Welfare Council's strategic role. The division itself was suspended in 1939 while the federal government carried out the massive reorganization necessitated by the outbreak of the Second World War. When it resumed operation after one year, it was forced to cut its information services to a minimum because of the financial exigencies of the war effort.

The Second World War had an even more direct and immediate impact on the movement. The war emergency took precedence over social issues with the general public as well as with the government. Child welfare concerns were never completely abandoned. Various supplications were made to Canadian mothers to perform their patriotic duties as "sentinels of the health of the family": "If Canada is to stand the pressure of modern war and make the all-out effort which will be required for victory, the health of her people must be built up and maintained." Every Canadian housewife and mother held a key position in the national war effort.[38] But magazines that had enthusiastically devoted feature articles and regular columns to child care now paid less attention to the previously fascinating motherhood topics. The *Canadian Home Journal* and *Chatelaine* retained their "expert advice" columns, but even these were published intermittently in the early war years.

Child welfare advocates soon realized that the international crisis boded ill for their campaign. Its most influential leaders in medicine and psychology, Alan Brown and W.E. Blatz, presented eloquent pleas in hopes of sustaining public and official interest. The campaign's ideologues used every patriotic argument in their repertoire to argue the special need for its continuation during wartime. Speaking before the Dominion Council of Health in 1939, Alan Brown acknowledged that an emergency often caused "defects in the systematic care of children." Calling forth the cherished concept of the child as "national asset," he reminded his predominantly medical audience that the century's universal and progressive decrease in births had prompted the democratic nations to compensate by saving the lives of babies and preventing childhood disease.[39] To allow anything to interfere with the health and development of Canadian children "who may be considered literally as our second line of defence" constituted "criminal neglect." The national cause required the state to protect the people's health that they might "give the best that is in them to the work they are doing, so that the highest efficiency at home may contribute to the efficiency of our armies abroad." War made healthy bodies the most valued national resource of all: health and health care should assume a position second only to that of the fighting forces.[40]

Similarly, child psychologist William Blatz, speaking to public health nurses, observed that Canadians not actually fighting for democracy still faced a vital duty: "There is one job which we cannot afford to neglect – bringing up our children to accept responsibility. Democracy is only strong when the individual is willing to contribute as much as he receives."[41] Just as their specific goals remained unchanged throughout the campaign's course, its participants unfailingly returned to the rhetoric of national efficiency, productivity, patriotism, and individual responsibility to draw the link between child welfare concerns and the "great causes" of the moment.

With the outbreak of war, special consideration was given to the part that the federal health department should play in conserving health while furthering the war effort. The matter was discussed with the various division heads in the interests of cooperation and rationalization of services. The federal department resolved, as always with the most honourable intentions, "That the highest possible level of good health must be maintained amongst our people and to this end it is imperative that all health departments, federal, provincial and municpal, shall maintain the present standard of health services and, where deemed advisable, expand such services to take care of our present problems and any new ones which may arise from time to time."[42] It could not be foreseen in 1939 that the war would continue for six years and that Canada's role at Britain's right hand would require a substantial economic and military contribution. The early 1940s saw a continuation of child welfare efforts along the lines laid out in the years just before the previous war to end all wars. Surveys were conducted, various advisory committees met and made recommendations, councils held conferences. But little was accomplished about any expansion of health services, with the exception of Ontario's organization of county units to provide for smaller municipalities that could not do it alone. While education continued to be important, publication of literature was also curtailed.

Nonetheless, the war years did see an important breakthrough for child and maternal welfare: by this time, the doctors' unrelenting faith in education as the one true remedy had weakened, as the testimony of Phair and Brown shows. At the same time, the combination of the Depression experience, full-scale state intervention for the war effort, and public pressure about reconstruction, pushed and pulled the nation on the road to the welfare state. Canadians who had suffered through the 1930s with minimal state assistance knew that "mysterious floodgates" would open "to promote the dance of universal death." They were not inclined to sacrifice themselves and their children unless money could be found to better their lives as well as to buy their participation in that dance.[43]

An ironic poem in the *Labour Leader* in 1938 foresaw the improved prospects for individuals and families once the state was obliged to invest in war. Called "Owed to the Future," Berton Brady's sardonic verse captured the real tragedy of state welfare measures devised for militaristic purposes and funded by war profits:

The Veteran of Future Wars began his lover's plea,
Our lives will be just dandy if you'll only marry me.
I am unemployed at present and I haven't got a cent
But we needn't let that bother us to any great extent.
For the government will loan us quite a tidy little sum
On my Future Soldier's Bonus for the War That's Yet to Come.

And we'll have your Wife's Allowance – paid us monthly, years before
I am drafted as a doughboy in the cause of Future War.
... Ah my love, you needn't worry, we'll have opulence galore,
On the income we may gather from the cost of Future War.
... and if you will wed me, honey
Be my little pal and mate
We can draw a lot of money
If you'll just collaborate.
Be a Future Gold Star Mother –
Do it often and repeat,
And our bonuses and pensions will be something pretty neat.
And as Patriotic Parents, we'll be compensated for
A flock of Future Veterans of every Future War![44]

Mackenzie King's Liberal government was at last prepared to consider the need for effective, coherent social security legislation.[45] Leonard Marsh's *Report on Social Security for Canada*, presented to the House of Commons Committee on Reconstruction and Rehabilitation in 1943, attempted to establish a justifiable social minimum for all Canadians. Marsh proclaimed that children "should have an unequivocal place in social security policy." After much criticism and consternation, the Family Allowances Act was passed in 1944.[46]

Unemployment insurance (1941) and family allowances marked the most unequivocal entry by the Canadian state into the sphere of social reproduction. Without disputing the desirability and benefit of these measures to Canadian families, both were inarguably significant reinforcements for the system. They were intended to mitigate class conflict, bolster the male breadwinner role and maintain the spending power of families. However modern and progressive their depiction, they also upheld the traditional family ethic and the traditional view of male and female roles both within the home and within the marketplace. The federal government would assist families in their reproductive activities and care of non-working members while assuring women's role in maintaining and reproducing the labour force, thereby institutionalizing its pattern of intervention in the family.[47]

Published the same year as the Marsh Report, Dr J.J. Heagerty's *Health Insurance Report* met an unfortunate fate. Its comprehensive measures for health insurance and public health grants were largely jettisoned due to the perpetual inability of the provincial and federal governments to agree on fiscal terms.[48] If the Depression had encouraged some doctors to look more favourably on "state medicine," the majority continued to insist that complete state control of health care services would undermine the quality of medical care and consequently the health status of the people.[49]

What mattered most to the doctors was professional autonomy. What mattered most to Canadians was affordable health care, as evidenced in a Gallup poll of 1942 that placed the state medicine question before them: "If the government should start a national health plan, would you be willing to pay a small part of your income every month so that you and your family would receive medical and hospital care whenever you needed it?" Seventy-five per cent of respondents answered yes, with only 7 per cent undecided. What is most surprising are the results by economic status: the "average" income group was 79 per cent in favour, the "wealthy" group was 76 per cent in favour, while the "poor" were 74 per cent in favour.[50] Canadians across the socio-economic spectrum wanted state medicine, but doctors and state policy-makers could not agree upon its necessity, the form it should take, or who should administer and underwrite it. During the war years, however, private health insurance plans were becoming more popular and affordable. As a result of this increase in insurance coverage and in the general standard of living, more Canadians were now able to meet the costs of medical attendance.[51]

Because the determinants of health are multifarious, it is not possible to provide a conclusive answer to the central question that remains: in what measure did the child and maternal welfare campaign that began with force during the Great War contribute to the decline in infant and maternal mortality? The campaigners could find some satisfaction in the statistical indications. The decline was real, for all that it masked continuing health inequalities rooted in persistent economic and regional inequalities. Yet the campaign's history was marked by many limitations that confounded its worthy aims. These limitations were apparent to the families skirted or touched only superficially by the campaigners' best efforts. As other developments began to hint at trouble for the campaign's future, they became equally evident to its directors.

The federal health department's Scientific Advisory Committee on Maternal Welfare undertook a special study on maternal mortality which was presented at its first meeting in April 1939. The report suggested that, in concrete terms, very little had been accomplished, despite more than a decade of educational activity. It underlined, first of all, a "lack of sustained and concerted effort." Even more importantly, facilities available for expectant and new mothers in 1939 differed little from those of the mid-1920s, except for "an improvement in educational lines." While hospital facilities had improved, the availability and distribution of prenatal and postnatal services had not. Postgraduate obstetrical studies were still insufficiently encouraged. Maternal welfare advocates had striven for the maximum of efficiency "but with a minimum of services." Further investigation and discussion were planned to consider "to what extent present methods are responsible for the lack of success."[52]

By the 1940s, the campaign's directors were admitting that further progress was contingent upon a change in strategy. Despite the improvement in the mortality figures, the exclusive focus on education had not brought about the desired results. Dr J.T. Phair recognized that official and professional efforts had to be redirected for any appreciable reduction in maternal and neonatal deaths: "It is now generally accepted that there are two major factors in a favourable outcome for pregnancy, namely the physical condition of the individual patient from conception to the conclusion of labour and the skill and judgment of the physician. The satisfactory control of these alone can permanently even out the statistical fluctuations of mortality curves and bring them to a more desirable level."[53] Couture also came to the view that "much waste of energy, time and money" had resulted from the educational focus, and that "we all know that the remedy for many situations lies not so much in educational efforts as in making services available."[54]

A comparative analysis of American and Canadian child welfare measures affirmed that, even accounting for population differences, Canadian efforts in the field lagged considerably behind those of the United States. As Couture lamented in 1945, "from all points of view – interest, performance and results – we have no cause for elation. One is inclined to wonder at such indifference towards the well-being of mothers and children, our most valuable resources."[55] This time the indifference that Couture decried was not that of the Canadian public in general, nor of parents in particular. It was the indifference of the state. Even public health officials now asserted that Canadian governments at every level had been notoriously tight-fisted with financial support for the campaign.[56] The result was a minimal degree of much-needed practical services and overvaluation of education.

Aversion to state intervention only goes so far in explaining the Canadian lag by comparison to the efforts of Great Britain and the United States. An equally important factor was the combined effect of the immaturity of the state apparatus in Canada, an infant nation in historical terms, and the unremitting constitutional haggling over division of powers. During the interwar period, when the United

States and Britain were consolidating their bureaucratic structures, Canada was only beginning to assemble its own. The weakness of the state was directly reflected in the paucity of welfare measures devised during this period, and in the growth of, and continued reliance on, voluntary participation in social welfare activities.[57] There was considerable debate and confusion in reform and state circles as to which level could and should be most responsible for health and welfare. Far from initiating and standardizing measures to ensure the maximum benefits for mothers and children across the land, the federal health department took on what was at best a support role by providing limited funding and much rhetorical encouragement for provincial efforts. With its Child Welfare Division and Council on Child Welfare given over largely to the publication of literature, there was considerable overlap not only between these two bodies, but also between them and their equivalent provincial agencies.

Since the federal department's commitment to child welfare was static and passive, the onus for provision of these services fell upon the province. Ontario's health department coordinated and supervised child welfare measures. But beyond providing free vaccine and free literature and sending nurses to demonstrate the possibilities of a child welfare program, its major goal was to encourage municipalities to hire their own nurses and establish their own clinics and visiting services. For the Ontario health department, the child welfare campaign of the interwar years became a drive for the hiring of local public health nurses.

The campaign ran out of steam by the 1940s because it had accomplished as much as its educational focus would permit. The child welfare campaign's attempts to awaken public, official, and professional interest had inspired greater efforts towards the adoption of such important measures as pure milk legislation, antiseptic conditions at delivery, improved hospital techniques, and prenatal and well-baby supervision. While there was still a long way to go in all these areas, by the 1940s Ontario families had more health options than they had had at the beginning of the period.

Medical innovation during this period also played a vital role in saving infant and maternal lives. No quarter of a century saw as many advances in medicine as occurred between 1925 and 1950. The discovery of insulin in the early 1920s was a watershed in the treatment of juvenile diabetes, previously a fatal illness. The widespread use of diphtheria toxoid beginning in the late 1920s saw the virtual eradication of that disease by the end of the interwar period.[58] Medical therapeutics made tremendous progress with the introduction of sulphonamides in the mid-1930s and antibiotics in the 1940s. Nutritional studies pointed out the importance of Vitamins c and d to prevent rickets, previously a ubiquitous ailment of childhood.[59]

By 1940, the medical understanding of the aetiology of intestinal diseases, the original bane of the child welfare campaigners, had advanced to the point where the emphasis on feeding as the key to the mystery of high infant mortality had greatly diminished. While studies of admissions to the Hospital for Sick Children revealed that over 70 per cent of infants were brought to the attention of doctors because of digestive disturbances, closer analysis showed that the digestive problems were symptoms and not diseases themselves. In the list of causative factors, feeding problems were close to the bottom. As Brown expressed it, "in other words, there is usually something wrong with the baby," something quite apart from intestinal upset. The treatment might involve feeding adjustments, but "the important point is to recognize and treat the cause."[60]

The major threat to infant life because of the dehydration associated with digestive symptoms was infection which decreased tolerance for food. It was now understood that the water balance in the body had to be adjusted to avoid the ketosis that meant the body was feeding off its own proteins. As far as Brown was concerned, better medical understanding of these two factors was "probably the greatest lifesaving advance in paediatrics during this period." He advised that, in the treatment of any infection of infancy, no matter how trivial, the employment of antiketogenic hydrating solutions by mouth and the discontinuation of feedings was "never an error and nearly always essential."[61] He still maintained that acute intestinal intoxication, formerly called *cholera infantum*, was largely due to the introduction of dysentery organisms through improper handling of milk. But it was not the type of feeding itself that mattered so much as attention to its purity. By 1945, the lifesaving use of potassium-containing fluid and electrolyte infusions in patients suffering from severe or prolonged diarrhaea greatly reduced mortality from the dreaded *cholera infantum*.

While prematurity remained a tremendous obstacle to further mortality reduction, new medical developments were proving effective in preventing associated deaths. In 1933, American medical researchers established optimum temperature and humidity requirements for premature infants. The Hospital for Sick Children began experimenting with ultraviolet light and air conditioning to maintain the sterility of air in the hospital's nursery for premature infants. The importance of early stabilization of the temperature of these babies was also understood, prompting more widespread use of incubators immediately after birth. For premature babies born at home, the hospital introduced in 1937 a special ambulance that was equipped with a portable incubator. The use of this portable incubator reduced the hospital's premature mortality rate by more than 10 per cent.[62]

And what of the state's contribution to the campaign? Broader-ranging public health legislation, particularly with respect to sanitation, the control of epidemic disease, and pasteurization, was another important contributing factor. Given the significance of milk as a carrier of infectious disease, the improved quality of the milk supply, furthered by compulsory provincial pasteurization laws in 1938, undoubtedly played a large part, not only in reducing infant mortality, but also tuberculosis, other childhood diseases such as scarlet fever, and a wide range of milk-borne infections.[63] As well, by the end of the Second World War, most towns in Ontario were served by some form of public health nursing, while more county health units were being created to minister to the needs of the "poor unfortunates" in unorganized rural and outpost districts.[64] In 1950, the provincial department's annual report noted "with gratification" the expansion of existing municipal programs and the growth in full-time health services. There were 381 full-time medical officers of health by this time, and the province was facing the problem of a shortage of trained public health personnel for the first time in its history.[65]

The clinic and visiting nurse services continued as before, expanding into the municipalities that were just acquiring public health organization. Their function was educational, as always, but the provincial government, in a 1946 amendment to the Public Health Act, provided for any expectant mother to obtain one free complete prenatal medical examination from the physician of her choice. That Ontario mothers were eager for medical attention of this kind is demonstrated by the fact that, by 1948, approximately 5,000 women per month, representing 396 municipalities, were taking advantage of this measure.[66] By 1950, the proportion of free prenatal examinations in relation to live births was 60 per cent. Maternal deaths reached an all-time low in 1946 of 1.64 per cent, and the rates for the three major causes also fell significantly. The toxaemias surpassed sepsis as the foremost cause of maternal mortality, with a rate of .35 per 1,000 live births; sepsis accounted for .24, and haemorrhage for .16 per 1,000 live births. Greater reliance on blood transfusions and antibiotics meant an improved survival rate, but the diminution of the figures is so striking by comparison to the 1940 levels that there must have been a very real drop in incidence.

In Norman Bethune's sweeping vision, "the best form" of health protection would demand that Canadians "change the economic system which produces ill health, to liquidate ignorance, poverty and unemployment."[67] Even if the medical profession had requested substantial state intervention on the grounds of national health and welfare, the state would not have been able to eliminate the factors accounting for the differential mortality and morbidity between social groups without wholesale reorganization of the economy. The best that the state can do in a system that commodifies health and health care is to attempt to reduce the worst effects of some of the threats to health.[68] Neither medicine nor the state were capable of attacking poverty effectively under the circumstances. But the evidence placed before them, and the example of other countries, allowed that there were more effective measures within their reach than those that they were using – measures that they consciously refused.

There is a considerable body of evidence which suggests that health standards are affected less by new discoveries and technologies than by improvement in the environment, that is, in the conditions in which people live.[69] Even taking into account the multiple contributory factors, the substantial decline in post-Second World War maternal and infant mortality figures suggests that the element of prosperity probably had the most significant repercussions for the improvement of health in Canadians of all ages. The construction of the war machine put an end to the unemployment crisis and introduced many Canadians to a higher standard of living than they had ever previously enjoyed. The postwar boom obviously did not eliminate class and regional disparities, but the improvement in real income was felt by more people than ever before.[70] Reconstruction measures such as hospital insurance, and, during the 1960s, provincial health insurance, spurred a concomitant improvement in the health of Canadians.[71] By 1949, the infant death rate in Ontario was 18.8 per 1,000 live births; today it hovers around 17. Recent medical studies on contemporary infant mortality consider the key variables to be socio-economic status, accessibility to and quality of health care, and parental level of education.[72]

By the 1940s, many of the afflictions originally at the root of high infant and maternal mortality had been reduced as much as possible by the means undertaken to that point. Their further reduction, and that of those which stubbornly remained, were not likely to be effected by education. Improved nutrition, better living conditions, and improved, accessible, and affordable medical care were essential. As Dr Couture pointed out, "the sudden improvement since 1939 suggests very strongly that education should have been coupled with the development of services, as delay in progress was evidently due to the inadequacy of services for the care of mothers."[73] Education was helpful, but it was seriously restricted in its ability to influence morbidity and mortality. It had reached the outer bounds of its efficacy. The campaigners were eventually forced to concede that progress in child welfare work was due largely to factors over which they had exercised little control: medical advances that could at least save those who made it to the doctor in time, and the improved economic situation that allowed more Canadian families a better basic level of health and greater access to needed medical services.

CHAPTER TEN

Conclusion

The improvement in infant and maternal mortality rates during the interwar period was real, although it masked the extent to which class and regional inequalities persisted. What remains to be considered is the campaign's impact on its participants in other than health terms, both with respect to its leadership and to its clients. As is true of the assessment of the state of health of Ontario mothers and children, it is difficult to measure with any precision the social and ideological effects of the new medical interest in child and maternal welfare. We know that concerted attempts were made by medicine and the state to intervene in the process of social reproduction. The extent to which these influenced the everyday lives of Ontario families, the role of women, and intrafamilial relationships, can only be inferred.

The campaign's impact on the medical profession suggests that it contributed significantly to the ongoing trend toward increased professional authority and medical dominance in society. Public and official interest in child welfare concerns inspired by physicians and nurses gave them new status as family advisers and state consultants. The profession's determination to make the state recognize its authority in all matters of public health, and its success in doing so, resulted in significant medical influence on state health and welfare policy. As we have seen, this influence was often in the interests of medicine rather than in the interests of health.

At the turn of the century, paediatrics was a new specialty struggling to establish itself both within the profession and in the public eye. By the end of the interwar period, paediatricians were still in short supply in Canada, but they had made themselves valued consultants to general practitioners, parents and health departments at all levels.[1] In 1939, the Royal College of Physicians and Surgeons accepted the responsibility of certifying Canadian specialists.[2] The immediate post-Second World War years saw an internal acknowledgment of this successful professionalization. The Canadian Society for the Study of the Diseases of Children, originally open to all physicians interested in child health, became the restricted Canadian Paediatric Society. As doctors, whether specialists or general practitioners, increasingly persuaded parents to look to them in childrearing matters, their power to influence social customs expanded.

Obstetricians not only maintained but fortified their hold over maternity and childbirth by their successful exclusion of midwifery, and by their campaign for medicalization of pregnancy and hospitalization of childbirth. By the Second World War, the care of expectant and parturient women and their children was firmly in the hands of the medical profession, creating a monopoly over health services that has only been challenged within the past few years. Institutionalized childbirth and well-baby supervision became the social norm for middle-class women, and increasingly for their working-class sisters as well. Hospital births were the experience of the majority of Canadian mothers by the mid-1950s.

Although the early twentieth century saw an increasing measure of state and public faith in medical leadership, both the profession's ideological unanimity and the passivity of the intended audience have been overplayed. Within the contours of the child welfare campaign, there is evidence of dissidence, not only among the clients themselves but also within medical ranks. The tension between doctors and nurses is a recurrent theme, as is that which arose between private practitioners and public health professionals, between competing child welfare agencies, and between the various levels of government. There was also the potential for conflict between the women's groups that occasionally called for specific remedies such as the provision of licensed midwives, and doctors who would not relinquish any measure of professional control. Mothers who wanted real medical services were at odds with doctors who insisted that education was the only answer. Although opposition was rarely actualized in open confrontation, it did make itself felt. Neither the profession nor the target audience can be viewed as a consensual whole.

Under state protection, the medical profession in twentieth-century Canada has made a vital contribution to the functioning of the economic and political system. The health care system, for its part, both reflects and supports the ideals and structures of the larger system.[3] Because modern medicine prefers to concentrate on the scientific basis of disease and mortality, and to regard individual behaviour as the source of class differences in health, it dismisses or evades the socio-economic causes of much illness that are contained in the structures of the system itself. Personal health choices are significant, but it must be recognized that people sometimes act in ways that they know are contrary to their best interests because the circumstances of their lives leave them little alternative. Since doctors failed to take this complicating factor into account in their profoundly individualist theories of health, they were able to make maternal ignorance the foremost cause of high infant and maternal mortality, and scientific motherhood the principal remedy.

The campaign's effects for women were contradictory. More than anything, it prescribed a new relationship for them with medicine and the state. Doubtless many women and their children gained from the services provided under the aegis of state child and maternal welfare divisions, limited as these were. Their own testimony indicates that they generally accepted their need for information about child care. Educated middle-class women also benefited from the new opportunities for social, economic, and political participation that arose out of the expansion of family-related health and welfare activities. But the overall effect for women was to enhance the focus on maternity as their reason for being, and especially on their feminine ineptitude in carrying out a social role that was supposed to be biologically determined.

Despite the fact that women's organizations took an active lead in child welfare efforts in the early twentieth century, women were relegated for the most part to subordinate positions in the campaign and its state agencies as child welfare increasingly became a professionally dominated and state-sponsored activity. Women like Mac-Murchy and Whitton at the federal level, Mary Power and Beryl Knox of Ontario's division, and many others in less visible roles, took official positions in health and welfare agencies. But with few exceptions, male leadership predominated both in medicine and the state. The public health nurses exemplify the subordination of women in the campaign's ranks and in the medical profession itself. While public health nursing achieved greater recognition than ever before as a result of expanded state activity in the period, the nurses who performed the dog work of conducting diagnostic clinics, visiting mothers and infants in their homes, and traversing sparsely populated areas in the name of child and maternal welfare, were ever conscious of their secondary status.

If women were making their mark in politics during these decades, in itself obviously an historical first, the force of that mark remained faint indeed. Thirteen women were elected to provincial legislatures between 1917 and 1939, but none were in Ontario. Agnes Macphail, one of only two women in the House of Commons during these years, struggled mightily on behalf of women and children, but against the mightiest of odds.[4] Doctors appreciated the support of the "female laity," but overrode its views on such issues as midwifery, maternity benefits and health insurance. They kept the women's organizations in line just as they did the nurses. Neither organized women nor nurses were innately deferential, but their opposition came up against the stone wall of medical dominance. As Seth Koven and Sonya Michel argue, women lost control over maternalist discourses when they were debated in male-dominated legislatures in Europe and America, and were then compelled to rely on male politicians to support their causes. Often they had to wait until national crises such as war permitted state attention to turn to matters like child welfare.[5] The pattern they uncovered holds true for Canada in this period.

For the majority of women, the ideology of scientific motherhood, if accepted and put into practice, would not only increase their already considerable burden of childrearing and household work, but would intensify it: as mothers they were now responsible to the state. In its idealized form, mothering was to be an all-consuming occupation for women of all classes. At the same time, mothers were not considered equipped to do the job without the help of experts who were largely male professionals. Medical regulation of motherhood was intended, and was carried out, to save babies. But in striving toward these goals, doctors provided modern scientific authorization for traditional gender roles and the traditional family ethic. Women themselves promoted and participated in the modernization of motherhood, at least to the degree that it served their individual needs and purposes. However, mothers were not the unquestioning automatons that doctors wanted them to be.

The same can be said of labour support of the campaign. As the primary targets of medical regulation, working-class families were subjected to the moral judgments of medicine and the state regarding their ignorance and indifference about the health and welfare of their children. Yet labour supporters who expressed their opinions on the subjects of public health and child welfare consistently upheld the need for education in these matters. Unlike their medical tutors, however, their understanding of health and their critique of the free-enterprise health care system underscored the relationship between health, health care and capitalism. They, too, were concerned about the impact of ill health on labour efficiency and productivity. As the most vulnerable of the population, they and their families stood to lose the most as a result of ill health. But the working-class critique of existing health care was premised on the concept of health as a fundamental human right, and medical services as rights of citizenship to which all should have equal access. As such, labour argued for attention to basic environmental issues such as working conditions, housing, and poverty, and for universal health care delivery supported by the state.

Labour commentators saw that true accessibility to health care could not be attained without its removal from the marketplace; in short, without the decommodification of health. Yet public protest along these lines was ineffectual because of the weakness of their political voice. The interwar years were a formative period for the Canadian left, but one that witnessed little political strength for leftist parties. Despite several promising moves by the Farmer-Labour coalition in Ontario in the early 1920s, including the introduction of mothers' allowances and the reorganization of the health department, the reign of the United Farmers was short-lived. After 1923, the Conservative provincial government of Howard Ferguson showed itself willing to take few initiatives in health and welfare areas.[6] The financial exigencies of the Great Depression and the overriding pressure of relief expenditures on provincial and municipal treasuries necessitated the curtailment of even the limited services that existed. By the mid-1920s, as James Naylor has shown, the Ontario working class was "demoralized and demobilized."[7] Although labour organization and activity in Ontario increased during the Depression years, the working class still did not manage to make political gains in the face of a repressive state. In the absence of a "massive electoral convulsion," even the destitution of the Depression years was not enough to prompt the policy-makers to confront the needs of the people with much more than rhetoric and brute force.[8]

The effect of the child welfare campaign on the parent/child relationship is an area that remains speculative. Not only is it difficult to know whether many mothers changed their parenting style according to medical dictates, but the impact of these changes on children can only be guessed at. Children raised "by the book" as it was written by medical experts during the interwar period became the parents of the 1940s and 1950s. By the early 1940s, there were already signs of a professional backlash against the strict scientific methods they espoused. The new childrearing ideas that influenced post-Second World War trends have been traced to the publication in 1938 of Charles and Mary Aldrich's *Babies Are Human Beings*.[9]

The Aldrichs' conception of childrearing foreshadowed the "permissive" modes that were popularized in the postwar years by the enormously influential Dr Benjamin Spock.[10] The book's title defined the new image of the child. No longer were babies "little machines" to be put into running order at birth, kept running efficiently, and generally left alone to do so. The Aldrichs did not present parents with ulterior motives for raising their children to be happy and healthy: the benefits to the child and its parents were sufficient without mention of national productivity or social degeneration. Nevertheless, they did not depart from the view that the physician was to be a central figure in the child's life, nor did succeeding advisers of the postwar generation of parents.[11] And mothers seemed eager to look to expert advice for assistance in their parenting duties, a pattern initiated in the interwar period that would become even more pronounced with the "baby boom" of the 1950s. By 1953, over 2 million copies of *The Canadian Mother and Child* had been distributed, while Spock's *Common Sense Book of Baby and Child Care*, published in 1945 and currently in its fifth edition, left its impress on an entire "Spock-marked" generation.[12]

Did the parents of the 1940s and 1950s turn to childrearing advice literature and expert supervision in imitation of their own parents? Were they inclined to be permissive in reaction to their own stringent upbringing? What role did the newfound prosperity of the period and the 1950s emphasis on domesticity play in changing family relationships and childrearing patterns? How much did the construction of the welfare state contribute to reducing class and regional differentials in health? What effect did the renewed immigration of these years have on childrearing patterns? These are questions that can only be raised by this study, but they point to the continuity of generational patterns of family organization and intrafamilial relationships, and to the die-hard persistence of traditional gender roles.

It is true that the intentions of the child welfare reformers did not always transform into the reality they envisioned. For all that the results of their campaign were disappointing, even from the perspective of some of its participants, its legacy was significant. Whatever the extent of its contribution, considerably more mothers and babies were surviving pregnancy, childbirth, and the early years of life on the eve of the Second World War than had done since the campaign commenced in earnest during the First World War. As to their vision of creating model citizens who would establish a social order based on scientific organization, forever free of violence and poverty, the child welfare campaigners clearly failed. An even more horrible war and social problems that persisted through the hopes of reconstruction underlined that failure. The utopian element of their vision sustained them, but the world they sought to create could not be realized by imperfect human beings whom no amount of medical regulation could turn into perfect machines.

The child welfare campaign's most lasting impact was ideological nonetheless. By directing attention to the child as the nation's most valuable resource, it brought about a new understanding of the vital social implications of parenting. As more and more mothers gave birth with reasonable confidence that they would survive, and that their children would grow to fulfil their own promise, effective parenting came to encompass a great deal more than the preservation of life and health. The post-Second World War years saw the institutionalization of health and welfare concerns at the state level. For the first time in Canadian history, the health and welfare of every child were recognized as its fundamental right. The "baby boom" generation would enjoy the benefits of greater health, optimism, and material well-being than had any previous generation – along with a substantial share of the individual and social troubles that reformers had hoped to vanquish forever.

It would be inaccurate as well as ahistorical to accuse the child welfare campaigners of having suffered from a naive and misplaced faith in science and technology. They believed wholeheartedly that, if Canadians could be persuaded that "nations are built of babies," and that they needed medical assistance to raise those individual babies, the nation as a whole would triumph in the modern world order. Just as were the children whose lives they were trying to reformulate, the makers of a modern Canadian childhood were products of the ideological, social and political forces of their time. Their intervention in the sphere of social reproduction was the direct outcome of their belief that the family was in danger. They recognized that its destiny and that of the system were so intertwined as to be one and the same. Their inability to accept that health is a function of structural problems like poverty, and limited access to medical care, is understandable in the context of the period's medical and social ideology, with its basis in individualism. Their failure lies in their refusal to accept, all evidence to the contrary, that real improvement in the health status and health care of Canadians was possible – even within the existing system – by expansion of citizenship rights.

In a time when 15 per cent of all Canadian families with children under the age of six are living in poverty, when 69 per cent of these families are headed by women, and when health and welfare benefits are facing mounting and ever more menacing attacks, it is well worth remembering the effects of that failure for Canadian mothers and children.[13]

Appendix

Table A1
Chief Causes of Infant Mortality in Ontario

Rank	Cause of Death	Average Annual No. of Deaths	%	Rate per Live Births
	1915–19			
1	Congenital debility	2,999	46.8	46.5
2	Pneumonia, bronchitis, influenza	993	15.5	15.4
3	Diarrhoea, enteritis, dysentery	848	13.2	13.2
4	Convulsions	297	4.6	4.6
5	Congenital malformations	227	3.6	3.5
6	Whooping cough	159	2.5	2.5
7	Meningitis	99	1.6	1.5
8	Tuberculosis	55	.9	.9
9	Measles	41	.7	.6
10	Diphtheria, croup	28	.4	.4
	Other causes	659	10.2	10.2
	TOTAL	6,405	100.0	99.3
	1925–29			
1	Prematurity	1,490	29.0	21.0
2	Pneumonia, bronchitis, influenza	730	14.2	10.7
3	Diarrhoea, enteritis, dysentery	609	11.8	8.9
4	Congenital malformations	475	9.2	6.9
5	Congenial debility	403	7.8	5.9
6	Injury at birth	278	5.4	4.0
7	Other diseases of early infancy	255	5.0	3.7
8	Whooping cough	136	2.7	2.0
9	Convulsions	89	1.7	1.3
10	Accidental causes	71	1.4	1.0
	Other causes	609	11.8	8.9
	TOTAL	5,145	100.0	74.3

Rank	Cause of Death	Average Annual No. of Deaths	%	Rate per Live Births
	1935–39			
1	Prematurity	1,027	31.1	16.2
2	Pneumonia, bronchitis, influenza	470	14.2	7.4
3	Congenital malformations	430	13.0	6.8
4	Diarrhoea, enteritis, dysentery	303	9.1	4.8
5	Injury at birth	270	8.2	4.3
6	Other diseases of early infancy	219	6.6	3.4
7	Congenital debility	121	3.6	1.9
8	Whooping cough	69	2.1	1.1
9	Accidental causes	68	2.1	1.1
10	Diseases of the thymus gland	56	1.7	0.9
	Other causes	274	8.3	4.3
	TOTAL	3,307	100.0	52.2

Source: Ontario, Department of Health, *Report of the Ontario Health Survey Committee* (Toronto 1952).

Table A2
Canadian Council on Child and Family Welfare,
Division of Maternal and Child Hygiene, Literature Distributed
in the Year Ending 30 September 1934

	Prenatal Letters	Postnatal Letters	Preschool Letters
Individuals, Church Groups, Misc. Organizations	6,251	6,672	2,602
Doctors, Nurses, Hospitals, Health Organizations	1,410	2,246	598
Government Departments	17,000	24,681	8,052
Outside Canada	95	102	—
Unrecorded	287	831	102
TOTAL	25,043	34,532	11,354

Source: NA, MG 28 I 10, Vol. 4, File 17, Canadian Welfare Council

Table A3
Canadian Council on Child and Family Welfare,
Division of Maternal and Child Hygiene,
Distribution of Health Literature in Canada, 1935–37

Province	Total 1935	% Cdn. Total	Total 1936	% Cdn. Total	Total 1937	% Cdn. Total
Ont.	61,614	32.5	49,348	21.0	84,067	33.9
Que.	48,103	25.3	93,562	40.7	44,556	18.0
Man.	9,310	4.9	11,669	5.1	12,684	5.1
Sask.	32,875	17.3	30,620	11.3	39,206	15.8
Alta.	11,437	6.0	13,265	5.8	11,708	4.7
B.C.	9,916	5.2	15,239	2.3	17,169	6.9
N.S.	8,224	4.3	5,236	2.3	17,169	6.9
N.B.	6,314	3.3	10,927	4.8	9,988	4.0
P.E.I.	1,827	1.0	99	.04	597	0.2
Yukon & N.W.T.	229	0.1	25	.01	64	.03

Source: NA RG 29, Vol. 991, File 499-3-2, Part 3, Maternal and Child Welfare

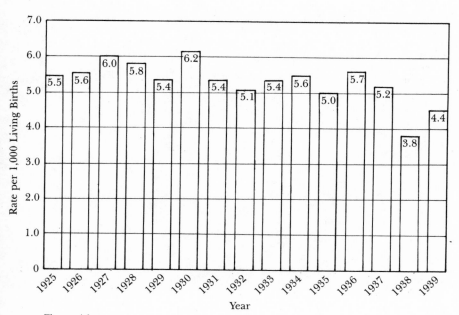

Figure A1
Infant Mortality in Ontario, 1925–39
Source: Ontario, Department of Health, *Annual Report*, 1940

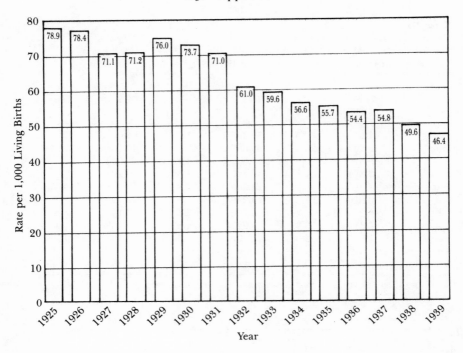

Figure A2
Maternal Mortality in Ontario, 1925–39
Source: Ontario, Department of Health, *Annual Report*, 1940

Notes

CHAPTER ONE

1 Jane Ursel presents a path-breaking analysis of state intervention in social reproduction in Canada by examining legislation directed at families over the last century; see J. Ursel, "The State and the Maintenance of Patriarchy," in J. Dickinson and B. Russell, eds., *Family, Economy and State: The Social Reproduction Process Under Capitalism* (New York 1986), and J. Ursel, *Private Lives, Public Policy: 100 Years of State Intervention in the Family* (Toronto 1992). See also Catharine A. MacKinnnon, *Toward a Feminist Theory of the State* (Cambridge, Mass. 1989), especially 157–70.

2 S. Kelman, "The Social Nature of the Definition of Health," in V. Navarro, ed., *Health and Medical Care in the United States* (New York 1977), 8–13; M. Renaud, "On the Structural Constraints to State Intervention in Health," ibid., 136; V. Navarro, "The Political Economy of Medical Care," ibid., 86–9.

3 E. Fee, "Women and Health Care," in Navarro, ed., *Health and Medical Care in the United States*, 128.

4 The work of medical sociologist Vicente Navarro is particularly valuable in illuminating the relationship between health, health care, and capitalism. See, for example, V. Navarro, *Medicine Under Capitalism* (New York 1976); *Class Struggle, the State and Medicine: An Historical and Contemporary Analysis of the Medical Sector in Great Britain* (London 1978); V. Navarro and D.M. Berman, eds., *Health and Work Under Capitalism* (New York 1981). See also B. Turner, *Medical Power and Social Knowledge* (London 1987), 196.

5 Turner, *Medical Power and Social Knowledge*, 195.

6 Ibid., 195.

7 B. Palmer, *A Culture in Conflict* (Montreal/Kingston 1979), 27. On miners' health in the early twentieth century, see D. Frank, "Company Town/Labour Town: Local Government in the Cape Breton Coal Towns," in D.J. Bercuson, ed., *Canadian Labour History: Selected Readings* (Toronto 1987), 146–7. On occupational health and safety, see A. Derickson, *Workers' Health, Workers' Democracy* (Ithaca, N.Y. 1989); E. Tucker, *Administering Danger in the Workplace: The Law and Politics of Occupational Health and Safety Regulation in Ontario, 1850–1914* (Toronto 1990).

8 E. Fee, "Women and Health Care," 128; Turner, *Medical Power and Social Knowledge*, 217.

9 D. Chunn, *From Punishment to Doing Good: Family Courts and Socialized Justice in Ontario, 1880–1940* (Toronto 1992), 45–7. Chunn describes the major social statutes relating to the protection of women and children, beginning with the Children's Protection Act, 1888. See also W. Mitchinson, "Early Women's Organizations and Social Reform:

Prelude to the Welfare State," in A. Moscovitch and J. Albert, eds., *The Benevolent State: The Growth of Welfare in Canada* (Toronto 1987), 77–92.

10 E. Blumenfeld and S. Mann, "Domestic Labour and the Reproduction of Labour Power," in B. Fox, ed., *Hidden in the Household: Women's Domestic Labour Under Capitalism* (Toronto 1980), 271, 301; J. Wayne, "The Function of Social Welfare in a Capitalist Economy," in Dickinson and Russell, eds., *Family, Economy and State*, 56–7; J. Dickinson, "From Poor Law to Social Insurance," ibid., 115; J. Ursel, "The State and the Maintenance of Patriarchy", ibid., 151; M. Abramovitz, *Regulating the Lives of Women* (New York 1987), 27–8; MacKinnon, *Toward a Feminist Theory of the State*, ix.

11 Until recently Marxist theorists neglected to develop a comprehensive theory of reproduction, despite warnings by Marx and Engels that a complete analysis of any social formation calls for such an understanding. See, for example, K. Marx, *Capital*, vol. 1, (Moscow n.d.), 356–7. In particular, Engels noted how family forms both reflect and sustain changes in economic organization, and explained the surbordination of women by the place accorded to their reproductive capacities under capitalism; F. Engels, "The Origins of the Family, Private Property and the State," in K. Marx and F. Engels, *Selected Works*, vol. 3 (Moscow 1970), 191. MacKinnon provides a feminist critique of Engels, and a larger discussion of feminism and Marxism, in *Toward a Feminist Theory of the State*, 19–24, 3–60; she sees the concept of social reproduction as "at most an uneven combination" of the biological and the material, 12. L. Vogel, *Marxism and the Oppression of Women* (New Jersey 1983), is a critical feminist review of the writings of Marx, Engels, and classical Marxists. See also J. Dickinson and B. Russell, "Introduction: The Structure of Reproduction in Capitalist Society," in Dickinson and Russell, eds., *Family, Economy and State*, 2–4; J. Ursel, "The State and the Maintenance of Patriarchy," ibid., 150, further developed in Ursel, *Private Lives, Public Policy*, 17–58; Abramovitz, *Regulating the Lives of Women*, 27–8. See also W. Seccombe, "The Expanded Reproduction Cycle of Labour Power in Twentieth Century Capitalism," in Fox, ed., *Hidden in the Household*, 225.

12 Canada, House of Commons, *Debates*, 13 February 1929, 88–9.

13 Wayne, "The Function of Social Welfare in a Capitalist Economy," 55; Navarro, "The Political Economy of Medical Care," 106.

14 Navarro, "The Political Economy of Medical Care," 104; D. Naylor, *Private Practice, Public Payment* (Kingston/Montreal 1986), 15; Turner, *Medical Power and Social Knowledge*, 155.

15 C. Heron, *The Canadian Labour Movement: A Short History* (Toronto 1989), 30–64; B. Palmer, *The Working Class Experience*, 2nd ed. (Toronto 1992), 214–63.

16 I am indebted to Robert Brain, University of California (Los Angeles) for bringing to my attention the research of German physiologists, who, in the 1890s, designed a science of physiological and mental work for implementation in schools, the military and factories (*Arbeitswissenschaft*). Max Weber's monograph, *The Psycho-Physics of Work* (1909) was a critical response to this movement; R. Brain, "The Extramural Laboratory Limited: German *Arbeitswissenschaft* versus Max Weber," paper presented to the British-North American Joint Meeting, Canadian Society for the History and Philosophy of Science/History of Science Society/British Society for the History of Science, University of Toronto, 26 July 1992.

17 E. Martin, *The Woman in the Body: A Cultural Analysis of Reproduction* (Boston, Mass. 1992), 54–67.

18 Fee, "Women and Health Care," 117–29, provides a summary of feminist approaches to health care. As Wendy Mitchinson has shown, nineteenth-century doctors reinforced patriarchal values by defining normal womanhood and supporting, both implicity and explicity, the traditional family structure; W. Mitchinson, *The Nature of Their Bodies* (Toronto 1991).

19 Blumenfeld and Mann,"Domestic Labour and the Working Class Household," 280; M. Luxton, *More Than a Labour of Love* (Toronto 1980), 14–19; J. Parr, *The Gender of Breadwinners* (Toronto 1990), 6–8.

20 Mitchinson, *The Nature of Their Bodies*, 153; Ursel, "The State and the Maintenance of Patriarchy," 155–7; MacKinnon, *Toward a Feminist Theory of the State*, 167–70; see also Abramovitz, *Regulating the Lives of Women*, 31; Blumenfeld and Mann, "Domestic Labour and the Working Class Household," 301–2; Seccombe, "The Expanded Reproduction Cycle of Labour Power in Twentieth Century Capitalism," 225–6; Wayne, "The Function of Social Welfare in a Capitalist Economy," 81.

21 On the role of doctors in social/moral reform campaigns, see A. McLaren, *Our Own Master Race* (Toronto 1990), 9, 28–9; M. Valverde, *The Age of Light, Soap and Water* (Toronto 1991), 47. Michel Foucault sees doctors replacing priests as custodians of social values; the ecclesiastical institutions of surveillance are replaced by those of scientific medicine. See M. Foucault, *Madness and Civilization* (London 1971); *The Birth of the Clinic* (London 1973); *The History of Sexuality* (London 1979).

22 See, for example, R. Allen, *The Social Passion* (Toronto 1971); R. Cook and R.C. Brown, *Canada 1896–1921: A Nation Transformed* (Toronto 1974); C. Bacchi, *Liberation Deferred? The Ideas of the English Canadian Suffragists* (Toronto 1983); and the essays in L. Kealey, ed., *A Not Unreasonable Claim: Women and Reform in Canada* (Toronto 1979), as

well as McLaren, *Our Own Master Race* and Valverde, *The Age of Light, Soap and Water.*

23 E. Zaretsky, "Rethinking the Welfare State," in Dickinson and Russell, eds., *Family, Economy and State,* 105.

24 Elizabeth Smith Shortt Collection, University of Waterloo, Box 46, File 1814, Letter of Shortt to Dr Peter Bryce, Chief Medical Officer, Department of Immigration, Ottawa, November 1914.

25 See M. Shore, *The Science of Social Redemption* (Toronto 1987), on the rise of the social sciences in Canada in the early twentieth century.

26 Editorial, "Health and Hygiene," *Canadian Trade Unionist,* 28 September 1927.

27 Elizabeth Smith Shortt Collection, University of Waterloo, Box 46, File 1813, undated manuscript, "Everyman's Child," 1.

28 Editorial, *Industrial Banner,* 20 April 1920.

29 Elizabeth Smith Shortt Collection, Box 47, File 1854, Shortt, undated speech, "Hygiene for Women."

30 J. Ursel, "The State and the Maintenance of Patriarchy," 177, 182–3; see also Zaretsky, "Rethinking the Welfare State," 105.

31 Mitchinson, *The Nature of Their Bodies,* 153. By the end of the nineteenth century, Canadian physicians were also well on their way to controlling the process of childbirth. On the medicalization of maternity in Canada, see J. Oppenheimer, "Childbirth in Ontario: The Transition from Home to Hospital in the Early Twentieth Century," *OH* 75, no. 1 (1983); V. Strong-Boag and K. McPherson, "The Confinement of Women: Childbirth and Hospitalization in Vancouver, 1919–1939," *BCST,* 69–70 (1986). Both are reprinted in K. Arnup, A. Levesque, and R. Pierson, eds., *Delivering Motherhood* (London 1990). For the United States and Britain, see J. Leavitt, *Brought to Bed: Childbearing in America, 1750–1950* (New York 1986); A. Oakley, *The Captured Womb* (Oxford 1984); R. Apple, *Mothers and Medicine: A Social History of Infant Feeding* (Madison, Wisc. 1987); J. Lewis, *The Politics of Motherhood* (Montreal 1980); D. Dwork, *War is Good for Babies and Other Young Children* (London 1987).

32 The issue of increasing professional and state intervention in the areas of motherhood and childhood has inspired a considerable historiography. See, for example, C. Lasch, *Haven in a Heartless World* (New York 1977), and J. Donzelot, *The Policing of Families* (New York 1979). No historian of childhood in Canada can fail to acknowledge the seminal work of N. Sutherland, *Children in English Canadian Society* (Toronto 1976). Veronica Strong-Boag describes how "eager tutors in medicine, education, and social work contrasted their superior professionalism with maternal amateurism:" V. Strong-Boag, *The New Day Recalled: Lives of Girls and Women in English Canada, 1919–1939*

(Markham 1988), 149. See also an earlier article, V. Strong-Boag, "Intruders in the Nursery," in J. Parr, ed., *Childhood and Family in Canadian History* (Toronto 1982). On infant and maternal mortality, see S. Buckley, "Efforts to Reduce Infant and Maternal Mortality Between the Wars," *Atlantis* 4 (1979); S. Buckley, "Ladies or Midwives?" in Kealey, ed. *A Not Unreasonable Claim*; S. Buckley, "The Search for the Decline of Maternal Mortality," in W. Mitchinson and J.D. McGinnis, eds., *Essays in the History of Canadian Medicine* (Toronto 1988); N. Lewis, "Creating the Little Machine," *BCST* 56 (1982–83); N. Lewis, "Reducing Maternal Mortality in British Columbia," in B.K. Latham and R.J. Pazdro, eds., *Not Just Pin Money* (Victoria 1984). For further treatment of child welfare efforts in British Columbia, see Lewis's unpublished doctoral thesis, "Advising the Parents: Childrearing in British Columbia during the Interwar Years," University of British Columbia (1980).

33 See V. Strong Boag, *The New Day Recalled*. See also B. Ehrenreich and D. English, *For Her Own Good: 150 Years of the Experts' Advice to Women* (New York 1978).

34 Ursel, "The State and the Maintenance of Patriarchy," 177, 182–3.

35 J. Lewis, "Motherhood Issues in the Late Nineteenth and Twentieth Centuries," in Arnup, Levesque, and Pierson, eds., *Delivering Motherhood*, 6; also Lewis, *The Politics of Motherhood*, 61–113. Lewis emphasizes medical politics without sufficiently analysing the actual state of contemporary medical science. Advances in immunology enabled doctors to prevent or at least diminish the impact of some diseases of childhood, but devastating bacterial infections were beyond medical control until the eve of the Second World War. Deborah Dwork's comprehensive examination of the bacteriological and epidemiological research conducted in this period to discover the cause of intestinal disease, the primary killer of babies in the world, establishes that maternal education had a fundamental medical basis. Dwork's essentially medical focus, however, leads her to dispute the notion that any other than medical concerns could have motivated the educational approach to child welfare; see Dwork, *War is Good For Babies and Other Young Children*, 228.

36 Their biographer is undoubtedly correct in asserting that "no other children in all history have had a remotely similar experience;" see P. Berton, *The Dionne Years* (Toronto 1977), 110–11. The tremendous publicity surrounding every aspect of the Quintuplets' lives certainly attracted the attention of Canadian parents to their professionally supervised and regulated upbringing; see Hon. H.J. Kirby, "A Message to the People of Ontario," *The Baby* (Toronto 1940), 4; Strong-Boag, "Intruders in the Nursery," discusses the impact of the Dionnes on Canadian parents.

37 See, for example, J. Sangster, *Dreams of Equality: Women on the Canadian Left* (Toronto 1989).

38 K. Arnup, "Educating Mothers: Government Advice for Women in the Interwar Years," 203, in Arnup, et. al., eds., *Delivering Motherhood*, suggests that the advisers may have "reduced women to slavish followers of their detailed advice."

39 On the high costs of medical care for "the average family," see Dr J. Stevenson, "The Costs of Medical Care," *The Canadian Doctor* 1, no. 11 (1935): 13; see also "Does Health Insurance Improve the National Health?" *The Canadian Doctor* 2, no. 12 (1936): 11, which discusses a statistical survey conducted by the Health Section of the League of Nations that "would appear to show it does." Naylor, *Private Practice, Public Payment*, analyses the profession's attitudes toward state medicine through the early twentieth century.

40 Paul Axelrod discusses the ideological development and social composition of the professional class in English Canada in the early twentieth century in his *Making A Middle Class: Student Life in English Canada During the Thirties* (Montreal/Kingston 1990), 9–11; see also Valverde, *The Age of Light, Soap and Water*, 29. On the attitudes of female doctors, see V. Strong-Boag, "Canada's Women Doctors: Feminism Constrained," in Kealey, ed., *A Not Unreasonable Claim*; Strong-Boag contends that female doctors tended to suscribe to the conservative professional ethos and thus upheld maternalism rather than equal-rights feminism.

41 See the theoretical discussion of social movements in the "General Introduction," S. Clark, J.P. Grayson, and L.M. Grayson, eds., *Prophecy and Protest: Social Movements in Twentieth-Century Canada* (Toronto 1975). While this study focuses on the campaign's medical participants, it nonetheless comprised a broad coalition of lay groups, including women's organizations, public health, social service, urban reform, and church-affiliated groups, as well as individual social scientists, educators, and clergy.

42 See Heather MacDougall's study of the Toronto Department of Health, *Activists and Advocates* (Toronto 1990), for a detailed consideration of child welfare initiatives in that city and their national influence.

43 The phrase comes from an early Ontario Board of Health pamphlet for new mothers: Dr Helen MacMurchy, *A Little Talk About the Baby* (Toronto 1913), 3.

CHAPTER TWO

1 Dr Alan Brown, "The Prevention of Neonatal Mortality," CMAJ 23, no. 9 (1933): 264.

2 Each of these topics has received consideration on its own merits with the increasing attention paid to Canadian social history in the past several decades. On social reform, for example, see R. Allen, *The Social Passion* (Toronto 1971), and more recently, M. Valverde, *The Age of Light, Soap and Water* (Toronto 1991); on medical professionalization in Canada, see D. Naylor, *Private Practice, Public Payment* (Kingston/Montreal 1986); W. Mitchinson, *The Nature of Their Bodies* (Toronto 1991); on public health, see H. MacDougall, *Activists and Advocates: Toronto's Health Department, 1883–1983* (Toronto 1990).

3 See, for example, the polemic by Swedish writer Ellen Key, *The Century of the Child* (New York 1909); similar views on the child as "the centre of life" can be found in Arthur W. Calhoun, *The Social History of the American Family*, 3 vols. (Cleveland 1919), 3:131.

4 N. Sutherland, *Children in English Canadian Society* (Toronto 1976), 11.

5 Dr B.K.F. Rashford, "The Child is Not a Little Man," *Canada Lancet* 29, no. 4 (1896): 208; see also Dr R.A. Bolt, "The Education of the Medical Student in His Relation to Child Welfare," *CPHJ* 9, no. 8 (1918): 304; Editorial, "The Gift of a Child," *Social Welfare* 7, no. 3 (1924): 1.

6 Editorial, "Progress in Paediatrics during the Victorian Age," *Canada Lancet* 30, no. 11 (1898): 575.

7 Editorial, "The Health of the Child," *CMAJ* 2, no. 7 (1912): 704; for similar views, see Dr B. Franklin Royer, "Child Welfare," *CPHJ* 12, no. 8 (1921): 293.

8 Sutherland, *Children in English Canadian Society*, 57; Editorial, "Save the Children", *Canada Lancet* 40, no. 10 (1907): 934.

9 The publication of Seebohm Rowntree's investigations into the living and working conditions of the York working class in 1901 also presented direct evidence of the intimate connection between poor health and poor living conditions; D. Dwork, *War is Good for Babies and Other Young Children* (London 1987), 3–5, 14–15.

10 Galton published *Hereditary Genius* in 1869; see A. McLaren, *Our Own Master Race: Eugenics in Canada, 1885–1945* (Toronto 1990), 13–27.

11 Dwork, *War is Good for Babies and Other Young Children*, 8–9. On the eugenics movement, see L. Farrell, *The Origins and Growth of the English Eugenics Movement* (New York 1985); M. Haller, *Eugenics: Hereditarian Attitudes in American Thought* (New Brunswick, N. J. 1963); for a thorough discussion of the Anglo-American eugenics movements, see D. Kevles, *In the Name of Eugenics: Genetics and the Uses of Human Heredity* (Berkeley, Calif. 1985).

12 A. McLaren, *Our Own Master Race*, details the Canadian eugenics movement. See also A. McLaren, "The Creation of a Haven for Human Thoroughbreds: Sterilization of the Feeble-Minded and the Mentally Ill in British Columbia," *CHR* 67, no. 2 (1986); T. Chapman,

"The Early Eugenics Movement in Western Canada," *Alta Hist* 24, no. 4 (1977); C. Howell, "Medical Professionalization and the Social Transformation of the Maritimes," *J Can Studies* 27, no. 1 (1992). On the eugenicist views of organized women, see C. Bacchi, *Liberation Deferred?: The Ideas of the English-Canadian Suffragists* (Toronto 1983). The NCWC established a Committee on the Care of the Feeble-minded, later renamed the Mental Hygiene Committee, in 1897; on the NCWC, see V. Strong-Boag, *The Parliament of Women* (Ottawa 1976). See also Valverde, *The Age of Light, Soap and Water*, 5, 104–28.

13 Dr P.H. Bryce, "The Scope of a Federal Department of Health," *CMAJ* 10, no. 1 (1920): 3. Actively involved in various reformist causes, Bryce was first secretary of Ontario's Board of Health, 1882–1904, then chief medical officer of the federal immigration department from 1904 until his retirement in 1921. On Bryce's participation in the Canadian Purity Education Association, see Valverde, *The Age of Light, Soap and Water*, 49. For similar medical views, see Dr A. Meyer, "The Right to Marry: What Can a Democratic Civilization Do About Heredity and Child Welfare?" *Canadian Journal of Mental Hygiene* 1, no. 2 (1919): 145; Dr H. MacMurchy, "The Parent's Plea," ibid. 1, no. 3 (1919): 211.

14 McLaren, *Our Own Master Race*, 30–45, discusses MacMurchy's eugenicist views in some detail. For MacMurchy's own views, see her reports on "The Feeble-Minded in Ontario" in Ontario, *Sessional Papers*, Board of Health, Annual Reports, 1907–15, and her larger study, *Sterilization? Birth Control?* (Toronto 1934). MacMurchy obtained a medical degree at the University of Toronto, and began her civil service career as medical inspector for the Toronto Board of Education. She acted as the provincial Board of Health's child health consultant, became assistant inspector of hospitals, prisons and public charities in 1913, and then inspector of the feebleminded. She became first chief of the federal Division of Child Welfare of the new Department of Pensions and National Health in 1919 and remained in that role until her retirement in 1934. See also "Dr Helen MacMurchy," *Child and Family Welfare* 9, no. 5 (1934). For a critical analysis of her reform career, see K. McConnachie, "Methodology in the Study of Women in History: A Case Study of Helen MacMurchy, MD," *OH* 75, no. 1 (1983); see also W. Roberts, "A Guide to the Mental Map of Women Reformers in Toronto," *Atlantis* 3, no. 1 (1977).

15 Editorial, *CMAJ* 17, no. 3 (1927): 347.

16 Dr W.W. Musgrove, "Problems of Childhood," *CMAJ* 17, no. 4 (1927): 441.

17 G.I.H. Lloyd, "The Relation of Preventable Sickness to Poverty," *CPHJ* 6, no. 5 (1915): 244.

18 McLaren, *Our Own Master Race*, 31.

19 Editorial, "Child Welfare," *CPHJ* 4, no. 4 (1913): 162.

20 Dr Alan Brown, "The Prevention of Neonatal Mortality," *CMAJ*, 264. Brown was involved in virtually every aspect of the child welfare campaign in the period and was undoubtedly the nation's leading paediatrician. He received his medical degree from the University of Toronto in 1909 and did postgraduate work under renowned American paediatrician L. Emmett Holt at the Babies' Hospital of New York City. A consultant to the federal and provincial child and maternal welfare divisions as well as to the Toronto Board of Health, he became physician-in-chief of the Hospital for Sick Children in 1920 and held that position until his retirement in 1950. He was chairman of the Department of Paediatrics at the University of Toronto, a founder of that university's Institute of Child Study, and one of the founders of the Canadian Society for the Study of the Diseases of Children. For a brief and celebratory biography, see Hospital for Sick Children Alumni Association, *Dr Alan Brown* (Toronto 1983). See also Dr J.H. Ebbs, "Alan Brown, the Man," *CMAJ* 121, no. 9 (1975). V. Strong-Boag also discusses Brown's child welfare efforts in *The New Day Recalled: Lives of Girls and Women in English Canada, 1919–1939* (Markham: 1988), 168, and in "Intruders in the Nursery," in J. Parr, ed., *Childhood and Family in Canadian History* (Toronto 1982).

21 Dr Alan Brown and Dr George Campbell, "Infant Mortality," *CMAJ* 4, no. 8 (1914): 693. Campbell received his medical degree from the University of Toronto, and did postgraduate training at the Hospital for Sick Children. He was the first director of the Division of Child Hygiene, Toronto Board of Health (1913–14); *Who's Who in Canada* (1931).

22 See, for example, Editorial, "The Cost of Sickness," *CPHJ* 4, no. 4 (1913): 163; J.S. Woodsworth, "The Significance of Human Waste in Modern Life and Its Causes," *CPHJ* 5, no. 1 (1914): 21. See also R. Cook and R.C. Brown, *Canada 1896–1921: A Nation Transformed* (Toronto 1974); T. Copp, *The Anatomy of Poverty* (Toronto 1974); M. Piva, *The Condition of the Working Class in Toronto* (Ottawa 1979), B. Palmer, *The Working Class Experience*, 2nd ed. (Toronto 1992).

23 For a comparative discussion of Progressive social reform in the United States during this period with a view to its impact on women, see M. Abramovitz, *Regulating the Lives of Women* (New York 1987), especially 181–213; see also J. Ursel, "The State and the Maintenance of Patriarchy: A Case Study of Family, Labour and Welfare Legislation in Canada," and E. Zaretsky, "Rethinking the Welfare State," in J. Dickinson and B. Russell, eds., *Family, Economy and State: The Social Reproduction Process Under Capitalism* (New York 1986), 188 and 105;

J. Ursel, *Private Lives, Public Policy: 100 Years of State Intervention in the Family* (Toronto 1992); C. Howell, "Medical Professionalization and the Social Transformation of the Maritimes," 10–16.

24 Editorial, "Free Mothers of a Free Race," *CPHJ* 4, no. 1 (1913): 40–1; see also B. Ehrenreich and B. English, *For Her Own Good: 150 Years of the Experts' Advice to Women* (New York 1978), 188.

25 On women and reform, see T.R. Morrison, "Their Proper Sphere: Feminism, the Family and Child-Centred Social Reform in Ontario," *OH* 68, nos. 1 and 2 (1976); S. Buckley, "Ladies or Midwives," in L. Kealey, ed., *A Not Unreasonable Claim: Women and Reform in Canada* (Toronto 1979) and S. Buckley, "Efforts to Reduce Infant and Maternal Mortality Between the Wars," *Atlantis* 4 (1979); on Quebec, see T. Copp, "The Child Welfare Movement in Montreal to 1920," in D.C.M. Platt, ed., *Social Welfare, 1850–1950: Australia, Argentina and Canada Compared* (London: 1989); for Great Britain, see Dwork, *War is Good for Babies and Other Young Children*, ll; A. Davin, "Imperialism and Motherhood," *Hist Workshop J* 2, no. 5 (1978). S. Koven and S. Michel, "Womanly Duties," *AHR* 95, no. 4 (1990), discuss the child welfare efforts of women in the United States, Great Britain, France, and Germany in the early twentieth century; see also the essays in H. Marland, L. Marks, and V. Fildes, eds., *Women and Children First: International Maternal and Infant Welfare* (London 1992). See also NA, MG 29, Vol. 1318, File 495–1–2, Victorian Order of Nurses, typescript, "Historical Development of Services on Behalf of Women and Children," September 1952, 1.

26 Dwork, *War is Good for Babies and Other Young Children*, 22. On the medicalization of childrearing in the United States in the early twentieth century, see R. Apple, *Mothers and Medicine: A Social History of Infant Feeding* (Madison, Wisc. 1987), especially 72–96; see also Ann Oakley, *The Captured Womb* (Oxford 1984).

27 Brown and Campbell, "Infant Mortality," 604; see also Howell, "Medical Professionalization and the Social Transformation of the Maritimes," 12.

28 Recent sociological assessments of the professionalization process have revised views about the professions as "sources of stability" in modernizing societies: B. Turner, *Medical Power and Social Knowledge* (London 1987), reviews the literature on professionalization with specific reference to physicians, 131–56. The older approach is exemplified by R. Wiebe, *The Search for Order* (New York 1967); B. Bledstein, *The Culture of Professionalism* (New York 1976). On the Maritimes, see Howell, "Medical Professionalization and Social Transformation"; on early twentieth-century midwifery, see C. Benoit, *Midwives in Passage* (St John's, Nfld. 1991).

29 Naylor, *Private Practice, Public Payment*, 8–9, 20–5; B.R. Blishen, *Doctors in Canada* (Toronto 1991). See also H.E. MacDermot, *One Hundred Years of Medicine in Canada* (Toronto 1967), 12. MacDermot sees Canadian medicine developing in two distinct phases. From 1867 to the early 1920s, medical schools were built and advances made elsewhere were assimilated; from 1921, Canadian physicians began to make significant contributions to the body of international medical research. C.M. Godfrey, *Medicine for Ontario* (Belleville 1979), 230, makes the same argument about the new era in Canadian medicine that opened with the immediate post-World War One years.

30 Editorial, "The Canadian Medical Association," *CMAJ* 2, no. 4 (1912): 696.

31 B. Haley, *The Healthy Body and Victorian Culture* (London 1978), 3–11; Apple, *Mothers and Medicine*, 97–113; Ehrenreich and English, *For Her Own Good*, 198–210; S.E.D. Shortt, "Physicians, Science and Status: Issues in the Professionalization of Anglo-American Medicine in the 19th Century," *Med Hist* 27 (1983): 68.

32 Turner, *Medical Power and Social Knowledge*, 38; see also Valverde, *Age of Light, Soap and Water*, 155–67; C. Lasch, "The New History of the Family," *New York Review of Books*, 11 December 1975: 52; C. Lasch, *Haven in a Heartless World* (New York 1977); J. Donzelot, *The Policing of Families* (New York 1979). Michel Foucault's work is instrumental in the discussion of these themes; see especially *Madness and Civilisation* (London 1971), *The Birth of the Clinic* (London 1973), and *The History of Sexuality* (London 1979).

33 Dr H. MacMurchy, "The Medical Inspection of Schools," *CMAJ* 3, no. 2 (1913): 111.

34 Dr A. Brown, "The General Practitioner and Preventive Paediatrics," *CPHJ* 21, no. 6 (1930): 268.

35 Dr J.H. Ebbs, "The Canadian Paediatric Society: Its Early Years," *CMAJ* 126, no. 12 (1980): 1235. The society was formed at a conference at the Hospital for Sick Children on 1 June 1922. The founding officers were Dr A.D. Blackader, president; Dr Alan Brown, vice-president; and Dr E.A. Morgan, secretary. The executive included Dr George Campbell, Dr H.P. Wright, and Dr A. Canfield. It became the Canadian Paediatric Association in 1951.

36 Brown, "The General Practitioner and Preventive Paediatrics," 267–8. Apple, *Mothers and Medicine*, 54, argues that, in the United States, paediatrics represented one-half the practice of the typical family physician by 1908.

37 Dr Alan Brown, "The Relation of the Paediatrician to the Community," *CPHJ* 10, no. 2 (1919): 54–5. For similar views, see Bolt, "Education of the Medical Student," 304. T. Cone, *History of American*

Pediatrics (Boston 1979), 158–9, notes that the opening address of the 1909 meeting of the American Pediatric Society saw Dr Thomas Rotch challenging the members to direct the society to assume an active role in social and public welfare work. In his 1923 presidential address to the society, Dr L. Emmett Holt argued "We must be teachers and leaders in all subjects related to the growth and health of children." By 1930, when President Herbert Hoover called the Third White House Conference on Children and Youth, paediatricians made up the majority of participants.

38 CMA, *Annual Report*, 1945, "Report of the Committee on Economics: Appendix, Presentation of the Canadian Society for the Study of the Diseases of Children," 66–7.

39 Naylor, *Private Practice, Public Payment*, 12; see also K.W. Jones, "Sentiment and Science," *JSH* 4, no. 18 (1983): 82.

40 In 1950 there were only 107 practising paediatricians in the entire country out of approximately 10,000 physicians, or 6.58 per cent of all physicians; Ontario, Department of Health, *Report of the Ontario Health Survey Committee* (Toronto 1952), 235.

41 Edwin Chadwick's *Report on the Sanitary Condition of the Labouring Population of Great Britain* (1842) fostered international interest in the relationship between environment and health. Louis Pasteur's discovery of the microbic origin of disease in 1870 and Robert Koch's isolation of the tubercle bacillus in 1882 prompted adoption of the microbic approach; see A. Grauer, *Public Health: Report of the Royal Commission on Dominion-Provincial Relations* (Ottawa 1939), 2. On the development of public health in Toronto, see MacDougall, *Activists and Advocates*.

42 See also R.D. Defries, ed., *The Development of Public Health in Canada* (Toronto 1940); P. Bator, "The Struggle to Raise the Lower Classes: Public Health Reform and the Problem of Poverty in Toronto, 1910–1921," *J Can Studies* 14, no. 1 (1979); P. Bator, "Saving Lives on the Wholesale Plan: Public Health Reform in the City of Toronto, 1900–1930," Ph.D. thesis, University of Toronto, 1979.

43 Dr A. G. Fleming, "The Education of the Public in Health Matters," *CMAJ* 20, no. 10 (1930): 562. Fleming received his MB degree from the University of Toronto in 1907, and a DPH degree in 1914; he became director of the Venereal Disease Prevention Division, Dominion Department of Health in 1920, and director of the Department of Public Health and Preventive Medicine at McGill University in 1928; *Who's Who in Canada* (1940–41).

44 Ibid.

45 For contemporary views on the value of preventive medicine, see E.M. Chapman, "Paying the Doctor to Keep You Well," *Maclean's*, 1 January

1921; E.M. Chapman, "The Soundest Kind of Prevention," *Maclean's*,
1 August 1921; A. Lampman, "What Price Health?" *Maclean's*, 15
September 1937; H.E. Spencer, "For a Healthy Canada," *Chatelaine*,
August 1930; J. Miller, "Preventive Pathology," *QQ*, October 1922.

46 H.M. Cassidy, "The Economic Value of Public Health," *CPHJ* 23, no. 2
(1932): 52.

47 NA, MG 28, Vol. 72, File 15, NCWC papers, pamphlet published by the
Health League of Canada. The Social Hygiene Council changed its
name to the Health League of Canada in 1936.

48 Dr J.H. McDermot, "The Control of Disease," *QQ*, January 1930: 386;
Editorial, "Public Health and Social Welfare," *CPHJ* 23, no. 10 (1932):
493.

49 See for example, Editorial, "Railways and Typhoid," *CMAJ* 1, no. 3
(1911): 261; also Editorial, "A Dominion Minister of Health," *Canada
Lancet* 37, no. 1 (1903): 243; Editorial, "The Lives of the People,"
CPHJ 4, no. 7 (1913): 422–3.

50 Grauer, *Public Health*, 14.

51 Ibid., 104.

52 Dominion Department of Health, *Report of the Deputy Minister*, 1922,
22; Editorial, "Child Welfare Activities in Canada," *CMAJ* 11, no. 5
(1921): 396. The council received $10,000 annually from the federal
government during the 1920s; the grant was cut 10 percent in 1931
due to Depression exigencies. The council changed its name several
times: in 1931, it became the Canadian Council on Child and Family
Welfare, then in 1935, the Canadian Welfare Council. It is presently
the National Council on Welfare. NA, MG 28 I 10, Vol. 40, File 175,
Canadian Welfare Council papers, Charlotte Whitton, Memorandum:
"To Combine Family and Child Welfare Services in Canada," 1929: 1.
Also, ibid., "Memorandum from the President and Secretary, Canadian Council on Child Welfare," 26 February 1929, in which the argument for the council's expansion is outlined.

53 Department of Health Act, *SC* 1919, c. 24.

54 Dr Helen MacMurchy, "A Safety League for Mothers," *Social Welfare*
13, no. 9 (1931): 184; *Canada Year Book* (1933), 993. The lay members
held three-year terms.

55 Bryce, "The Scope of a Federal Department of Health," 5–6.

56 Estimates indicate that in 1913, total federal government expenditure
on public health was about $15 million, amounting to only 6 per cent
of all government expenditure and only .6 per cent of the gross
national expenditure on public health: Dr Eric J. Hanson, *Public
Finance Aspects of Health Services in Canada: Royal Commission on Health
Services* (Ottawa 1964), 21. See A. Irving, "Federal and Provincial
Issues in Social Policy," in S.A. Yelaja, ed., *Canadian Social Policy*

(Waterloo 1987), 328; C. Charles and R.F. Badgley, "Health and Inequality: Unresolved Policy Issues," ibid., 49.

57 The Public Health Act, *so* 1882, c. 29.

58 Dr J.J. Heagerty, "Public Health in Canada," in Defries, ed. *The Development of Public Health in Canada*, 8. Heagerty received an MD (1905) and DPH (1912) from McGill; in 1928, he became the chief executive assistant of the Department of Pensions and National Health; in 1939, he became director of that department's Division of Public Health Services; *Who's Who in Canada* (1938–39).

59 Ontario, Ministry of Health, *Annual Report*, 1981–82, Special Feature: "A Century of Caring," 59.

60 "Canada's Health," *CCJ* 19, no. 9 (1940): 41; Ministry of Health, *Annual Report*, 1981–82, 57–9. The board became the Department of Health in 1924.

61 In a letter to Carrie Carmichael of the NCWC, Dr Elizabeth Smith Shortt, also an NCWC member, comments at length about "the very serious problem" of the high cost of medical care, and advises the Health Committee of the NCWC to study this problem; see Elizabeth Smith Shortt Collection, University of Waterloo, Correspondence, File 77, Letter of Smith Shortt to Carrie Carmichael, 12 May 1924; see also Editorial, "State Medicine," *CPHJ* 25, no. 3 (1934): 88; Editorial, "The Cost of Sickness," *Canadian Trade Unionist*, 26 July 1929; A.A. Perry, "The High Cost of Sickness," *Chatelaine*, September 1929; Perry, "What Woman Can Do To Combat the High Cost of Sickness," *Chatelaine*, January 1930. See also M.S. Gould, "A Standard of Health and Decency as a Living Wage," *Social Welfare* 8, no. 10 (1926): 220–2; CMA, *Annual Report*, 1934, 62.

62 During World War One, for example, some local medical societies throughout the country committed themselves to free treatment of soldiers' dependents. As early as 1916, the CMA was warning that "the time has come when it is desirable to look the situation calmly in the face and see if there is not a great danger of pauperising these people." See Editorial, "Soldiers' Wives and Free Medical Treatment," *CMAJ* 6, no. 1 (1916): 47–8.

63 The CMA study indicated that the average cost of carrying a practice was $2,934.46. The average amount of medical service supplied gratuitously in one year was $814.82, while unpaid medical accounts amounted to $1,246.57; CMA, *Annual Report*, 1934, 62; see also Naylor, *Private Practice, Public Payment*, 47. The regular "Medical Economics Column" published during the interwar years in the *CMAJ* kept up a constant refrain of exploitation of the profession by individuals and an irresponsible state; see, for example, "Medical Economics," *CMAJ* 30, no. 10 (1939): 403, which quotes an American study

claiming that "the wage rate for physicians is less than for skilled labour."

64 The pages of *The Canadian Doctor* (the "business journal" of the profession) are filled with largely negative arguments on this issue; see, for example, "Costs of Medical Care," *The Canadian Doctor* 1, no. 11 (1935): 14–17. See also Naylor, *Private Practice, Public Payment*, 32–3; C.H. Shillington, *The Road to Medicare in Canada* (Toronto 1972) and Malcolm G. Taylor, *Insuring National Health Care: The Canadian Experience* (Chapel Hill 1990).

65 "Medical Economics," *CMAJ* 30, no. 10 (1939): 403.

66 On "deskilling," see Turner, *Medical Power and Social Knowledge*, 141.

67 Editorial, "Unemployment Relief," *CMAJ* 23, no. 7 (1933): 71; Dr H. McPhedran, "The Difficulties of the Profession," *CMAJ* 24, no. 4 (1934): 436; "Organized Medicine Ready for Health Insurance," *The Canadian Doctor* 1, no. 10 (1935): 18–20; Naylor, *Private Practice, Public Payment*, 47.

68 League for Social Reconstruction Research Committee, *Social Planning for Canada* (Toronto 1935), 390.

69 In 1933, the CMA sent a delegation to Ottawa to discuss with Bennett the medical care of the unemployed. The delegation argued that doctors were willing to accept one-half their regular fee if the provinces and the federal government would contribute the other half as a relief measure. The prime minister expressed "every sympathy" but replied that "the matters you have presented are strictly the business of the provinces" and any federal contribution would be decided "according to the merits of the case presented by the province." "Delegation to Ottawa Re Medical Care of the Unemployed," *CMAJ* 23, no. 11 (1933): 555. Bennett's Employment and Social Insurance Act of 1935 contained the framework for a national health and welfare plan that also included health insurance; the plan was declared ultra vires by the Judicial Committee of the Privy Council; see Shillington, *The Road to Medicare in Canada*, 20, 21. See also L.C. Marsh, *Health and Unemployment* (Montreal 1938), 214–16; H.E. MacDermot, *One Hundred Years of Medicine in Canada*, 83–4.

70 Dr T.C. Routley, "Medical Relief for the Unemployed and Their Dependents in the Province of Ontario," *CMAJ* 25, no. 7 (1935): 85. The plan was administered by the OMA under the supervision of the Department of Public Welfare; Routley was president of the OMA. Despite medical control of the plan, complaints by doctors persisted: see "When Sick It Pays to Be Poor," *The Canadian Doctor* 1, no. 10 (1935): 16; Dr J. Stevenson, "This Must Be Remedied," ibid., 17; "Medical Relief Payment: Continued Failure to Recognize the Rights of Doctors," ibid., 2, no. 3 (1936): 12.

71 Dr J. Roberts, "Does Vaccination Protect?" *CPHJ* 4, no. 8 (1913): 443; E. Shorter, *The Health Century* (New York 1987), 3–5.

72 Between 1910–19, the death rate for children under five due to tuberculosis averaged about 5 per cent, which was reduced to 3.8 per cent by 1931. While not insignificant, the death rate due to intestinal infections averaged about 20 per cent in this period; see Dr R.E. Wodehouse, "On the Necessity for the Careful Medical Oversight of Children of the School and Pre-school Age," *CMAJ* 12, no. 6 (1922): 429; M.A. Ross, "Tuberculosis Mortality in Ontario," *CPHJ* 25, no. 2 (1934): 78–9. See Ontario, Board of Health, *Annual Report*, 1916, 4, for tuberculosis mortality statistics from 1906–15; Ross provides statistics from 1880–1931.

73 Editorial, "The Tuberculosis Problem," *Canada Lancet* 42, no. 2 (1908): 58–9; Dr J.H. Elliot, "The Prevention of Tuberculosis," *CPHJ* 4, no. 1 (1913): 28–30; Dr M.F. McPhedran, "Tuberculosis in Childhood as a Problem of Preventive Medicine," *CPHJ* 21, no. 10 (1930): 455. See also K. McCuaig, "From Social Reform to Social Service. The Changing Role of Volunteers: The Anti-tuberculosis Campaign, 1900–1930," *CHR* 61, no. 4 (1980).

74 Dr F. Tisdall, "The Aetiology of Rickets," *CMAJ* 11, no. 11 (1921): 943; Dr F. Tisdall, "Inadequacy of Present Dietary Standards," *CMAJ* 25, no. 12 (1935): 627. By 1935 it was "universally acknowledged" that Vitamin D was essential during the first two years of life in order to prevent rickets, and that this vitamin could be provided safely and inexpensively by means of cod-liver oil.

75 Diseases reported were smallpox, scarlet fever, diphtheria, measles, whooping cough, typhoid, tuberculosis, infantile paralysis, and cerebrospinal meningitis; Board of Health, *Annual Report*, 1912, 12–13. For the eight-year period, the total death rate from communicable diseases from birth to age one was 790 per year; from one to two, it was 459; from five to nine, it was 462. See also Ontario, Department of Health, *Annual Report*, 1940. I have grouped together under infectious diseases the respiratory diseases (12.4 per cent) and the contagious diseases (10 per cent), since these categories are not further defined in the report. In 1921, children under fifteen years formed 30.8 per cent of the population of Ontario.

76 "Public Health in Ontario," *CMAJ* 2, no. 10 (1912): 929. The Public Health Act of Ontario of 1912 listed the following as reportable diseases: smallpox, diphtheria, scarlet fever, measles, German measles, glanders, cholera, erysipelas, tuberculosis, mumps, anthrax, bubonic plague, rabies, poliomyelitis, and cerebrospinal meningitis. The difficulties posed by the official statistics were a constant refrain in health care circles in the early 20th century. See, for example, Dr N.E.

McKinnon and M.A. Ross, "Whooping Cough: The Public Health Problem," *CPHJ* 25, no. 11 (1935): 533; Editorial, "Provincial Board of Health Report," *Canada Lancet* 38, no. 3 (1904): 274–5; A.B. Baird, "Problems in Infant Hygiene and What Statistics Reveal," *CPHJ* 22, no. 3 (1931): 120–9; M.A. Ross, "The Mortality in Ontario of Four Communicable Diseases of Childhood," *CPHJ* 23, no. 7 (1932): 331; Dr J.G. Fitzgerald, "The Specific Prevention of Measles, Scarlet Fever and Diphtheria," *CPHJ* 24, no. 10 (1933): 455.

77 In the 1880s, communicable diseases accounted for more than 1 in 3 of all deaths in the under-fourteen age group; in 1932, they were still responsible for 600 deaths annually in Ontario, concentrated largely in the under-ten age group; see M.A. Ross, "The Mortality in Ontario of Four Communicable Diseases of Childhood," 340.

78 "Report of the Medical Officer of Health for Windsor," Board of Health, *Annual Report*, 1916, 146.

79 "Report of the Medical Officer for Chatham," ibid., 1915, 220.

80 "Report of the Medical Officer of Health for Hamilton," ibid., 1916, 129.

81 Ross, "The Mortality in Ontario of Four Communicable Diseases of Childhood," 341; "Vaccination Against Diphtheria," advertisement for diphtheria toxoid by Connaught Laboratories, University of Toronto, published in *CMAJ* 18, no. 8 (1928). On the role of the Connaught Laboratories in the manufacture and distribution of diphtheria anti-toxin and toxoid, see J. Lewis, "The Prevention of Diphtheria in Canada and Britain, 1914–1945," *JSH* 20, no. 1 (1986); P. Bator and A.J. Rhodes, *Within Reach of Everyone: A History of the University of Toronto School of Hygiene and Connaught Laboratories* (Ottawa 1990).

82 Ontario, Department of Health, *Prevention of Diphtheria*, 3rd ed. (pamphlet) (Toronto 1930), 1.

83 Department of Health, *Annual Report*, 1930, 2.

84 "Report of the Medical Officer of Health for Hamilton," Board of Health, *Annual Report*, 1920, 246; "Report of District I," Department of Health, *Annual Report*, 1924, 65; ibid., "District II," 67.

85 Ibid., 35. Paul Bator, "The Health Reformers Versus the Common Canadian: The Controversy over Compulsory Vaccination against Smallpox," *OH*, 75, no. 4 (1983): 349–73. See also Lewis, "The Prevention of Diphtheria in Canada and Britain, 1914–1945," 169. H. MacDougall, *Activists and Advocates*, 116, discusses anti-vaccination activists in Toronto in this period.

86 Department of Health, *Annual Report*, 1929, 81–3; 1930, 118. The 1933 *Annual Report*, 27, noted a marked reduction in the incidence of diphtheria. A total of 529 cases were reported, whereas the median for the previous six years was 2,918.

87 Department of Health, *Annual Report*, 1936, 36, 38. From a death rate of
   31.32 per 100,000 in the years 1900–1904, the death rate had dropped
   to an average of .65 per 100,000 in the years 1935–39; Fitzgerald, "The
   Specific Prevention of Measles, Scarlet Fever and Diphtheria," 456.
88 Ontario Department of Health, *Scarlet Fever* (pamphlet) (Toronto
   1928), 1, 2. Scarlatina, or scarlet fever, is an acute communicable disease characterized by sudden onset of sore throat, fever, and vom-
   iting, with the development of a scarlet rash which appears soon after
   the initial symptoms.
89 The breakthrough for a test came with the investigations of George
   and Gladys Dick at the University of Chicago; see H.F. Dowling,
   Fighting Infection (Boston 1977), 58–9.
90 Department of Health, *Annual Report*, 1927, 15.
91 Department of Health, *Scarlet Fever*, 2. Dowling also points out that
   even in the large series of cases reported from the hospital associated
   with the Dicks' laboratory, the case fatality rate was the same for the
   patients treated with antitoxin as for those who had received none.
   He argues that, from a public health standpoint, the antitoxin was
   harmful because it prevented the rash from developing, thus complicating diagnosis; *Fighting Infection*, 60–1, 65. Dr C.D. Farquharson,
   Medical Officer of Health, "Controlling Smallpox, Diphtheria, Scarlet
   Fever and Measles in Scarborough Township," *CPHJ* 22, no. 8
   (1931):422, indicates that five children who tested negative got the
   disease, while retesting after the series of five innoculations showed
   immunity in only 70 per cent of cases.
92 Department of Health, *Report of the Ontario Health Survey Committee*,
   385.
93 Fitzgerald, "The Specific Prevention of Measles, scarlet Fever and
   Diptheria," 456–8, 464; Ross, "The Mortality of Four Communicable
   Diseases of Childhood," 341. Human convalescent serum was developed from the blood of a case recently recovered, or whole blood
   from the child's parents, 95 per cent of whom had had the disease in
   childhood. It was believed particularly effective if given within four
   days after exposure; see also Dr W.H. Hattie, "Etiology of Measles,"
   CMAJ 17, no. 8 (1927): 952. Hattie discusses American experimentation with measles antitoxin, which had been "used successfully as a
   prophylactic in a limited number of exposed persons."
94 McKinnon and Ross, "Whooping Cough: The Public Health Problem,"
   533.
95 Ontario, Department of Health, *Whooping Cough* (pamphlet) (Toronto
   1930), 2–3.
96 McKinnon and Ross, "Whooping Cough: The Public Health Problem,"
   537.

97 Department of Health, *Whooping Cough*, 2–3.
98 Department of Health, *Report of the Ontario Health Survey Committee*, 385.
99 Dr A.L. McKay, "The Control of Measles and Whooping Cough," *CPHJ* 22, no. 7 (1931): 351; Ross, "The Mortality in Ontario of Four Communicable Diseases," 331.
100 Baird, "Problems in Infant Hygiene and What Statistics Reveal," 168. On influenza, see E. Pettigrew, *The Silent Enemy: Canada and the Deadly Flu of 1918* (Saskatoon 1989); J.P. Dickin McGinnis, "The Impact of Epidemic Influenza: Canada, 1918–1919," in S.E.D. Shortt, ed., *Medicine in Canadian Society* (Montreal/Kingston 1981).
101 C. Webster, "Healthy or Hungry Thirties?" *Hist Workshop* 13, no. 4 (1982): 124. Webster provides a critical analysis of the reliability of official health statistics as a true measure of public health. See also M. Mitchell, "The Effects of Unemployment on Women and Children in the 1930s," *Hist Workshop* 19, no. 5 (1985): 107, and L. Bryder, "The First World War: Healthy or Hungry?" *Hist Workshop* 24, no. 6 (1987): 141.
102 Webster, "Healthy or Hungry Thirties?" 124.
103 Ibid., 118.
104 Dr J.H. Mason Knox, "Infant Care," *CMAJ* 23, no. 8 (1933): 151. Knox was chief of the Bureau of Child Hygiene, Maryland State Department of Health, Baltimore, Maryland. MacMurchy participated in the formation of the American Association for the Study and Prevention of Infant Mortality in 1909, and was considered "from the beginning an honoured member and counsellor."
105 Dr H. MacMurchy, *Infant Mortality: First Special Report* (Toronto 1910); *Infant Mortality: Second Special Report* (1911), *Infant Mortality: Third Special Report* (1912).
106 Dr C.A. Hodgetts, "Infantile Mortality in Canada," *CMAJ* 1, no. 8 (1911): 720.
107 Ibid., 722. Hodgetts produced much the same analysis as chief health officer of Ontario; see Board of Health, *Annual Report*, 1906, "Review of Vital Statistics," 99–102.
108 Dwork, *War is Good for Babies and Other Young Children*, 26.
109 Hodgetts, "Infantile Mortality in Canada," 723.
110 Ibid.
111 Brown and Campbell, "Infant Mortality," 692–3.
112 See also Dr E.A. Morgan, "The Summer's Experience with Infectious Diarrhaea," *CMAJ* 10, no. 6 (1920): 531; Dr Albert Jobin, "Heat and Infant Mortality," *CMAJ* 10, no. 7 (1920): 661; Dr Stanley Graham, "The Bacteriology of Infectious Diarrhaea," *CMAJ* 11, no. 8 (1921): 529.

113 MacMurchy, *Infant Mortality* (1912), 16–17.

114 Brown and Campbell, "Infant Mortality," 693.

115 See, for example, B. Palmer, *The Working Class Experience*; Copp, *The Anatomy of Poverty*, and Piva, *The Condition of the Working Class in Toronto*.

116 "Changes in the Cost of Living in Canada from 1913 to 1937," *Labour Gazette*, June 1937, 819–21.

117 PAO, Acc. 16383, Ontario Welfare Council papers, T.R. Robinson, "Report on Industrial Relations," Social Service Council of Ontario, *Annual Meeting and Conference*, Hamilton, May 1920, 72–3.

118 Ibid., F. Almy, "The Meaning of Poverty," 87.

119 "Worker's Hard Struggle," Letter to the Editor, from Kincardine, *Industrial Banner*, 20 May 1921.

120 "Earnings and Infant Mortality in the United States," *Labour Gazette*, January 1924, 5.

121 Copp, *The Anatomy of Poverty*, 93–100; Piva, *The Condition of the Working Class in Toronto*, 113–23.

122 Canada, House of Commons, *Debates*, 15 March 1926, 1567. Woodsworth described his examination of a spot map of Winnipeg that showed the concentrations of disease, relief cases, and incidence of juvenile crime in poor areas of the city.

123 Brown, "The Prevention of Neonatal Mortality," 265.

124 Jones, "Sentiment and Science," 81–2.

125 Hodgetts, "Infantile Mortality in Canada," 725.

126 MacMurchy, *Infant Mortality* (1912), 30.

127 For contemporary views, see R. Howe, "A Woman's Place," *Industrial Banner*, 20 February 1920; E. Morton, "Can Women Solve Unemployment," *Canadian Trade Unionist*, 30 August 1932; see also J. Sangster, *Dreams of Equality: Women on the Canadian Left* (Toronto 1989), 13–25; L. Kealey, "Canadian Socialism and the Woman Question, 1900–1914," *Labour* 13 (1984).

128 "How to Produce a Better Race," *Labour News*, 29 June 1925.

129 "Health A Worker's Asset," *Canadian Trade Unionist*, 24 May 1928; "Forestalling Disease Ravages," *Canadian Trade Unionist*, 27 January 1928; "The Prevention of Disease," ibid., 27 January 1928. For similar promotion of the value of health education, see "Vaccination Truths," *Industrial Banner*, 30 January 1920; "Fighting Against White Plague Menace," ibid., 27 May 1921; "Health and Housing," *Canadian Trade Unionist*, 26 July 1929; "Cost of Sickness," ibid., 26 July 1929; "Maternal and Infant Welfare," ibid., 29 May 1929; "Defeating Disease," ibid., 31 January 1930; "How Science Can Add Years to Your Life," ibid., 20 August 1930; "Maternal Mortality in Canada," *Labour News*, 27 April 1929; "Health Study in Montreal," ibid., 31 May 1929;

"Health Methods Will Save Canadians," *Industrial Banner*, 29 August 1931; "Penny Wise and Pound Foolish," *Oshawa Labour Press*, 13 July 1939.

130 See, for example, "Sickness Insurance," *Labour News*, 15 June 1934, an editorial insisting that "compulsory state health insurance will have to be enacted."

131 Dr H. Little, "Intestinal Intoxication," *CMAJ* 13, no. 11 (1923): 806. A London paediatrician, Little noted that "in spite of the best known methods of treatment, the mortality in this condition at the Hospital for Sick Children [Toronto] in 1920 was 131."

132 Dr A. Brown and Dr G. Boyd, "Acute Intestinal Intoxication in Infants," *CMAJ* 13, no. 12 (1923): 802.

133 Baird, "Problems in Infant Hygiene," 169.

134 Brown and Boyd, "Acute Intestinal Intoxication in Infants," 801–3. See also M.M. Johnston, A. Brown, and M.J. Kaake, "Further Studies of the Aetiology of Acute Intestinal Intoxication in Infants and Children," *CPHJ* 22, no. 9 (1931): 441.

CHAPTER THREE

1 It was not until 1945 that the cause of gastroenteric disease was established conclusively with the discovery of the pathogenic role of *escherichia coli* by Dr John Bray, Middlesex; see D. Dwork, *War is Good for Babies and Other Young Children* (London 1987), 50.

2 Dr A. Brown and Dr G. Boyd, "Acute Intestinal Intoxication in Infants," *CMAJ* 13, no. 12 (1923): 800–1. Based on research conducted in the wards and laboratories of the Hospital for Sick Children and the Department of Paediatrics, University of Toronto, this paper was read at the first annual meeting of the Canadian Society for the Study of Diseases of Children held in Montreal, June 1923. Brown and Boyd noted that "numerous bacteriological researches have failed to reveal a pathognomonic organism." Their own experimental work suggested that the cause was "a circulating toxin produced in the mucous membrane of the bowel," but further work was being done to determine whether the symptoms were due to an overproduction or increased absorption of this substance. In a later study, M.M. Johnston, A. Brown, and M.J. Kaake, "Further Studies of the Aetiology of Acute Intestinal Intoxication in Infants and Children," *CPHJ* 22, no. 9 (1931): 452, the researchers concluded that the causative organisms "are members of the colon-paratyphoid-paradysentery group." Dwork, *War is Good for Babies and Other Young Children*, 36–51, provides an in-depth discussion of international medical research to locate the spe-

cific disease-causing organism. See also "Kill Flies and Save Lives," *The Canadian Nurse* 16, no. 4 (1920): 215.

3 "Report of the Medical Officer of Health for Brantford," Ontario, Board of Health, *Annual Report*, 1913, 443.

4 Dr A. Cochrane, "The Importance of Clean Bottles," *Canada Lancet* 45, no. 8 (1912): 58.

5 "Report of the Medical Officer of Health for Guelph," Board of Health, *Annual Report*, 1913, 445.

6 Editorial, "The Milk Commission," *CPHJ* 1, no. 10 (1910): 459–60; J.H. Elliott, "Shall We Have Pure Milk in Canada?" *CPHJ* 2, no. 8 (1911): 353; "Hygiene and the Ontario Legislature," *CPHJ* 2, no. 4 (1911): 170; L.C. Bilmer, "Municipal Milk Inspection," *CPHJ* 5, no. 7 (1914): 500–4; Editorial, "Solving the Milk Problem," *CPHJ* 5, no. 7 (1914): 504–6; Editorial, "The Value of Pasteurization," *CMAJ* 30, no. 12 (1939): 603; Dr M.F. McPhedran, "Tuberculosis in Childhood as a Problem of Preventive Medicine," *CPHJ* 21, no. 10 (1930): 475; Dr. R.M. Price, "Milk and Its Relation to Tuberculosis," *CPHJ* 25, 1 (1934): 13. A rough estimate of 1915 suggested that one-quarter of tuberculous children under five had been infected by milk and that at least one-quarter of Ontario dairy herds had the disease; see K. McCuaig, "From Social Reform to Social Service: The Changing Role of Volunteers in the Anti-Tuberculosis Campaign, 1900–1930," *CHR* 61, no. 4 (1980): 484; also K. McCuaig, "Tuberculosis: The Changing Concepts of the Disease in Canada," in C.G. Roland, ed., *Health, Disease and Medicine: Essays in Canadian History* (Hamilton 1982); see also Dr C.D. Parfitt, "An Address Before the Canadian Tuberculosis Association," *CMAJ* 14, no. 7 (1924): 573–9, for the association's history. The association was formed in 1901.

7 K.W. Jones, "Sentiment and Science," *JSH* 4, no. 18 (1983): 80; N. Sutherland, *Children in English Canadian Society* (Toronto 1976), 59. See also Dr W.J. Deadman and Dr F.J. Elliott, "Clean Bottles, A Factor in Clean Milk," *CPHJ* 25, no. 1 (1934): 32–3.

8 Dwork, *War is Good for Babies and Other Young Children*, 59–88, discusses the anti-tuberculosis campaign in Britain in some detail.

9 Newspaper clipping, Toronto *Globe*, 2 April 1909, in Ontario Legislative Library, *Newspaper Hansard*.

10 Board of Health, *Annual Report*, 1910, 137–71; "Hygiene and the Ontario Legislature," 170; Toronto *Globe*, 27 January 1910. This early pure milk legislation involved enforcing strict standards of cleanliness and purity (certification) but did not actually require pasteurization. N. Lewis, "Advising the Parents: Childrearing in British Columbia during the Interwar Years," Ph.D. thesis, University of British

Columbia 1980, 70, discusses efforts to clean up the milk supply in that province.

11 Newspaper clippings, from the Toronto *Globe*, 11 March 1910; 16 March 1910; 24 February 1911; 24 February 1917, in Ontario Legislative Library, *Newspaper Hansard*. The legislation provided for the substitution of a "pooling" system for one of paying by "test," so that dairy farmers would be paid according to quality, not quantity. The Western Ontario Dairymen's Association was in favour, but the Eastern Ontario Association argued that it had "not sufficient time to remove prejudices against such a radical change."

12 Dairy Standards Act, so 1916, c. 52. In 1922, for example, under the United Farmers of Ontario (UFO) government of E.C. Drury, the UFO member for Dundas called for the indefinite suspension of the Act due to its "impracticality." The vote was 60 to 14 against him; Toronto *Globe*, 31 March 1922.

13 Dr T.P. Shaw, "Sanitary Milk," CMAJ 1, no. 12 (1911): 1138; Dr C.S. Edgett, "Milk and Meat Inspection," CMAJ 3, no. 5 (1913): 373; Editorial, "Clean Milk," CMAJ 5, no. 4 (1915): 318; Dr H.W. Hill, "The Relation of Sanitation to Death and Disease," CMAJ 6, no. 5 (1916): 452; Editorial, "Pasteurization of Milk," CMAJ 20, no. 11 (1930): 637; Dr A.L. McKay, "A Clean Milk Supply for Small Towns," CPHJ 16, no. 6 (1925): 409; Dr. B Evan Parry, *Pasteurization of Milk for Small Communities* (pamphlet) (Ottawa 1928); Dr K.W. McHenry, "The Nutritional Value of Pasteurized Milk," CPHJ 25, no. 1 (1934): 22–3.

14 Editorial, "Pasteurization of Milk," CMAJ, 20, no. 11 (1930): 637. Mackay, "A Clean Milk Supply for Small Towns," 409, found "over twenty towns in Ontario of a population around 2,500 inhabitants have over 80% of their milk pasteurized and most of them 100%." R.H. Murray, "The Extent of Pasteurization in Canada," CPHJ 25, no. 1 (1934): 30–1; Murray's survey of 24 cities found 19 with 60 per cent of their milk supply pasteurized and only 5 with 100 per cent pasteurization.

15 Parry, *Pasteurization of Milk for Small Communities*, 61–2. Controversy continued even after pasteurization was made compulsory; see for example, Editorial, "Pasteurization Does Not Clean Dirty Milk," *Labour Press* (Oshawa) 3 November 1938. The mayor of Collingwood argued that milk dealers were being pushed out of business because of this unfair legislation. Like the Waterloo town council, Collingwood's town council voted 7 to 2 to request immediate repeal. The *Labour Press* editors expressed hesitation. See Ontario, *Report of the Ontario Health Survey Committee*, vol. 1, (Toronto 1950), 1.

16 Editorial, "Clean Milk," 316; Shaw, "Sanitary Milk," 1140.

17 The Local Council of Women in Ottawa also lobbied for Sunday milk delivery, arguing that "the poorest of the population" could not keep milk for their babies fresh over the weekend during the summer; Elizabeth Smith Shortt collection, University of Waterloo, File 2210, Letter to *Ottawa Evening Journal*, 11 July 1912, unsigned (newspaper clipping); also File 4, Letter of Shortt to *Ottawa Free Press*, 28 August 1916, "Sunday Milk and the Babies" (newspaper clipping).

18 Dr A. Brown and Dr G. Campbell, "Infant Mortality," *CMAJ* 4, no. 8 (1914): 697; Dr J.H. Mason Knox, "Infant Care," *CMAJ* 23, no. 8 (1933): 150; Dwork, *War is Good for Babies and Other Young Children*, 95–8.

19 Dr Henry Koplik established the first distribution centre on the Lower East Side of New York City in 1889. By 1893, wealthy New York philanthropist Nathan Straus was supporting and directing the construction of several pasteurizing plants that distributed prepared milk formulas through stations set up in various areas of New York. See Brown and Campbell, "Infant Mortality," 698; Knox, "Infant Care," 150; R. Apple, *Mothers and Medicine: A Social History of Infant Feeding* (Madison, Wisc. 1987), 57–8.

20 The St Helen's milk depot was established in England in 1899, although the French example was not really imitated until the organization of a weekly consultation clinic for babies at Battersea in 1905; Dwork, *War is Good for Babies and Other Young Children*, 107–12. For an international perspective, see the collection of essays in V. Fildes, L. Marks, and H. Marland, eds. *Women and Children First: International Maternal and Infant Welfare* (London 1992).

21 Brown and Campbell, "Infant Mortality," 699. They argued that "efforts in other cities to be successful" had to incorporate the British and American fundamentals of extensive development of the milk depot and infant consultation, federation of all the agencies engaged in infant welfare work, and home visits by trained nurses.

22 Dr W.L. Cody, "The Scope and Function of the Medical Staff of the Babies' Dispensary, Hamilton," *CPHJ* 6, no. 11 (1915): 545; Dr J. Heurner Mullen, "Child Welfare in a Democracy," *CPHJ* 9, no. 10 (1918): 448; Enid M. Forsythe, "Child Welfare Clinics", *CPHJ* 9, no. 4 (1918): 170.

23 Brown and Campbell, "Infant Mortality," 707. A similar view is expressed in Dr R. Wodehouse, "Municipal Health Work Pertaining to Infant Welfare," *CMAJ* 3, no. 3 (1913): 186.

24 Dr A. Brown, "The Relation of the Paediatrician to the Community," *CPHJ* 10, no. 2 (1919): 51.

25 Editorial, "Baby Clinics," *CPHJ* 4, no. 2 (1913): 94.

26 Dr G. Smith, "The Result of Three Years' Work in the Department of Child Hygiene, Toronto," *CPHJ* 9, no. 7 (1918): 310–11.

27 Ibid., 313.

28 Forsythe, "Child Welfare Clinics," 169.

29 Smith, "The Result of Three Years' Work in the Department of Child Hygiene, Toronto," 313; Forsythe, "Child Welfare Clinics," 170.

30 Elizabeth Smith Shortt collection, University of Waterloo, Correspondence, Box 6, File 317, Letter of Dr J. Heurner Mullen to Dr Elizabeth Smith Shortt, 22 August 1910.

31 Cody, "The Scope and Function of the Medical Staff of the Babies Dispensary, Hamilton," 546–7. See also V. Bruegerman, RN, "With the Babies Dispensary, Hamilton," *The Canadian Nurse* 22, no. 5 (1926): 256; P. Bowman, RN, "A Child Welfare Clinic," ibid. 22, no. 9 (1926): 484–5.

32 Mullen, "Child Welfare in a Democracy," 449. See also "Teaching Methods in Public Health Nursing," *The Canadian Nurse* 16, no. 1 (1920): 29–31; A. Thomson, RN, "The Value of Health Training in the Home," ibid., 22, no. 8 (1926): 415–16; B.E. Merson, RN, "A Day with the Clinic's Visiting Nurse," ibid., 28, no. 1 (1932): 24–5.

33 Grace E. Moore, RN, "Report of the Superintendent of Milk Stations," Board of Health, *Annual Report*, 1914, 247–8.

34 London Child Welfare Association, "Report of the Supervising Nurse," *Canadian Child Welfare News* 1, no. 5 (1925): 27.

35 PAO, RG 10, 30-A-3, Box 7, file 7.4, Supervisors' Reports, N.E. Howey, London, "Amalgamation of Services," 6 October 1938, 1–3. The Board of Health assumed responsibility for the clinics in 1936. Three of the 8 clinics then in existence were closed.

36 "The Well-Baby Clinics in London, Canada," *CPHJ* 16, no. 5 (1925): 202.

37 Brown and Campbell, "Infant Mortality," 699.

38 Ibid., 707.

39 Dr C.A. Hodgetts, "Statistics and Publicity in Child Welfare Work," *CPHJ* 12, no. 3 (1921): 111. See also Lewis, "Advising the Parents," chap. 2.

40 Hodgetts, "Statistics and Publicity in Child Welfare Work," 111.

41 Editorial, "Infant Mortality," *CPHJ* 6, no. 10 (1915): 510.

42 Dwork, *War is Good for Babies and Other Young Children*, 114.

43 Ibid., 114; Jane Lewis, *The Politics of Motherhood* (Montreal 1980) also focuses on the educational aspects of the campaign in Great Britain.

44 Editorial, "Infant Mortality," 510.

45 Editorial, "These Little Ones," *Social Welfare* 1, no. 3 (1918): 53; see also Editorial, "Child Welfare," *CPHJ* 6, no. 3 (1915): 162.

46 Editorial, "Human Sacrifice," *CPHJ* 4, 2 (1913): 95.

47 Dr B.F. Royer, "Child Welfare," *CPHJ* 12, no. 7 (1921): 293.

48 Dr L. M. Lindsay, "Secretary's Report: 1919," *CPHJ* 11, no. 2 (1920): 80.

49 Dr W.W. Chipman, "The Infant Soldier," *Social Welfare* 4, no. 3 (1921): 48–9.

50 Dr R.A. Bolt, "The Education of the Medical Student in His Relation to Child Welfare," *CPHJ* 9, no. 2 (1918): 309.

51 See, for example, Dr M. Sherwood, "Some Problems of Child Hygiene," *CPHJ* 4, no. 4 (1921): 54; M. Power, "Child Welfare," *Social Welfare* 1, no. 9 (1919): 100; Editorial, "A Children's Bureau for Canada," *Social Welfare* 1, no. 4 (1919): 84; Dr H. MacMurchy, "The Baby's Father," *CPHJ* 9, no. 7 (1918): 318; Dr A.C. Jost, "The Conservation of Child Life," *CPHJ* 11, no. 11 (1920): 503; M.H. Malcolmson, "How We Reduced Infant Mortality in St Catharines," *Social Welfare* 5, no. 10 (1922): 215; Dr A.D. Blackader, "Fundamental Facts in Organization," *CPHJ* 12, no. 3 (1921): 97–8; Editorial, "The Gift of a Child," *Social Welfare* 7, no. 3 (1924): 1; C.S. Walters, "The Duty of the City to the Child," *CPHJ* 6, no. 11 (1915): 540. On the impact of war in Great Britain, see Dwork, *War is Good for Babies and Other Young Children*, and A. Davin, "Imperialism and Motherhood," *Hist Workshop* 2, no. 5 (1978).

52 NCWC, "Report of the Public Health Committee," *NCWC Yearbook*, 1915, 235.

53 R. Torrington, "Presidential Address," *NCWC Yearbook*, 1917, 16; see also V. Strong-Boag, *The Parliament of Women* (Ottawa 1976), 311.

54 *Women's War Conference* (pamphlet) (Ottawa 1918), 33. Helen Reid became director of the Victorian Order of Nurses as well as Director of the Child Welfare Association of Montreal during the First World War; *Who's Who in Canada* (1930–31).

55 Ibid., 44.

56 Royer, "Child Welfare," 290–1.

57 "Things Editorial," *Social Welfare* 2, no. 1 (1919): 3.

58 See for example, Dr S.W. Hewetson, "National Defence and the Medical Profession," *CMAJ* 4, no. 10 (1914): 886; Col. Guy Carleton Jones, "Importance of the Balkan Wars to the Medical Profession in Canada," *CMAJ* 4, no. 10 (1914): 779; Editorial, "The War," *CMAJ* 4, no. 10 (1914): 803; Editorial, "The Canadian Mother," *Social Welfare* 5, no. 8 (1923): 158; Bolt, "Education of the Medical Student,": 309; Dr P. Bryce, "Two Problems in Child Welfare," *Social Welfare* 3, no. 7 (1921): 187–8.

59 Jost, "The Conservation of Child Life," 503.

60 Dr O.A. Cannon, "Health Opportunities in Industry," *CPHJ* 21, no. 1 (1930): 2–3.

61 Dr A. Brown, "Infant and Child Welfare Work," *CPHJ* 9, no. 4 (1918): 149; also A.W. Coone, "The Child as an Asset," *Social Welfare* 1, no. 2 (1918): 38. For similar comments on the economic and military necessity of saving infant lives, see Dr P.H. Bryce, "Infant Mortality and Disease," *Social Welfare* 1, no. 6 (1919): 133.

62 Walters, "The Duty of the City to the Child," 540. One Canadian estimate declared that 36 per cent of those examined for service were found to be physically fit; 23 per cent were pronounced "fairly good"; 31 per cent were "unsound" and 10 per cent were declared "absolutely no good." Rev. A.H. Sovereign, "Report of the Child Welfare Association of British Columbia," October 1919, cited in Strong-Boag, *The Parliament of Women*, 345; "Social Hygiene," *Social Welfare* 7, no. 3 (1924): 48. Concerns about the implications of these figures also inspired the women's organizations in their child welfare and general public health efforts; see Strong-Boag, *The Parliament of Women*, 311–12.

63 Cited in H.E. Spencer, "For a Healthy Canada," *Chatelaine*, August 1930. Currie was speaking before the Taxation and Civil Service Convention held in Montreal in 1924. Spencer was a Conservative MP (Battle River) and active in urging the federal government to take the initiative in public health concerns. See, for example, his part in the debates on federal health policy, Canada, House of Commons, *Debates*, 3 March 1930, 217–19.

64 A poor military performance in the Boer War combined with reports of high numbers of army rejects in both that and the Great War had exposed the poor health of the British working class and the threat of national deterioration in health and achievement. See Dwork, *War is Good for Babies and Other Young Children*, 208–20; Davin, "Imperialism and Motherhood," 12. Reports that 40 per cent of the youth examined for the American army had been found unfit had similar effects in the United States: Sherwood, "Some Problems of Child Hygiene," 54. On Canadian anxiety about Western degeneration, see *Women's War Conference*, 32. These worries about the physical state of recruits in the Great War persisted well after 1918; see, for example, the debate in the House of Commons over federal health policy, House of Commons, *Debates*, 3 March 1930, 221–2, where the statistics are again cited.

65 Dr A.G. Fleming, "Study of Infant Deaths in Toronto During the Summer of 1921," *CPHJ* 13, no. 5 (1922): 199; Dr J. Halpenny, "One Phase of the Foreign Invasion of Canada," *Canadian Journal of Mental Hygiene* 1, no. 3 (1919): 224–6. Halpenny blames "capitalists" for the "invasion." See also J. Crosbie, RN, "The Foreign Problem as Related to Public Health," *The Canadian Nurse* 26, no. 3 (1920): 136–7. For the

views of organized women, see "Report of the Provincial Vice-President for Ontario," NCWC *Yearbook*, 1913, 35, and C. Bacchi, *Liberation Deferred? The Ideas of the English Canadian Suffragists* (Toronto 1983), 104–16. M. Valverde, *The Age of Light, Soap and Water* (Toronto 1990), 104–28, and A. McLaren, *Our Own Master Race* (Toronto 1990), 46–67, discuss eugenic concerns about immigration and racial degeneration on the part of social reformers in general and doctors in particular.

66 Editorial, J.E.D., *Industrial Banner*, 20 April 1920; ibid., "Health Methods Will Save Canadians," 29 August 1931. On business support of immigration, see D. Avery, *Dangerous Foreigners* (Toronto 1979).

67 Coone, "The Child as an Asset," 38.

68 D. Avery, *Dangerous Foreigners*, 12; on labour nativism in the 1920s, see J. Naylor, *The New Democracy* (Toronto 1991), 55.

69 As one Winnipeg observer expressed it, "We need a strong organization of middle-class Canadians and British-born in Canada today to fight the shallow and perverted arguments of labour"; Elizabeth Smith Shortt collection, University of Waterloo, Correspondence, Box 6, File 342, Letter to Shortt from Mrs. V. Patriarche, Winnipeg, 21 December 1918. Patriarche was an NCWC member and sat on the Manitoba Censor Board. On working-class militancy in Ontario, see Naylor, *The New Democracy*, 42–55.

70 Fleming, "Study of Infant Deaths in Toronto During the Summer of 1921," 199; *Women's War Conference*, 33.

71 Dr J.J. Heagerty, "Birth Control," *Social Welfare* 6, no. 3 (1924): 57; Editorial, "Birth Control," *Social Welfare* 5, no. 12 (1923): 243–4; A. McLaren, "Birth Control and Abortion in Canada," in S.E.D. Shortt, ed., *Medicine in Canadian Society* (Toronto 1983), 288; A. McLaren, "What Has This to Do with Working-Class Women?" *Hist Soc* 14 (1981); A. McLaren and A.T. McLaren, *The Bedroom and the State* (Toronto 1986). See also D. Dodds, "The Canadian Birth Control Movement on Trial," *Hist Soc* 16 (1983): 422–3. In England, working-class women saw birth control as a vital means of ensuring child and maternal welfare; see J. Lewis, *The Politics of Motherhood*, 197–200. See also J. Henripin, *Trends and Factors of Fertility in Canada* (Ottawa 1977), 21. In the opening decade of the twentieth century, population increase due to births alone was 21 per cent. Between 1921 and 1931, this rate dropped to 17 per cent and then decreased again to 11 per cent during the tumultuous Depression decade; Dominion Bureau of Statistics, *Trends in Vital Statistics, 1921–1954* (Ottawa 1956), 8.

72 Joan Sangster, *Dreams of Equality* (Toronto 1989), 120–1, discusses the CCF's advocacy of birth control, and the Communist Party of Canada's view, 39–41; see also McLaren, "What Has This to Do With Working-

Class Women" and McLaren and McLaren, *The Bedroom and the State,* 65. For a favourable working-class feminist point of view, see Elizabeth Hunting, "Birth Control or Unemployment," *Canadian Trade Unionist,* 27 November 1930.

73 Editorial, "On Birth Control," CMAJ 16 no. 10 (1926): 1063–4.

74 Ibid., 1064.

75 McLaren and McLaren, *The Bedroom and the State.*

76 Chipman, "Infant Soldier," 48.

77 Dr A. Brown, "Child Health," CPHJ 11, no. 2 (1920): 49.

78 Dr A. Sand, "Social Medicine," *Social Welfare* 2, no. 12 (1919): 526. On the Great War and modernism, see P. Fussell, *The Great War and Modern Memory* (Oxford 1975) and M. Ecksteins, *Rites of Spring: The Great War and the Birth of the Modern Age* (Toronto 1989). J.H. Thompson, *The Harvests of War* (Toronto 1978) examines the impact of war on Western Canadian reform movements.

79 M. Power, "The Management of a Child Welfare Week in Small Cities and Towns with Results," CPHJ 9, no. 7 (1918): 363, refers to the opening of clinics in Port Hope, Windsor, Brantford, Galt, St Catharines, and Oshawa. Power was first director of the Ontario Board of Health's public health nurses.

80 Dr P. Bryce, "Recent Constructive Developments in Child Welfare," Child Welfare Report of the Ontario Social Service Council, *Social Welfare* 2, no. 10 (1920): 19.

81 Brown, "Relation of the Paediatrician to the Community," 51; Forsythe, "Child Welfare Clinics," 169. See also Dr D. Forsyth, "The Care of Children Under School Age," CPHJ 7, no. 5 (1916): 384; Blackader, "Fundamental Facts in Organization," 97–8.

82 Brown, "Infant and Child Welfare Work," 147; Forsyth, "The Care of Children Under School Age," 381.

83 Mullen, "Child Welfare in a Democracy," 450–1; Sutherland, *Children in English Canadian Society,* 68.

84 Brown, "Relation of the Paediatrician to the Community," 52.

85 Dwork, *War is Good for Babies and Other Young Children,* 208–14.

86 Knox, "Infant Care," 151. See also M. Ladd Taylor, "Why Does Congress Wish Women and Children to Die?: The Rise and Fall of Public Maternal and Infant Health Care in the United States," in Fildes, Marks, and Marland, eds. *Women and Children First,* 121.

87 D. Guest, *The Emergence of Social Security in Canada,* 2nd ed. (Vancouver 1985), 48–9.

88 F.J. Flatman, "A Reconstruction of the Ruling Class," *Ontario Labour News,* 1 June 1919. The paper was the organ of the Ontario Provincial Council of the International Association of Machinists. On Flat-

man's role in the Ontario labour movement, and labour's views on reconstruction, see Naylor, *The New Democracy*, 67, 214.

89 Ibid.

90 S. Koven and S. Michel, "Womanly Duties," *AHR* 95, no. 4 (1990): 1078–80. Koven and Michel point out that this was the pattern in Germany, France, the United States, and Great Britain.

91 Dr A. Blackader, "The Problem of the Nervous Child," *CPHJ* 14, no. 3 (1924): 97–8. A founding member of the Canadian Society for the Study of the Diseases of Children, Blackader was a Montreal paediatrician and McGill professor of paediatrics. Similar views were expressed by Dr J.T. Phair, Director, Ontario Division of Maternal and Child Hygiene: "Child Hygiene," Radio Talk prepared for the Canadian Social Hygiene Council, 8 March 1927, published in *CPHJ* 18, no. 5 (1927): 132.

CHAPTER FOUR

1 Dr Alan Brown, "The Prevention of Neonatal Mortality," *CMAJ* 23, no. 9 (1933): 264; for a comparison with the United States, see Dr J.H. Mason Knox, "Infant Care," *CMAJ* 23, no. 8 (1933): 154.

2 Dr A. Brown, "A Decade of Paediatric Progress," *CMAJ* 31, no. 10 (1940): 305.

3 Dr W. Pelton Tew, "Recent Advances in Obstetrics and Gynaecology," *CMAJ* 24, no. 11 (1934): 525.

4 Ibid.; Brown, "The Prevention of Neonatal Mortality," 266. Brown cites the effects of the prenatal supervision and "skilful midwifery attendance" given by the Maternity Centre Association of New York to nearly 9,000 women as having "greatly diminished" neonatal deaths due to all three causes. A study of the eleven-year record of the Dalhousie University Public Health Centre Prenatal Clinic in Halifax also indicated that women having prenatal care had a 4.6 per cent fetal mortality rate and those without had an 11.9 per cent rate; see Dr A.L. McLean and Dr W.G. Colwell, "Prenatal Care," *CMAJ* 30, no. 10 (1939): 383.

5 Dr H. MacMurchy, "The Baby's Father," *CPHJ* 30, no. 10 (1918): 315. Although this quote is frequently attributed to MacMurchy, she is in fact citing the pronouncement of Dr John Burns, who presided over Britain's First National Council on Infantile Mortality in 1906; see D. Dwork, *War is Good for Babies and Other Children* (London 1987), 114. On maternal mortality in Canada, see N. Lewis, "Reducing Maternal Mortality in British Columbia," in B.K. Latham and R.J. Pazdro, eds., *Not Just Pin Money* (Victoria 1984); J. Oppenheimer, "Childbirth in

Ontario," *OH* 75, no. 1 (1983); C.L. Biggs, "The Response to Maternal Mortality in Ontario, 1920–1940," M.Sc. thesis, University of Toronto 1982; S. Buckley, "The Search for the Decline of Maternal Mortality," in W. Mitchinson and J.D. McGinnis, eds., *Essays in the History of Canadian Medicine* (Toronto 1988); A. McLaren and A.T. McLaren, "Discoveries and Dissimulations: The Impact of Abortion Deaths on Maternal Mortality in British Columbia," in K. Arnup, A. Levesque, and R.R. Pierson, eds., *Delivering Motherhood* (New York 1990). On the experience of childbirth in this period, see V. Strong-Boag and K. McPherson, "The Confinement of Women: Childbirth and Hospitalization in Vancouver, 1919–1939," *BCST* 69–70 (1986), reprinted in Arnup, Levesque, and Pierson, eds., *Delivering Motherhood*; W. Mitchinson, *The Nature of Their Bodies* (Toronto 1991), especially chap. 6; see also J. Walzer Leavitt, *Brought to Bed: Childbearing in America, 1750–1950* (New York 1986); A. Oakley, *The Captured Womb* (Oxford 1984).

6 Dr W.G. Cosbie, "The Obstetrical Causes and Prevention of Stillbirth and Early Infant Mortality," *CMAJ* 13, no. 11 (1923): 877–8.

7 Dr W.B. Hendry, "Report of the Committee on Maternal Welfare," *CMAJ* 25, no. 9 (1935): 26. Hendry was professor of obstetrics and gynaecology at the University of Toronto, chief obstetrician at the Toronto General Hospital, and consultant to the Toronto Board of Health; *Who's Who in Canada* (1930–31). The committee was established by the CMA in 1930.

8 Dr P McLeod, "Maternal Mortality from the Viewpoint of the Obstetrician," *CMAJ* 31, no. 6 (1940): 54.

9 Dr K.C. McIlwraith, "Nutrition and Pregnancy," *CPHJ* 21, no. 19 (1930): 513. By the early 1930s, British studies recognized that malnutrition played an important role in maternal mortality, and an even more important one in stillbirths and neonatal mortality; C. Webster, "Healthy or Hungry Thirties?" *Hist Workshop* 13, no. 4 (1982): 117. See also E. Peretz, "The Costs of Modern Motherhood to Low-Income Families in Interwar Britain," in V. Fildes, L. Marks, and H. Marland, eds. *Women and Children First: International Maternal and Infant Welfare, 1870–1945* (London 1992), 257–77.

10 On the postwar celebration of maternalism, see N. Lewis, "Advising the Parents," Ph.D. thesis, University of British Columbia 1980, 45–6; V. Strong-Boag, "Intruders in the Nursery," in J. Parr, ed., *Childhood and Family in Canadian History* (Toronto 1982), 161; V. Strong-Boag, *The New Day Recalled* (Markham 1988), especially chap. 5; J.H. Thompson and A. Seager, *Decades of Discord* (Toronto 1985), 153; M. Vipond, "The Image of Women in Canadian Mass Circulation Magazines during the Twenties," in A. Prentice and S. Trofimenkoff, eds.,

The Neglected Majority (Toronto 1981), 117. The "cult of motherhood" was international: see E. Key, *The Century of the Child* (New York 1909), 100, for a contemporary description of the "entirely new conception of the vocation of mother." See B. Ehrenreich and D. English, *For Her Own Good: 150 Years of the Experts' Advice to Women* (New York 1978), 189–96 for American trends, and A. Dally, *Inventing Motherhood* (London 1982) for Britain. See also R. Bridenthal, "Something Old, Something New: Women Between the Two World Wars," in R. Bridenthal and C. Koonz, eds., *Becoming Visible: Women in European History* (Boston 1977).

11 R. Torrington, "Presidential Address," *NCWC Yearbook*, 1917, 16. V. Strong-Boag, *The Parliament of Women* (Ottawa 1976) provides a thorough discussion of the NCWC's promotion of modern motherhood.

12 Editorial, "A Splendid Move," *Industrial Banner*, 7 May 1920; also Editorial, "The Value of Motherhood," *Industrial Banner*, 26 March 1920. The United Women's Educational Association was formed at the convention of the Labour Educational Association in Brantford in May 1920. The *Industrial Banner*, 21 May 1920, published a directive "To Women Readers of the *Banner*: Your Cooperation is Requested in the Formation of a Great Women's Federation in the Cause of Motherhood, Childhood and the Home." See J. Naylor, *The New Democracy* (Toronto 1991), 129–55; Joan Sangster *Dreams of Equality: Women on the Canadian Left* (Toronto 1988) also discusses the maternalism of women on the left.

13 Ehrenreich and English, *For Her Own Good*, 26–9, discuss the medical discourse on the woman question; for Canada, see W. Mitchinson, *The Nature of Their Bodies*, and W. Mitchinson, "The Medical Treatment of Women in Canada: An Historical Overview," in S. Burt, L. Code, and L. Dorney, eds., *Changing Patterns: Women in Canada* (Toronto 1988).

14 Dr B. Atlee, "The Menace of Maternity," *Canadian Home Journal*, (May 1932): 8.

15 C.E. Hamilton, "The Scientific Management of Household Work and Wages," *CPHJ* 4, no. 1 (1913): 30–1. This concept of "efficient housekeeping" based on the principles of scientific management was also supported by the NCWC; see Strong-Boag, *The Parliament of Women*, 187; Strong-Boag, "Discovering the Home: The Last 150 Years of Domestic Work in Canada," in P. Bourne, ed., *Women's Paid and Unpaid Work: Historical and Contemporary Perspectives* (Toronto 1985). For a discussion of Helen MacMurchy's support of "scientific management" in the home, see K. McConnachie, "Methodology in the Study of Women in History: A Case Study of Helen MacMurchy, MD," *OH* 75, no. 1 (1983). Also on "scientific motherhood" in Canada, see Strong-Boag,

The New Day Recalled, 148–52; for the United States, see R. Apple, *Mothers and Medicine: A Social History of Infant Feeding* (Madison, Wisc. 1987), 97–113; Ehrenreich and English, *For Her Own Good*, 196–210.

16 Dr W.W. Chipman, "Some Conclusions After a Symposium in Obstetrics," CMAJ 14, no. 8 (1924): 705. Chipman was professor of obstetrics and gynaecology at McGill University, Montreal.

17 An editorial in the CMAJ on the occasion of Ballantyne's death in 1923 pays homage to him for the "new midwifery": "Ballantyne and the New Midwifery," CMAJ 13, no. 6 (1923): 441. Ballantyne wrote *Antenatal Pathology and Hygiene* (Edinburgh 1902), and *Expectant Motherhood* (London 1914).

18 Dr J.R. Torbert, "The Prenatal Care of Obstetric Cases," CMAJ 4, no. 10 (1914): 1,086. See the rather less optimistic assessment of Dr H.C. Swartzlander, "The Medical Treatment of Obstetric Cases," CMAJ 6, no. 10 (1916): 222. See also Dr C.B. Oliver, "Obstetrical Practice Yesterday and Today," *The Canadian Nurse* 22, no. 5 (1926): 301–2; "Preventable Maternal Mortality," ibid., 254.

19 Dr K.C. McIlwraith, "Obstetrics and the State," paper delivered before the Section on Obstetrics and Gynaecology, Academy of Medicine, Toronto, October 1919; published in CMAJ 10, no. 4 (1920): 307. They were also verified by Dr W.J. Bell of the provincial health department, who reported on the Ontario situation in 1922. The Bell report showed that maternal deaths in Ontario in 1920 had attained a record high of 489 or 6.75 per 1,000 live births. The city of Toronto revealed an average of 7.61 per 1,000 live births. See Ontario, Board of Health, *Annual Report*, 1922, 184. Bell's study was presented at the Annual Meeting of the American Child Hygiene Association that year. See also Dr J.G. Gallie, "Antenatal Work and Stillbirths," CPHJ 11, no. 2 (1920).

20 Board of Health, *Annual Report*, 1921, 184–91.

21 McIlwraith, "Obstetrics and the State," 310. See also Dr. R Ferguson, "A Plea for Better Obstetrics," CMAJ, 10, no. 10 (1920): 901.

22 McIlwraith, "Obstetrics and the State," 312–13.

23 Ibid., 313. See also L. Marks, "Mothers, Babies and Hospitals: 'The London' and the Provision of Maternity Care in East London, 1870–1939," in Fildes, Marks, and Marland, eds. *Women and Children First*, 48–73.

24 A. McLaren, *Our Own Master Race* (Toronto 1990), 34, discusses professional concerns with respect to hospitalization, as do Strong-Boag and MacPherson, "The Confinement of Women."

25 Dr W.G. Cosbie, "The Obstetrical Causes and Prevention of Stillbirth and Early Infant Mortality," CMAJ 13, no. 11 (1923): 877–80. Employing the term "meddlesome midwifery" as well, Ferguson, "A

Plea for Better Obstetrics," 903, also implicates the routine use of pituitrin and anaesthesia.

26 Dr W.B. Hendry, "Maternal Mortality," *CMAJ* 13, no. 4 (1923): 253.

27 Ibid., 254.

28 Dr H. MacMurchy, "Neonatal Mortality," *CPHJ* 17, no. 9 (1926): 44.

29 Dr H. MacMurchy, "On Maternal Mortality in Canada," *CPHJ* 16, no. 9 (1925): 411.

30 Dr H. MacMurchy, *Maternal Mortality in Canada* (Ottawa 1928), 60–5.

31 Ibid., 445; see also MacMurchy, "The Relation Between Maternal Mortality and Infant Mortality," *CPHJ* 16, no. 8 (1925); MacMurchy, "On Maternal Mortality in Canada," *CPHJ* 16, no. 9 (1925); MacMurchy, "Classification of Maternal Deaths," *CPHJ* 22, no. 8 (1931); Dr J.T. Phair, "Maternal Mortality: A General Survey," *CPHJ* 23, no. 4 (1932). See also McLaren, *Our Own Master Race*, 32–4; S. Buckley, "The Search for the Decline of Maternal Mortality," in Mitchinson and McGinnis, eds., *Essays in the History of Canadian Medicine*, 151–4. One doctor found that, of 5,000 applicants for life insurance, 246 had lost a mother or sister, or both, in childbirth, a figure almost equal to that of the combined mortality from tuberculosis and cancer: see Dr J.N. Nathanson, "Prophylaxis in Obstetrics, with Special Reference to the Value and Importance of Prenatal Care," *CMAJ* 15, no. 6 (1924): 494.

32 Dr H. MacMurchy, "Child Welfare Work in Canada and Maternal Mortality," Dominion Council of Health, *Report of the 7th Meeting*, October 1922, 10.

33 MacMurchy, *Maternal Mortality in Canada*, 27; McLaren, *Our Own Master Race*, 34; Buckley, "The Search for the Decline of Maternal Mortality," 153, 161.

34 For example, Dr W.W. Chipman, "Some Conclusions After a Symposium in Obstetrics," 705; Editorial, "Maternal Mortality and the Practice of Obstetrics," *CMAJ* 19, no. 2 (1929): 181.

35 Dr J.R. Goodall, "Maternal Mortality," *CMAJ* 19, no. 10 (1929): 447. Goodall examines an analysis of maternal mortality for Aberdeen, Scotland, which "forms the basis of most of the learned discussions upon maternal mortality," and accepts its findings for Canada. The Aberdeen study concluded that there was "no significant association" between puerperal mortality and "cleanliness of house, size of house, crowdedness of house and congested areas." Also upholding the Aberdeen study's findings on this issue are Dr A.D. Blackader, "Thoughts on Maternal Mortality," *CMAJ* 19, no. 6 (1929): 656; Editorial, "The Problem of Maternal Mortality," *CMAJ* 19, no. 10 (1929): 432. Webster, "Healthy or Hungry Thirties?" provides a critical perspective on these British findings.

36 MacLaren, *Our Own Master Race*, 35; McLaren and McLaren, "Discoveries and Dissimulations," 127. On the relation of abortion deaths to maternal deaths in Britain see J. Lewis, *The Politics of Motherhood* (Montreal 1980), 36–8, 209–11.

37 McLaren and McLaren, "Discoveries and Dissimulations," 134, 146.

38 In 1934, two studies on maternal mortality that surveyed Ontario and Manitoba revealed an abortion death rate of approximately 17 per cent for each province: Dr J.T. Phair and Dr H. Sellers, "A Study of Maternal Deaths in the Province of Ontario," *CPHJ* 25, no. 5 (1934): 566; Dr F.W. Jackson and Dr R.D. Jeffries, "A Five Year Study of Maternal Mortality in Manitoba," *CPHJ* 25, no. 5 (1934): 105. An examination of Manitoba's vital statistics from May 1938 to April 1939 indicated 9 abortion deaths out of a total of 31 maternal deaths. Yet one Winnipeg doctor claimed that abortions "do not carry a high mortality:" Dr J.D. McQueen, "Report of the Committee on Maternal Welfare," *CMAJ* 30, no. 9 (1939): 18. See also Dr R. Mitchell, "The Prevention of Maternal Mortality in Manitoba," *CMAJ* 18, no. 9 (1928): 293. Mitchell suggested that compulsory notification of pregnancy would afford a means of determining the frequency of abortions.

39 See, for example, Dr P.A. McLeod, "Maternal Mortality from the Viewpoint of the Obstetrician," *CMAJ* 31, no. 1 (1940): 54. Dr J.T. Phair, Director of Ontario's Division of Maternal and Child Hygiene and Public Health Nursing, found in 1935 that 86 per cent of those dying from abortion-related deaths died from sepsis; Ontario, Department of Health, *Annual Report*, 1936, 50.

40 Canadian Council on Child and Family Welfare, *Need Our Mothers Die?* (Ottawa 1935) 6, 36–7, 43.

41 Department of Health, *Annual Report*, 1935, 31.

42 A. McLaren and A.T. McLaren, *The Bedroom and the State* (Toronto 1986), 65, note the Women's Labour League petition of 1936 demanding birth control clinics and warning that poverty was forcing working class mothers to "resort to the most crude and dangerous means in order to procure abortions." The McLarens argue that the key supporters of birth control in the interwar period were socialist feminists.

43 Dr W.G. Cosbie, "Maternal Mortality," *CMAJ* 31, no. 7 (1940): 38–9; see also Dr P.A. McLeod, "Maternal Mortality from the Viewpoint of the Obstetrician," *CMAJ* 31, no. 1 (1940): 54.

44 McLaren and McLaren, *The Bedroom and the State*, 35.

45 Dr R.E. Wodehouse, "Maternal Deaths," *CMAJ* 26, no. 5 (1936): 526. Wodehouse became health officer of Fort William in 1910, and district medical officer of Western Ontario in 1912 (to 1921). He was executive secretary of the Canadian Tuberculosis Association

from 1921 to 1933, when he was made deputy minister of the Department of Pensions and National Health; *Who's Who in Canada* (1945–46).

46 Mitchell, "The Prevention of Maternal Mortality in Manitoba," 294.

47 Doctors' concerns about declining population grew during the Depression; see Dr E.L.Chicanot, "Canada's Falling Birth Rate," *The Canadian Doctor* 7, no. 11 (1935): 22; "Does Canada Face Birth Subsidization?" ibid., 8, no. 11 (1936): 30.

48 Goodall, "Maternal Mortality," 449, was one of the few who felt that "the laity must be taught the frightful risks that accompany abortions" by bringing to the public's attention "the exceedingly high death rate."

49 On the theme of law and family, see J. Snell and C. Comacchio Abeele, "Regulating Nuptiality," *CHR* 69, no. 4 (1988).

50 M. Shore, *The Science of Social Redemption* (Toronto 1987), provides a thorough discussion of the development of the social sciences in Canada and their impact for the study of contemporary social conditions.

51 B.G. Hall, RN, "Must 1,532 Mothers Die?" *Chatelaine*, July 1928; "The Chatelaine's Comment," ibid.

52 M. Muldoon, "Mother and Child Are Well!" *Canadian Home Journal*, May 1929.

53 Dr W.B. Hendry, "Maternal Welfare," *Social Welfare* 13, no. 9 (1931): 181.

54 S. Buckley, "Efforts to Reduce Infant and Maternal Mortality Between the Wars," *Atlantis* 4 (1979): 80.

55 McLaren, *Our Own Master Race*, 34; Buckley, "The Search for the Decline of Maternal Mortality," 155.

56 Dr M. Patterson, "Women's Institutes: Report of the Standing Committee on Health and Child Welfare in Ontario," Department of Agriculture, *Annual Report*, 1928, 65.

57 Ibid., 63–4.

58 Dr H. MacMurchy, "A Safety League for Mothers," *Social Welfare* 13, no. 9 (1931): 185; Canada, Department of Pensions and National Health, *Annual Report*, 1929–30, 63, reported the publication of two pamphlets to popularize MacMurchy's findings, *Mother—A Little Book for Women*, and *Mother—A Little Book for Men*.

59 Dr H. MacMurchy, "Maternal Mortality," Dominion Council of Health, *Report of the 20th Meeting*, November 1930; see the report by a medical participant from Hamilton, Dr Sarah McVean, "The Pageant of Motherhood," *CPHJ* 21, no. 11 (1930): 579.

60 Dr W.B. Hendry, "Maternal Welfare," 179.

61 Dr G.P. Jackson, "Maternal Mortality," *Social Welfare* 13, no. 9 (1931): 186. Jackson was Toronto's medical officer of health.

62 Department of Health, *Annual Report*, 1930, 47. Phair became district medical officer with Toronto's health department in 1917; in 1920, he became director of the city's child hygiene division. He was appointed director of the Division of Maternal and Child Hygiene of the provincial health department in 1925, became chief medical officer of health in 1935, and deputy minister of health in 1945; *Who's Who in Canada* (1958–59).

63 Canada, Department of Pensions and National Health, *Annual Report*, 1939, 137–8.

64 Canada, House of Commons, *Debates*, 5 June 1928, 3783. The minister of health was J.H. King. Macphail was elected to the House of Commons for Southeast Grey by the United Farmers of Ontario. On her life and career, see T. Crowley, *Agnes Macphail and the Politics of Equality* (Toronto 1990).

65 Dominion Council of Health, *Report of the 20th Meeting*, November 1930. See also the report on maternal welfare-related activities by voluntary groups in Department of Pensions and National Health, *Annual Report*, 1928–29, 125–6.

66 "Report of the Committee on Maternal Welfare," CMA *Annual Report*, Winnipeg 1930, 272.

67 Dr W.B. Hendry, "Report of the Committee on Maternal Welfare," CMA *Annual Report*, Vancouver 1931, 324. Similar arguments can be found in Editorial, "The Problem of Maternal Mortality," *CMAJ* 19, no. 10 (1929): 432; Goodall, "Maternal Mortality," 450; Editorial, "Maternal Mortality and the Practice of Obstetrics," *CMAJ* 19, no. 2 (1929): 180–1; Dr M.R. Bow, "Maternal Mortality as a Public Health Problem," *CMAJ* 20, no. 8 (1930): 170; Chipman, "Some Conclusions after a Symposium in Obstetrics," 704; Dr F.H. Coppock, "State Obstetrics," *CMAJ* 25, no. 12 (1935): 671.

68 The report was summarized in the *Toronto Daily Star*, 14 August 1931. Biggs, "The Response to Maternal Mortality in Ontario," 88, discusses the negative reaction of many of the city's physicians, including members of the Academy of Medicine, who argued strongly in favour of education.

69 Dr. G. Fleming, "The Future of Maternal Welfare in Canada," Dominion Council of Health, *Report of the 26th Meeting*, June 1933, 3–4.

70 "Obstetrical Procedures and Practices in Hospitals," CMA *Annual Report*, June 1937, 286. Many of the same doctors who argued the point of professional responsibility also insisted on mothers' responsibility to avail themselves of prenatal care: see Dr J.N. Nathanson, "Prophylaxis in Obstetrics, with Special Reference to the Value and Importance of Prenatal Care," *CMAJ* 14, no. 6 (1924): 494; Editorial,

"Mainly about Complacency," *CMAJ* 18, no. 5 (1928): 712; Editorial, "Maternal Mortality and the Practice of Obstetrics," *CMAJ* 19, no. 2 (1929): 181; Editorial, "The Problem of Maternal Mortality," *CMAJ* 19, no. 10 (1929): 433.

71 Dr H.E. Young and Dr J.T. Phair, "Maternal Mortality in Canada," *CPHJ* 19, no. 3 (1928): 135.

72 Dominion Council of Health, *Report of 7th Meeting*, October 1922, 10. See also the report of the CMA's Committee on Economics, CMA, *Annual Report*, 1934. The editors of *Chatelaine* echoed the profession's worries; see "The *Chatelaine's* Comment," July 1928.

73 Swartzlander, "The Medical Treatment of Obstetric Cases," 306. British physicians accepted that approximately 50 per cent of all obstetrical work in England and Wales was in the hands of midwives and urged legislation to ensure their proper training and regulation in the interests of maternal welfare. The Midwives Bill of 1912 required that midwives undergo three months' training at an obstetrical centre (later increased to six months), examination by the medical instructors, registration, and supervision by public health officials. Registered midwives were also compelled by law to call in medical aid in difficult cases and to report all cases of sepsis; see Dwork, *War is Good for Babies and Other Young Children* and Lewis, *The Politics of Motherhood*.

74 M. Ladd Taylor, "Introduction," *Raising a Baby the Government Way* (New Brunswick, N.J. 1987), 27–8.

75 Dr Elizabeth Smith Shortt, "Maternity Nursing and Trained Midwives," 2, undated typescript, (mid-1920s) File 1844, Elizabeth Smith Shortt Collection, University of Waterloo. Shortt provides this estimate; see also C. Benoit, *Midwives in Passage* (St. John's, Nfld. 1991).

76 W. Mitchinson, *The Nature of their Bodies*, especially chap. 6. On the gradual decline of midwifery, see C. L. Biggs, "The Case of the Missing Midwives," in K. Arnup, et al., *Delivering Motherhood*.

77 S. Buckley, "Ladies or Midwives," in L. Kealey, ed., *A Not Unreasonable Claim* (Toronto 1979), 149. The history of midwifery in Newfoundland is detailed in C. Benoit, *Midwives in Passage*. See also S. Reverby, *Ordered to Care: The Dilemma of American Nursing, 1850–1945* (Cambridge 1987).

78 D. Naylor, *Private Practice, Public Payment* (Kingston/Montreal 1986), 23; also Biggs, "The Case of the Missing Midwives."

79 Dr W.B. Hendry, "Maternal Welfare," 182; see also Phair and Young, "Maternal Mortality in Canada," 135; Coppock, "State Obstetrics," 671; Editorial [Dr J.T. Phair], "Why Maternal Deaths?" *CPHJ* 25, no. 3 (1934): 142, in which Phair pronounces midwives "a distinct menace."

80 Dr H. MacMurchy, *Supplement to the Canadian Mother's Book* (Ottawa 1923), 139–40.

81 McLaren, *Our Own Master Race*, 34.

82 Dominion Council of Health, *Report of the 7th Meeting*, October 1922, 11. On the NCWC's interest in midwives and medical opposition to them, see Buckley, "The Search for the Decline of Maternal Mortality," 156–7. For a contemporary nurse's viewpoint, see E. Johns, "The Practice of Midwifery in Canada," *The Canadian Nurse* 21, no. 1 (1925). On the efforts of nurses to disassociate themselves from the negative image of midwives, see Buckley, "Ladies or Midwives?" 149. Strong-Boag and McPherson, "The Confinement of Women: Childbirth and Hospitalization in Vancouver, 1919–1939," discuss the opposition of British Columbia doctors to midwifery.

83 Dr Elizabeth Smith Shortt, "Maternity Nursing and Trained Midwives," 3–5, undated typescript (mid-1920s), Elizabeth Smith Shortt Collection, University of Waterloo, File 1844.

84 Buckley, "The Search for the Decline," 156.

85 Ibid., 157.

86 Some physicians remarked that births attended by trained midwives or graduate nurses consistently showed a lower maternal and neonatal death rate than those attended by doctors because of the latter's propensity for "meddlesome midwifery"; see Dr H.M. Little, "An Address on Obstetrics During the Past Twenty-five years," *CMAJ* 14, no. 10 (1924): 904. An editorial in the *CMAJ*, "The Problem of Maternal Mortality," 19, no. 10 (1929): 432, makes the same point, as do Goodall, "Maternal Mortality," 448; Editorial, "What's the Matter with Obstetrics?" *CMAJ* 19, no. 6 (1929): 647; Dr A.D. Blackader, "On Maternity Teaching and the Obstetric Nurse," *CMAJ* 19, no. 6 (1929): 648. See also Blackader, "Thoughts on Maternal Mortality," ibid., 656.

87 Maternal mortality in VON cases in 1928 was 1.6 per 1,000, infant mortality was 19 per 1,000, in stark contrast to the national rates of 5.6 and 104 respectively. In 1930, the rates were 1.2 and 22 respectively; from 1935 to 1940, the rate averaged 2.1, while the national maternal mortality rate for this period was 4.2; the infant mortality rate averaged 20 per 1,000, while the national average was about 80 per 1,000. See VON, *Annual Reports*, for the years 1928 to 1940 inclusive. See the positive assessment of the VON's role as obstetric nurses by Mitchell, "The Prevention of Maternal Mortality in Manitoba," 294, and Blackader, "On Maternity Teaching and the Obstetric Nurse," 648.

88 Editorial, "Mainly About Complacency," *CMAJ* 18, no. 5 (1928): 712.

89 Dr R.E. Wodehouse, "Maternal Deaths," *CMAJ* 26, no. 5 (1936): 525–6. The nursing services Wodehouse refers to are the VON, the Red Cross Society, and the Assistance Maternelle of Quebec.

90 "Married Women Workers," *Labour Herald*, 30 September 1927.

91 "Why Married Women Have to Leave Home," *Labour Herald*, 31 July 1928.

92 C. Smith, "Women Workers and Their Health," *CCJ* 11, no. 1 (1932): 44.

93 J. Ursel, "The State and the Maintenance of Patriarchy," in J. Dickinson and B. Russell, eds., *Family, Economy and State* (New York 1986), 161; also Ursel, *Private Lives, Public Policy: 100 Years of State Intervention in the Family* (Toronto 1992), 83–95, 125–42.

94 W. Tite, "Married Women in Industry," paper read before the Conference of the Employment Service Council of Ontario, published in *CCJ* 3, no. 10 (1924): 40.

95 Ibid., 41.

96 Dr H. MacMurchy, *Infant Mortality: First Special Report* (Toronto 1910), 17.

97 Tite, "Married Women in Industry," 40.

98 Ibid., 41.

99 See B. Palmer and G. Kealey, *Dreaming of What Might Be: The Knights of Labour in Ontario* (Cambridge 1982), 318.

100 E. Zaretsky, "Rethinking the Welfare State," in Dickinson and Russell, eds., *Family, Economy and State*, 104–5; see also F.F. Piven and R. Cloward, *Regulating the Poor* (New York 1971).

101 MacMurchy, *Infant Mortality* (1910, 1911, 1912).

102 PAO, MU 16383 3/14, Ontario Welfare Council papers, Dr J.T. Phair, "Report of the Child Welfare Committee: Points Which Seem to Arise from the Discussion of Certain Standards of Child Welfare Services," Ontario Social Hygiene Council, *Annual Report*, January 1930, 1. On maternity benefits in Europe during the interwar period, see Bridenthal, "Something Old, Something New," 433–4. See also Dr W.B. Hendry, "Report of the Maternal Welfare Committee," CMA, *Annual Report*, 1934, 227.

103 McIlwraith, "Obstetrics and the State," 311.

104 Ibid., 301.

105 See the warnings against state medicine in Editorial, "Dollarless Doctors and Penniless Patients," *CMAJ* 25, no. 12 (1935): 674.

106 Dominion Council of Health, *Report of 18th Meeting*, December 1928.

107 Cited in McIlwraith, "Obstetrics and the State," 305.

108 "Would Bonus Every Birth," Toronto *Globe*, 15 March 1921. Rollo was one of the early leaders of the ILP, formed in 1908; see B. Palmer, *A Culture in Conflict* (Kingston/Montreal 1979), 228; also Naylor, *The New Democracy*, 153. On Drury's health and welfare efforts, see C.M. Johnston, *E.C. Drury: Agrarian Idealist* (Toronto 1986), especially chap. 11.

109 Toronto *Globe*, 15 March 1921. The Labour members were J. McNamara (Riverdale) and R.R. Hall (Parry Sound).

110 J. Parr, *The Gender of Breadwinners* (Toronto 1990), 241–4, discusses
the persistence of the "breadwinner myth." McLaren and McLaren,
The Bedroom and the State, 84, point out that many workers opposed
birth control because they believed it interfered with their rights to
enjoy a large family, a "patriarchal existence" that, in effect, had never
existed for most workers. Joan Sangster, *Dreams of Equality*, also discusses working-class attachment to the patriarchal ideal. See also
Naylor, *The New Democracy*, 129.

111 Hett's arguments were published in four parts in the *Industrial
Banner*, organ of the Trades and Labour Congress, from May to July
1920, and released in pamphlet form the following year. See Dr J.E.
Hett, "The Nationalization of the Medical Profession," *Industrial
Banner*, 21 May 1920, 28 May 1920, 4 June 1920 and 11 July 1920.
The editors indicated their complete support of his views and urged
readers to consider them seriously; see Editorial Comment, 21 May
1920. Naylor, *The New Democracy*, 97, briefly mentions Hett's involvement in the ILP.

112 "United Women Hold Convention," *Industrial Banner*, 3 June 1921. On
the United Women, see Naylor, *The New Democracy*, chap. 5.

113 *Industrial Banner*, 3 June 1921. The *CMAJ* also noted that "labour
women" at a "recent conference at Winnipeg" were clamouring for
state medicine; see Editorial, "Labour Women and Medical Problems,"
CMAJ 20, no. 6 (1930): 849.

114 Buckley, "The Search for the Decline," 157.

115 Dominion Council of Health, *Report of the 18th Meeting*, December
1928. Merson had presented a similar opinion a few years previously
in the *CCJ* 4, no. 4 (1925): 18.

116 Dr P. Bryce, "Two Problems in Child Welfare," *Social Welfare* 3, no. 7
(1921): 188. On mothers' allowances, see V. Strong-Boag, "Wages for
Housework," *J Can Studies* 14, no. 1 (1979). The issue of maternity
benefits and the British Columbia debate over their value is discussed
in Strong-Boag and McPherson, "Childbirth and Hospitalization,"
159–60. On labour's views, see Naylor, *The New Democracy*, 227.
Minnie Singer of the United Women's Educational Association became
one of the first mothers' allowances commissioners in Ontario.

117 Dr Elizabeth Smith Shortt, "Report on Mothers' Pensions," 1914, 2–3,
Elizabeth Smith Shortt papers, University of Waterloo, Box 4, File
1847. The annual meeting of the NCWC in 1913 had appointed a
Committee on Mothers' Pensions, with Shortt as its convener, and had
asked for a report for the following year. Shortt was also one of the
first mothers' allowances commissioners in the province.

118 T. Moore, "Preface," in M. Cohen, *Mothers' Allowances in Canada*
(Toronto 1927), 8. Moore was president of the Trades and Labour
Congress of Canada.

119 McIlwraith, "Obstetrics and the State," 313.
120 Dr W. Pelton Tew, an obstetrician from London, Ontario, noted the effects of poor maternal nutrition on the outcome of pregnancy for both mother and infant in his "Recent Advances in Obstetrics and Gynaecology," 521–2. Dr W.R. Campbell, "Dietary Factors in Health and Disease," *CMAJ* 25, no. 10 (1935): 384, argued that "we should see to it that every expectant and lactating mother is supplied with an adequate caloric intake" but made no practical suggestions beyond public education. Studies on the health repercussions of nutrition began to appear regularly in the *CMAJ* in the 1930s. In 1937, the CMA established a committee on nutrition and began publishing a new regular feature called "Diet and Nutrition". Medical interest in this area was spurred by advances in nutritional sciences and anxieties about Depression-induced deprivation. See, for example, Dr E.C. Robertson and Dr F.F. Tisdall, "Nutrition and Resistance to Disease," *CMAJ* 30, no. 3 (1939): 282; Dr E.V. McCollum, "Better Nutrition as a Health Measure," *CMAJ* 30, no. 4 (1939): 393; Sir Edward Mellaney, MD, "Proper Feeding and Good Health," *CMAJ* 30, no. 6 (1939): 597. In Great Britain, the Maternal and Child Welfare Act of 1918 provided for free meals and milk for pregnant and nursing mothers; see Dwork, *War is Good for Babies and Other Young Children*, 213–14.
121 Dominion Council of Health, *Report of the 7th Meeting*, 11.
122 A.B. Baird, RN, "Statistical Indications in Some Problems in Maternal and Child Hygiene," *Canadian Child and Family Welfare* 9, no. 3 (1933): 6.
123 Hendry, "Report of the Maternal Welfare Committee," 181.
124 Editorial, "Puerperal Mortality: Success or Failure?" *CPHJ* 25, no. 12 (1934): 599–600, comments on the lack of success in the fight against maternal mortality; see also Dr F.W. Jackson, Dr R.D. Defries and Dr A.H. Sellers, "A Five Year Study of Maternal Mortality in Manitoba," *CPHJ* 25, no. 3 (1934): 103; Dr J.T. Phair and Dr A.H. Sellers, "A Study of Maternal Deaths in the Province of Ontario," *CPHJ* 25, no. 12 (1934): 563.
125 Department of Health, *Annual Report*, 1933, 51; ibid., 1936, 50. Twenty-four per cent of the deaths in 1935 were reported as due to the toxaemias, compared to 20 percent in 1933. In 1935 puerperal septicaemia was 23 per cent, compared to 15 per cent in 1933; haemorrhage deaths declined from 13 per cent to 11 per cent in the same two year period. See also ibid., 1937, 60.
126 Ibid., 1935, 31.
127 Webster, "Healthy or Hungry Thirties?" and Mitchell, "The Effects of Unemployment," make this point for Britain in this period.
128 Dominion Council of Health, *Report of the 36th Meeting*, June 1938, 10.

129 Young and Phair, "Maternal Mortality in Canada," 136.
130 Toronto, Department of Public Health, *Care of the Infant and Young Child* (Toronto 1935), 2.
131 Phair, "Report of the Child Welfare Committee: Points Which Seem to Arise from the Discussion of Certain Standards of Child Health Services," 2.
132 "Report of the Committee on Maternal Welfare," CMA, *Annual Report*, 1936, 265. The report, *Obstetrical Procedures and Practices in Hospitals*, was published in 1937. It made recommendations for patient accomodation, clinical facilities, staff conferences to review morbidity and mortality and proper procedures for prenatal, intranatal, and post-natal care. See also 1937, 286.
133 Strong-Boag and McPherson, "Childbirth and Hospitalization," 145. British Columbia's rate rose from 48.3 per cent to 84.4 per cent of live births between 1926 and 1940; the second highest rate in 1940 was found in Alberta, with 72.9 per cent. Ontario saw a shift from 24.9 per cent to 62.1 per cent during the 1926–1940 period. The authors note that Vancouver's preference for hospital births began early in the century. N. Lewis, "Advising the Parents," 52, argues that as early as 1931, even in British Columbia's rural districts, the majority of maternity cases were sent to hospital.
134 Oppenheimer, "Childbirth in Ontario," 36; Biggs, "The Response to Maternal Mortality in Ontario, 1920–1940," 25; Strong-Boag and McPherson, "The Confinement of Women," 151; Lewis, "Advising the Parents," 52. C. Scholten, *Childbearing in American Society, 1650-1850* (New York 1985), 105–8, argues that hospitalization of birth in the United States was due largely to physician concern with maintaining antiseptic conditions and with the scientific management of childbirth.
135 See, for example, Dr W.M. Wilson, "The Care of the Premature Child," *CMAJ* 31, no. 2 (1940): 133–7; McLeod, "Maternal Mortality from the Viewpoint of the Obstetrician," 53.
136 Oppenheimer, "Childbirth in Ontario," 52–3. Dr A.F. McKenzie, "Notes on One Hundred Obstetrical Cases in Rural Practice," *CMAJ* 24, no. 8 (1934): 178, notes that in 1929 in Ontario, 34.1 per cent of the births were institutional. This had risen to 39.4 per cent by 1932 and "at the same rate of increase by 1938 they will be about equal." McKenzie counts only one hospital delivery, but remarks that there was "no special reason why this patient should have gone to the hospital" except that she thought the hospital "was the proper place for a woman to have a baby." Leavitt, *Brought to Bed*, points out that American women themselves played an important role in the trend towards institutionalization of childbirth in the early 20th century. D. Gagan, *A Necessity Among Us: The Owen Sound General and Marine Hospital*

(Toronto 1990), 37–8, found that middle-class women in Owen Sound were instrumental in arguing for a maternity ward, established in 1911, at the hospital.

137 Dr A.F. McKenzie, "Notes on One Hundred Obstetrical Cases in Rural Practice," 178, reveals that the maternal mortality in Ontario in 1932 was 5.1 per 1,000 live births for the entire province; the non-institutional rate was 2.3 and the institutional rate was 9.3, or four times as great. Dr G. Jackson's report for the Toronto Committee on Maternal Welfare indicated that, in Toronto, of 7,771 institutional births in 1930, there were 73 deaths as compared to 8 deaths for 5,180 home births. See also Biggs, "Response to Maternal Mortality," 88. Biggs points out that many Toronto physicians explained hospital deaths as a result of the fact that more complicated cases were sent to hospital. This is an unsatisfactory explanation, since many parturient women received medical attention only at the time of confinement.

138 Lewis, "Reducing Maternal Mortality in British Columbia," 349, also finds the educational solution uppermost in British Columbia during this period.

139 Dr A. Brown, "Certain Features of Child Welfare Not Sufficiently Emphasized," *CPHJ* 14, no. 9 (1923): 240; Dr A.G. Fleming, "Child Hygiene," *CPHJ* 14, no. 7 (1923): 300; MacMurchy, "Neonatal Mortality," 446; Baird, "Statistical Indications," 10.

140 Dr W.W. Chipman, Editorial Comments, "Maternal Mortality," *CMAJ* 26, no. 5 (1936): 553.

141 "Preliminary Trends," *Canadian Welfare Summary* 15, no. 5 (1940): 55.

142 Dr J.T. Phair, "Radio Talk," *CPHJ* 18, no. 3 (1927): 133.

CHAPTER FIVE

1 B. Turner, *Medical Power and Social Knowledge* (London 1987), 10–12, discusses the knowledge/power relationship as developed by Michel Foucault. For Foucault's discussion, see *Discipline and Punish: The Birth of the Prison* (London 1977), 27–8. See also C. MacKinnon, *Toward a Feminist Theory of the State* (Cambridge, Mass. 1989), ix, on the relationship between power, knowledge, and the social inequality of women and men.

2 K.W. Gorrie, "Parent Education and Social Work," *Canadian Child and Family Welfare* 11, no. 5 (1936): 33–4; S.M. Carr Harris, "Reasons for Parental Education," *The Canadian Nurse* 22, no. 6 (1926): 312–14.

3 Dr E.K. Clarke, "Community Responsibility for Habit Training in Children," *Social Welfare* 13, no. 11 (1931): 228.

4 O. Brim, *Education for Childrearing* (New York 1965), 17–18.

5 J. Mechling, "Advice to Historians on Advice to Mothers," *JSH* 9, no. 1 (1973): 65.

6 S. Comstock, "The New Baby's Wardrobe," *Maclean's*, 15 November 1920.

7 Brim, *Education for Childrearing*, 17–18.

8 In Canada, with the usual lag behind American and European developments, the child study movement was officially launched in the late 1920s with the establishment of the University of Toronto's Institute of Child Study; see V. Strong-Boag, "Intruders in the Nursery," in J. Parr, ed., *Childhood and Family in Canadian History* (Toronto 1982), 169–73.

9 Gorrie, "Parent Education and Social Work," 33.

10 D. Beekman, *The Mechanical Baby* (Westport, Conn 1977), 110.

11 On the subject of advice literature and its dissemination in Canada, see V. Strong-Boag, "Intruders in the Nursery;" V. Strong-Boag, *The New Day Recalled* (Markham 1988); K. Arnup, "Educating Mothers," in Arnup, A. Levesque, and R.R. Pierson, eds., *Delivering Motherhood* (New York 1990); N. Lewis, "Creating the Little Machine," *BCST* 56 (1982–83).

12 "Babies–Life Patients: How Young Doctors May Build Up a Permanent Clientele," *The Canadian Doctor* 2, no. 10 (1937): 28.

13 D. Beekman, *The Mechanical Baby*; C. Hardyment, *Dream Babies* (New York 1983) and B. Ehrenreich and D. English, *For Her Own Good: 150 Years of the Experts' Advice to Women* (New York 1978) provide surveys of the period's advice literature in the United States and Western Europe.

14 Dominion Department of Health, *Report of the Deputy Minister*, 1925, Division of Child Welfare, Sessional Paper No. 19, 36–37. The mother's series of the "little blue books" included *The Canadian Mother's Book, How to Take Care of the Mother, How to Take Care of the Baby, How to Take Care of the Children, How to Take Care of the Father and the Family*. In 1922, 55,000 were sent to district registrars. A supplement to *The Canadian Mother's Book*, for distribution by doctors and nurses only and intended for use in outpost homes, was published in 1923: see Dominion Department of Health, *Report of the Deputy Minister*, 1925, Division of Child Welfare, Sessional Paper No. 19, 39.

15 Ibid. (1923), 37.

16 Ibid. (1924), 42–3.

17 Whitton had a degree in education from Queen's University (1918), and an honourary Master's degree in history, but was not trained as a social worker. On her life and career, see P. Rooke and R.T. Schnell, *No Bleeding Heart* (Vancouver 1987). By the early 1930s, the council had absorbed the Social Service Council of Canada, the federal health

department's child welfare division, and the Canadian Association of Child Protection Officers. It also gained control over the Canadian Association of Social Workers and the Canadian Conference of Social Work; see D. Chunn, *From Punishment to Doing Good: Family Courts and Socialized Justice in Ontario, 1880–1940* (Toronto 1992), 31–3.

18 Dominion Department of Health, *Report of the Deputy Minister*, 1924, Sessional Paper No. 19, 12. See also, "Lo, the Poor Parent Whose Untutored Mind," *Social Welfare* 12, no. 7 (1930) on the extent of pamphlet literature, and "The Work of the Child and Maternal Hygiene Section," *Child and Family Welfare* 8, no. 5 (1933): 35; A.B. Baird, "1933 with the Division," *Child and Family Welfare* 10, no. 1 (1934): 14; S. Buckley, "Efforts to Reduce Infant and Maternal Mortality Between the Wars," *Atlantis* 4 (1979): 80.

19 See Appendix (Tables A2, A3) for distribution statistics of the council's material. See also, "Child Hygiene Section," *Child and Family Welfare* 7, no. 4 (1931): 14; "The Work of the Child Hygiene Section," 33; "14th Annual Report," *Child and Family Welfare* 11, no. 1 (1935): 3; "Summary of 17th Annual Report," *Child and Family Welfare* 12, no. 5 (1937): 53, and "Child Hygiene Section," *Canadian Welfare Summary* 14, no. 3 (1938): 40. The council's journal changed its name to the latter in May 1938.

20 A. Mackay, "Caring for the Children," *Maclean's*, 15 August 1928.

21 "Maternal and Child Health Still a Challenge to Voluntary Programmes," *Canadian Welfare Summary* 14, no. 3 (1938): 11. On Charlotte Whitton's role in the council, see P. Rooke and R. Schnell, "Making the Way More Comfortable: Charlotte Whitton's Child Welfare Career, 1920–48," *J Can Studies* 17, no. 4 (1982–83). Distribution was arranged with the Local Councils of Women throughout Canada, the IODE in each province, the Women's Institutes in Ontario, the Homemakers' clubs, the "Welcome" and Welfare departments of the Anglican Church, the United Church, the Catholic Women's League, the Salvation Army Hospital Service, the Missionary Society of the Baptist Church, and the Women's Missionary Society of the Presbyterian Church.

22 The labour press also promoted the council's literature: see, for example, "Maternal and Infant Welfare," *Canadian Trade Unionist*, 29 May 1929.

23 Dr J. Puddicombe, "The Importance of Prenatal Care," *Child and Family Welfare* 10, no. 1 (1934): 11.

24 Ibid., 12.

25 NA, MG 28 I 10, Vol. 4, File 17, Child Hygiene Section, "Summary of Minutes," Division on Maternal and Child Hygiene, Canadian Council on Child and Family Welfare, Meeting, Ottawa, 14 June 1934, 3. See

also MG 28 I 10, Vol. 4, File 19, Child Hygiene Section, Statistical Information: "Medical Inquiry Service: Number of Requests Answered," 1 January 1934–30 September 1934: January (12), February (9), March (31), April (36), May (29), June (29), July (18), August (15), September (20): Total, 199.

26 Puddicombe, "The Importance of Prenatal Care," 17.

27 Canada, Department of Pensions and National Health, *Annual Report*, 1933–34, 112; Rooke and Schnell, *No Bleeding Heart*, 93–4.

28 Department of Pensions and National Health, *Annual Report*, 1933–34, 112.

29 NA, MG 29, Vol. 1318, File 495–1–2, VON, Memorandum to the Honourable Murray MacLaren, MD, Minister of Pensions and National Health, from Dr J.J. Heagerty, Re Abolition of Child Welfare Division, 11 October 1933, 6.

30 Ibid., 6.

31 Ibid., 7. Rooke and Schnell, *No Bleeding Heart*, 94, discuss medical opposition to the transfer.

32 CMA, *Annual Report*, 1934, "Committee on Public Health Resolutions," 75. The CMA reiterated its opposition to the transfer at the annual meeting of 1935 (187), and applauded the reinstitution of the Division of Maternal and Child Hygiene within the federal Department of Health in 1938 by recapitulating its 1934 resolutions; ibid., 1938, 70.

33 Dr R.E. Wodehouse, Letter to the Editor, *CMAJ* 24, no. 9 (1934): 323–4.

34 Rooke and Schnell, *No Bleeding Heart*, 81–2.

35 NA, MG 28 I 10, Vol. 4, File 17, Child Hygiene Section, Letter to Dr J.T. Phair from Charlotte Whitton, 5 July 1934; Reply of Phair, 9 July 1934. Whitton had apparently heard rumours that Phair had resigned as the director of the Ontario division in protest against the transfer at the federal level; Phair replied that "at no time have I viewed this change with disfavour nor have I changed my mind since the transfer became effective." Whitton does not appear to have been convinced, however; four months later she sent Eunice Dyke to Toronto "to make certain contacts of a political significance with a view to strengthening the Division's relationship with the Ontario Department"; Memorandum for Files, Eunice Dyke, Secretary, Canadian Council on Child and Family Welfare, 27 December 1934.

36 Turner, *Medical Power and Social Knowledge*, 137–9, discusses the sociological literature on deskilling in the medical profession.

37 King appointed the Royal Commission on Dominion-Provincial Relations (the Rowell-Sirois Commission) in 1937 with just that end in mind; D. Guest, *The Emergence of Social Security in Canada* (Vancouver 1980), 133–4.

38 "Maternal and Child Health Still a Challenge," 13. Couture, an obstetrician, was previously in charge of the maternity department of the Ottawa General Hospital.

39 NA, MG 28 I 25, Vol. 75, File 8, National Council of Women of Canada papers, letter of Charlotte Whitton to NCWC President Mrs. G.O. Spencer, 13 June 1938. Whitton urged Spencer to complain to the minister of health, C.G. Power, about this reintegration. Spencer complied immediately; ibid., Letter of Spencer to Power, 13 June 1938.

40 Department of Pensions and National Health, *Annual Report*, 1938–39, 141.

41 Between 1930 and 1935, doctors constituted 29 of 245 MPs; in 1935, Ontario had 6 medical MPPs out of 112. See "Doctors in Government," *The Canadian Doctor* 1, no. 2 (1935): 42–3.

42 Department of Pensions and National Health, *Annual Report*, 1938, 141. The secretary of the committee was the divison's chief, Dr Ernest Couture.

43 Ibid., 142. Dr Alan Brown was among the committee's members; the secretary, again, was Couture.

44 In 1939 the editing of *The Canadian Mother and Child* was completed and the book replaced *The Canadian Mothers' Book*. The advisory committee endorsed its publication for free distribution to visitors to the quintuplets at Callander. By 1940, 80,000 of the 90,000 copies printed had been sent out to applicants for a distribution of 11,000 copies a month. Specimen copies were also sent to 10,000 doctors; see Department of Pensions and National Health, *Annual Report*, 1940, 154.

45 S. Buckley, "Efforts to Reduce Infant and Maternal Mortality Between the Wars," *Atlantis* 4 (1979): 82; Rooke and Schnell, *No Bleeding Heart*, 108. The expense involved in its continuation and the exigencies of another war emergency meant that the Canadian Council on Child and Family Welfare's own health education efforts virtually ended by the early 1940s. Whitton resigned as its executive director in 1941.

46 Ontario, Board of Health, *Annual Report*, 1917, 11; Mary Power was its director. She would become director of the new Division of Maternal and Child Hygiene and Public Health Nursing after the war. See also ibid., 1919, "Report of the Bureau of Child Welfare," 37. Brief mention is given to the bureau in P. Oliver, *G. Howard Ferguson: Ontario Tory* (Toronto 1977), 216–17.

47 Ibid., 1920, 40. The director was Mary Power; Beryl Knox, RN, was in charge of public health nursing; Dr W.J. Bell was in charge of child welfare; Dr Alan Brown was the paediatric consultant. See also C.M. Johnston, *E.C. Drury: Agrarian Idealist* (Toronto 1986), 153–4.

48 As late as 1939, the department's annual report noted the "gratification expressed by medical officers of health and public health nurses
   engaged in infant hygiene work throughout the province as they had
   come to depend on the provincial baby book;" see Department of
   Health, *Annual Report*, 1939, 139.

49 Board of Health, *Annual Report*, 1921, 62.

50 Ibid., 1922, 39, 106; See also ibid., 1929, 63, and 1939, 158, for publication and distribution statistics.

51 C.M. Johnston, *E.C. Drury: Agrarian Idealist*, 149–65; Chunn, *From
   Punishment to Doing Good: Family Courts and Socialized Justice in Ontario,
   1880–1940*, 49–50.

52 P. Oliver argues that Ferguson's record in health and welfare was a
   "reflection in equal parts of traditionalism and parsimony;" see *G.
   Howard Ferguson: Ontario Tory*, 155–6; 215–30.

53 On Hepburn, see J. Saywell, *"Just Call Me Mitch:" The Life of Mitchell F.
   Hepburn* (Toronto 1991), a comprehensive biography that nonetheless
   pays little attention to Ontario outside of legislative politics.

54 Ontario, Department of Health, *The Baby*, 6th ed. (Toronto: 1924);
   new introductory page with new emphasis on prenatal care, 4. See
   also Dr Alan Brown, "The Prevention of Neonatal Mortality," CMAJ 31,
   no. 10 (1940), and Dr A.L. McLean and Dr W.G. Colwell, "Prenatal
   Care: An Eleven Year Study of the Dalhousie University Public Health
   Centre Prenatal Clinic," CMAJ 30, no. 10 (1939): 385, which found a
   significant difference in the neonatal mortality rate between mothers
   having prenatal care and those who did without. For the nurses' point
   of view, see I.S. Manion, RN, "Outline for an Introductory Talk to
   Expectant Mothers," *The Canadian Nurse* 26, no. 2 (1930): 87; A.
   Ahern, RN, "The Importance of a Prenatal Program in a Visiting
   Nurse Service," ibid. 26, no. 9 (1930): 601.

55 Toronto, Board of Health, *Prenatal Care* (Toronto 1922), 7. Also,
   Canadian Council on Child and Family Welfare, *Prenatal Letters* (1929)
   Letter No. 1, 2.

56 Department of Health, *The Baby*, introductory page.

57 Dr W.B. Hendry, "Maternal Welfare," *Social Welfare* 13, no. 9 (1931):
   180; Dr G. Jackson, "Maternal Mortality," *Social Welfare* 13, no. 9
   (1931): 183.

58 Dr W.P. Tew, "Antenatal Hygiene," *Social Welfare* 4, no. 10 (1922): 215;
   A. Morceau, RN, "Minor Abnormalities," *The Canadian Nurse* 26, no. 2
   (1930): 141–3.

59 Dr W.W. Chipman, "Some Thoughts After a Symposium on Obstetrics," CMAJ 14, no. 8 (1924): 380.

60 Canadian Council on Child and Family Welfare, *Prenatal Letters*,
   Letter No. 1, 1.

61 Ibid., 2.

62 Ibid., Letter No. 2, 1.

63 Toronto, Board of Health, *Prenatal Care*, 3.

64 On Victorian neurasthenia, see A.D. Wood, "The Fashionable Diseases: Women's Complaints and Their Treatment in Nineteenth-Century America," in L. Banner and M. Harman, eds., *Clio's Consciousness Raised* (New York 1974); W. Mitchinson, *The Nature of Their Bodies* (Toronto 1991).

65 Department of Health, *The Baby*, 5.

66 Dr A. Brown, "Certain Features of Child Welfare Work Not Sufficiently Emphasized," *CPHJ* 14, no. 9 (1923): 243.

67 Ibid. See also Dr J.W.S. McCullough, "The Prevention of Maternal Mortality," *Chatelaine*, October 1930.

68 Dr J.T. Phair, "Radio Talk," *CPHJ* 18, no. 3 (1927): 201; E. Smellie, RN, "Diet and Hygiene of Pregnancy from the Nurse's Standpoint," *The Canadian Nurse* 22, no. 6 (1926): 300–4.

69 Dr E. Guest, "Problems of Girlhood and Motherhood," *CPHJ* 18, no. 5 (1927): 195–8. For a contemporary non-medical version of the same opinion, see E. Chapman, "The Luxury of Children," *Maclean's*, 15 March 1921. There is also an interesting discussion of family limitation from the purely economic viewpoint, presented by a young middle-class mother: "Just One Baby?" *Chatelaine*, March 1931. For the racial repercussions of non-marriage and birth control, see Dr W. Hutchinson, "The Saner, Kinder Worship of the Race," *Maclean's*, 1 July 1920.

70 Dr W.W. Chipman, "Preparing Women for the Greatest of Professions," *Maclean's*, 15 October 1921.

71 Dr Woods Hutchinson, "The Modern Mother," *Maclean's*, 15 July 1920. Chipman, "Preparing Women for the Greatest of Professions," and Chapman, "The Luxury of Children," cite similar charges against Canadian motherhood. See also Editorial, "The Health of Women," *CMAJ* 26, no. 11 (1936): 572, quoting with approval the views of American obstetrician Dr G. Theobald: "The freedom that has resulted from the achievement of economic independence of women has played and continues to play ... a distinct role in the causation of maternal mortality ... that independence has probably resulted in a marked increase in the number of abortions."

72 Hutchinson, "The Modern Mother," 69.

73 F.L. Johnson, "What of Your Child?" *Chatelaine*, April 1928.

74 F. Webb, "Troubles and Triumphs," *Canadian Magazine*, July 1932. This was the first of a regular column that would act as a "department for parents where children's problems and how they are combatted may be discussed." Parents were to send a letter relating at

least one problem and how it was solved, along with a snapshot of the child.

75 E.S. Chesser, "Perfect Babies," *CCJ* 3, no. 12 (1924): 59.

76 S.N. Pines, RN, "We Want Perfect Parents," *Chatelaine*, September 1928.

77 Ibid.; See "Babies–Life Patients," for details on routine office visits.

78 Dr A. Brown, *The Normal Child: Its Care and Feeding* (Toronto 1923), 205.

79 "Mother and Baby," *Family Herald*, 26 July 1919; S. Comstock, "Getting the Baby's Viewpoint," *Maclean's*, 1 December 1920: "An amazing number of women don't know that a baby is born deaf and blind." For similar views, see also Brown, *The Normal Child*, 22. Paediatricians now take a less extreme view of the newborn's ability to see, hear and respond, arguing that these senses are minimal at birth but develop quickly within the first few days of life. See Dr Benjamin Spock, *Baby and Child Care*, 4th ed. (New York 1982), 268. For a discussion of the evolution of the "vegetable hypothesis," see L. Rappoport, *Personality Development: The Chronology of Experience* (Glenview, Ill. 1972), 112–13.

80 On Froebel, see N. Sutherland, *Children in English Canadian Society* (Toronto 1976), 18.

81 Brown, *The Normal Child*, vii–viii, 25.

82 By their "second summer," children were weaned and exposed to an even greater possibility of contracting the deadly gastro-intestinal infections through tainted milk and food affected by summer heat and poor refrigeration. "Summer complaint" was the first cause of deaths from the second to the twelfth months through the 1920s, and the second cause in the second year of life for the same period in Ontario; see Dr J.W.S. McCullough, "Summer Complaint," *Chatelaine*, August 1937.

83 Sutherland, *Children in English Canadian Society*, chap. 3, discusses the medical inspection of schools.

84 Editorial, "On the Necessity for the Careful Medical Oversight of Children of the School and Preschool Age," *CMAJ* 11, no. 6 (1922): 428.

85 M. Clark, "Helping the Preschool Child," *Canadian Magazine*, September 1928, 26.

86 E. Wallace, "During the No-Man's Land of Childhood," *Chatelaine*, February 1931.

87 For example, a study conducted by the Canadian Tuberculosis Association of Dundas Region preschoolers in 1925 revealed that, of 1,392 children examined, non-tuberculous defects alone were as follows: 33 per cent were 7 per cent or more under normal weight; 36 per cent showed lymph gland enlargement; 9 per cent showed definite defective vision; 2 per cent had defective hearing; 20 per cent had

diseased tonsils; 23 per cent had enlarged adenoids; 32 per cent had diseased primary teeth. See PAO, Pamphlet No. 64, 1925, 12. See also Dr F.S. Burke, "The Preschool Child and School Medical Inspection," *CPHJ* 24, no. 4 (1933): 170–5.

88 Toronto City Hall Archives, RG 11, F 1, Box 1, Historical Material on Maternal and Child Hygiene, typescript, Dr G. Jackson, Toronto, "The Preschool Child," presentation to Local Council of Women, Toronto, 19 March 1929, 1. For similar arguments, see Public Health Relations Committee, Academy of Medicine, "The Preschool Child," *Social Welfare* 11, no. 9 (1929): 201; Dr L. MacHaffie, "Health Pitfalls and Tragedies of the Preschool Child," *Child and Family Welfare* 12, no. 1 (1936); NA RG 29, Vol. 993, File 499–3–7, Part 10, Child Hygiene, MacHaffie, "The Mortality Trend of the Preschool Child," typescript, undated.

89 MacHaffie, "The Mortality Trend of the Preschool Child," 2. The Academy of Medicine's study, "The Preschool Child," provided a catalogue of potentially serious and frequently overlooked problems in young children, particularly with respect to hearing, sight, tonsils, adenoids, and teeth; see also Jackson, "The Preschool Child," 6; Department of Health, *The Baby* (1940), 5.

90 Council on Child and Family Welfare, "Preschool Letters," No. 1, 1; ibid., No. 9, 1.

CHAPTER SIX

1 J. Mechling, "Advice to Historians on Advice to Mothers," *JSH* 8, no. 1 (1975): 45–6.

2 Attempts to correlate bodily strength and motion with production preoccupied German medical researchers in the early twentieth century: R. Brain, "The Extramural Laboratory Limited," paper presented to the British North American Joint Meeting, Canadian Society for the History and Philosophy of Science/American History of Science Society/British Society for the History of Science, University of Toronto, 26 July 1992.

3 B. Palmer, *The Working Class Experience*, 2nd ed. (Toronto 1992), 160–1. On the international impact of Taylorism, see E. Andrew, *Closing the Iron Cage* (Montreal 1981), 72–5.

4 K. Derry, "Morale, National and Industrial," *CCJ* 12, no. 3 (1933): 23; Dr W.A. Evans, "Human Efficiency," *CPHJ* 4, no. 3 (1913): 138. See also the parody of Taylorism literally gone mad in N.S. Rankin, "100 Percent Efficient," *CCJ* 3, no. 12 (1924): 78.

5 See, for example, C.E. Hamilton, "The Scientific Management of Household Work and Wages," *CPHJ* 4 no. 1, (1913): 30.

6 K. McConnachie, "Methodology in the Study of Women in History," *OH* 75, no. 1 (1983): 61–70.

7 D. Beekman, *The Mechanical Baby* (Westport Conn 1977), and B. Ehrenreich and D. English, *For Her Own Good: 150 Years of the Experts' Advice to Women* (New York 1979), analyse the scientific management trend in American childrearing literature.

8 Dr A. Brown, *The Normal Child: Its Care and Feeding* (Toronto 1923), 223; Dr F.F. Tisdall, *The Home Care of the Infant and Child* (New York 1931), 242, and Ontario, Department of Health, *The Baby* (Toronto 1933) all employ this "little machine" metaphor. It seems to have been introduced to Canada by Brown in his *The Normal Child*, and was quickly adopted by other medical and popular advisors. The concept was prevalent in international child welfare circles during this period. See D. Beekman, *The Mechanical Baby*, C. Hardyment, *Dream Babies* (New York 1983), and B. Ehrenreich and D. English, *For Her Own Good*. See also Lewis, "Creating the Little Machine," *BCST* 56 (1982–83). Tisdall was a paediatric specialist in nutrition working out of the University of Toronto and the Hospital for Sick Children.

9 J. Ellul, *The Technological Society* (New York 1964), 325; Ellul remains the foremost critic of "technique."

10 S.N. Pines, RN, "We Want Perfect Parents," *Chatelaine*, September 1928.

11 NA, MG 28 I 10, Vol. 40, File 173C, Canadian Council on Child and Family Welfare, "Postnatal Letters," No. 1, 1. All the manuals provided similar schedules based on feedings every four hours.

12 Ibid., 2; child psychologists W. Blatz and H. Bott, *Parents and the Pre-school Child* (Toronto 1928), viii, also note the importance of using the "kitchen timepiece."

13 This isolation of the baby extended to the unprecedented measure of providing a separate sleeping chamber for it from birth. Previously, infants had often shared bedrooms with parents even in middle-class households where space was not a problem. The advisers acknowledged that this was a radical departure, but justified it as necessary for the baby's health; I. Glenn, "A Room of One's Own," *Canadian Magazine*, October 1934, 30.

14 Council on Child and Family Welfare, "Postnatal Letters," No. 10, 3.

15 Brown, *The Normal Child*, 25.

16 S. Comstock, "Getting the Baby's Viewpoint," *Maclean's*, 1 December 1920.

17 Dr R.P. Kinsman, "Mental Hygiene and Its Relation to Infants and Children," *CMAJ* 26, no. 11 (1936): 540. Kinsman argued that this branch of medicine had been grossly neglected.

18 Comstock, "Getting the Baby's Viewpoint;" B. France, RN, "Why Baby Cries," *National Home Monthly*, June 1936; Dr A. Brown and Dr F. Tis-

dall, *Common Procedures in the Practice of Paediatrics* (Toronto 1926),
111. John B. Watson, founder of behaviourism, argued that children
should never be hugged or kissed or allowed to sit on their mother's
lap; see J.B. Watson, *Psychological Care of Infant and Child* (New York
1928), 81–2. For an assessment of Watson's impact on American psychology, see J.M. O'Donnell, *The Origins of Behaviourism* (New York
1985).

19 Council on Child and Family Welfare, "Postnatal Letters," No. 2, 2.

20 The Council on Child and Family Welfare published a special series
of "diet folders" in the late 1920s; these covered every aspect of the
child's feeding and nutrition up to and including school age. They
were reprinted in their entirety in the *CCJ* 6, nos. 2–6 (1927).

21 Hospital for Sick Children, *Annual Report*, 1920, 12. See also "Nutri-
tion as a Health Problem," *The Canadian Nurse* 22, no. 4 (1926): 198;
Dr E.M. Watson, "Some Present Day Views on Diet," *The Canadian
Nurse* 26, no. 6 (1930): 309.

22 See Dr F.F. Tisdall, "Inadequacy of Present Dietary Standards," *CMAJ*
25, no. 12 (1935): 384; Dr K.C. McIlwraith, "Nutrition and Pregnancy," *CPHJ* 2, no. 10 (1930): 513. In 1938, the CMA established a
comittee on nutrition and began publishing special articles; see Dr E.
Chant Robertson and Dr F. Tisdall, "Nutrition and Resistance to Disease," *CMAJ* 30, no. 3 (1939): 282; Dr E.V. McCollum, "Better Nutrition as a Health Measure," *CMAJ* 30, no. 4 (1939): 393. These regular
nutrition columns were also broadcast on CBC radio. See also Dr A.
Brown and Dr G.A. Davis, "The Prevalence of Malnutrition in the
Public School Children of Toronto," *CMAJ* 11, no. 2 (1921): 121.
Brown and Davis found that, of 2,843 children examined, 1,256 (44
per cent) were 7 per cent or more underweight; 751 (26 per cent)
were 10 per cent to 12 per cent underweight; they studied two
"middle-class" and two "working-class" schools, but do not indicate
how they were categorized as such. See also Dr E.W. McHenry, "Nutrition in Toronto," *CPHJ* 30, no. 1 (1939): 4–13. Various nutrition surveys conducted by Toronto's health department during the 1920s and
the early 1930s revealed clear evidence of malnutrition in poor children, but health officials advised only public education to improve
dietary habits. H. MacDougall, *Activists and Advocates* (Toronto 1990),
169, indicates that the Toronto health department's awareness of malnutrition, especially in families on relief during the Depression, was
not confronted due to the city's budgetary constraints.

23 In 1922 a jury investigating the death of a child of two-and-one-half
months at Orillia brought in the "unique verdict" that the infant had
died due to "enteric trouble caused by food not suitable for a child of
her age." The public health nurse had offered her services at the
request of the local physician, but had been unable to gain access to

the house. This "unique verdict" was believed to be universally applicable to cases of preventable infant death; PAO, RG 10, 30-A-1, file 3–3, Historical Literature and Pamphlets, Division of Maternal and Child Hygiene and Public Health Nursing, *Bulletin*, October 1922; see also PAO, RG 10, 30-A-3, Public Health Nursing Correspondence and RG 62 series, Field Reports, which outline countless instances in which ailing infants taken to clinics were diagnosed as feeding cases.

24 Elizabeth Smith Shortt Collection, University of Waterloo, Correspondence, File 15, Letter to Smith Shortt from Virginia, Loudreau, Ontario, undated. Smith Shortt noted in the margin that the baby died two weeks later, evidently of influenza. R. Apple, *Mothers and Medicine: A Social History of Infant Feeding* (Madison, Wisc. 1987), provides many such examples of American mothers' attempts to feed their babies according to medical dictates.

25 Dr J.J. Middleton, "Mothers! Breastfeeding of Infants is Best," (Toronto 1921); published in *CPHJ* 12, no. 7 (1921): 312.

26 PAO, RG 62, Vol. 468, File 1-D-1, Correspondence, letter of Dr Middleton, Director, Division of Public Health Education, to Public Health Nursing Division, regarding nurses' distribution of his pamphlet.

27 Dr A. Goldbloom, "A 25 Year Retrospective of Infant Feeding," *CMAJ* 36, no. 4 (1945): 279. See also Dr D.J. Evans, "The Scientific Principles Underlying Milk Feeding of Infants," *Canada Lancet* 39, no. 5 (1906): 543–4; for a detailed description of a typical artificial formula, see Dr R.J. Ewart, "A Cheap Food for Babies," *CPHJ* 6, no. 9 (1915): 440–1. See Apple, *Mothers and Medicine*, 54.

28 Brown introduced this formula to the Hospital for Sick Children upon his return from postgraduate paediatric studies in Germany just before the outbreak of World War One. During the perennial summer epidemics of this disease, Brown would go down to the hospital milk lab at night and make the formula himself; Hospital for Sick Children Alumni Association, *Dr Alan Brown* (Toronto 1983), 30.

29 Dr R.R. Struthers, "The Use of Acid Milk Mixtures in Infant Feeding," *CMAJ* 14, no. 8 (1924): 712. Lactic acid milk was made by adding a bacterial culture to boiled whole cow's milk to break down the indigestible lactose in it; Hospital for Sick Children, *Dr Alan Brown*, 31.

30 Editorial, "Infant Mortality," *CMAJ* 17, 3 (1927): 347; J. Chisholm, RN, "The Advantages of Breastfeeding," *The Canadian Nurse* 26, no. 3 (1930): 139–41. Katherine Arnup argues that the medical focus on education was due to this insistence on breast-feeding; see "Educating Mothers," 192.

31 Dr H. MacMurchy, *A Little Talk About the Baby* (Toronto 1913), 3. The "breast versus bottle" controversy is an eternal theme in the history of

childrearing. Before the advent of bottle feeding, it was a case of maternal versus wet-nursing; see V. Fildes, *Breasts, Bottles and Babies: A History of Infant Feeding* (London 1986), and V. Fildes, *Wet Nursing: A History from Antiquity to the Present* (London 1988). For a discussion of the medical profession's concern with breastfeeding in the United States in the early twentieth century, see C.E. Vincent, "Trends in Infant Care Ideas: The Breast versus Artificial Feeding Controversy", *Child Development*, September 1951. The "breast is best" argument continues to resurface; see Editorial, Toronto *Globe and Mail*, 8 August 1992.

32 Brown, *The Normal Child*, 60.

33 Dr A.G. Fleming, "Child Hygiene," *CPHJ* 14, no. 7 (1923): 295.

34 Brown, "The Prevention of Neonatal Mortality," 266.

35 R. George, "Milk as an Essential Food," *Social Welfare* 3, no. 11 (1921): 50.

36 Editorial, *CPHJ* 6, no. 10 (1915): 511; see also Dr A. Brown, "The Ability of Mothers to Nurse Their Infants," *CMAJ* 7, no. 3 (1917): 241; Dr R.D. Rudolph, "Low Percentages in Infant Feeding," *CMAJ* 2, no. 3 (1912): 174.

37 Apple, *Mothers and Medicine*, 131, argues that by 1950 the majority of American mothers were bottle-feeding.

38 Dr A. Brown, "Infant and Child Welfare Work," *CPHJ* 9, no. 4 (1918): 150. Brown conducted the study in Toronto in 1916. The Montreal study is discussed in "Breastfeeding Continues to Decline," *Child Welfare News* 6, no. 1 (1930): 218. The latter revealed that only 48 per cent of the babies surveyed were nursed to six months, only 46 per cent until the advised weaning time of nine months; 7 per cent of those weaned early were weaned because their mothers were employed outside the home. There was more breastfeeding among mothers who attended child welfare clinics than among non-attenders. The study was compared with Brown's; even beside Montreal's rather poor showing, Toronto's was worse. The impressions of the public health nurses seem to support this contention that a large percentage of Ontario infants were being artificially fed; see PAO, RG 62, 1-F-1-B, Box 473, Correspondence, letter of B. Knox, Associate Director of Public Health Nursing, to F.I. MacEwan, Public Health Nurse, March 25, 1926, from Elsace. It is now estimated that about 70 per cent of mothers nurse their infants for at least one month; see T. Pitman, "Nursing the Newborn," *Great Expectations*, July 1986. See also Brown, "The Prevention of Neonatal Mortality," 266.

39 MacMurchy, *Infant Mortality: First Special Report* (Toronto 1910), 17.

40 Brown, "The Prevention of Neonatal Mortality," 267.

41 Editorial, *CPHJ* 6, no. 10 (1915): 511; Brown, "The Prevention of Neonatal Mortality," 267.

42 Dr A. Brown, "Keeping the Well Child Well," *Maclean's*, 15 October 1922. Brown condemned the "exploiting of photographs of crowing, fat, red-cheeked babies" by the manufacturers of infant foods composed mostly of maltose who "stoop to steal the credit which belongs to a cow." The CMAJ did not publish formula advertisements, but the Ontario Medical Association's organ, the *Canadian Medical Quarterly*, occasionally did so; see, for example, advertisements for Dennos Food and CMP Protein Milk Powder, *Canadian Medical Quarterly* 5, no. 2 (1919); advertisement for Borden's Eagle Brand ("When Mother's Milk Fails"), *Canadian Medical Monthly* (new name) 5, no. 11 (1920). See also Apple, *Mothers and Medicine*, 72, 84–5, 94.

43 Dr F. Royer, "Child Welfare," CPHJ 12, no. 7 (1921): 292–3.

44 Dr F. Tisdall, *The Home Care of the Infant and Child*, 67.

45 Dr L.A. Chase, "Comparing the Breastfed and the Bottle-fed Infant," CMAJ 20, no. 12 (1930): 868. In summarizing the findings of a study based on detailed examination of 217 infants attending baby clinics in Boston and the vital statistics of 1,566 infants followed for one year, Chase notes that the frequency of infection and mortality was most common among the bottle-fed group in the poorer district, least common among the bottle-fed in the better district. She concludes that "In districts where economic and hygienic conditions are fairly good, the average bottle-fed infant does as well as the average breastfed infant." See also Apple, *Mothers and Medicine*, 56.

46 Brown, "The Prevention of Neonatal Mortality," 268; see also Dr A. Goldbloom, "Modern Tendencies in Infant Feeding," CMAJ 14, no. 8 (1924): 704; Dr F.M. Fry, "Fixed Principles in the Feeding of Infants," CMAJ 14, no. 6 (1924): 503. Both Goldbloom and Fry were paediatricians associated with McGill University. See also Dr H. Spohn, "Infant Feeding," *Canadian Medical Monthly* 5, no. 9 (1920); Dr W.J. Denney, "Infant Feeding: A Consideration of Cow's Milk, Its Chemistry and Chemical Modifications," *Canadian Medical Monthly* 5, no. 11 (1920): 472.

47 Board of Health, *The Baby* (1920), 17; Council on Child and Family Welfare, "Postnatal Letters," No. 2, 1.

48 Editorial, CPHJ, 6, no. 10, 512.

49 PAO, RG 10, 30-A-1, Field Reports, A.L. Campbell, Report of Demonstration in Espanola, 1923; see also Dr A.B. Chandler, "Recent Studies in Problems Connected with Lactation and Infant Feeding," CMAJ 11, no. 1 (1921): 62. Chandler, a paediatrician working out of Children's Memorial Hospital, Montreal, contended that "if the doctor does not dominate, the neighbour will."

50 For example, at the Canadian National Exhibition's annual child welare display and at various local fairs where the Canadian Welfare

Council or the provincial health department sent exhibits. The Hospital for Sick Children's nutritional clinic also weighed and measured babies weekly and "to stimulate interest a prize is awarded for the child who best attains the result in view"; Hospital for Sick Children, *Annual Report*, 1920, 12.

51 Goldbloom, "A Twenty-Five Year Retrospective of Infant Feeding," 279.

52 Brown, "The Prevention of Neonatal Mortality," 267; Apple, *Mothers and Medicine*, 67.

53 Hospital for Sick Children, *Dr Alan Brown*, 31; Sunwheat Biscuit royalties were also turned over to Sick Children's. Pablum is still a popular "first solid" for infants, and Sunwheat biscuits, modified in accordance with today's nutritional knowledge (and in order to remove the bonemeal of the original recipe, which is no longer allowed in food for human consumption) have recently been reintroduced by Galen Weston's Loblaws/Zehrs supermarket empire.

54 S.R. Laycock, "The Relation Between Psychology and Medicine," *CMAJ* 26, no. 10 (1936): 435.

55 Brown and Tisdall, *Common Procedures in the Practice of Paediatrics*, 109–10. See also Dr W.M. Musgrove, "Some Problems of Childhood," *CMAJ* 17, no. 4 (1927): 438; Laycock, "The Relation Between Psychology and Medicine," 435; N. Lewis, "Advising the Parents: Childrearing in British Columbia in the Interwar Years," Ph.D. thesis, University of British Columbia 1980, 81–4.

56 Council on Child and Family Welfare, "Postnatal Letters," Introductory letter, 1.

57 See, for example, Tisdall, *The Home Care of the Infant and Child*, 265; in his chapter on habit training, Tisdall "highly recommends" that parents read W. Blatz and H. Bott, *Parents and the Preschool Child* (1928) and *The Management of Young Children* (1930). Blatz and Bott also acknowledged the influence of paediatric medicine on childrearing patterns: *The Management of Young Children*, 3. Blatz himself was the embodiment of this cross-influence: he received a Master's degree in physiology in 1917 and a Bachelor of Medicine in 1921 from the University of Toronto before taking a Ph.D. in psychology from the University of Chicago in 1924. See also Dr R.M. Matthews, "Permissiveness and Dr Blatz," *CMAJ* 126, no. 1 (1980). As foremost authorities on childrearing during the 1930s, Blatz and Dr Alan Brown were together responsible for the regimen imposed on the famous Dionne quintuplets; see V. Strong-Boag, "Intruders in the Nursery," 174–7. Under Brown's direction, the Hospital for Sick Children established a "clinic for Psychological Medicine" in January 1937, the first of its kind in Canada, in order to treat emotional and psy-

chological disorders in young children: Hospital for Sick Children, *Annual Report*, 1937, 5.

58 Musgrove, "Some Problems of Childhood," 438.

59 B. Palmer, *A Culture in Conflict* (Montreal/Kingston 1979), 98.

60 P. Sandiford, "Parental Responsiblity," Radio Talk prepared for the Social Hygiene Council, broadcast at CKCL Toronto, 4 August 1925; published in *CPHJ* 16, no. 8 (1925): 387.

61 "Good Habits for Baby," *CCJ* 11, no. 1 (1932): 29.

62 Dr E. Clarke, "Community Responsibility for Habit Training in Children," 228.

63 Brown and Tisdall, *Common Procedures in the Practice of Paediatrics*, 109; Tisdall, *The Home Care of the Infant and Child*, 237.

64 Toronto City Hall Archives, RG 11, F1 Box 1, Historical Material on Maternal and Child Hygiene, typescript of talk given at Local Council of Women luncheon, Toronto, 19 March 1929, Dr G. Jackson, Toronto, "The Preschool Child," 6.

65 Tisdall, *The Home Care of the Infant and Child*, 6.

66 Toronto City Hall Archives, RG 11, Box 4, File 1, A. Thomson, "Changing Practices in Public Health Nursing," late 1930s, 1.

67 N. Weiss, "The Mother-Child Dyad Revisited," *JSI* 34, no. 2 (1978): 35.

68 This was undoubtedly more important to the mothers who could not afford outside help for household duties. See "Baby's Day and Yours," *CCJ* 4, no. 8 (1925): 46; also "A Day in Baby's Life," *CCJ* 8, no. 1 (1929): 40.

69 Council on Child and Family Welfare, "Postnatal Letters," (1933), Introductory letter, 2.

70 M.C. Ringland, "You Can't Blame the Old Adam," *Maclean's*, 15 March 1928.

71 Council on Child and Family Welfare, "Postnatal Letters," No. 7, 2–3.

72 "The Importance of Mothers," *CCJ* 11, no. 3 (1932): 29.

73 B. France, RN, "Cultivating Habits," *National Home Monthly*, October 1934, 22; "Preschool Letters," No. 10, 1–2; S.N. Pines, RN, "Irregularities of Babyhood," *Chatelaine*, February 1929.

74 On eugenics, see chap. 1, notes 10–11; N. Sutherland, chap. 5, *Children in English Canadian Society* (Toronto 1976) provides an excellent discussion of mental hygiene with respect to Canadian school children.

75 The highly influential Alan Brown contended that, if mothers assigned negative qualities to certain aspects of child behaviour, it was important that "the parent shall strive to recognize the inborn traits of character which lie back of behaviour." Yet Brown was an avid proponent of early habit training. So was psychologist Dr E. Clarke, although he also

argued that "heredity has a definite part to contribute in personality development." See Brown, *The Normal Child*, 206; Clarke, "Community Responsibility for Habit Training in Children," 228.

76 O. Brim, *Education for Childrearing* (New York 1965), 32–3.

77 J.B. Watson, *Behaviourism* (New York 1928), 4.

78 C. Hardyment provides a good review of behaviourism's main tenets in *Dream Babies*, as does D. Beekman in *The Mechanical Baby*.

79 Blatz was definitely influenced by Watson, although he never admitted to being a behaviourist. More importantly, Blatz believed that "Insofar as the hereditary equipment of a human being is so meagre, it is obvious that the environmental influences are exceedingly important;" Blatz, *Understanding the Young Child* (Toronto 1944), 36. He argued as well that "all social patterns in the human being are learned;" *Human Security: Some Reflections* (Toronto 1966), 5.

80 Brim, *Education for Childrearing*, 34. Freud's views on early life experience were becoming influential; see D. Chunn, *From Punishment to Doing Good: Family Courts and Socialized Justice in Ontario, 1880–1940* (Toronto 1992), 38.

81 M.C. Ringland, "As the Twig is Bent," *Maclean's*, 1 May 1929.

82 Tisdall, *The Home Care of the Infant and Child*, 239.

83 F.L. Johnson, "What of Your Child?" *Chatelaine*, April 1928.

84 Tisdall, *The Home Care of the Infant and Child*, 239; Ringland, "You Can't Blame the Old Adam," 70.

85 Watson, *Behaviourism*, 303–4. For an analysis of Watson's impact on child study in Canada, see P.J. Miller, "Psychology and the Child," in P.T. Rooke and R.L. Schnell, eds., *Studies in Childhood History* (Calgary 1982).

86 Brown, *The Normal Child*, 206.

87 Blatz and Bott, *Parents and the Preschool Child*, 11.

88 Ringland, "As the Twig Is Bent," 79.

89 Brown, *The Normal Child*, 208.

90 Ibid., 208.

91 Tisdall, *The Home Care of the Infant and Young Child*, 241.

92 For example, M.C. Ringland, "To Spank or Not to Spank," *Maclean's*, 1 April 1928; Ontario, Department of Health, *The Baby* (1940), 64–5. Blatz stated it forcefully: blind obedience was "the fundamental basis of fascism"; *Understanding the Young Child*, 5.

93 Theodor Adorno and Max Horkheimer began one such study, *Authority and the Family*, at the Institute for Social Research in Frankfort; it was published in Paris in 1936 after its authors fled Nazism. Psychoanalyst Wilhelm Reich drew similar conclusions in his *The Mass Psychology of Fascism* (1933). See R. Bridenthal, "Something Old,

Something New: Women in Europe Between the Two World Wars," in R. Bridenthal and C. Koontz, eds., *Becoming Visible* (Boston 1977), 442.

94 Toronto, Department of Health, *Care of the Infant and Young Child* (1931), 45; Ontario, Department of Health, *The Baby* (1940), 65.

95 Tisdall, *The Home Care of the Infant and Child*, 241–2.

96 Ibid., 242.

97 Ringland, "To Spank or Not to Spank," 82.

98 Tisdall, *The Home Care of the Infant and Child*, 242.

99 Brown, *The Normal Child*, 209–10.

100 "Postnatal Letters," No. 7, 3.

101 "The Importance of Mothers," 29. See also F.L. Johnson, "Shall We Punish Our Children?" *Chatelaine*, January 1930; "Don't Punish Your Children," *CCJ* 8, no. 11 (1929): 41.

102 Brown, *The Normal Child*, 208; *The Baby* (1920), 35.

103 D. Saunders, "To Spank or Not to Spank," debate on corporal punishment featuring Blatz and Judge Hosking of the Toronto Court of Family Relations, *Maclean's*, 15 April 1932. Saunders is quoting Blatz.

104 Ibid.

105 M. Emerson, "Parent Education in a Family Casework Agency," *Child and Family Welfare* 10, no. 5 (1935): 46.

106 M.E. Anstey, "If It Were Not for the Kiddies," *Social Welfare* 14, no. 2 (1931): 26.

107 "Cries—Every Kind," *CCJ* 4, no. 4 (1925): 51.

108 France, "Cultivating Habits," 22; also B. France, "Why Baby Cries," *National Home Monthly*, June 1936.

109 Tisdall, *The Home Care of the Infant and Child*, 29.

110 Ibid., 246.

111 "Cries—Every Kind," 51.

112 *The Baby* (1933), 29.

113 Ibid. (1940), 30.

114 Turner, *Medical Power and Social Knowledge*, 85.

115 PAO, RG 10, 30-A-1, File 3–3, Historical Literature, A. Thomson, RN, Supervisor, Division of Maternal and Child Hygiene, Toronto Board of Health, "The Infant and Preschool Child," *News Exchange* (Bulletin of the Ontario Division of Public Health Nursing), 24.

116 E. Wallace, "During the No-Man's Land of Childhood," *Chatelaine*, February 1931.

117 Brown, *The Normal Child*, 112.

118 Council on Child and Family Welfare, "Preschool Letters," No. 2, 1; Dr J.W.S. McCullough, "Doctor He Won't Eat," *Chatelaine*, February 1937; L.P. Bell, "Cultivating Right Habits," *National Home Monthly*, October 1933, 59; "A Battle of Wills," *CCJ* 8, no. 5 (1929), 42.

119 L.P. Bell, "Applesauce," *National Home Monthly*, May 1933, 59.

120 Ibid., 59.

121 "A Battle of Wills", 42.

122 Brown, *The Normal Child*, 143–4.

123 "A Battle of Wills", 42.

124 Council on Child and Family Welfare, "Postnatal Letters," No. 2, 3.

125 Ibid., 2, "A Hint for Fathers."

126 "But What of the Fathers?" *Family Herald*, 9 July 1919.

127 M.C. Ringland, "What About Father?" *Maclean's*, 1 August 1928.

128 Council on Child and Family Welfare, "Postnatal Letters," No. 11, 213.

129 Ibid., "A Hint to Mothers," 3.

130 "Father Doesn't Count!" *CCJ* 10, no. 11 (1931): 39.

131 Ibid.

132 V. Strong-Boag, *The New Day Recalled: Lives of Girls and Women in English Canada, 1919–1939* (Markham 1988), 164.

CHAPTER SEVEN

1 See E.C. Carter, RN, "The Present Day Relation of Doctors and Nurses," *The Canadian Nurse* 22, no. 2 (1926): 67–72; E. Cryderman, RN, "The Relationship of the Visiting Nurse to the Medical Profession," ibid. 26, no. 6 (1930): 309–11. See also S. Buckley, "Ladies or Midwives?" in L. Kealey, ed., *A Not Unreasonable Claim: Women and Reform in Canada* (Toronto 1979), 149. See also J. Coburn, "'I See and Am Silent': A Short History of Nursing in Ontario," in J. Acton, P. Goldsmith, and B. Shepard, eds., *Women at Work: Ontario, 1850–1930* (Toronto 1974), 139: Coburn stresses that nurses were trained in the "need for complete subservience to the doctor." The entire gamut of nursing services across the nation is catalogued in J.M. Gibbon's *Three Centures of Canadian Nursing* (Toronto 1947).

2 J. Struthers, *No Fault of Their Own: Unemployment and the Canadian Welfare State* (Toronto 1983), 202–3.

3 Canada, House of Commons, *Debates*, 5 June 1928, 3782. The speaker was M. McGibbon (Muskoka).

4 Ibid., 3784.

5 Ibid., 23 May 1929, 2811. As another MP commented, "In relation to the Department of Health, the government has stood still for ten years; and what is more, it will stand still for twenty years longer unless someone comes along and wakes it up."

6 Ibid., 2812–13. The Honourable Member was Dr T.E. Kaiser (Ontario township).

7 Ibid., 2815.

8   Ibid., 3 March 1930, 217. The resolution was presented by H.E. Spencer (Battle River).

9   Ibid., 219; Canada, Department of Pensions and National Health, *Annual Report*, 1930–31, 137.

10 Ibid., 235.

11 Ibid., 24 January 1935, 172; 31 January 1935, 352. Bennett's health minister was D.M. Sutherland.

12 Ontario, Board of Health, *Annual Report*, 1919, 37, 42.

13 The new Division of Maternal and Child Hygiene and Public Health Nursing created as a result of this restructuring included one paediatrician, Dr William J. Bell; Mary Power, Director of Nursing; Beryl Knox, Associate Director; and eight staff nurses paired with eight nurses supplied by the Red Cross Society, or two for each provincial health district. In 1925, the division was amalgamated with that of the School Medical Services, formerly under the aegis of the Department of Education. Dr J.T. Phair became the division's director. See Ontario, Department of Health, *Annual Report*, 1982, "A Century of Caring."

14 PAO, RG 10, 30-A-L, Box 11, File 11.3, Historical Files, typescript, undated, unsigned, "Maternal and Child Hygiene." Each of the eight public health nurses was paired with a Red Cross nurse and sent to a district for a three-to-six month tour. See also Board of Health, *Annual Report*, 1921, 171.

15 Board of Health, *Annual Report*, 1922, Report of Associate Director Beryl Knox, 177–9. Knox summarizes the total work done between October 1920 and December 1921: instructive, 14,970, nursing, 1,512; infant, 3,827; postnatal, 430; and prenatal, 767.

16 Ibid.; by 1938, 36 centres had clinics and a total public health nursing staff of 73; Toronto employed 96 nurses. PAO, RG 62, 1-f-1-b, Box 473, Correspondence, "List of Municipalities Employing Public Health Nurses in 1921": Windsor, London, Chatham, St Thomas, Galt, St Mary's, Kitchener, Stratford, Owen Sound, Orillia, Barrie, Welland, St. Catharines, Niagara Falls, Toronto, Hamilton, Peterborough, Ottawa, Kingston, Sudbury, Timmins, Sturgeon Falls, Blind River, and Sault Ste Marie.

17 See, for example, Board of Health, *Annual Report*, 1921, Welland, 260; 1922, District 1 (counties of Lambton, Essex, Kent, Elgin, Oxford, and Middlesex), 195; District 2 (Galt, Owen Sound, St Mary's, Kitchener, Stratford, Collingwood, Barrie, Orillia, Guelph, Walkerton, and Goderich), 202; District 6 (Temiskaming, Nipissing, Parry Sound, part of district of Sudbury), 220; District 8 (Algoma, Manitoulin, and Sudbury West), 238; North Bay, 347; 1923, District 8 (Sault Ste Marie area), 185.

18 PAO, RG 10, 30-A-1, Box 6, File 6–4, Public Health Nursing, Historical Literature, undated typescript, probably early 1920s, 2–3, outlining official goals in establishing child welfare clinics in Ontario.

19 PAO, RG 10, 30-A-1, Box 1, File 1.7, typescript, unsigned, "Living Conditions in Belleville," read at Open Forum Meeting, Belleville Chamber of Commerce, 22 March 1922.

20 Dr A. Brown, "Toronto as a Paediatric Centre," *The Canadian Medical Monthly* 5, no. 6 (1920): 204–9. H. MacDougall, *Activists and Advocates* (Toronto 1990), provides thorough coverage of Toronto's child welfare clinics and visiting nurse services for the period.

21 Although of a celebratory and "centennial" nature, Max Braithewaite's *Sick Kids: A History of the Hospital for Sick Children* (Toronto 1975) outlines some of the major developments of its history.

22 Hospital for Sick Children Archives, Brown file, Dr A. Brown, typescript, "How the Children's Hospital Can Best Meet Community Needs," read at 41st convention of the American Hospital Association, Toronto, 25–9 September 1939, 1–4. On the establishment of the Toronto School of Hygiene, see Editorial, *CMAJ* 14, no. 8 (1924): 878–9. The school included the University of Toronto's Departments of Hygiene and Preventive Medicine and Public Health Nursing as well as the Connaught Laboratories.

23 Ibid., 8; Brown, "Toronto as a Paediatric Centre," 209.

24 Hospital for Sick Children, *46th Annual Report*, 1921, 4; ibid., *47th Annual Report*, 1922, 5.

25 Dr A.G. Fleming, "Child Hygiene," *CPHJ* 14, no. 7 (1923): 300.

26 Nor was the situation better in other provinces: in 1931, only 4 of 43 hospitals in a national survey (excluding Ontario) indicated that they provided prenatal supervision; see Dr W. B. Hendry, "Maternal Welfare," *Social Welfare* 13, no. 9 (1931): 181. This does not include prenatal clinics held outside hospitals; no figures have been located to indicate how many of these were in existence either in the province or outside. The impressions given by the public health nurses' field reports support my contention that there were few of them. Dr G. Fleming declared that "the present programme for maternal care has failed because it has not been applied to a sufficiently large percentage of mothers;" see Department of Pensions and National Health, *Annual Report*, 1931–32, 106. See also C.L. Biggs, "The Response to Maternal Mortality in Ontario, 1920–40," M.Sc. thesis, University of Toronto 1982. For a discussion of such clinics in British Columbia, see N. Lewis, "Reducing Maternal Mortality in British Columbia," in B.K. Latham and R.J. Pazdro, eds., *Not Just Pin Money* (Victoria 1984), 340.

27 Dr G. Smith, "The Result of Three Years' Work in the Department of Child Hygiene, Toronto," *CPHJ* 9, no. 7 (1918): 312; *Canadian Child Welfare News*, 2, no. 1 (1926): 35.

28 PAO, Pamphlet Collection, Dr J.T. Phair, Chief Medical Officer of Health, Ontario, "Report of a Survey of the Services Extended by the Health Department of the City of Toronto," December 1943.

29 Toronto City Hall Archives, RG 11, Box 1, A. Thomson, Director, Toronto Public Health Nurses, "Changing Practices in Public Health Nursing," undated typescript, probably early 1930s, 1.

30 Ibid., 3. The department's own manual, *Care of the Infant and Young Child*, was largely the work of Dr Alan Brown and closely resembled his own *The Normal Child* (Toronto 1923).

31 "Report of the Medical Officer of Health for Hamilton," Board of Health, *Annual Report*, 1922, 329. See also B. Emerson, RN, "A Day With the Clinic's Visiting Nurse," *The Canadian Nurse* 28, no. 1 (1932): 24–5; A. Thomson, RN, "The Value of Health Training in the Home," ibid. 22, no. 8 (1926): 415–16.

32 Dr J.T. Phair, "Points Which Seem to Arise from the Discussion of Certain Standards of Child Health Service," 2; PAO, 16383, 3–14, Ontario Welfare Council, *Annual Report*, January 1930, Report of the Child Welfare Committee.

33 PAO, Typescript outlining scope and function of baby clinics, 1. See also Dr A.M. Jeffery, "The Private Physician Looks at Public Health Nursing," *CPHJ* 23, no. 10 (1932): 459–60.

34 In 1907, the New Zealand Society for the Health of Women and Children was established by Dr Frederick Truby King. Its goal was to provide prenatal care and motherhood training, with particular emphasis on breastfeeding, the cornerstone of the Truby King method. By the end of World War One, New Zealand boasted the lowest infant mortality rate in the world, a feat widely attributed to Truby King's movement. His system was similar to those urged on mothers in North America in the early decades of this century. He advocated breastfeeding, or if all else failed, a professionally modified cow's milk formula prepared to exacting requirements, rigid feeding schedules, strict habit training, minimal handling, and plenty of fresh air. The New Zealand government "lent" Truby King to the British government in 1918. He founded the Mothercraft Training Society at Cromwell House in London, with the Duchess of York as its president. See E. Cryderman, RN, "Mothercraft," *Canadian Child Welfare News* 3, no. 3 (1927): 20; C. Hardyment, *Dream Babies* (New York 1983) and A. Dally, *Inventing Motherhood* (London 1982); both the latter discuss the ideas and impact of Truby King.

35 Cryderman, "Mothercraft," 26.

36 Toronto City Hall Archives, RG 11, Box 1, Letter from A. Thomson to L. Holland, Department of Public Welfare, Victoria, British Columbia, 10 December 1942, 1. In describing the Mothercraft Society's work and the department's long-held policy of ignoring it, Thomson wrote, "Honesty compels me to state that I believe [Dr. Brown] was prejudiced against them and that his decision was not an entirely objective one." When the Mothercraft Centre first opened its Toronto base, two public health nurses were sent by the city to take a training course in Truby King methods. At the conclusion of this course, they provided Brown with a summary of some of the basic differences between Truby King methods and Brown's own; Toronto City Hall Archives, RG 11, File 1, Box 1, Memorandum from Public Health Nurse Elsie Hickey re The Canadian Mothercraft Society, 11 August 1938. As Hickey summarized the major points of contention from the nurses' report, they were as follows: 1. All babies should be nursed at both breasts at every nursing regardless of the supply of breast milk. Dr Brown: No; only if the supply of breast milk is inadequate; 2. Mattresses of babies' beds should be made of bran. Dr Brown: No; 3. Babies' beds should be made by putting bedding under mattress, putting baby on mattress and bringing clothing over him, one covering from one side, one from the other. Dr Brown: No. There is no indication given as to whether Brown explained the reasons for his objections; the memo simply records his negative response.

37 Ibid., 1.

38 Toronto City Hall Archives, RG 11, Box 1, File, 1, Reply of Dyke to Brown, 9 July 1932. Dyke would become Charlotte Whitton's secretary on the Council on Child and Family Welfare the following year; for an account of Dyke's career, see M. Royce, *Eunice Dyke: Health Care Pioneer* (Toronto 1982). Otherwise positive views are given by some nurses: see E. Cryderman, RN, "The Mothercraft Training Society," *The Canadian Nurse* 22, no. 5 (1926): 227; G. Bain, RN, "The Mothercraft Training Centre," ibid. 28, no. 2 (1932): 77–8.

39 Reply of Dyke to Brown, 1.

40 The university, the academy and the hospital were, of course, Brown strongholds. This policy of non-cooperation is discussed in the letter of Thomson to Holland, 10 December 1942, 2. See also ibid., A. Thomson, Memorandum re The Canadian Mothercraft Society, 20 June 1945.

41 PAO, RG 10, 30-A-1, Box 6, File 6.4, Public Health Nursing, Historical Literature, typescript outlining scope and function of baby clinics in Ontario, 2.

42 M. Power, "The Scope of the Public Health Nurse," Division of Maternal and Child Hygiene and Public Health Nursing, *Bulletin*, September-October 1924, 20.

43 PAO, RG 62, Vol 483, Field Reports, M.I. Foy, Public Health Demonstration in Galt, November 1920.

44 Ibid., 1-f-2, Box 486, Field Reports, O.M. Gipson, letter to Director Mary Power, Hawkesbury, 8 August 1921.

45 Ibid., F-2, Vol. 481, Public Health Nurses' Correspondence, letter from Beryl Knox, Toronto, 9 March 1926, in response to letter of B.E. Johnson from Little Current, 16 February 1926.

46 B.E. Harris, RN, "The Public Health Nurse Looks at Herself," *CPHJ* 23, no. 10 (1932): 467.

47 PAO, RG 62, 1-f-1-b, Box 473, Correspondence, letter marked "confidential," to Mary Power from M.R. Heeley, Bowmanville, 5 January 1922.

48 Ibid., F.I. McEwan, Report on Bracebridge, 11 January 1926.

49 Ibid., RG 10, 30-A-3, Box 17, Supervisors' Reports, H.G. Pennock, Report of Visit to St Thomas, June 1938. In an interview with the town's hospital nurses three years previously (ibid., Visit to St. Thomas, June 1935), Pennock had been told that "there is no possibility of establishing a child health conference in the city because of the attitude of the physicians." She also discovered what was probably the source of the chairman's opposition: "They also say that Dr M., the Chairman of the Board of Health, is very anxious to have the local hospital initiate an out-patient clinic service and he feels that a conference might further delay this."

50 Ibid.

51 Ibid., Box 19, H.G. Pennock, Sturgeon Falls, September 1934; see also ibid., 30-A-1, Box 1, M.R. Heeley, Report of the Demonstration of Public Health Nursing in Kitchener, 7 June-22 July 1921.

52 Ibid., Box 19, H.G. Pennock, Report of Visit to Chatham, February 1935.

53 Ibid., Box 17, H.G. Pennock, Report of Visit to St Mary's, 21–25 March 1939.

54 Ibid., Box 7, N.E. Howey, Report of Visit to Hamilton, 31 January-13 February 1936.

55 Ibid., RG 62, 1-f-1-b, Box 473, Correspondence, letter from B. Knox to M.R. Heeley at Barrie, 12 July 1922L-11. This letter was in response to Heeley's question, cited above, as to how much could be done at clinics without hurting the family physician.

56 Dr A.G. Fleming, "Organized Medicine and Public Health," *CMAJ* 24, no. 3 (1934): 664–5. See also Dr W.J. Bell, "Trends in Public Health and Medical Care in Canada," *CPHJ* 25, no. 7 (1934): 316–7. See the

altogether negative views on public health work expressed in Dr B. Cuddihy, "The Patients That Do Not Come to Me," *The Canadian Doctor* 11, no. 6 (1936): 9–14; Cuddihy complains bitterly about clinics and visiting nurses.

57 Fleming, "Organized Medicine and Public Health," 664–5.

58 PAO, RG 62, 1-f-1-b, Box 469, Correspondence, letter of Dr J.T. Phair to Nurse H. Lunn at Gore Bay, 5 November 1926: "I feel Dr B [local medical officer of health] is allowing a nurse much more freedom than we actually approve. If you will consult your regulations regarding infant and preschool hygiene, I think you will see that we do not allow or agree to have any nurse prescribe formulae. This means diagnosing the condition, which you will agree, no nurse can do!" Similarly, in RG 10, 30-A-3, Box 23, Supervisors' Reports, E. M. Squires, "Report of Visit to East York, 15–16 May 1935, 3, Squires reported "The one criticism would be the same as last year, that Mrs. C. [local public health nurse] orders feedings and simple home remedies for infants ... Had a serious talk with her regarding this." Mac-Dougall, *Activists and Advocates*, 66–7, argues that within the Toronto department, "nurses remained subordinate until the 1970s."

59 Ibid., RG 10, 30-A-3, Box 7, H.G. Pennock, Report of Visit to Cochrane, November 1936.

60 PAO, RG 10, 30-A-3, Box 23, D. Mickleborough, Report on East York, 16–17 April 1934. This is the same situation reported upon by Squires, cited above. Mickleborough, like Squires, felt that "[Mrs. C.] is inclined to diagnose cases and to give advice which is not within her province." See also ibid., Box 19, H.G. Pennock, Visit to Strathroy, 19–23 February 1934.

61 B. Turner, *Medical Power and Social Knowledge* (London 1987), 140–1, surveys the sociological literature on nursing.

62 See for example S. Schulman, "Mother Surrogate," in E.G. Jaco, ed., *Patients, Physicians and Illness* (New York 1972), 233–9; B. Ehrenreich and D. English, *Complaints and Disorders: The Sexual Politics of Sickness* (London 1976); S. Reverby, *Ordered to Care: The Dilemma of American Nursing* (New York 1988); Turner, *Medical Power and Social Knowledge*, 147–9.

63 Dr H. MacMurchy, "Neonatal Mortality," CPHJ 17, no. 9 (1926): 447.

64 A.B. Baird, RN, "Statistical Indications in Some Problems in Maternal and Child Hygiene," *Canadian Child and Family Welfare* 9, no. 3 (1933): 7.

65 Dr H. MacMurchy, "A Safety League for Mothers," *Social Welfare* 13, no. 9 (1931): 185.

66 PAO, RG 62, 1-f-1-b, Box 473, Correspondence, letter of M.R. Heeley to M. Power from Barrie, 9 July 1921.

67 Editorial, "Public Health and the Economic Depression," *CPHJ* 23, no. 31 (1932): 139–40; also Dr J.J. McCann, "Some Public Health Activities and Needs in Ontario," *CPHJ* 25, no. 6 (1934): 259. The cut-backs affected the VON as much as much as official public health agencies: see VON, *Annual Report*, 1931, 37. In 1932, special classes were discontinued, clinics and mothers' conferences were cut down, and home visits for child welfare purposes were reduced through the earlier transfer of the oversight of babies delivered to other agencies; see VON, *Report of Board of Governors*, 1932, 31.

68 Toronto City Hall Archives, RG 11, File 1, Box 4, J. Nielson, Public Health Nurse, "The History of Public Health Nursing in Toronto," January 1944, 12. Similarly, the VON noted a large increase in the number of free visits and obstetrical cases: free visits were up by 25,262 since the previous year; VON, *Annual Report*, 1930, 32. The Hospital for Sick Children made the same observation for its outpatient services, which performed much the same duties as the child welfare clinics, but also treated minor illnesses and injuries. In 1931, the "Chairman's Address" pointed out that, "In the out-patient department there was a very large increase, the treatments given being 10,000 more than the year before. In the absence of any great epidemic … it seems probable that this increase resulted from the fact that many came to us who were formerly in better circumstances and able to engage their own doctor"; Hospital for Sick Children, *56th Annual Report*, 1931, 13.

69 Thomson, "Changing Practices in Public Health Nursing," 1.

70 Ibid., 2.

71 Dr J.T. Phair, "Effectiveness of Child Health Programs in Ontario by Survey Methods," *AJPH* 30, no. 1 (1933): 127.

72 PAO, National Committee for Mental Hygiene, *Distribution of Medical Care and Public Health Services in Canada* (Toronto 1939), 93.

73 "Sickness and the Economic Depression," *Labour Gazette*, June 1934, 496–7.

74 A. Baird, "1933 with the Division of Maternal and Child Hygiene," *Child and Family Welfare* 10, no. 1 (1934): 14. Analysis of weekly relief food orders in an unnamed Ontario city, July-August 1933, showed that, for the eight families studied, the total caloric deficiency ranged from 10 per cent to 34 per cent; see M.S. McCready, "Analysis of Weekly Relief Food Orders in a Southern Ontario City," *CPHJ* 25, no. 4 (1934): 181; the same was found in Toronto; see MacDougall, *Activists and Advocates*, 169.

75 Canadian Welfare Council, *Annual Report*, 1935–36, in *Proceedings and Reports*, 19th Annual Meeting (Ottawa 1939), 41; see also "Child Health and the Depression," *CCJ* 13, no. 11 (1934): 32.

76 Canadian Welfare Council, ibid., 41.
77 League for Social Reconstruction Research Committee, *Social Planning for Canada* (Toronto 1935), 390.
78 Canada, House of Commons, *Debates*, 25 January 1935, 204.
79 Ibid., 207 (G.D. Stanley, East Calgary); see also ibid., 22 February 1935 (J.K. Blair, North Wellington), 1139.
80 Ibid., 24 January 1935, 180; 22 February 1935, 1137. The minister was D.M. Sutherland.
81 Editorial, "Unemployment Relief," *CMAJ* 23, no. 7 (1933): 71; Dr H. McPhedran, "The Difficulties of the Profession," *CMAJ* 24, no. 4 (1934): 436; D. Naylor, *Private Practice, Public Payment* (Kingston/Montreal 1986), 47.
82 Toronto City Hall Archives, RG 11, File 1, Box 4, Report of the Advisory Committee to the Local Board of Health on Maternal Welfare, June 1933; ibid., Box 1, A. Thomson, "City of Toronto Maternal Welfare Service," October 1940, 1. In 1931, at the suggestion of Dr Gordon Jackson, the city's medical officer of health, a committee was formed to act in an advisory capacity to the Board of Health in the field of maternal welfare. The committee's report was adopted by the city in June 1933. The advisory committee consisted of Jackson, Dr Alan Brown, Dr A.W. Canfield of the newly formed Canadian Mothercraft Society, and representatives of the departments of obstetrics, paediatrics and dentistry from the University of Toronto.
83 Thomson, "City of Toronto Maternal Welfare Service," 3.
84 PAO, MU 6373, Box 12, Series F, Toronto Local Council of Women, Mrs. W.K. Fraser, "Report of the Child Welfare Committee," *Yearbook*, 1935, 52. The service was continued until 1940.
85 Toronto City Hall Archives, RG 11, Box 4, File 1, Memorandum from the Public Health Nursing Division to Dr. Jackson Re Attached Request from the Board of Control Re Maternal Welfare Service, undated.
86 Thomson, "City of Toronto Maternal Welfare Service," 5.
87 National Committee for Mental Hygiene, *Study of the Distribution of Medical Care and Public Health Services in Canada* (Toronto 1939), 82.
88 Dr D.R. McClenahan, "Observations on Rural Public Health Work in Ontario," *CPHJ* 23, no. 4 (1932): 170–1.
89 National Committee, *Study of the Distribution of Medical Care and Public Health Services in Canada*, 8; see also "Canada's Health", *CCJ* 19, no. 9 (1940): 39.
90 See, for example, CMA, *Annual Report*, 1931, 324; ibid., 1933, 415. Saskatchewan adopted this plan in the early 1930s, but nothing ever came of the proposition in Ontario. See also Editorial: "Go Rural Young Man," *The Canadian Doctor* 5, no. 5, (1939): 21–6.

91 Department of Pensions and National Health, *Report of the Deputy Minister*, 1923, 39; House of Commons, *Debates*, 3 March 1930, 223. F.W. Gershaw (Medicine Hat) raised this point of the necessity of providing rural mothers and children with medical assistance.

92 D. Mickleborough, "Health Services Outside the City," *Social Welfare* 14, no. 6 (1933): 197.

93 Department of Health, *Annual Report*, 1927, 24.

94 Wodehouse, "Public Health Information Bearing Upon Prenatal Subjects," *CPHJ* 10, no. 5 (1920): 196: "In Ontario there are 27 cities, 51 towns, 7 villages, 12 townships and 7 combined rural and urban areas in which some type of public health nursing is in effect"; PAO, RG 62, 1-f-1-b, Box 473, Public Health Nursing Correspondence, District IV file, list of municipalities employing public health nurses in 1921. See also M. Stuart, "Ideology and Experience: Public Health Nursing and the Ontario Rural Child Welfare Project," *Canadian Bulletin of Medical History* 6, no. 1 (1989).

95 National Committee, *Study of Distribution of Medical Care and Public Health Services in Canada*, 84.

96 Department of Health, *Annual Report*, 1929, 39–40.

97 PAO, RG 10 30-A-3, Box 16, Public Health Nursing Field Reports, Manitoulin Island and Apsley files, Report of Red Cross Outposts at Apsley, Wilberforce, Bancroft, Coe Hill, and Whitney, visited June 1935; Report of Visit to Red Cross Outpost Hospital, Mindemoya, 1940. The *Canadian Almanac*, 1940, 351, lists these outpost centres: Apsley, Armstrong, Atikokan, Bancroft, Blind River, Bracebridge, Coe Hill, Dryden, Emo, Englehart, Espanola, Haliburton, Hawk Junction, Hornepayne, Jellicoe, Kakabeka Falls, Kirkland Lake, Lions Head, Loring, Mindemoya, Nakina, New Liskeard, Quibell, Rainy River, Redditt, Richard's Landing, Thessalon, Whitney, and Wilberforce.

98 CMA, *Annual Report*, 1934, 34.

99 Public Health Nursing Field Reports, Apsley file, June 1935. Apsley is 40 kilometres north of Peterborough. See also W.F. Marshall, RN, "The Red Cross Outposts," *The Canadian Nurse* 26, no. 3 (1930): 128–30; An Ontario Outpost Nurse, "Experiences in a Red Cross Outpost," ibid. 22, no. 2 (1926): 76–7.

100 Dr A.G. Fleming, *Report of the 26th Meeting*, Dominion Council of Health, June 1933, 3.

101 Department of Health, *Annual Report*, 1924, 16. For similar views see the report of the chief officer of health of Ontario, Dr. J.W.S. McCullough, "The Necessity of Effective Organization in Public Health Departments," *CMAJ* 16, no. 10 (1926): 151.

102 Board of Health, *Annual Report*, 1923, 16. See also Dr R.B. Jenkins, "Municipal Health Expenditures in Canada," *CPHJ* 25, no. 3 (1934):

120–3. Jenkins found that, of 15 cities, Toronto led with $1.51 per capita; the average was $.50 per capita.

103 Mickleborough, "Health Services Outside the City," 198.

104 PAO, RG 62, F-2, Vol. 488, Field Reports, "Public Health Work in the Thunder Bay District," to Beryl Knox, Supervisor, 19 September 1922, from G. Bastedo, Public Health Nurse.

105 Department of Health, *Annual Report*, 1927, 70. See also M.E. Wilkinson, RN, "The Rural Community and the Nursing Outpost," *The Canadian Nurse* 22, no. 6 (1926): 306–8.

106 In 1928, a visiting journalist noted the sort of grateful welcome that these "messengers of mercy" could expect to receive from Northern Ontario mothers; Mona Clark, "Messengers of Mercy to the Women and Children of the North," *Canadian Magazine*, June 1928, 26.

107 PAO, RG 10 30-A-1 Box 1, File 1–24, Field Reports, Detailed Report of Summer Work 1922 of S.M. Carr Harris, Rainy River District, 7; PAO, Pamphlet No. 64, *A Survey of Preschool Children in Dundas Region*, 1925.

108 House of Commons, *Debates*, 3 March 1930, 225.

109 Dr A. Brown, "Certain Features of Child Welfare Not Sufficiently Emphasized," *CPHJ* 14, no. 6 (1923): 248; Dr. J.W.S. McCullough, "City the Safest Place," 33; A. Brown, "Problems of the Rural Mother," *CPHJ* 9, no. 7 (1918): 299–300.

110 Brown, "Certain Features of Child Welfare Work Not Sufficiently Emphasized," 248.

111 Editorial, "Health Units in Outlying Districts," *CMAJ* 15, no. 10 (1925): 1060.

112 House of Commons, *Debates*, 3 March 1930, 228. The resolution was presented by J.P. Howden (St Boniface).

113 Dr J.W.S. McCullough, Letter to the Editor, *CMAJ* 20, no. 4 (1930): 575.

114 H.M. Cassidy, *Public Health and Welfare Reorganization* (Toronto 1945), 345. In 1944, the province provided grants to cover from 25 to 50 per cent of total budgets in organized municipalities, and in some cases 100 per cent of costs in unorganized territory.

115 PAO, RG 62, 1-F-2, Box 486, Field Reports, O.M. Gipson and D. Hally, Report on Visit to Rockland, Gipson, 1921.

116 Ibid., RG 10, 30-A-1, Box 1, Field Reports, Hastings County file, Report to Mary Power from E. Corbman, March 17, 1925, 1–5. This nurse had come upon two families in Bancroft, consisting of 21 people, who occupied a house of six rooms. There was one active case of tuberculosis among them and six contacts. In nearby Musclow, she found a one-room shack with a narrow built-in cot that was the only sleeping place for a father and his two young daughters. In Hybla,

she discovered a poor farm with a two-room house, nine people sharing the only bedroom. A two-room shack in the same town housed seven children and their parents; this family also served meals to the miners and kept an occasional boarder.

117 Ibid., RG 62, F-2, Vol. 488, Public Health Nurses Field Reports, Report sent to Assistant Director Beryl Knox, from Nursing Supervisor Gladys Bastedo, "Public Health Work in the Thunder Bay District," 3.

118 Ibid., F-1-b, Vol. 475, E.M. Squires file, Public Health Nursing Correspondence, letter of E.M. Squires to M. Power, from Hawkesbury, 17 November 1922.

119 Ibid.

120 PAO, RG 10, 30-A-3, Box 2, Field Reports, Bruce County file, Report of Demonstration of Public Health Nursing in Bruce Peninsula: St. Edmunds and Tobermory, O.M. Gipson, undated, 1930s.

121 Ibid., 30-A-1, Box 1, Field Reports, Rainy River and Thunder Bay file, "Summer Work in Thunder Bay 1926." The agricultural portion of Rainy River, in the early 1920s, had about 32 townships of which 6 were well-settled, 6 fairly well and the remainder "sparsely or not at all." The more prosperous settlers were along the railway, roads, and river and the less prosperous in the townships behind. See ibid., File 1–24, "Rainy River District," Miss Broadfoot, Public Health Nurse, in "General Report of Work of Three Temporarily Appointed Nurses in District No. VII," Summer 1922.

122 Ibid., Field Reports, Miss Veitch, Public Health Nurse, "General Report of Work of Three Temporarily Appointed Nurses in District No. VII," Summer 1922 (Dryden District).

123 Reprinted in "The Canadian Mother," *Social Welfare* 5, no. 8 (1923): 160. In response to the publication of this letter in *Social Welfare*, a letter to the journal's editor confirmed the arduous conditions endured by rural mothers. The government and the medical profession were roundly criticized for their apparent lack of involvement in maternal and child welfare issues outside urban limits; see Letter to the Editor, "Benefits for Rural Mothers," *Social Welfare* 5, no. 12 (1923): 256.

124 Department of Pensions and National Health, *Annual Report*, 1928–29, 126.

125 Letter to the Editor, "Benefits for Rural Mothers," 256.

126 Dr Helen MacMurchy, *Supplement to the Canadian Mothers' Book* (Ottawa 1923), 139.

127 PAO, RG 10, 30-A-1, Box 1, File 1–24, Detailed Report of Summer Work (1922) of S.M. Carr Harris, Bergland, Rainy River District, 11.

128 Ibid., Field Reports, Northumberland and Durham file, A.L. Campbell, Report of the Demonstration of Public Health Nursing in Penetang, 6 December 1921 to 13 April 1922; ibid., RG 62, F-2, Vol. 488,

Field Reports, Bastedo. See also P. Jackson, RN, "Public Health and the Small Town," *The Canadian Nurse* 20, no. 5 (1924): 215–16; M.A. Rutherford, RN, "A Day's Work in a Rural District," ibid. 36, no. 5 (1940): 279–81.

129 Dr W. Woolner (Ayr, Ontario), "A Few Observations on the Medical Care of Residents in Rural Areas of Ontario," *CMAJ* 24, no. 4 (1934): 437. Dr Woolner argues that half of farm families in Waterloo, Brant and Oxford counties were unable to pay for medical care. See also Dr W. Woolner, "Medical Economics in Rural Districts of Ontario," *CMAJ* 24, no. 3 (1934): 307; Dr W.E. Park, "Rural Medical Relief," *CMAJ* 24, no. 4 (1934): 438. Park, a Brownsville physician, reported receiving one-half his regular fee when attending families on relief.

130 NA, RG 29, Vol. 991, File 499–3–2, pt. 2, Canadian Welfare Council, letter addressed to "Minister of Health, Ottawa, Ontario," signed "A worried expectant mother", Mrs. L.R., Wawbewawa, Ontario, 3 pages.

131 Ibid., 1.

132 Ibid., 2.

133 See "Heroines of the Depression," *CCJ*, 12, no. 12 (1933): 19–20, for a description of letters from poverty-stricken mothers expressing their anxiety about their situation and the suffering of their families to the Canadian Welfare Council. Unfortunately, most of these letters seem to have been destroyed; only a handful have been found in the National Archives of Canada.

134 NA, RG 29, Vol. 991, File 499–3–2, Pt. 2, letter of Charlotte Whitton, Director, Canadian Welfare Council, to Dr Robert Wodehouse, Deputy Minister of Health, 5 September 1935, 1. There is no evidence as to whether such an inquiry ever took place; Wodehouse's reply was not found.

135 The nurses' visit to Smith Falls revealed the mothers' indifference to purely educational nurse visits; see PAO, RG 62, 1-f-2, Box 486, Field Reports, O. Gipson and M. Halley, Report to the Local Council, Smith Falls, 15 April 1921; a similar response was met in Thessalon, see ibid., f-2, Box 488, Field Reports, F.M. Bagshaw, Report on Sault Ste Marie District, 11 April 1921 and Sturgeon Falls, ibid., RG 10, 30-A-3, Box 19, Supervisors' Reports, H.G. Pennock, Sturgeon Falls, December 1935, 2.

136 Ibid., 30-A-1, Box 1, File 1–24, S.M. Carr Harris, "Detailed Report of Summer Work of 1922," 5.

137 Ibid., Box 7, File 7, Annual and Monthly Reports, Division of Maternal and Child Hygiene and Public Health Nursing, *Annual Report*, 1933, Dr J.T. Phair, Director, and Edna Moore, Chief Public Health Nurse, "A Survey of Effectiveness of Child Welfare Measures," 3.

138 Ibid., 3.

139 Ibid., 4.
140 See V. Strong-Boag, "Wages for Housework": Mothers' Allowances and
the Beginnings of Social Security in Canada," *J Can Studies* 14, no. 1
(1979).
141 "The Effects of Unemployment on Children and Young People," *Child
and Family Welfare* 10, no. 9 (1934): 31.
142 Funding for the unit was helped by a grant of $33,000 from the
Laura Spelman Rockefeller Foundation, an American agency dedicated to furthering public health efforts; the foundation also provided
funding for the St George's School of Child Study at the University of
Toronto, and the School of Hygiene at the University of Toronto; PAO,
RG 10, 30-A-3, Box 3, Eastern Health Unit file, "Varied Activities of
Health Unit in 1937," newspaper clipping, unknown source/date,
obviously 1937.
143 Ibid., "Report on Child Welfare Work in the Eastern Ontario Health
Unit," 1.
144 Ibid., Field Reports, Minutes of Staff Meeting, Eastern Health Unit,
Alexandria, 27 November 1936.
145 Ibid.,"Report on Child Welfare Work," 2.
146 Ontario, Department of Health, *Annual Report*, 1935, 41.
147 Ibid., 1935, 43.
148 Ibid., 45.
149 J. Struthers discusses the state's view of public relief in this manner in
No Fault of Their Own (Toronto 1983),
150 PAO, RG 62, f-2, Box 488, Field Reports, I.J. Grenville, Report of Visit
to Thessalon, December 1920 to March 1921.

CHAPTER EIGHT

1 R. Williams, *Culture and Society* (London 1990), 320–2, points out that
cultural change is a process involving reshaping and resistance as well
as acceptance and adaptation.
2 See V. Strong-Boag, "'Wages for Housework': Mothers' Allowances and
the Beginnings of Social Security in Canada," *J Can Studies* 14, no. 1
(1979) on monitoring of allowance recipients.
3 NA, MG 28 I 25, Vol. 7, File 8, National Council of Women of Canada
papers, Canadian Welfare Council, *Proceedings and Reports*, 1 May
1939, 10; see V. Strong-Boag, "'Wages for Housework'," 24. See also
D. Guest, *The Emergence of Social Security in Canada* (Vancouver 1985),
49; P. Rooke and R. Schnell, *Discarding the Asylum* (Calgary 1982).
4 Toronto City Hall Archives, RG 11, Box 1, File 1, Historical Material
on Maternal and Child Health, A. Thomson, "Changing Practices in
Public Health Nursing," undated manuscript, 1930s, 1.

5 Ibid., 2.

6 Cited in K.W. Gorrie, "Parent Education and Social Work," *Child and Family Welfare* 11, no. 5 (1936): 39.

7 Ibid., 38.

8 The Canadian Welfare Council regularly broadcast childrearing programs on CBC radio, as did the Canadian Public Health Association; by the mid-1930s, the CMA also began broadcasting health information programs. The journals of these organizations published their "radio talks."

9 S. Fox, *The Mirror Makers* (New York 1984) argues that the 1920s were the high point of advertising in America and the peak of its ability to influence consumer purchasing patterns. See also N. Lewis, "Advising the Parents: Childrearing in British Columbia during the Interwar Years," Ph.d. thesis, University of British Columbia 1980, 27; J. Ellul, *The Technological Society* (New York 1964), 323.

10 Parke, Davis and Company advertisement, "Are Two Pairs of Hands Enough?" *Maclean's* 15 September 1937. Different versions of these ads ran in *Maclean's* from 1932–39.

11 B. Palmer, *The Working Class Experience*, 2nd ed. (Toronto 1992), 229–36.

12 Isobel Ecclestone Mackay, "Where Are We Leading Them?" *Canadian Magazine*, October 1918, 160–2.

13 Ibid., 162.

14 Ibid.

15 V. Strong-Boag, "Pulling a Double Harness or Hauling a Double Load: Women, Work and Feminism on the Canadian Prairies," *J Can Studies* 21, no. 3 (1986) makes this observation for mothers in western Canada.

16 An Average Mother, "Psychology Does Not Always Work," *National Home Monthly*, December 1932, 54.

17 Ibid., 54, where she talks about losing her temper with a stubborn child and upsetting "the whole psychological applecart."

18 Ibid., 55.

19 Enid Griffis, "Who's Boss in Your Home?" *National Home Monthly* March 1933, 55.

20 Mackay made the same observation: "Perhaps some of the pieces are still missing:" Mackay, "Where are We Leading Them?" 164.

21 Griffis, "Who's Boss in Your Home?" 55.

22 F. Edwards, "An Old-Fashioned Father," *Maclean's*, 1 March 1934.

23 "Follow the Baby Not the Book," *CCJ* 6, no. 9 (1927): 41.

24 See, for example, M.C. Ericson, "Childrearing and Social Status," *AJS* 52 (1946): 191. Ericson interviewed 48 middle-class and 52 working-class parents. See also E. Ross, "Labour and Love: Rediscovering Lon-

don's Working Class Mothers," in J. Lewis, ed., *Labour and Love: Women's Experience of Home and Family* (Oxford 1986), 79–80. Ross argues that early twentieth-century childrearing practices in London's working class were warmer, more lenient, and "worlds apart" from the regimented methods of the "progressive" middle class.

25 "About Barbara's Baby," *CCJ* 11, no. 2 (1932): 27.

26 Ibid.

27 See, for example, Robert Howe, "A Women's Place," *Industrial Banner*, 20 February 1920.

28 "Leave Jack and Jill Alone," *CCJ* 10, no. 1 (1931): 41.

29 For a discussion of the quints' daily schedule and observations made on their behaviour, see W. Blatz and D. Millichamp, et al., *Collected Studies on the Dionne Quintuplets* (Toronto 1937) and W. Blatz, *The Five Sisters* (Toronto 1938). For a contemporary Canadian analysis of the quints' experience, see L. Dempsey, "What Will Become of Them?" *Chatelaine*, June 1937. V. Strong-Boag, "Intruders in the Nursery," in J. Parr, ed., *Childhood and Family in Canadian History* (Toronto 1982) provides an interesting analysis of the system imposed on the quints and its public effect. P. Berton, *The Dionne Years* (Toronto 1977) chronicles the anger, anxiety, and pain that their parents endured while watching them raised by "experts" in a manner completely foreign to their own beliefs, their determination to raise them in their own "traditional" manner once they received custody, and the tragic effects.

30 This was recognized by contemporary sociologists; see E.M. Duvall, "Conceptions of Parenthood," *AJS* 52 (1946): 202–3.

31 "Editorial Snippets," *Industrial Banner*, 13 February 1920.

32 Pro Bono, "Denied A Chance," *Industrial Banner*, 16 April 1920.

33 See also Olive G. Owen, "A Child" (poem), *Industrial Banner*, 26 March 1920.

34 J. Farrant, "What of My Children?" *Canadian Trade Unionist*, 30 August 1932.

35 See for example, B. Palmer, *A Culture in Conflict* (Montreal/Kingston 1979) and J. Parr, *The Gender of Breadwinners* (Toronto 1990). Parr details arrangements for child care and housekeeping made among working women.

36 "Maple Leaf Auxilliary," *Bulletin*, June 1914. The *Bulletin* was the official organ of the IAM. On the auxilliary, see S. Murray, "Quand les menageres se font militantes: la Ligue auxiliaire de l'Association internationale des machinistes, 1905–30," *Labour* 29 (1992).

37 Mrs W. Singer, President, Maple Leaf Auxilliary, "Tidings from Toronto," *Bulletin*, April 1915.

38 Mrs W. Singer, "Women Are Needed in the Labour Movement," *The People's Cause* (Toronto), 27 April 1926. Minnie Singer was an execu-

tive member of the IAM Ladies Auxilliary, president of its Maple Leaf branch, president of the United Women's Educational Federation of Ontario, and a Mothers' Allowance Commissioner. See Murray, "Quand les ménagères se font militantes."

39 D. Naylor, *Private Practice, Public Payment* (Kingston/Montreal 1986), 49. See also the special issue of *Polyphony* 2, no. 2 (1979), on benevolent and mutual aid societies among immigrants in Ontario.

40 Dr Peter Bryce, "The Scope of a Federal Department of Health," *CMAJ* 10, no. 1 (1920): 7. Bryce, the chief medical officer of the Department of Immigration, indicates that there were 172,000 members, of which 33,468 were sick; there were 166,872 weeks of illness in 1917. The societies spent $90,621 that year.

41 Naylor, *Private Practice, Public Payment*, 32–3.

42 On welfare capitalist measures, see Parr, *The Gender of Breadwinners*, and J. Naylor, *The New Democracy* (Toronto 1991); also C. Heron, "Hamilton Steelworkers and the Rise of Mass Production," in B. Palmer, ed., *The Character of Class Struggle* (Toronto 1986), 81.

43 Editorial, "The Value of Motherhood," *Industrial Banner*, 26 March 1920. See also "Infant and Maternal Welfare," *Canadian Trade Unionist*, 29 August 1929.

44 Editorial, "The Cost of Sickness," *Canadian Trade Unionist*, 26 July 1929.

45 "Women Urge State Medicine," *Canadian Trade Unionist*, 29 February 1932.

46 "Women Are Needed in the Labour Movement," *The People's Cause*, 27 April 1926. On the efforts of organized labour women, see also J. Naylor, *The New Democracy*, 137–9.

47 Editorial, "Bread for Health," *Canadian Trade Unionist*, 23 May 1931.

48 Ibid.

49 Elizabeth Smith Shortt Collection, University of Waterloo, Correspondence, File no. 4, letter to Shortt, June 1918, signed "A Farmer of Nepean."

50 "Hygiene or Fussiness," *CCJ* 7, no. 9 (1928): 38. For similar sentiments see "Those Vital Vitamins," *CCJ* 11, no. 5 (1932): 25.

51 See, for example, "Are We Fair to the Child," *Industrial Banner*, 18 June 1920; "Infant and Maternal Welfare," ibid., 29 August 1929; "How Science Can Add Years to Your Life," ibid., 20 August 1930; "How to Produce a Better Race," *Labour News*, 29 June 1925; "Maternal Mortality in Canada," ibid., 27 April 1929.

52 M. Ladd Taylor, *Raising a Baby the Government Way* (New Brunswick, N.J. 1987) 3–5, notes the many letters from working-class and farm mothers, showing that the American Children's Bureau bulletins were read by the poor, many of whom sought information about child-

rearing. See also M.L. Davies, ed., *Maternity* (New York 1978). The latter is a collection of letters from English working-class mothers originally published by the Women's Cooperative Guild in 1915 as part of a campaign to improve welfare and services for poor families. Unfortunately, although various government reports remark on the numbers of letters sent to the Canadian Welfare Council requesting information, few seem to have survived.

53 NA, MG 28 I 10, vol. 35, file 168, letters to the Canadian Welfare Council, from Norwich, Ontario, 25 August 1933.

54 Ibid., London, 21 August 1933; see also NA, MG 28 I 10, vol. 35, file 168, Rainy River, 1 April 1929, expressing another father's gratitude after the birth of twins.

55 NA, MG 28 I 10, vol. 35, file 168, Canadian Welfare Council, from Toronto, September 1933.

56 Ibid., Oakville, 9 June 1933.

57 Ibid., Maxewood, 26 June 1933.

58 Ibid., Kapuskasing, 16 December 1935.

59 NA, RG 29, vol. 991, file 499–3–2, pt 2, 26 December 1935.

60 Ibid., MG 28, I 10 vol. 35, file 168, no address given, marked "Ontario, 1932."

61 Ibid., from Maloy, 28 August 1935.

62 Ibid., Ayr, November 1928.

63 Ibid., Richwood, Ontario, 6 November 1928; see also testimony to this effect from a public health nurse to the council, ibid., RG 29, vol. 993, file 499–3–7, pt 10, Canadian Welfare Council files, letter from Sault Ste Marie to Charlotte Whitton, 3 June 1935.

64 Ibid., MG 28 I 10, vol. 39, file 168, Canadian Welfare Council, "Maternal and Child Hygiene," Canadian Life Officers Association file, letter from Lucknow, 28 September 1928.

65 Ladd Taylor, *Raising a Baby the Government Way*, 5.

66 PAO, RG 10. 30-A-1, Box 1, Unorganized Victoria and Waterloo counties file, 1921–24, Report on the Nursing Demonstration in the Town of Lindsay, September to December 1923.

67 Ibid., RG 62, F-2, vol. 488, Public Health Nurses Field Reports, Report sent to Nursing Director Beryl Knox, 19 September 1922, from nursing supervisor Gladys Bastedo, "Public Health Work in the Thunder Bay District," 3.

68 Ibid., RG 10, 30-A-1, Historical Pamphlets and Literature, Division of Maternal and Child Hygiene and Public Health Nursing, *Bulletin*, October 1922, 3.

69 Ibid., RG 62, F-1-b, vol. 471, Public Health Nurses Correspondence, District II, A.L. Campbell file, Penetang, 16 January 1922.

70 See N. Lewis, "Goose Grease and Turpentine: Mother Treats the Family's Illnesses," in V. Strong-Boag, A.C. Fellman, eds., *Rethinking Canada*, 2nd ed. (Toronto 1991). In their famous study, Robert and Helen Lynd also found a wide variety of folk medicine practised; see *Middletown: A Study in Contemporary American Culture* (New York 1929), 435.

71 Dr E. Morgan, "Some Traditional Beliefs Encountered in the Practice of Paediatrics," *CMAJ* 24, no. 12 (1934): 666.

72 In Canadian historiography, Bryan Palmer has made most effective use of Raymond Williams' ideas about residual/emergent cultural strains; see B. Palmer, "Most Uncommon Common Men: Craft and Culture in Historical Perspective," *Labour* 1 (1977): 19–20, further developed in Palmer, *A Culture in Conflict.*

73 PAO, RG 62, 1-f-1-b, Box 473, Public Health Nurses Correspondence, District IV file; Nurse D. Heeley, from Barrie, Ontario to Beryl Knox, Nursing Supervisor, Toronto, 23 July 1921.

74 NA, RG 29, vol. 991, file 499–3–2, pt. 2, Canadian Welfare Council, letter addressed to Minister of Health, Ottawa, Ontario, signed "a worried expectant mother," Wawbewawa, Ontario, 10 July 1935. This woman's situation was discussed in more detail in Chapter 6.

75 Ibid., pt 3, Canadian Welfare Council, from Sudbury, 8 January 1937. Unfortunately, no reply was found.

76 Ibid., 3.

77 O. Brim, *Education for Childrearing* (New York 1964), vii.

78 Ibid., viii.

79 Ibid., 17; see also Duvall, "Conceptions of Parenthood," 203. Duvall refers to this as the "see-saw process."

CHAPTER NINE

1 Canada, Department of Pensions and National Health, *Annual Report*, 1940, Deaths of infants under one year, 156. Rate per 100,000 live births: scarlet fever 1931, 6; 1939, 6; whooping cough 1931, 209; 1939, 167; diphtheria 1931, 22; 1939, 14; diarrhaea/enteritis 1931, 1,813; 1939, 691; pneumonia 1931, 900; 1939, 764. See also Ontario, Department of Health, *Annual Report*, 1940, 90: Deaths of children birth to age four, per 1,000 live births: contagion 1920, 10; 1939, 6.1; respiratory diseases 1920, 12.4; 1939, 11.5; diarrhaea/enteritis 1920, 18; 1939, 7.6.

2 C. Webster, "Healthy or Hungry Thirties?" *Hist Workshop* 13, no. 4 (1982); M. Mitchell, "The Effect of Unemployment on Women and Children," ibid., 19, no. 5 (1985). The most adamant proponent of the

view that there was no direct correlation between economic insecurity and infant and maternal mortality in Britain is Winter; see Winter, "Unemployment, Nutrition and Infant Mortality in Britain," in J.M. Winter, ed., *The Working Class in Modern British History* (Cambridge 1983). Although not concerned specifically with infant mortality, I. Drummond, *Progress Without Planning: The Economic History of Ontario From Confederation to the Second World War* (Toronto 1987), 236, argues that falling death rates in the early twentieth century suggest that "things were, on the whole and in the long run, getting better."

3 See, for example, Department of Pensions and National Health, *Annual Report*, 1931–32, 129; also Department of Health, *Annual Report*, 1935, 32.

4 The same was true of Britain: Webster, "Healthy or Hungry Thirties?" 115; Mitchell, "The Effect of Unemployment on Women and Children," 107.

5 Dr E. Couture, *A Study of Maternal, Infant and Neo-Natal Mortality* (Ottawa 1942), 5. The material was prepared by the Dominion Bureau of Statistics in collaboration with the Department of Pensions and National Health "for use in the medical schools, by physicians in private practice and by public health workers and educators in Canada." The statistical analysis was performed by Couture himself. All population figures were based on census returns.

6 Ibid., 10, 16. J. Struthers, *No Fault of Their Own* (Toronto 1983), provides tables showing the average annual unemployment rate in Canada, 1920–40, Appendix 1. Between 1936 and 1939 the unemployment rate declined from 16.7 to 14.l; it dropped to 9.3 in 1940.

7 Department of Pensions and National Health, *Annual Report*, 1940, 157.

8 Couture, *A Study of Maternal, Infant and Neo-Natal Mortality*, 10. The potential of abortion figures for inflating maternal mortality figures must also be considered; there is no way of telling, for example, the extent to which puerperal sepsis and haemorrhage, two of the primary killers, were abortion-related. See A. McLaren and A.T. McLaren, "Discoveries and Dissimulations: The Impact of Abortion Deaths on Maternal Mortality in British Columbia," BCST (64 1984–85): 13, 25; the authors argue that although maternal deaths in British Columbia were declining in the 1930s, abortion deaths were reaching unprecedented highs. For the national scene, see A. McLaren and A.T. McLaren, *The Bedroom and the State* (Toronto 1986).

9 Couture, *A Study of Maternal, Infant and Neo-Natal Mortality*, 22, 32, 38.

10 Ibid., 28. Between 1926 and 1930, the average number of infant deaths during the first month was 10,530; 1931–35, the average was

8,507; 1936–40, the average was 7,296. For the first four months of life, the averages for the same five-year periods were 15,975, 12,621, and 10,844 respectively. From the second to the twelfth months, the averages were 11,533, 8,594, and 7,405 respectively. See also Department of Pensions and National Health, *Annual Report*, 1942, 146.

11 Webster, "Healthy or Hungry Thirties?" 117. Birth weight is a significant factor in the survival rate of premature and newborn infants, and is also closely linked to maternal nutrition; see P. Ward and P.C. Ward, "Infant Birth Weight and Nutrition in Industrializing Montreal," *AHR* 89, no. 2 (1984): 324–45. The Wards found that malnutrition among poor women in Montreal increased in their sample from 1851–1905, with evident results in lower birth weights.

12 Department of Health, *Annual Report*, 1939, 138–9.

13 In his 1936 report, Phair commented that toxaemias seemed to be on the increase; Department of Health, *Annual Report*, 1936, 50; 1940, 88.

14 Department of Pensions and National Health, *Annual Report*, 1931–32, 129.

15 Ibid., 1939, 139, 140.

16 Ibid., 155.

17 Ibid, 1936, 50; ibid., 1940, 87–9.

18 Webster, "Healthy or Hungry Thirties?" 123.

19 For example, PAO, RG 62, f-l-b, Vol. 475, Public Health Nursing Correspondence, letter of E.M. Squires to M. Power, from Hawkesbury, 17 November 1922.

20 Rockland's workers endured deplorable living and health conditions in the 1920s; see ibid., 1-f-2, Box 486, Public Health Nursing Field Reports, O.M. Gipson, "Report on Visit to Rockland," 1921. Both this and the Hawkesbury report are cited in Chapter 6.

21 Department of Health, *Annual Report*, 1935, "Report of the Eastern Ontario Health Unit," 37.

22 Ibid., 39. There were 11 maternal deaths recorded in Stormont county in 1931, 4 in 1933; in Glengarry, 3 and 4 respectively; in Prescott, 4 and 4; in Russell, 5 and 2. No more mention is made of maternal deaths in subsequent years.

23 Webster, "Healthy or Hungry Thirties?" 116.

24 Department of Health, *Annual Report*, 1935, 41; 1936, 54, 58, 59.

25 Canada, House of Commons, *Debates*, 22 May 1939, 4380–1. The speaker was Denton Massey (Greenwood). See also "An Equal Opportunity for Health," *The Canadian Doctor* 3, no. 12 (1938): 29.

26 Dr N. Bethune, "Take Private Profit Out of Medicine," *The Canadian Doctor* 3, no. 1 (1937): 11.

27 A.E. Grauer, *Public Health: A Study Prepared for the Royal Commission on Dominion-Provincial Relations* (Ottawa 1939), 1, 36.

28 L.C. Marsh, Dr A.G. Fleming, and C.F. Blackler, *Health and Unemployment* (Montreal 1938), 141.

29 Canadian Welfare Council, *Need Our Mothers Die?* (Ottawa 1935), 7.

30 House of Commons, *Debates*, 22 May 1939, 4383.

31 Dr A. Brown, "Child Care During War," *CMAJ* 31, no. 3 (1940): 259. "Lower-income" families were defined as those whose total family income did not exceed $1,500 per annum; the minimum income was $10 per week. The average number of children per family was 4.2. Reference is also made to this study in House of Commons, *Debates*, 22 May 1939, 4382. For a report on the study itself, see E.W. McHenry, "Nutrition in Toronto," *CPHJ* 30, no. 1 (1939): 4–13. McHenry, of the School of Hygiene at the University of Toronto, was part of the committee; he indicates that it was formed in 1937 under the auspices of the Council on Child and Family Welfare. Its membership included A.E. Grauer, who completed the public health study for the Rowell-Sirois Commission, and Dr F.F. Tisdall, Hospital for Sick Children.

32 McHenry, "Nutrition in Toronto," 8.

33 Dr A. Brown, "A Decade of Paediatric Progress," *CMAJ* 31, no. 10 (1940): 305–6.

34 Ibid., 306.

35 Brown, "Child Care During War," 259.

36 McHenry, "Nutrition in Toronto," 9–11.

37 Brown, "Child Care During War," 260.

38 A. McEachern, "Health for Victory," *National Home Monthly*, June 1941, 63.

39 Dr A. Brown, "Child Care in Wartime," *Canadian Welfare Summary* 15, no. 8 (1939): 40–3. This was the new name of the journal of the Council on Child and Family Welfare (now called the Canadian Welfare Council). The journal was previously called *Child and Family Welfare*. This is much the same speech published in the *CMAJ* 31, no. 3 (1940). For similar views, see Editorial, "War Interrupts Social Progress," *The Canadian Doctor* 5, no. 12 (1939): 32–2.

40 See D. Dwork, "Conclusion," *War is Good for Babies and Other Young Children* (London 1987), for the effects of the Second World War on child and maternal welfare in Great Britain.

41 Dr W.E. Blatz, *News Exchange*, Division of Public Health Nursing, September 1940, 2.

42 Department of Pensions and National Health, *Annual Report*, 1940, 84.

43 Editorial, "What of the Future?" *Labour Press* (Oshawa), 9 February 1939.

44 Berton Brady, "Owed to the Future," *Labour Leader*, (Oshawa) 16 June 1938.

45 J.L. Granatstein, *Canada's War* (Toronto 1975), chap. 5. See also D. Guest, *The Emergence of Social Security in Canada* (Vancouver 1985), chap. 8.

46 Granatstein, *Canada's War*, 260. The outspoken Conservative critic of the Act was Charlotte Whitton, who believed that ensuring a "reasonable wage" to workers would allow family maintenance to remain where it belonged, in the hands of the chief breadwinner of each family.

47 M. Abramovitz, *Regulating the Lives of Women* (New York 1987), 4–5, and 234–5, discusses American social security provisions in this context; see also J. Ursel, *Private Lives, Public Policy* (Toronto 1992), for full discussion of the Canadian situation.

48 Guest, *The Emergence of Social Security in Canada*, 140.

49 Even doctors who favoured health insurance insisted that it was feasible only as long as its administration remained in private hands–their own. See, for example, the ongoing debate in the pages of their "business journal:" "CMA President Advocates Health Insurance," *The Canadian Doctor* 4, no. 1 (1938): 16; "American Medicine Moves Toward Socialization," ibid., 17; "National Health Insurance Comes Nearer," ibid., 13; "Ontario Favours Compulsory National Health Insurance," ibid., 5, no. 7 (1939): 28–9. See also Naylor, *Private Practice, Public Payment* (Montreal/Kingston 1986), 131–2.

50 H. Cantrill, ed., *Public Opinion, 1935–1946* (Princeton N.J. 1951), 440. The income qualifications for each group are not indicated.

51 "Budgeting for Health in Toronto," *The Canadian Doctor* 4, no. 6 (1938): 13; the author indicates that one such private company, Associated Medical Services, Inc. (established by Dr Joseph Hannah in 1937), had registered 1,100 clients in less than twelve months in the Toronto area. See also C. Shillington, *The Road to Medicare in Canada* (Toronto 1972), 34–6.

52 Department of Pensions and National Health, *Annual Report*, 1940, 143.

53 Department of Health, *Annual Report*, 1939, 2.

54 Dr E. Couture, "Some Aspects of the Child Health Program in Canada," *CPHJ* 30, no. 12 (1939): 584.

55 NA, RG 29, Vol. 1318, File 495-1-2, Dr E. Couture, "A Comparison of Activities Under Official Auspices in the Field of Maternal and Child Hygiene Between the United States and Canada," 1945, 6.

56 Grauer, *Public Health*, 72.

57 S. Koven and S. Michel, "Womanly Duties," *AHR* 95, no. 4 (1990): 1079–80. By comparison to the four states that they consider – Germany, France, Great Britain, and the United States – Canada's was easily the weakest.

58 For a detailed discussion of medical, and especially paediatric, advances during this period, see T. Cone, *History of American Pediatrics* (Boston 1979), 202–5. See also M. Bliss, *The Discovery of Insulin* (Toronto 1985).

59 Brown, "A Decade of Paediatric Progress," 312.

60 Ibid., 307.

61 Ibid.

62 Ibid., 306. See also Department of Pensions and National Health, *Annual Report*, 1942, 145. The Dominion Council of Health passed a resolution recommending the provision of not less than 200 incubators in locations deemed by the provincial health authorities to be most readily available for care at home, transportation to hospital, or care in a hospital not equipped with incubators.

63 Thomas McKeown argues that the improved quality of the milk supply was the main reason for the reduction of deaths from infantile gastroenteritis in the twentieth century; see T. McKeown, *The Role of Medicine* (London 1979), 57.

64 Department of Health, *Annual Report*, 1982, "The Fifth Decade," discusses advances in public health during the 1940s and 1950s.

65 Department of Health, *Annual Report*, 1950, 6.

66 Ibid., 79, 81.

67 Bethune, "Take Private Profit Out of Medicine," 15.

68 M. Renaud, "On the Structural Constraints to State Intervention in Health," in V. Navarro, ed., *Health and Medical Care in the United States* (New York 1977), 136.

69 Renaud, "On the Structural Constraints to State Intervention in Health," 136; T. McKeown, "A Historical Appraisal of the Medical Task," in T. McKeown and G. McLachlan, eds., *Medical History and Medical Care* (New York 1971), 32.

70 See R. Bothwell, I. Drummond, and J. English, *Canada Since 1945* (Toronto 1981), 9–26.

71 Sociological studies of the British working class have found that state welfare benefits brought about a significant improvement in their general health in the 1950s; B. Turner, *Medical Power and Social Knowledge* (London 1987), 179.

72 Department of Health, *Annual Report*, 1950, 81; Dr J. Balog, "A New Look at Our Infant Mortality," *Birth and the Family Journal* (1976): 15. See also "Baby Deaths Puzzlingly High: Despite Education, Black Mortality Rate is Double Whites," Toronto *Globe and Mail*, 4 June 1992, which discusses a recent study by American researchers that suggests "the subtle effects of racism" – lower pay even for college-educated blacks, the "intergenerational effects" of malnutrition, etc. – may be a factor in high black infant mortality (under one year).

73 Couture, "A Comparison of Activities Under Official Auspices in the Field of Maternal and Child Hygiene Between the United States and Canada," 5; "Some Aspects of the Child Health Program in Canada," 584.

CHAPTER TEN

1 On the increasing importance of paediatric specialists within the profession and society, see Dr H.P. Wright, "Whither Paediatrics?" *The Canadian Doctor* 2, 6 (1936): 19–21.

2 Until 1947, specialist certificates were awarded without examination to individuals with appropriate qualifications. Commencing in 1944, an increasing number of disciplines were recognized by specialty examinations at fellowship and certification level. By 1951, the college was holding examinations in 17 different specialties. See R. Gunton, "The Development of the Specialties," in A.W. Andison and J.G. Robichon, eds., *The Royal College of Physicians and Surgeons of Canada* (Toronto 1979), 74.

3 E. Fee, "Women and Health Care," in V. Navarro, ed., *Health and Medical Care in the United States* (New York 1977), 128.

4 See V. Strong-Boag, *The New Day Recalled: Lives of Girls and Women in English Canada, 1919–1939* (Markham 1988), 205–8. The other female MP, Martha Black, was elected in 1935, at the age of seventy, to hold her husband's Conservative seat during his illness, and was firmly committed to the "unequal relationship of women and men." On Macphail, see T. Crowley, *Agnes Macphail and the Politics of Equality* (Toronto 1990). Five women were elected to the federal Parliament before 1950; at the provincial level only a total of 23 women won seats between 1916 and 1949; see A. Prentice, P. Bourne, G.C. Brandt, B. Light, W. Mitchinson, and N. Black, *Canadian Women: A History* (Toronto 1988), 281.

5 S. Koven and S. Michel, "Womanly Duties," AHR, 95, no. 4 (1990): 1106–7. See also Catharine MacKinnon's astute feminist critique of the liberal state in C. MacKinnon, *Toward a Feminist Theory of the State* (Cambridge, Mass. 1989), especially 155–70.

6 P. Oliver, *G. Howard Ferguson: Ontario Tory* (Toronto 1977), 213–15; J. Schull, *Ontario Since 1867* (Toronto 1978), 258, 290–2.

7 J. Naylor, *The New Democracy* (Toronto 1991), 252. See also C. Heron, *The Canadian Labour Movement: A Short History* (Toronto 1989), 61; B. Palmer, *The Working Class Experience*, 2nd ed. (Toronto 1992), 219–21.

8 F.F. Piven and R. Cloward, *Regulating the Poor* (New York 1971), 77; Palmer, *The Working Class Experience*, 259.

9 C.A. and M. Aldrich, *Babies Are Human Beings* (New York 1938). Aldrich was a paediatrician and professor of paediatrics at the esteemed Mayo Foundation. On the Aldrichs, see C. Hardyment, *Dream Babies* (New York 1983), 213–15.

10 Spock's childrearing manual, the bible of countless mothers of the baby boom generation, was *Common Sense Book of Baby and Child Care* (New York 1945).

11 Aldrich, *Babies Are Human Beings*, viii. They argued that parents, physicians, and nurses are the foremost influences in children's lives.

12 Prentice, *Canadian Women*, 310; on Spock's influence, see M. Zuckerman, "Dr Spock: The Confidence Man," in C. Rosenberg, ed., *The Family in History* (Philadelphia 1975).

13 A. Rashid, *Statistics Canada, Analytic Reports: The Changing Profile of Canadian Families with Low Incomes, 1970–1985* (Ottawa 1990). The findings are based on 1986 census returns. Low-income families are those earning less than $20,812 annually in 1985. The Canadian Council on Social Development's research (1992) shows that Canada has the second highest rate of poverty among single-parent households out of seven Western nations, just behind the United States; see A. Mitchell, "Divorce a Ticket to Poverty For Women," *Globe and Mail*, 4 June 1992.

Index